IN SEARCH OF
GREAT
PLANTS

Published by Cool Springs Press, Inc.
A Division of Thomas Nelson, Inc.
P.O. Box 141000, Nashville, Tennessee 37214

LIBRARY OF CONGRESS CATALOGING-IN-PUBLICATION DATA

Earl, Betty.
  In search of great plants : the insider's guide to the best plants in the Midwest / Betty Earl.-- 1st ed.
  p.cm.
  Includes bibliographical references and index.
   ISBN: 1-59186-094-6 (pbk.)
   1. Nurseries (Horticulture)--Middle West--Directories. 2. Nursery growers--Middle West--Directories. 3. Nursery stock--Middle West--Directories. 4. Ornamental plant industry--Middle West--Directories. I. Title.
   SB118.487.M6285E25 2004
    631.5'2'02977--dc22
                          2004012090
First printing 2004
Printed in the United States of America
10 9 8 7 6 5 4 3 2 1

Managing Editor: Ramona Wilkes
Horticulture Editor: Troy Marden
Copyeditor: Sally Graham
Production Artist: S.E. Anderson
Visit the Thomas Nelson website at: www.ThomasNelson.com

Bonica®, Carefree Delight™, Carefree Wonder™ and Meideland™ are registered trademarks of Meilland International, France. Canadian Explorer™, and Canadian Morden Parkland™ are registered trademarks of Agriculture Canada. Carefree Beauty™ is a registered trademark of Dr. Griffith J. Buck. Crayolas® is a registered trademark of Binney & Smith. Crystal Fair™, Fairy Queen™, and Lovely Fairy™ are registered trademarks of R.A. Vurens, the Netherlands. David Austin™ is a registered trademark of David Austin. Echinacea 'Doppelganger'™ is a registered trademark of Jackson & Perkins. Echinacea 'Razzmatazz'® is a registered trademark of Darwin Plants. Gaillardia 'FanFare'® is a registered trademark of Plant Haven (Richard Read), England. Hydrangea 'Endless Summer'® is a registered trademark of Bailey Nurseries. Knock Out™ and Blushing Knock Out™ are registered trademarks of Conard Pyle. Luminaire™, Suncatcher™, Verbna Aztec™, Wildfire™ and Wave™ are registered trademarks of Ball Seed Co. Million Bells®, Super Bells™, Supertunia®, Surfina®, Superbena™, Tapien™, Temari™, Babylon™, and Tiny Tunias™ are registered trademarks of Euro American. Nashville™, Natchez™, Pebble Beach™, Santa Barbara™, and Town & Country™ are registered trademarks of Poulson, Denmark. Starry Night™ is a registered trademark of Pierre Orard.

IN SEARCH OF
GREAT PLANTS

THE
INSIDER'S GUIDE
TO THE
BEST PLANTS
IN THE MIDWEST

BETTY EARL

COOL SPRINGS PRESS
A Division of Thomas Nelson Publishers
Since 1798

www.thomasnelson.com

BIBLIOGRAPHY

Clausen, Ruth Rogers and Nicolas H. Ekstrom, *Perennials for American Gardens*. ISBN: 0-39455-740-9, Random House, New York, NY, 1989.

Davis, Brian. *The Gardener's Essential Plant Guide*. ISBN: 1-57145-601-5, Laurel Glen Publishing, San Diego, CA, 1997.

Gardner, JoAnn. *The Heirloom Garden*. ISBN: 0-88266-752-1, Storey Communications, Inc., Pownal, VT 1992.

Lawson-Hall, Toni and Brian Rothera. *Hydrangeas, a Gardeners' Guide*. ISBN: 0-88192-327-31, Timber Press, Portland, OR, 1996.

Mills-Hicks, James. *The Plant Book: The World of Plants in a Single Volume*. Random House, Milsons Point, Australia, 2001.

Overy, Angela. *The Foliage Garden*. ISBN: 0-51759-173-1, Harmony Books, New York, NY, 1993.

TABLE OF CONTENTS

⚬ ⚬ ⚬

INTRODUCTION

In Search of Great Plants: The Insider's Guide to the Best Sources in the Midwest is dedicated to my fellow Midwest gardeners. Whether you are a beginner, a seasoned pro, a weekend gardener, or a full-time plant enthusiast—this book was written with you in mind. Its main purpose is to provide you with a regional guide to beautiful, healthy, and well-grown plants. So whether you wish to indulge in something new—a bewitching fragrance that makes you swoon, an enchanting blossom, a leaf you're compelled to touch—or you just have wanderlust in your horticultural soul, there's a plant for you waiting to be discovered. I'm confident *In Search of Great Plants* will help you find it.

In addition to all of the practical reasons for seeking out great nurseries, I want you to have fun! Half the fun of finding sought-after plants is enjoying the journey. That's why I've also included information on nursery display gardens and fun "side trips" you can make during your search. Many of these nurseries offer "extras" such as wonderful classes, seminars, and festive events. As a plant lover, take advantage of the fun that could just be a short drive away. Or make it a day trip! I have accumulated many great stories while on the road getting my facts for this book. Go get some stories of your own!

GARDENING IN THE MIDWEST

The climate of the Midwest, with its fluctuating seasonal extremes, can present significant barriers to newbie gardeners and frustrate experienced pros. If alternating cycles of intense summer heat and muggy humidity, or periods of serious drought doesn't kill our plants, then they run the risk of drowning in our violent summer storms. And as if this weren't stressful enough, the subtle problems of winter's treacheries take their devastating tolls. We have January thaws followed by frigid February storms, late winter warming soils and gusty March winds that rip at plant roots. As the ground freezes and thaws (again and again), perennials, especially newly planted ones, run the risk of being heaved out of the ground, exposing tender roots to the ravages of winter.

Yet many plants not only survive but actually thrive in our environment. Obviously, in the right spot, indigenous plants will flourish—sometimes even to the point of aggressiveness. And it is a poorly kept secret that our Midwestern soils grow bigger and "better" weeds than any other place in the world. But as our horticultural horizons expand beyond native plants, we welcome other "where did *you* come from?" garden-worthy plants with open arms. In our immense universe full of exquisite plants, there are many choices that are somewhat different, sometimes peculiar, but always gorgeous.

MY GARDENING ROOTS

When I first started gardening—young, inexperienced, and easily swayed by pictures of vividly dazzling petals and flashy leaves—I sloshed pell-mell through the immense stacks of slick and glossy nursery catalogs, ordering everything and anything that caught my eye. Armed only with a very rudimentary knowledge of USDA zones rather than a good understanding of a plant's needs, I was continually seduced by the pretty faces of the latest flora. I helplessly answered the hypnotic calls of variegated-foliage sirens, and eagerly succumbed to a perceived notion of floriferous gratification. I did not know the importance of locally grown plants—nor did I care. I killed more plants than I care to confess.

Meanwhile, visiting local nurseries was a hit or miss affair. It took a little while, but the demise of a prized catalog purchase made me sit up and take notice. That singular loss led to an appreciation of the difference between a flourishing, locally grown plant and a doped-up product of the horticulture industry. I had learned the value of a judicious purchase.

I turned a critical eye. No longer did it suffice to know that the nursery offered my latest perceived "heartthrob." I wanted to know if it was healthy. Did the leaves project robust vigor, or were they chewed or damaged, diseased or insect infested? I wanted to see roots. Not a mass of twisty potbound roots but good, healthy roots.

Once I understood, I realized there were no shortcuts. A successful garden or landscape involves robust, healthy, well-grown plants. I needed plants acclimated to our regional

CONTACT ME

I warmly welcome feedback from my readers, no matter the reason. Everyone has an opinion and judgment calls are never absolute. Correspondence to correct an entry or expand coverage in a future edition is always appreciated. Most of all, I want to hear about your experiences. Online gardeners may contact me at www.BettyEarl.com.

Heartfelt Disclaimer

I have made every effort to present information that is accurate, state observations that will pique your interest, and give conclusions that are honest and impartial. I have tried hard to verify all facts, but there are always time limitations and unforeseen changes when creating a guide like this. I do not pretend that my information is totally without error or that every exceptional nursery in the five Midwestern States is listed in this book. In fact, I'm sure that I have left some out, but their absence is not necessarily meant as a negative comment. As a general rule, I have personally visited each and every open-to-the-public nursery, garden center, grower, and hybridizer featured (as well as many others that didn't make it in this edition).

weather—plants that would actually prosper and flourish in my suburban garden. But who grew these plants? I started asking questions...poking around...visiting nurseries. I talked to professionals...to trained horticulturists... to exceptional gardeners. I gathered the information, did some investigating for myself, and put together this guide that will hopefully open your eyes to new possibilities.

What I Looked For

The intention of this book is to offer you honest, informative, and useful facts toward finding exemplary regional sources for whatever garden plants you are searching for. Granted, I admit to some prejudices. I prefer nurseries that grow their own plants—container or field grown—because generally this produces a stronger, healthier plant than the trucked-in, force-fed hothouse divas of the standard nursery trade. I like nurseries with hands-on, accountable pest control. I love nurseries that seek out the unusual, strut the interesting, and embrace both the classic and "newbie" ornamental plants with the same zestful passion. I admire the tenacity and dedication of devoted hybridizers. I favor nurseries whose owners respect their customers, provide well-labeled plants, and have clearly visible pricing. I seek out nurseries with knowledgeable and helpful staff.

Obviously there is no one single nursery that can meet all the needs and expectations of anyone truly obsessed with gardening and all its pleasures. It is not my intent to proclaim a "best" source for any *specific* plant. Rather, it is to introduce you to nurseries and their owners; people who live with the soil and the climate, producing a mind-boggling array of well grown, even superb choices. However, there is no definitive Mecca. Big or small, every nursery has some unique feature, collection, or pursuit that sets it apart from all others. That fact in itself is a good thing.

HOW TO USE THIS BOOK

At the beginning of each nursery entry, there is a box with general information for that nursery, including address, phone number, and the hours they are open. Listings under the **"Specialties"** heading in this box are plants or needs on which the nursery particularly focuses.

When planning your itinerary I hope this book encourages you to explore that which is unfamiliar by visiting locales and establishments listed in the **"Side Trips" boxes**. All locations mentioned in these boxes are set within a radius of 30 to 40 minutes from the featured nursery. The joy of visiting great nurseries is further enhanced when the trip is filled with enticing public gardens, stops of historical significance, a few places to shop, or good food to share.

In some entries you'll find an **"Extras" box**. These are used to highlight something special that the nursery offers, such as services, classes, or festive events. In very few cases, a plant source listed in this book was not open to the public, but was exceptional and therefore included. The heading for each of these entries is clearly labeled **"Armchair Shopping Only."**

Though I acknowledge the existence of reputable garden centers and outstanding mail-order sources, for the most part I have not included them in this book unless they offer something exceptional. My main focus is on the wonderful, regional growers who, besides growing commonly known plants, also grow those that can't be found in your typical garden centers, box stores, or franchised green centers. I hope to help you broaden your horizons; and diversify your sources.

ACKNOWLEDGEMENTS

༄ ཉ

In their own individual ways, an extraordinary group of people has helped me in the preparation of this manuscript. Some by providing information, others by their support and inspiration. I would like to thank them all.

In particular I would like to thank my husband, David C. Earl, without whose encouragement and support this book could not have been written.

Gardening is an awesome adventure, and along the winding roads and rural pathways of the Midwest I had the incredible privilege of meeting the most wonderful people. Plant enthusiasts, nursery owners, hybridizers, "plant nuts" and just "plain folks" with whom I shared moments of laughter, pleasant experiences, or a brief moment of connection. You have left me with fond memories of my days on the road, and for that, I would like to extend a special thank you.

I also wish to thank Ramona Wilkes and Jenny Andrews for their help, astute observations, and memorable contributions to the book.

SEARCHING ILLINOIS

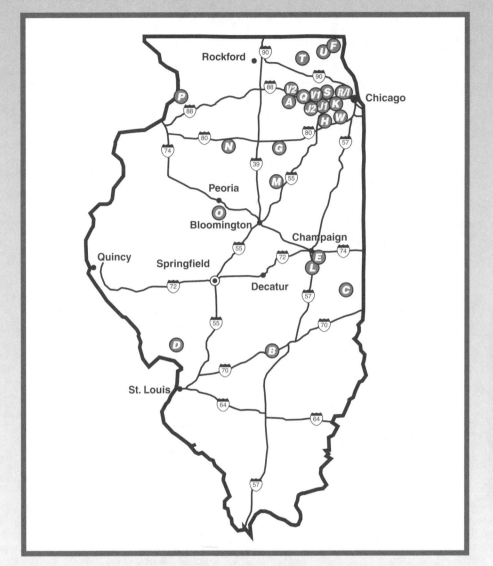

ILLINOIS

AAA ORNAMENTALS

৵৩৶ ৶৩৵

AAA Ornamentals, located in rural Big Rock (a mere speck on the map), is a treasure trove of healthy and hardy plants, and is a great place to procure a plant at a very reasonable price. Greg Miller, sole proprietor, is a self-confessed ornamental grass and hosta fanatic whose love affair with these plants got so out of hand that starting a nursery was the only sane solution.

In 2000, when the business finally outgrew its original residential roots, Greg purchased 5 acres of farmland on the edge of town and relocated both home and nursery to their new environs. For a small nursery, AAA Ornamentals grows an impressive array of the latest hosta varieties. Prices are very reasonable, making it a good place to tempt your garden budget.

Visitors are welcome to stroll the half-acre display garden, still in its infancy, where Greg practices tough love. His simple philosophy: "Plants that don't do their job, don't thrive as expected, and aren't attractive at any time during a typical growing season, are replaced." He states his case plainly, "Plants have to look good all season long. If they don't, out they go."

OWNERS: Greg Miller
TYPE: Small specialty nursery
SPECIALTIES: Hosta; grasses; perennials (small selection)
OPEN: End of April through Sep.: Wed.-Fri. 8:00 am to 4:00 pm, Sat. 8:00 am to 4:00 pm, Sun. Noon to 4:00 pm. Other hours by appointment.
CATALOG AVAILABLE: Printed price sheets and online information
MAIL-ORDER AVAILABLE: Yes
DISPLAY GARDEN: Yes
CLASSES: No

CONTACT
8S953 Jericho Road
Big Rock, IL 60511
PHONE: (630) 556-4507
WEB ADDRESS: www.hostas.com
EMAIL: mailorder@hostas.com

DIRECTIONS
FROM I-88: Exit Rt. 56 westbound. (Rt. 56 exit is one exit west of Orchard Rd.) Continue westbound on Rt. 56, which turns into Rt. 30 as you cross over Rt. 47,—past Aurora Airport—to Dugan Road. (Dugan Road is the first road past the airport. Watch for it. Though marked, it tends to sneak up on you.) Turn south (left), cross the railroad tracks, and continue to a "T" which is Jericho Road. Turn west (right) for approx. 0.5 miles. The nursery is on the right hand side of the road in the middle of a big "S" curve. Look for the hoop houses.

GPS: N 41° 44.08', W 88° 29.97'

WHAT YOU'LL FIND

AAA Ornamentals offers 167 varieties of **hosta**, 85 varieties of hardy (Zone 5) ornamental grasses, and a smattering of companion perennials—primarily hardy cranesbill, coral bells, and astilbe. Most of the stock is grown in the nursery's three hoop houses, with the rest brought in as needed.

The nursery has acquired a good selection of ornamental grasses. According to Greg, bold form is a quality that makes many grasses garden worthy, and there are none as bold as Miscanthus 'Giganteus' and **Taiwan grass** (Arundo formosana), both topping out at 96 inches—without the plumes. *Miscanthus*, also known as

> *"Grass is the hair of the earth."*
> —THOMAS DEKKER

maiden grass or **silver grass**, is the showy diva in any landscape production. It has narrow, graceful foliage—some with striking variegation, showy fan-shaped flower tassels, orange-red fall color; and bleached fountains of deciduous winter foliage. It is one of the most interesting plants in the winter garden. Of the 26 miscanthus available at AAA Ornamentals, some particularly noteworthy cultivars include 'Variegatus', 'Morning Light', 'Zebrinus', 'Cabaret', 'Adagio', and 'Gracillimus'. New-comers 'Huron Sunrise', 'Kaskade', and 'Kirk Alexander' caught my attention. Besides maiden grass, AAA Ornamentals carries 12 varieties of **fountain grass** (Pennisetum), 9 of **switch grass** (Panicum), and an excellent sampling of all others.

Though the nursery is open Wednesdays through Fridays (as well as Saturday and Sunday), Greg is gainfully employed full-time elsewhere. So if you're in the market for a serious discussion of hosta or ornamental grasses, need specific cultural advice, or want help integrating these two plants into your landscape, visit the nursery on a weekend. If, however, there is no need for hand-holding, weekdays offer a pleasant, leisurely experience.

ILLINOIS

ALWERDT'S GARDENS

✧

Alwerdt's Gardens is a popular nursery in Southern Illinois. Its roots are grounded in pheasants, not ornamental plants. Started fifty years ago by the elder Alwerdt raising pheasant for the gaming industry, today's fifteen-year old garden center is a second-generation offshoot, experiencing robust growth side-by-side with its thriving parent industry.

Nik Alwerdt, a sculptor and painter by trade, and his wife, Lisa, found their interests directed first to dried flowers and then, in their continual search for "new, better, and exciting plant varieties," expanded to encompass ornamentals, shrubs, and water plants. Most recently they have added miniature and dwarf conifers ideal for bonsai, rock trough gardens, and railroad gardens.

Visitors are encouraged to stroll the 4 acres of Alwerdt's Gardens' attractive display gardens, as well as the All-America Selections (AAS) Display Garden adjoining the parking area. Plants are well labeled with markers interspersed along the easily navigated pathways. (Each year the All America Selections program identifies praise-worthy seed grown flowers, vegetables, roses, and perennials—similar to an "American Idol" presentation. There are presently approximately 200 All-America Selections Display Gardens located in 30 states and provinces throughout North America.) Alwerdt's Gardens is one of those well run garden centers that

OWNERS: Nik and Lisa Alwerdt
TYPE: Large retail nursery
SPECIALTIES: Perennials—sun and shade; annuals; hanging baskets; shrubs; vines; grasses; aquatics; roses; trees; herbs; containers; garden art; hypertufa troughs
HOURS: April 1 to April 14: Mon.-Sat. 10:00 am to 5:00 pm, Sun. Noon to 4:00 pm, April 15 to June 21: Mon.-Sat. 8:00 am to 6:00 pm, Sun. Noon to 4:00 pm; June 22 to (approx.) end of Oct.: Mon.-Sat. 10:00 am to 5:00 pm, Sun. closed; Nov. thru March: By chance or appointment.
CATALOG AVAILABLE: Printed every two years with an annual updated supplement insert. Annuals and tropicals are not included.
MAIL-ORDER AVAILABLE: No
DISPLAY GARDENS: Yes (including an AAS Display Garden)
CLASSES: Yes

CONTACT
3238 E. 80th Avenue
Altamont, IL 62411
PHONE: (618) 483-5798

DIRECTIONS
FROM I-70: (West of Effingham, East of Vandalia) to Altamont Exit, Rt. 128 (Exit #82). Take Rt. 128 south approximately 1 mile to 800th Street. Left (East) on 800th Street for approx. 1/8 mile. Nursery entrance on left just past the pheasant farm.

GPS: N 39° 01.81', W 88° 44.76'

ILLINOIS

immediately pops to mind, because even though they may not carry everything, they always seem to have exactly what is needed.

WHAT YOU'LL FIND

Alwerdt's has a good selection of common perennials such as **yarrow**, **bellflower** (*Campanula*) **blue star** (*Amsonia*), **barrenwort** (*Epimedium*) **false indigo** (*Baptisia*), **marguerite daisy** (*Anthemis*), **clove pink** (*Dianthus*), **purple coneflower** (*Echinacea*) and **hardy geranium** (*Geranium*).

Also available are: *Heuchera* 'Amber Waves' (a color break-through of ruffled, amber-gold foliage); *H.* 'Amethyst Myst' (a cool fog of shimmering silver nestled on glossy, amethyst colored foliage); *H.* 'Chocolate Ruffles' (incredibly ruffled leaves, chocolate on top, burgundy underneath); *H.* 'Harmonic Convergence' (a bold silver and bronze marble pattern); the award winning *H.* 'Regina' (stunning colored foliage of silver, burgundy, and bronze); and the ever so vigorous *H.* 'Stormy Seas' (excellent landscape plant endowed with an incredible mix of colors in frothy shades of pewter, burgundy, and olive).

Other inspiring choices for woodland or shade gardens included 2 distinct **bleeding hearts**—*Dicentra* 'King of Hearts' (a new hybrid cross) and *D.* 'Gold Heart' (sporting bright golden foliage, an excellent contrast to the above mentioned *Heucheras*). There was also **hardy oxalis**, (*Oxalis crassipes* 'Rosea'); pasque flower, (*Pulsatilla* 'Papageno'), *P.* 'Heiler Hybrids'; comfrey, (*Symphytum grandiflorum* 'Hidcote Variegated'); 12 varieties of **foam flower**, *Tiarella* (a plant enjoying a new wave of popularity); **astilbe**, *Astilbe arendsii* 'Flamingo' (a standout, flaming flamingo-pink blossoms immediately catching one's eye, slightly fragrant); and **columbine**, *Aquilegia*.

Although by far most of Alwerdt's Gardens selection is of garden perennials, it also carries a heady mix of **roses** such as tea, hardy shrub, climbing, and antique. They also have some interesting ornamental grasses such as **sedge** (*Carex*), **reed grass** (*Calamagrostis*), **hardy pampas** (*Erianthus*), a large selection of maiden grass (*Miscanthus*), **switch grass** (*Panicum*), and a fair choice of native grasses, such as little **bluestem** (*Andropogon scoparius*) and **prairie dropseed** (*Sporobulus heterolepsis*). One can find a good selection of hosta cultivars, ferns, annuals, tropical marginals, herbs, evergreens, and perennial and annual vines. Interesting shrubs include: *Deutzia* × 'Monzie' (multi-stemmed, with pendulous, showy pink flower clusters); the rarer mint shrub, *Elsholtzia* (flouting rosy-purple panicles from summer through

ILLINOIS

fall); and *Hydrangea macrophylla* 'Goliath' (important for northern gardens because it blooms on both old and new wood).

> *"If you would be happy all your life, plant a garden."*
> —CHINESE PROVERB
> ᴂᴥᴥᴂ

For smaller gardens, the front of the border, or as a ground cover, Alwerdt's offers: *Forsythia* × 'Courtasol' (heavy blooming dwarf **forsythia** from France); **potentilla** (*Potentilla fruticosa* 'Fargo'); *Weigela florida* 'Tango' (compact); *Spirea* × *bumalda* 'Dart's Red' (a low growing spirea); and *Salix caprea* 'Weeping Sally' (with its trailing mound).

Among the temptations on my last visit, exceedingly late in the growing season, were a specimen-sized **hosta**, *Hosta* 'Hoosier Harmony' (a real show-stopper of white edged chartreuse leaves and fragrant, white flowers), and the vigorous *H.* 'Potomac Pride' (amazingly glossy black-green leaves, heavy substance, and puckering). There was an incredible selection of **basil** for that late in the season, *Ocimum basilicum* (too late for the garden but wonderful potted up for the kitchen windowsill), including lettuce-leaf 'Mammoth', dark purple 'Osmin', and the ever so excellent 'Sweet Genovese', my favorite heirloom variety. Additionally, I claimed *Clematis* 'Blue Ravine' (a robust vine cloaked in a profusion of large, lilac-blue flowers with contrasting red anthers) and *Ginkgo biloba* 'Autumn Gold', (a hard to find, non-fruiting male maidenhair tree decked out in bright golden yellow autumn finery).

The perennials at Alwerdt's Gardens are supplemented by annuals (Proven Winners, Flower Fields, and All America Selections), water garden plants, hanging baskets, vegetable flats (in spring), vines, trees, and shrubs. Rocks, stone, hardwood bark mulches, mushroom compost, potting mixes, planters and pots, specialized garden tools, and custom containers are also available.

For those who enjoy a creative outlet, Alwerdt's suggests hand crafting a hypertufa trough. (Just ask them about it—they are happy to share lots of information on the subject.) These relatively lightweight pots, made with the basic ingredients of peat, Portland cement, perlite, synthetic reinforcement fibers, and water, are easy to make and fun to do. Though the pots themselves are visually stunning, planted out with Alwerdt's selection of miniature and dwarf conifers, herbs, succulents, or other "precious" little plants, each container presents a miniature landscape. Think fairy gardens! Don't feel like messing around with cement? Alwerdt's carries a great selection of the finished product.

ILLINOIS

ALTAMONT LIVING MUSEUM (618-483-5348), South Main & Lincoln, is justifiably famous for its large, elaborate, stained glass windows. **BEN WINTER MUSEUM** (619-483-6665) RR1, is open most days, but it's advisable to call ahead. This museum has ten full scale steam engines, five scale model steam engines, and twelve stationary engines—all in working order. There are other antiques, or you can ride in your choice of steam or gasoline-powered train through fruit and nut orchards. **WRIGHT HOUSE** (618-482-6216), North Main and Jackson Streets, is listed in the National Register of Historic Places. This stately 1889 Renaissance Revival Home holds three generations of Wright family furnishings. It's advisable to call for an appointment. **CAMEO VINEYARDS** (217-923-9963) 400 Mill Road, Greenup, is open Memorial Day through Labor Day, Tues.-Thurs. (www.cameowine.com). It's located on a picturesque hillside overlooking the Embarrass River (pronounced "umbraw") and the Embarrass River Covered Bridge, a 200 ft. long bridge originally built by Abe and Thomas Lincoln, and Dennis Hanks. It's accessible from Greenup on Rt. 40 or I-70 east of Effingham. **COWDEN COVERED BRIDGE** is a pre-civil War Bridge over the Kaskaskia River near Cowden, northeast of Effingham on Rt. 33. **LINCOLN LOG CABIN STATE HISTORIC SITE**, Greenup (217-345-6489) is the last home of Thomas and Sarah Lincoln, Abraham Lincoln's parents. The site is shared with the Stephen Sargent Farm, an 1840's living history farm. Take I-70 east to Greenup exit and follow the signs.

ILLINOIS

Alwerdt's grows out scads of spectacular hanging baskets—1500 or more—in all forms, colors, and combinations. These baskets fly out the doors on weekends during the month of May. Additionally, specialized landscape design and installation, water garden design and installation, and commercial landscape maintenance are available.

BARKLEY FARMS NURSERIES

"...let us dwell in fair Ithilien and there make a garden. All things will grow with joy there..."
—FARAMIR TO EOWYN IN
The Lord of the Rings

Enjoy a relaxing drive out into the country to a delightful spot tucked back off the main roads. Rest in a lavishly planted landscape magically conjured up by a wonderful horticultural magician, smack dab in the center of acres and acres of corn.

Barkley Farms Nurseries, a family-run greenhouse nursery located behind the Barkley vintage farmhouse, offers an expansive selection of trees, shrubs, vines, roses, ornamental grasses, perennials, and annuals.

The lush display gardens promote plant marriages you won't be able to resist, and owner Dyke Barkley's skill in companion plantings will send you home with exciting plans for your own garden. I highly recommend a visit in May and June to view his dazzling combinations.

The staff is friendly and helpful, and there is a garden gift shop stocked with a little of everything from tools to stepping stones, garden books to herbal soaps, garden ornaments to unique gardening gifts, and garden-inspired decorating accessories.

WHAT YOU'LL FIND

Barkley specializes in perennials, both as wholesale growers and as a retail nursery, and concentrates on plant varieties well suited to the weather vagaries of the Midwest. Barkley Farms offers a tribe of **astilbe**, **hosta**,

OWNER: Dyke Barkley
TYPE: Specialty nursery. Retail and wholesale
SPECIALTIES: Perennials—sun and shade; grasses; shrubs; annuals
HOURS: April and May: Tues.-Fri. 9:00 am to 5:00 pm, Sat. 9:00 to 4:00 PM, Sun. Noon to 4:00 pm; June to end of Sept.: Wed.-Fri. 9:00 am to 5:00 pm, Sat. 9:00 am to 5:00 pm; Oct.: Sat. 9:00 am to 4:00 pm. Other hours by appointment. (Times are seasonal and may change. If coming from a distance, call and check.)
CATALOG AVAILABLE: No
MAIL-ORDER AVAILABLE: No
DISPLAY GARDENS: Yes
CLASSES: No

CONTACT
11200 East 1300 Road
Paris, IL 61944
PHONE: (217) 463-7003
FAX: (217) 466-4040
WEB ADDRESS: www.barkleyfarms.com
EMAIL: dbarkley@barkleyfarms.com

DIRECTIONS
See the facing page for directions.

GPS: N39° 39.59', W 87° 45.39'

hardy **geranium**, **daylilies**, **salvia**, **sedum**, and **veronica**. Woodland plants include **bleeding heart**, **columbine**, **monkshood**, **Virginia bluebells**, **forget-me-not**, and **pasque flower**. English garden devotees will find **phlox**, **peonies**, **bellflower**, **lavender**, **dame's rocket**, **delphinium**, **foxglove**, **catmint**, **valerian**, and **pinks**.

For shade lovers out there, the nursery offers quite an abundance for you: **fern**, **spiderwort**, **toad lily**, **anemone**, **coral bells**, and **bergenia**; for those with sunny yards: **yarrow**, **aster**, **coreopsis**, **coneflower**, **babies breath**, and **daisy**. Barkley Farms offers specialized collections of unusual varieties of good-sized trees and old-fashioned flowering shrubs such as **bottlebrush**, **buckeye**, **lilacs**, **hydrangeas**, **viburnums**, and **mockorange**.

Dyke Barkley, an avid plantsman and self-confessed plant junkie, has an ever-evolving palette of more than 800 perennials that includes both old favorites as well as the rare and sought-after new varieties. In spring, they are bursting with top quality annuals, and **pansies** and **primrose** when in season. The nursery carries a growing selection of hardy **geraniums**, and lots and lots of ornamental grasses. They have a lovely form of **monkshood** (*Aconitum* × *cammarum* 'Bicolor') with spikes of bicolored flowers instead of the more common bluish-purple ones. Other plants include an **English daisy** (*Bellis perennis* 'Pomponette Mix') not generally available, a cute **dwarf meadow cranesbill** (*Geranium pratense* 'Midnight Reiter'), and a **Far East Japanese Silver Grass** (*Miscanthus sinensis* 'Ferner Osten').

Dyke Barkley is a genius with ornamental grasses. Anyone interested in them should spend some time with him. He notes that grasses, "unlike perennials, are most effective when backlit by the sun. Just one plant can change a garden from formal to informal, or completely shift the garden's balance and scale." On several

> ## DIRECTIONS
> **FROM CHAMPAIGN:** Take I-57 south to Hwy 36 (Tuscola exit), take Hwy-36 east to Hwy 1 south (left) to 1200th Rd. Turn west (right) onto 1200th Rd. driving to 1200th St. Turn north (right) on 1200th St. and drive 1 mile to 1300th Rd. Turn west (left) on 1300th Rd. and drive 0.7 miles to the nursery on your left. (**NOTE:** at the intersection of I-1 and 1200th Rd. there is a blue Tourist Activities sign for Barkley Farms. You can follow the blue signs from this point to the nursery, a total of 4.5 miles away.) **FROM CHARLESTON:** Take Hwy-16 east to Hwy 49. Turn north (left) on Hwy 49 to Hwy 133. Turn east (right) on Hwy 133 to 1200th Rd Turn north (left) on 1200th St. driving to 1300th Rd. Turn west (left) on 1300th Rd. driving 0.7 miles to the nursery which will be on your left. (Note: There is a blue Tourist Activities sign for Barkley Farms at the intersection of Hwy 133 and 1200th St. which you could follow to the nursery.) **CAUTION:** A majority of the roads leading up to the nursery are rural dirt roads heavily used by farm machinery.

Saturday mornings in early spring, Barkley hosts a garden walk through the nursery's 2-acre display gardens (call for a schedule). These informal ramblings, while an exceptional opportunity to learn about plants in general, are an incredible opening into the world of grasses. On these tours, Dyke says one can learn how "weaving groups of grasses throughout the landscape can create calm—or create excitement." You can also learn how to use grasses to their best autumn and winter advantage. These gatherings are entertaining, informative—and free.

EXTRAS

Barkley Farms hosts fun potting parties (reservations needed, call for schedules). Bring your own containers, select plants right from the greenhouses, purchase the nursery's high quality potting soil at a minimal cost, and have the benefit of a professional staff to guide you. Leave the mess behind! Cap the evening off with goodies, conversation, and laughter. The nursery also hosts an annual Ornamental Grass Blast in mid-September, as well as a perennial garden party the first Saturday in June. Come enjoy the vendors, food, tours, and speakers.

COTTAGE GARDEN

❧ ❧

One could easily miss this small nursery, tucked away like a secret at the end of a long driveway, in the middle of the rural countryside. Located just outside the quaint town of Piasa in the extreme southwestern part of Illinois, Cottage Garden is an incredibly captivating and tantalizing source of the latest in "tropicalissmo." Much of these types can be seen growing and blooming profusely in magnificent urns and planters tastefully clustered in various groupings about the premises. They also have the most cutting-edge perennials, hosta, shrubs, and vines. "Plantaholics," plant nerds, and just plain plant lovers of the rare, the unusual, the new, and the exceptional should make their way here.

The heart and soul of Cottage Garden is owner Chris Kelley, a self-confessed "plant nut" who spends every waking moment during the winter months wandering up and down the information superhighway. She's always in search of uncommon, noteworthy, and interesting plants. Her specialties are container plants and hosta; however, she also dabbles (successfully, I might add) in perennials, flowering shrubs, vines, and ornamental grasses.

I enjoy container gardening, planting out a number of pots for placement on the deck, patio, and garden. Kelley, on the other hand, goes absolutely "pot crazy," planting up a covey of awesome combinations of really cool and bodacious plants. In

OWNER: Chris Kelley
TYPE: Specialty nursery.
SPECIALTIES: Tropicals; annuals; perennials—shade and sun; ornamental grasses; vines; shrubs; hosta
HOURS: March 15 through Oct. 15: Mon.-Sat. 9:00 am to 5:00 pm, Sun. 10:00 am to 5:00 pm. Closed Easter Sunday, 4th of July, and Wednesdays July through Oct..
CATALOG AVAILABLE: Printed and online
MAIL-ORDER AVAILABLE: Yes
DISPLAY GARDENS: Yes
CLASSES: Yes

CONTACT

6967 Rt. 111 (Formerly Rt. 67)
Piasa, IL 62079
PHONE: (618) 729-4324
FAX: (618) 729-2188
WEB: cottgardens.com
EMAIL: infor@cottgardens.com

DIRECTIONS

FROM ST. LOUIS AREA: Take Hwy 67 north through Alton and Godfrey, IL. As you leave Godrey veer right onto Hwy.-111 and drive 8 miles to Brighton. The nursery is located 3 miles north of Brighton on Hwy-111. Watch for sign. Take the long driveway to the residence; the nursery is in back. **DIRECTIONS FROM THE NORTH:** Take I-55 south to Hwy-16 (Litchfield exit). Follow Hwy-16 west to Piasa to Hwy-111. Turn south (left) onto Hwy-111, the nursery is 1 mile down on your right. Watch for sign. Take the long driveway to the residence; the nursery is in back.

GPS: N 39° 06.09', W 90° 08.51'

ILLINOIS

her words, "I feel like a kid with a package of Crayolas®! I can't remember a time when gardening was ever more fun or satisfying." Wait until you see what she has at her disposal to play with—it's plant nirvana.

The nursery offers well-grown plants, propagated from seed, cuttings, and plugs, in various sized containers. The Cottage Garden catalog offers informative plant descriptions; however, the web site is far superior to the printed page due to the addition of color photographs for a majority of the plants. This is an intriguing, colorful nursery—definitely worth the extra time and effort needed to seek it out.

WHAT YOU'LL FIND

For starters, there's the "Grand Poobah of all angel trumpets," *Brugmansia* 'Super Nova' (humongous white blossoms—a whopping 16 inches long—gushing fragrant perfume); several gargantuan **elephant ears**, *Alocasia* 'Greenshield' (celadine green leaves and deep green veins); *A.* 'Purpley', (an Amazonian hybrid of glossy, eggplant-purple leaves brazenly streaked with silver veins); and *A. × portodora* 'Portore' (huge, ruffle-edged jungle frosted buttery-cream and violet leaves). There's a bevy of flowering **maple** (*Abutilon*), **copper leaf** (*Acalypha*), **four o'clocks** (*Mirabilis*), **shamrock** (*Oxalis*), and summer **snapdragon** (*Angelonia*). Cottage Garden has an ocean of **petunias** (*Callibrachoa*, Million Bells®, Wave™); **sage** (*Salvia*), including the color-challenged *Salvia microphylla* 'Hot Lips; **cigar plant** (*Cuphea*); various striking cultivars of **verbena**; and 51 varieties of **coleus** (*Solenostemon*) in every interesting shape, mouthwatering color, and dizzying pattern imaginable.

I admired a dainty, captivating **ginger** (*Globba wintii* 'Dancing Ladies'); delighted in a flurry of hummingbirds surrounding the **Texas firecracker** (*Anisacanthus wrightii*); and was awed by the red striped **banana** (*Musa acuminata* 'Zebrina'). I was inspired by the brilliant orange blooms of **yellow bells** (*Tecoma ×* 'Orange Jubilee'); and immediately coveted the Cuban show-off, *Brunfelsia nitida*, (fountains of flaring, creamy white trumpets). I was also drawn to the **butterfly magnet**, *Caesalpinia pulcherrima*, (a siren of brilliant, orange red, mimosa-type blossoms and impressive red stamens).

Nothing speaks such volumes of "tropicalismo" like a canopy of cavorting, elaborate, exotic, outrageous, winding vines dripping in luscious blossoms. Cottage Garden offers its customers a marvelous collection as bait: For sweet perfume, there are the awesome "corkscrew" blooms of the **snail vine** (*Vigna cara-caclla*)—Thomas Jefferson was a devotee—and the heavily perfumed **star jasmine** (*Trachelospermum asiaticum*), with star-like blossoms giving off clouds of sweet perfume.

For foliage, there is the ultimate exotic **rex begonia vine** *Cissus discolor*, flaunting velvety oval leaves hand painted by the mighty jungle gods in forest green, pewter, and deep purple. For colorful blooms, see the **winged beauty vine** (*Dalechampia*) with its

> *"We must cultivate our garden."*
> — VOLTAIRE

end of season waterfall of wing-petaled violet-pink blossoms. They have an impressive selection of **passion flowers** (*Passiflora* spp.) with intricate, exotic bloom structures in a rainbow of seductive colors. Especially notable is the luscious raspberry red *P.* 'Lady Margaret'. For sheer curiosity, you'll be attracted to a bewildering group of **Dutchman's pipes**, including burgundy and cream *Aristolochia giganteum*, and glowing *A. fimbriata* with its velvety red and yellow "pipes." You'll also find *A. ringens*, with bizarre blooms mimicking the head of an exotic bird.

Cottage Garden began life eighteen years ago with a plethora of perennials—something that is still very close to Kelley's heart. Today, she has refreshing collections of sun perennials: **yarrow, bugleweed, old-fashioned hollyhock, columbine, wormwood, aster, tickseed, pinks, globe thistle, cranesbill, peony,** and **phlox**. This nursery is the only place I've actually seen the deep blue spikes of **hummingbird mint** (*Agastache urticifolia* 'Honey Bee Blue'). Other plants I saw were the exemplary blue blooming plant **blue star** (*Amsonia* 'Blue Ice'); the incredible **coneflower** (*Echinacea pupurea* 'Double Decker') with the quirky curiosity of a double row of rosy-pink petals atop cone centers; and the compact, drooping yellow petalled coneflower (*E. p.* 'Paranoia'). There was a short, lovely native **joe-pye-weed** (*Eupatorium dubium* 'Little Joe'); the colorful, unique, and much touted **blanket flower** (*Gaillardia* 'Fanfare'™); the biennial, night flying moth magnet, **evening primrose** (*Oenothera* 'Tina James Magic'); and a pristine white **clary sage** (*Salvia sclarea* 'Swan Lake'). You'll find an incredible tribe of cottage garden divas, such as the stately **mulleins** *Verbascum* × *hybridum* 'Banana Custard', 'Caribbean Crush', 'Bold Queen', 'Sixteen Candles', and 'Jackie in Pink').

Noteworthy plants for the shade include two varieties of **hardy begonia**, desirable **bugbane**, spectacular **bleeding hearts**, numerous **hellebores**, excellent herbaceous **lamium**, some stunning **lungwort**, and the cheery spring bloomer celandine poppy. **Hosta** is another specialty of the nursery, and each year Kelley wows her customers with winsome cultivars such as: 'Earth Angel' (a 'Blue Angel' with wide-irregular white borders); 'Rosedale Golden Goose' (golden, puckered leaves); and 'Fujiboton' (sporting stunning fully double blooms of lavender pink). With my penchant for very large hostas, I couldn't leave without 'Wooly Mammoth' (a gold-edged sport of 'Blue Mammoth'); 'Grand Canyon' (bred from 'Sum and Substance'); and 'Paradise Power' (golden leaves edged in a narrow green margin).

Cottage Garden carries a select assortment of flowering shrubs such as *Hydrangea macrophylla* 'Penny Mac' (touted as a **hydrangea** that blooms on new and old wood); *Diervilla* 'Butterfly' (a North American native with rich yellow blossoms); and *Lespedeza* 'Yakushima' (an adorable dwarf bicolor **bush clover**). There is a good assortment of own-root **roses**, perennial vines, **clematis**, and ornamental grasses, both perennial and tender.

★ **SIDE TRIPS** ★

MISSOURI BOTANICAL GARDEN, 4344 Shaw Blvd., St. Louis, MO. This is an outstanding botanical garden full of inspirational display gardens and the latest perennials, tropicals, and woody plants. www.mobot.org. **RIVERLANDS,** Hwy-111 just south of the Clark Bridge in Alton. This is a wetland ecosystem for birders and nature lovers. **MOONLIGHT RESTAURANT,** 3400 Fosterburg Rd., Alton, IL, is home of "talk n chic" fried chicken (518) 462-4620. **MY JUST DESSERTS,** 31 E. Broadway (near Visitor's Center), Alton, IL, has good food and desserts that will have you drooling.

ILLINOIS

COUNTRY ARBORS NURSERY

❧ ❧

Country Arbors Nursery, located southeast of Urbana, is a popular nursery and garden center offering its customers an innovative diversity of plant material. Owners Donna and P. Terence Cultra have built their nursery's outstanding reputation in the field by growing perennials that are rare, unusual, and typically hard to find in the horticultural trade. Situated on 50 acres of fertile farmland, the nursery specializes in choice perennials, annuals, trees, and shrubs of the kind that flourish and thrive in the Midwest.

The perennials, propagated in pots on site at Country Arbors, are set out alphabetically on long tables, grouped by type. A large section of the garden center is devoted to the ornamental trees and shrubs and the ever-expanding collection of hosta. Repeat visits are advisable as new and different stock, appearing as if by magic, can be found at every turn. The sales staff is a group of well-trained and experienced horticulturists who are friendly, helpful, and more than willing to share their knowledge. Their well-constructed website is easy to navigate and offers a full line of plants and accessories.

Robert Blain Cultra, upon his return from the Civil War in 1865, sold strawberry and raspberry plants

OWNERS: Donna and P. Terence Cultra

TYPE: Large retail and wholesale nursery

SPECIALTIES: Perennials—sun and shade; annuals and tender perennials; hanging baskets; herbs; trees; shrubs

HOURS: Jan. 1 through mid-Apr.: Mon.-Fri. 9:00 am to 4:30 pm, Sat. & Sun.: closed; mid-Apr. through Oct.: Mon-Fri. 8:00 am to 6:00 pm, Sat. 9:00 am to 5:00 pm, Sun. 10:00 am to 4:00 pm. Closed Fourth of July and Labor Day. Nov.: Mon.-Fri. 8:00 am to 5:00 pm, Sat. & Sun.: closed. Dec.: closed.

CATALOG AVAILABLE: Online

MAIL-ORDER AVAILABLE: No

DISPLAY GARDENS: Yes

CLASSES: No

CONTACT

1742 Country Road 1400 North
Urbana, IL 61802

PHONE: (217) 367-1072

FAX: (217) 367-2472

WEB ADDRESS: www.countryarbors.com

EMAIL: via website

DIRECTIONS

FROM I-74: Take I-74 to University Exit (it only goes East). Drive to the first stoplight, which is the intersection of Rt. 150 & E. University Ave. Turn left and follow the road until Rt. 130 breaks off to the south as High Cross Rd. Turn south (right) onto Rt. 130 and drive to Windsor Road. Turn east (left) onto Windsor Rd which becomes C.R. E 1400 North. Nursery is 1.4 miles down on your left.

FROM I-57: Take I-57 to I-74 East. Follow directions above.

GPS: N 40° 05.03', W 88° 08.14'

ILLINOIS

as well as various fruit trees by toting his wares to customers in the surrounding rural areas on foot. Today, the 45,000 square feet of greenhouses, growing more than 850 varieties of perennials and annuals, is run by the fourth and fifth generation of Cultra nurserymen.

WHAT YOU'LL FIND

Country Arbors is a dynamic horticultural resource that carries such fashionable newcomers as: **snow-in-summer** *Cerastium tomentosum* 'Yo Yo' (undemanding, smothered in luminous white flowers); *Dianthus gratianopolitanus* 'Spotty' (cute, little, pale pinkish-red with white spots); and *Astilbe chinensis* 'Veronica Klose' (brilliant rose-purple bloomer).

> *"The flower that follows the sun does so even in cloudy days."*
> —ROBERT LEIGHTON

It has unusual holdings of **yarrow**, **blanket flower**, **coneflower**, **aster**, **butterfly bush**, **tickseed**, **hardy geranium**, **catmint**, **lungworth**, and **toad lily**. Gardeners in the know scurry to the nursery for rare treasures such as: **globeflower**, *Trollius* × *cultorum* 'Commander in Chief' (lovely buttercup relative); **foamflower**, *Tiarella* 'Skeleton Key' (interesting woodlander sporting extensively cut leaves and generous blooms of fuzzy blush-pink flowers); *Sanguisorba dodecandra* (unusual mountain burnet); and **forget-me-not**, *Myosotis sylvatica* 'Royal Blue Compact' (dwarf, compact carpet of tiny, brilliant blue flowers).

The nursery carries a good array of **ferns** and **peonies**, including the tree peony (*Paeonia suffruticosa* 'Shimaniski'). On this day, my traveling companion could barely contain her enthusiasm at finding a number of containers of *Lilium* 'Ballroom' and *L.* 'Blackbird' (two outstanding bulb **lilies**). She was also excited to find *Leucanthemum* × *superbum* 'Crazy Daisy' (a taller **daisy** and the first variety of this height to produce a high percentage of double flowers; and *Phlox divaricata* 'Clouds of Perfume' (extremely fragrant, laven-

★ SIDE TRIPS ★

Champaign County Forest Preserve District—LAKE OF THE WOODS BOTANICAL GARDENS, RT. 47, Mahomet, IL. (217) 586-4389. FRASCA AIR MUSEUM, (217) 328-6088, 1402 Airport Rd., Urbana, IL. MUSEUM OF NATURAL HISTORY, (217) 333-2157, 1301 West Green St., Urbana, IL.

ILLINOIS

der phlox). I, on the other hand, laid claim to *Sedum robustum* 'Oregon Sunset' (blazing yellow **sedum**); *Phlomis russelliana* (large flowered **Jerusalem sage**); three varieties of *Phlox paniculata* 'Miss Jo-Ellen', *P.p.* 'Miss Karen', and *P.p.* "Miss Wilma' (new fragrant, smaller flowered **phlox**); and the definite "find" for my woodland collection, *Asarum speciosum* 'Buxom Beauty' (native **ginger** with green arrowhead-shaped leaves marbled with a muted silver pattern).

EXTRAS

A totally awesome 5-acre arboretum, the Mary Jane Teller Cultra Arboretum adjoins the garden center. Maintained by a staff of trained horticulturists, the landscaped arboretum affords every gardener the ability to view the true beauty of a plant in a land-scaped setting. Seeing plants in this setting helps gardeners understand how specific plants relate to each other in a garden setting as well as appreciate the special attributes the plant brings to the overall landscape design. Each year, Country Arbor continues to expand the gardens by incorporating more diverse plant material into the design.

ILLINOIS

CRAIG BERGMANN'S COUNTRY GARDEN

ocated midway between Chicago, Illinois and Milwaukee, Wisconsin, Craig Bergmann's Country Garden is a perennial farm and garden center considered by many to be *the* pre-eminent, upscale nursery of the Chicagoland area and neighboring suburbs. This rural 12-acre nursery was founded on the premise that quality plants are essential for successful gardening. Known for its imaginative selection of more than 1,200 herbaceous perennials and 900 unusual seasonal plants, Craig Bergmann's Country Garden is the perennial garden and nursery of (guess who) Craig Bergmann. Craig is an esteemed author, lecturer, garden designer, professional horticulturist, and merchandiser extraordinaire. Mr. Bergmann has received numerous horticultural awards.

Craig Bergmann's Country Garden has a private garden surrounding the Bergmann home, and 6 demonstration gardens. The sun garden consists of informal plantings of sun-loving perennials surrounding a clematis bower. The herb and rose garden is an ambitious undertaking of espaliered apple trees, semi-formal plantings of herbs, clipped boxwood hedging, cherry trees, and roses. The shade garden is a richly planted area with more than 3,000 woodland plants and spring bulbs. The rock garden is a small area planted out with dwarf

OWNER: Craig Bergmann
TYPE: Specialty retail nursery and garden center
SPECIALTIES: Perennials—sun and shade; vines; herbs; ornamental grasses; ferns
HOURS: Mid-April through Mid-Oct.: Wed., Fri., Sat 9:00 am to 6:00 pm, Thurs. 9:00 am to 7:00 pm, Sun. 10:00 am to 6:00 pm.
CATALOG AVAILABLE: Yes
MAIL-ORDER AVAILABLE: No
DISPLAY GARDENS: Yes
CLASSES: Yes

CONTACT
700 Kenosha Road *
Winthrop Harbor, IL 60096
PHONE: (847) 746-0311
WEB ADDRESS: www.craigbergmann.com
EMAIL: craig@craigbergmann.com

DIRECTIONS
FROM I-94: I-94 to Rosecrans Rd /IL-173. Take eastbound Rosecrans Rd. for 4.8 miles to Kenosha Rd./CR-53. Turn north (left) onto Kenosha Rd and drive 1.1 miles to the nursery on your left.

*If you are using mapquest.com to map out your route, please plug in the following address: 42732 North Kenosha Road, Zion, IL 60099. This "idiosyncrasy" of our numbering systems will insure that mapquest locates the nursery at its correct location.

GPS: N 42° 28.76', W 87° 51.80'

ILLINOIS

conifers, shrubs, and spring blooming perennials. The autumn garden is the largest of the demonstration gardens, designed to peak during the months of August, September, and October. The newest garden, the James Garden, consists of four garden rooms—the shaded entry, the woodland, the kitchen, and the rose room.

WHAT YOU'LL FIND

Craig Bergmann's Country Garden is fashioned to resemble European nurseries and specializes in perennial classics, be they new introductions or old standards They also have some roses, vines, and "woodies" that interplant well with perennials. There are 16 Courtyard Squares filled with sun-loving perennials. The nearby domed structure, the Shade Pavilion, is devoted to

> *"You cannot understand a garden unless it has soiled your hands."*
> —TEXAS B. BENDER

shade-loving perennials. The Old Greenhouse and Lath Structure are filled with seasonal plants (annuals and tender perennials). The Herb House displays over 80 seasonal and perennial herbs, and the topiary collection. Visitors are welcome to stroll the gardens (many come repeatedly) taking note of the many unusual and creative ways of combining plants in the garden.

The nursery's informative plant lists are actually booklets that feature new introductions and old standards that have been trialed and tested in the nursery's fields and gardens before inclusion in the catalogs and sales areas. The nursery cultivates superior varieties of **yarrow, columbine, aster, astilbe, bellflower, pinks, cranesbill, daylily, hosta, monarda,** and **phlox.** Other favorites include: *Artemesia arborescens* 'Huntington' (a hardier form of **artemisia**); *Aster puniceus* (an uncommon aster with true architectural stature); *Astrantia major* 'Rose Symphony' (a dramatic pink **masterwort**); the giant *Cephalaria gigantea* (with its primrose-yellow, scabiosa-like flowers), *Epimedium* × *youngianum* 'Roseum' (dusky lavender-pink blooms, a worthy **barrenwort** reintroduction); and a **Helen's flower,** *Helenium* 'Rubinswerg' (sporting deep burnt-red petals surrounding yellow and brown centers). Helen's flower must surely be one of the very best perennials for late summer color).

Craig Bergmann's is renowned for its "English" **delphiniums**. Grown at the nursery from the finest, hand-pollinated seed procured annually from an English source, the resulting plants are offered in separate colors and are superior in type

ILLINOIS

and garden performance. Also of note are the indisputably elegant **irises** including: crested (*Iris cristata*), orris root (*I. florentina*), stinking (grown for the unusual seed heads) (*I. foetidissima*), bearded (*I. × germanica*), variegated (*I. pallida* 'Variegata' and *I. pseudacorus* 'Variegata'), dwarf bearded (*I. pumila*), and Siberian (*I. sibirica*). The nursery is appreciated for its collections of uncommon **allium**—I was particularly enamored of *Allium schoenoprasum* 'Schnittlauch', a dwarf version of common chives. They also have good collections of hardy ferns, ornamental grasses, and bamboos.

The perennials at Craig Bergmann's, many available only in small quantities, are a wide range of blooming-size plants mainly grown out in 1-gallon containers. Others, primarily the nursery's greenhouse plants and a limited number of other perennials, are sold in 1-quart containers. For on-site customers and "plantaholics," there are always some new surprises since innovative additions are ongoing.

Craig Bergmann's is a good source for vines, and die-back shrubs such as **buddleia**, **caryopteris** and **lespedeza**. There are "woodies" (shrubs and trees) selected for fragrance, for all season foliage interest, or strictly for their intensely gorgeous fall foliage.

ILLINOIS

DOWIS RANCH

❦ ❦

Dowis Ranch is a two-generation nursery owned by Janell Denham and her son Eric. Each member of this engaging duo is immersed in his or her own specialty. Janell Denham grows more than 500 varieties of iris while her son Eric, with more than 1,000 named daylily cultivars growing in the propagation fields, pursues an amazingly aggressive daylily breeding program. In the past five years, Eric has registered no less than 25 outstanding cultivars. Eric's specialty is breeding winter hardy, dormant tetraploids using only cultivars from the breeding lines of the late Brother Charles Reckamp, Rudolph, and Walt Stackman to produce "a thing of great beauty." His holy grail is a variegated daylily (currently unamed) with good color intensity, branching, and bud count. A measure of Eric's success is the introduction of 'Variegated Jackpot', a registered (2001), variegated, glowing melon daylily he introduced in conjunction with Walt Stackman. And with 30 or so understudies anxiously waiting in the wings for their moments in the spotlight, we may soon see many more variegated daylily stars taking center stage.

The beginnings of Eric's hybridization efforts are rather humble. Eric showed an early curiosity in crossing flowers he simply thought were "pretty." Noticing this interest, Janell introduced him to the noted hybridizer Walt Stackman, a man Eric credits with teaching him everything he knows about hybridizing daylilies.

OWNERS: Janell Denham, Eric Denham
TYPE: Specialty nursery
SPECIALTIES: Daylilies; iris.
HOURS: May thru mid-Aug.: Hours are flexible; it is requested that you call a day or two before coming out. Other times by special appointment.
CATALOG AVAILABLE: Separate b&w catalogs; partial listings online
MAIL-ORDER AVAILABLE: Yes
DISPLAY GARDENS: Yes
CLASSES: No

CONTACT
2576 N 28th Road
P.O. Box 124
Marseilles, IL 61341
PHONE: (815) 795-5681
WEB ADDRESS:
www.GardenEureka.com/DOWIS
EMAIL: pollen@mtco.com

DIRECTIONS
FROM I-55: Take I-55 to I-80 west. Take I-80 (west) to Marseilles Exit south (24th Rd.). Drive south on 24th Rd. to 30th Rd. (first flashing light), turn east (left) on 30th Rd. to the second intersection (no street sign, but an old radio tower on the southwest corner), turn south (right) and drive to the "T" in the road (N28th Rd). Turn east (left) on N 28th Rd) and make a quick right down the long driveway at 2576. Nursery is at the end of a long driveway.

GPS: N 41° 20.35', W 88° 40.41'

ILLINOIS

The display gardens at Dowis Ranch are rich in color and design. Both Eric and Janell are accomplished gardeners with all manner of new, rare, exciting, and unusual plants interspersed throughout the gardens surrounding the house. Be sure to make this a part of your visit.

WHAT YOU'LL FIND

Eric follows the charming tradition, common among daylily hybridizers, of naming introductions after his surroundings. Consider his 'Dowis Cranberry Merchant' (a tall, stunning cranberry bicolor), 'Dowis Grove Street' (an orange with gold blend), and 'Dowis Snow Cap' (a mesmerizing cream polychrome with diamond dusting and ruffling), among others.

Other Denham **daylily** hybrids honor nieces and other relatives: the cute and tiny 'Emmy Jo Cunico E.' (adorable pink with gold ruffling), saucy 'Evee Marie Cunico E.' (a hot pink with ruffled gold edge), and serendipitous 'Janice Dowis E.' (a striking ruffled fuschia with white edge). I can only wonder what prompted the circumstances leading up to the very late bloomer 'Mom Is Late E.' (a beautiful golden yellow with fringed edge).

One of the pleasures of my visit to Dowis Ranch was seeing 'Rain of Fire', an incredibly vibrant red daylily. I cannot think of a better addition to my hot, sunny border than this sunfast cultivar—bold red blossoms thrust upright in the sunshine, unfazed by heat and afternoon sun (Eric has measured a petal heat index of 106 degrees Fahrenheit with nary a smidgen of fading).

Through its catalog, Dowis Ranch offers those daylily cultivars whose numbers are great enough to support mail-order customers. The catalog lists the breeder, year of introduction, and bloom habits of each plant. The list includes most Denham and Denham/Stackman introductions, many distinctly hardy hybrids developed by other breeders, and a bevy of pastel beauties from the hybridization efforts of the late Brother Charles. Worthy seedlings from the Denham's efforts, rejects from the registration program but far superior to many of the daylily plants available today, are sold at the nursery for $10 a "shovel full." Daylilies are shipped freshly dug, by double divisions or greater, unless noted otherwise. Bonus plants, chosen by the nursery from a customer's substitution list (if sent), are included with each order. Eric maintains a reasonable number of pre-potted daylilies that are perfect choices for housewarmings, dinner parties, or to be held by the side of your garage for a leisurely dig in the garden.

Janell Denham's love affair with the genus *Iris* began more than thirty years ago, and today's nursery is the by-product of a hobby gone wild. Though interested in all aspects of the plant, Janell's specialties are the historic, the reblooming, and the tall bearded **iris**. There are a great many tales of how the iris got its name, yet all are in agreement that the origins lie in Greek mythology and the myths surrounding the Rainbow Goddess—Iride or Iris. Though the stories differ slightly in detail, they are all incredibly romantic.

> *"Gardening is an instrument of grace."*
> —MAY SARTON

Historical irises come only in white, yellow, or purple, or occasionally a combination of all three colors. Since then hybridizers have expanded the range into a rainbow of colors and a variety of shapes and sizes. The flowers now come in a full spectrum of colors, ranging from pure white and creamy yellow to bright yellow and vivid orange. There are red-browns and chestnut-browns, hues that are nearly white to those considered "black" (but in reality varying from very dark blue to dark purple). The petals, which were once smooth and delicate in shape, are now ruffled, fluted, and thick in substance. The tall bearded iris contains the greatest numbers of hybrids in the widest variety of colors. Some are flamboyant, clothed in bright hues; others are more tranquil with colorations in gentle pastels.

The Dowis Ranch catalog offers 139 named iris cultivars, a mere fraction of the admirable collection of more than 500 varieties growing throughout the 10-acre parcel of land. Dowis Ranch carries: 'Amas' (a blue bitone introduced in 1885); *Iris pallida* subsp. *pallida* (a lilac blue species iris); and 'Lord of June' (a blue bicolor from 1911). Admirable tall bearded irises include: 'Superstition' (a "black" flowered plant that is more rich purple than black); the red 'Indian Chief'; and another red, 'Rip City'. Gorgeous rebloomers (hybrids that flower at least twice a year) include 'Cham-

EXTRAS

Although new daylily hybrids can run upwards of $150, Dowis Ranch also offers stout, wonderfully named cultivars at $5, $6, and $7. The nursery also carries hundreds of daylilies not listed in the catalog, giving on-site visitors a distinct advantage. Irises and daylilies are shipped to all parts of the country, but local customers always enjoy a much greater selection of cultivars.

ILLINOIS

pagne Elegance' (small, frilly flowers of white and soft peach) and 'Immortality' (pristine, pure white).

Depending on the season, the stars of the garden could be the iris or the daylily, but the best supporting actors are always Eric's interesting **hostas**, a variegated pagoda **dogwood**, unusual perennials, and, without a doubt, Janell's uniquely braided **poplar** trees.

The Denhams encourage guests to tour the seedling beds and production fields. Iris may be viewed in bloom during the month of May (peaking mid-May), while daylilies are at their best early to mid-July. (Bloom is always dependent on weather and one must consider the vagaries of Mother Nature, so it is advisable to call ahead for peak bloom periods.)

THE FIELDS ON CATON FARM ROAD

❧ ❧

The Fields on Caton Farm Road, located on 150 acres of fertile farmland, is a wholesale grower and retail nursery full of color-laden, broadly sweeping gardens of fanciful flowers and breathtaking daylily displays. The Fields is also an approved American Hemerocallis Society (AHS) Display Garden, with more than 150 daylily varieties growing throughout the garden's 10-acre site. I once read somewhere that, judging by the vast numbers of daylilies hybridized and introduced each year, it is probably God's favorite plant. And standing in the center of The Fields' 60 acres of daylily production fields abutting the retail nursery, I can't help but agree.

During the height of the daylily growing season, The Fields is awash in the splendor of nature's boldest colors. These field-grown plants, adapted to the Midwest's growing conditions, offer good color choices and interesting flower shapes from various major breeders. Acres of daylilies (more than 100,000 plants) bloom in waves from the darkest black-red to orange, yellow, purple, raspberry, and cream coloring, with ruffled edges, striped petals, colored throats, water markings, and eyes.

OWNERS: Greg Newmann, Diane Hucek
TYPE: Large Specialty growers. Wholesale and retail
SPECIALTIES: Daylilies; hosta; shrubs; perennials—shade and sun annuals; herbs; hanging baskets
HOURS: April through mid-Aug.: Mon.-Sat. 9:00 am to 6:00 pm, Sun 10:00 am to 4:00 pm; closed July 4th. (Closed Sundays in August) End of Sept. through end of Oct.: Mon.-Sat 9:00 am to 6:00 pm, Sun. 10:00 am to 4:00 pm. (Call for hours mid-August through end of September)
CATALOG AVAILABLE: Yes
MAIL-ORDER AVAILABLE: No
DISPLAY GARDENS: Yes (AHS Display Garden)
CLASSES: No

CONTACT
1850 Caton Farm Road
Joliet, Il 60435
PHONE: (815) 744-7841
WEB ADDRESS: www.fieldsnursery.com
EMAIL: hefields@worldnet.att.net

DIRECTIONS
FROM I-55: I-55 to Weber Road south to Caton Farm Road. Turn west (right) on Caton Farm Road and drive 0.4 miles to nursery on your right.

GPS: N 41° 33.97', W 88° 07.32'

During this peak period, The Fields designates a daylily "du jour," which is then sculpted into sometimes stunning, sometimes unusual, but always interesting

ILLINOIS

flower arrangements. The credit goes to the gifted floral designer responsible for the daily cut-flower displays exhibited in the shade of the nursery's main sales building. This gives the customer the opportunity to experience the beauty of the daylilies as they would grow in their gardens and as they would look gracing the family's table. The garden center sales area, referred to as the Arbor Center, offers uncommon annuals and tender perennials, premium organic herbs, beautiful hanging baskets, hardy perennials, interesting pottery, and creative garden sculpture.

WHAT YOU'LL FIND

The Fields boasts of being "the world's largest grower of 'Stella d'Oro' **daylilies**." As popular as this hybrid is, some of the more flamboyant daylily cultivars available at the nursery include: the shimmering amber-orange 'Mauna Loa'; the rosy-pink 'Cherry Cheeks'; the big, bright yellow 'Big Bird'; and the golden 'Bonanza'. But that's not all. They also have the fragrant, orchid blend 'Lavender Blush'; the ruffled pink 'Chicago Petticoats'; the burnt-orange with darker orange veins 'Staghorn Sumac'; and the brilliant red 'Baltimore Oriole'. They offer the cute, yellow, fragrant, reblooming 'Mini Stella' appropriate for walkways, border edgings, small spaces, or for those gardeners looking for diversity yet still hooked on 'Stella d'Oro'.

Besides daylilies, the nursery also grows a good selection of garden-worthy **hostas**, shade and ornamental trees, and a general line of nursery stock. Though The Fields does carry some of the latest hosta hybrids, the majority of the selection is classics: 'August Moon', 'Gold Standard', 'Golden Tiara', 'Royal Standard', 'Sagae', 'Francis Williams', and 'Sum & Substance', to name but a few.

This nursery is known for growing landscape-worthy, but mainly standard, shade and street deciduous trees such as **flowering pear**, **maple**, **oak**, **magnolia**, **crabapple**, **honeylocust**, **birch**, **linden**, **hawthorn**, and seedless **ash**. However, in the mix are a number of classics: slow growing **ironwood** (*Ostrya virginiana*); **pagoda dogwood** (*Cornus alternifolia*); **Kentucky coffeetree** (*Gymnocladus dioicus*); the disease resistant **crabapple** (*Malus* 'Prairiefire'); yellow **buckeye** (*Aesculus flava*); **red horse chestnut** (*Aesculus* × *camea* 'Fort McNair'); and for brilliant red fall color,

ILLINOIS

a worthy **maple** (*Acer rubrum* 'Red Sunset').

The Fields' select shrub yard includes good hardy shrub **roses**, **hydrangea**, **sandcherry**, **witchhazel**, **spirea**, **viburnum**, and **lilac**. Noteworthy selections that managed to find their way into my trunk were white **fringetree** (*Chionanthus virginicus*), and for two-season enjoyment, the **wayfaring tree** (*Viburnum lantana* 'Mohican') with creamy white flowers in spring and reddish purple leaves in autumn. Most of the shrubs and trees are mature specimens, priced accordingly. Customers can select plants at the nursery or call and have them dug to order.

An annual Open House kicks off the spring and summer planting seasons, complete with gardening advice, demonstrations, complimentary refreshments, door prizes, and giveaways. The well attended, annual fall tree sale also showcases giant **mums**, **asters**, **pansies**, and, of course, **pumpkins**.

EXTRAS

During the year, The Fields hosts many fun events such as Art in the Garden and the Jack Frost Festival. The nursery comes together with local community groups for fun and fundraising. Art in the Garden, held during peak bloom times, features artists, live music, and entertainment scattered about the colorful gardens. The Jack Frost Festival celebrates the fall season with hayrides, guided tours, pumpkin decorating, storytelling, the haunted maze, and the very popular haunted house— Ghouls by the Pool.

ILLINOIS

FOX VALLEY ORCHIDS, LTD.

❧ ❧

Fox Valley Orchids is a small independent nursery specializing in tropical Lady's Slipper orchids. Fifteen years ago, the nursery got its start in a small backyard greenhouse purchasing these rare and expensive orchids, propagating them, and selling the resulting seedlings at a reasonable price. (Note: The nursery does not deal in or sell native American Lady Slipper orchids.)

These Lady's Slipper orchids *(Paphiopedilum)* are not as well known as the butterfly orchids *(Phalaenopsis)*, but they make great windowsill plants. The flowers last at least six weeks, look like an exquisite drawing with their spotted or striped sepals, and possess a lip whose delicate curves give rise to the common name "lady's slipper."

When it comes to the subject of orchids, gardeners are divided: some adore them, others don't. Orchids have an erroneous reputation for being temperamental beauties that require meticulous care, plus tons of luck, for their survival. In reality, few other plants adapt as well to the conditions of the average homes as orchids do.

OWNERS: Tom Kalina
TYPE: Small specialty nursery
SPECIALTIES: Orchids
HOURS: Mon.-Sat. 9:00 am to 5:00 pm, Sun. 11:00 am to 3:00 pm.
CATALOG AVAILABLE: Online
MAIL-ORDER AVAILABLE: Yes
DISPLAY GARDENS: No
CLASSES: No

CONTACT
2N134 Addison Rd.
Villa Park, IL 60181
PHONE: (630) 458-0636
FAX: (630) 458-1030
WEB ADDRESS: www.foxvalleyorchids.com
EMAIL: info@foxvalleyorchids.com

DIRECTIONS
FROM I-355: I-355 to North Avenue east for 2.5 miles to Addison Road. Turn north (left) onto Addison Rd., the nursery is immediately on your left. (Turn into the long driveway to Orchids by Hausermann. Fox Valley Orchids is located within the Hausermann complex.)

GPS: N 41° 54.33', W 87° 59.31'

WHAT YOU'LL FIND

Currently Fox Valley Orchids propagates not only "paphs" but also "phrags" *(Phragmipedium* spp.), focusing on the production of unusual grexes. (A grex is a hoticultural term referring to the group of offspring produced from hybridizing orchids. According to Fox Valley, these **orchids** are rarely offered by large commercial growers because of the limited number of seedlings produced. The nursery grows spectacular orchid hybrids, including many from their own hybridization program. All plants are greenhouse propagated and sold as seedlings or mature plants.

Fox Valley Orchids carries novelty *Paphiopedilum* hybrids, vini-color *Paphiopedilum* hybrids, *Paphiopedilum* species, *Paphiopedilum sanderianum* hybrids, coloratum *Paphiopedilum* hybrids, complex *Paphiopedilum* hybrids, *Parvisepalum* hybrid seedlings, and *Phragmipedium* species and hybrids.

Note: Fox Valley Orchids is located on the property of Orchids by Hausermann, so online orders from Fox Valley are processed through the Orchids by Hausermann system.

ILLINOIS

THE GROWING PLACE

❧ ❧

The Growing Place is a family owned second-generation business that caters to the needs of upscale gardeners in Naperville and surrounding suburbs. Regarded as a "Naperville institution," old-timers may remember this nursery as Emma's Perennials. In 1972, after the passing of both Emma and her husband Fritz, their nephew Rich Massat and his wife Carol expanded the nursery with the addition of annuals, trees, shrubs, and ground covers. In 1976, with the business flourishing and growing, they changed the name to The Growing Place to better reflect its new direction.

Twelve years later, the Massats purchased 18 acres of farmland for a second location in Aurora and dubbed it, "The Farm." A barn was built, along with numerous greenhouses and perennial frames, enabling The Growing Place to grow a greater diversity of plants. In the year 2000, Carol attended a nearby farm auction for the specific purpose of picking up a few minor farm implements to add charm and character to The Farm. Instead, she purchased a whole farmhouse—DuPage County's last 1800s farmhouse—moving it the 4½ miles to The Farm. Today, the preserved farmhouse and its formidable heirloom gardens are the crown jewels of that location, adding considerable character to the environment.

Both the Naperville and Aurora sites are densely populated with well-labeled plants that are attractively integrated into the nursery and display

OWNERS: Rich and Carol Massat
TYPE: Large retail nursery
SPECIALTIES: Perennials—sun and shade; annuals—tender perennials; tropicals; summer bulbs; hanging baskets; trees; shrubs; roses; herbs; aquatics; vines; grasses; garden art; containers
HOURS: April 1 thru Oct.: Mon.-Fri. 9:00 am to 6:00 pm; April 15 to June 14: Mon.-Fri. 9:00 am to 7:00 pm, Sat. 9:00 am to 5:00 pm, Sun. 11:00 am to 5:00 pm. Closed Sundays in July and August. Nov. 8 to Dec. 21: Mon.-Sat. 9:00 am to 4:00 pm.
CATALOG AVAILABLE: Printed
MAIL-ORDER AVAILABLE: No
DISPLAY GARDENS: Yes
CLASSES: Yes

CONTACT
25W471 Plank Road
Naperville, IL 60563
PHONE: (630) 355-4000
WEB ADDRESS: www.growingplace.com

DIRECTIONS
DIRECTIONS FROM I-88 (EAST-WEST TOLLWAY): Exit at Naperville Exit (Naperville Road/Naper Blvd) and go south (right) on Naper Blvd to Plank Road. At Plank turn west (right) and proceed for approximately 5 blocks. Nursery is on the left.

GPS: N 41° 47.34', W 88° 07.33'

ILLINOIS

gardens. The Growing Place has a knack for offering intriguing newcomers yet still retaining the old favorites. Grouped according to category, all plants are attractively displayed in alphabetical order by horticultural names on long tables. Informative and descriptive, plant placards strung on wires above each variety are clear, concise, and easy to read.

Both sites are perpetually crowded on weekends and jam-packed the weeks leading up to Mother's Day and Memorial Day. For these two holidays, full, large, impressive hanging baskets are wisked out the door in numbers too great to count.

WHAT YOU'LL FIND

Among the shade perennials are numerous **hosta** and **coral bells** (*Heuchera*) delicate **tunica** (*Petrorhagia*), a dozen airy and graceful **columbines**, nearly 20 varieties of **astilbe**, the greatly underused **barrenwort**, undemanding **cranesbill**, Japanese *Kirengishoma*, and early flowering **hellebores**. On a recent spring visit, I also noticed an uncommon **bluebell** (*Mertensia pterocarpa* var. *yezoensis*) as well as **gentians, forget-me-nots**, and **Japanese toad lilies**. Cottage or Victorian gardeners will find a good selection of **pinks, foxgloves, bleeding hearts**, and **peonies**. Looking to spice up a sun border, I found superior varieties of perennial **snapdragon** (*Antirrhinum*), a yellow wild **indigo**, and the variegated **phlox**, 'Becky Towe'.

For container gardeners, a wide range of colorful annuals, tropicals, and tender perennials is stocked throughout the season. Masterful container gardens and seasonal displays illustrating decorative uses of the nursery's plants are clustered throughout the property. Also available are impressive hanging baskets, geraniums, a long list of vines, a reasonable selection of grasses, herbs, vegetable flats (in spring), and other ornamental plants. The nursery grows much of its annual stock from seed or plugs, including such mainstays as **alyssum, tuberous begonia, verbena, cleome, salvia, lobelia, petu-**

SATELLITE LOCATION

CONTACT
2000 Montgomery Road
Aurora, IL 60504
PHONE: (630) 820-8088

DIRECTIONS
FROM I-88: (East-West Tollway): Exit at Kirk/Farnsworth Road and go south (right) to Montgomery Road. At Montgomery turn east (left) approximately 1/2 mile. Nursery is on the left. **FROM OGDEN AVENUE (IN NAPERVILLE):** Take Ogden Ave. southwest to Montgomery Road. Turn west (right) for approximately 1/4 mile. Nursery is on the right. ("The Farm" is approximately. 3.5 miles southwest of the Fox Valley Mall.)

ILLINOIS

nia, **marigold**, and **pansy**. Excellent selections of well-branched and bushy **impatiens** and delicate snapdragon-like **diascia** are also on hand.

For gardeners with upscale tastes, I noticed 7 varieties of free-flowering **bacopa**, 11 of brightly colored **lantana**, 8 of **Million Bells**® (*Callibrachoa*), 15 of the oh-so-colorful sun **coleus**, a couple of eye-catching **skullcaps** (*Scutellaria*), and the incredibly captivating **cat's whiskers** (*Orthosiphon*).

> *"Nothing is more completely the child of art than a garden"*
> —Sir Walter Scott

The herb section has traditionally been excellent, combining common culinary herbs with such exotics as **sweetleaf** (*Stevia*), **sorrel** (*Rumex*), **lovage** (*Levisticum*), **lemongrass** (*Cymbopogon*), and scented **mints** (*Mentha*). Best of all are the ornamental herbs that hold their own in low maintenance perennial beds: **thyme**, **hyssop**, **lavender**, and **salvia**.

Both Growing Place locations carry an incredible array of **roses**. Included in the selection are many of the newest and the oldest. According to the catalog, the rose selection is the result of extensive research for hardiness and disease resistance. Varieties that have shown themselves to be of merit are the David Austin™ series of English roses; fragrant Generosa from France, and Renaissance from England. They also have the Explorer™ and Parkland™ series from Canada; the Romantica series from the Meilland breeders; Buck roses; Scotch roses popular in cottage gardens; very fragrant Portland roses; and the extremely hardy Rugosa roses, to name a few.

There is an outstanding selection of ornamental trees, woody shrubs, and evergreens brought in from outside sources. Most trees and evergreens are large one-of-a-kind specimens in impressive health, with freshly balled-and-burlapped root systems.

The Garden Treasures Shop in both locations is a good source for practical and decorative products for the garden, and for garden themed accents for the home. Among the items: birdbaths, statuary, benches, tools, metal accent pieces, troughs, fountains, and much more. The Naperville shop, open for the Christmas season, is renowned for it natural decorating ideas and fresh greens—distinctive wreaths, swags, and containers. Each location has an estimated acre of display gardens, each one designed and lovingly tended by the staff. Many of the gardens have themes, such as rose, bog, butterfly, fragrant, respite, water, white, and old house. For kids (or those who are kids at heart), The Growing Place at the Aurora facil-

★ SIDE TRIPS ★

Stroll the grounds of **NAPER SETTLEMENT** (630-420-6010), a museum village of nineteenth century homes, shops, and gardens where costumed interpreters tell the story of daily life in Naperville during the period of change from a frontier outpost to a turn-of-the-century community. Naper Settlement is located near downtown Naperville. **RIVERWALK** (near Naper Settlement) is a landscaped path along the DuPage River, 2 blocks west of Washington St. at Aurora Ave. (Follow signs along major Naperville Streets.) Across Aurora Ave. from Naper Settlement is the impressive **MILLENNIUM CARILLON BELL TOWER** (call 630-355-4141 for a schedule of free concerts). This is one of only four Bell Towers world-wide whose bells span six full octaves. A short distance east, in Lisle, **THE MORTON ARBORETUM** (630-968-0074) is a 1,700-acre non-profit outdoor museum of more than 3,300 kinds of trees, shrubs, and other plants in woodlands, wetlands, and gardens. There is a restored native prairie that offers more than 10 miles of roads and hiking trails. There is an admission charge. From The Growing Place, go east (right) on Plank Rd., turn north (left) at Naper Blvd., east (right) at Warrenville Road, north (left) at Rt. 53. The arboretum entrance is immediately on your right.

ity maintains a hypnotic outdoor train garden in which a miniature garden railroad winds its way through a Lilliputian landscape.

The Growing Place's dense, annual newsprint catalog is an informative resource. At a hefty 170 pages, it has the feel of a good-sized periodical. The friendly, smiling staff at both locations is adept at assisting both novice and expert gardeners in selecting the right plant for the right site or container. There is a comforting sense of un-rushed, yet purposeful and efficient, activity. The crowded annual Open House, held on a Saturday in June, offers interesting seminars, exciting new plant introductions, master gardeners, creative garden crafters, and, of course, music and refreshments.

ILLINOIS

HIDDEN GARDENS NURSERY

✦

Aptly named, Hidden Gardens Nursery is a horticultural find for any discerning gardener. Though located next to a major expressway, the convoluted path leading to the nursery could be a somewhat tricky endeavor for the first time visitor without instructions. Nevertheless, gardeners should not be deterred from seeking out this secluded treasure.

The nursery's impressive plant list includes many uncommon trees, shrubs, perennials, bonsai, hanging baskets, annuals, and vines. The diverse selection, while managing to offer gardeners an enticing bit of everything, nonetheless concentrates principally on trees and shrubs. At Hidden Gardens the emphasis is primarily on those ornamental plants commonly sought out by visionary landscape architects and designers.

In addition to plants, Hidden Gardens carries new and creative beautiful garden ornaments such as whimsical iron art, tuteurs, obelisks, and rusty iron benches. There is an interesting gift shop located in the vintage farmhouse. For garden interest, it offers a variety of trellises, cement urns, statuary, garden art, and a unique selection of birdhouses. For someone like me, who collects birdhouses, this is truly a dangerous place.

Customers are encouraged to tour the elegant display gardens showcasing staff design talents as well as the witty plant combinations that are cleverly integrated inside the nursery.

OWNERS: Gladys Schutz
TYPE: Retail nursery
SPECIALTIES: Trees; shrubs; annuals; perennials; hosta; grasses; bonsai
HOURS: April through Sept.: Mon.-Fri.: 7:00 am to 7:00 pm, Sat.: 7:00 am to 5:00 pm, Sun.: 10:00 am to 3:00 pm. Closed Fourth of July. Oct. through Nov.: Mon-Fri: 7:00 am to 5:00 pm, Sat.: 7:00 am to 5:00 pm, Sun: 10:00 am to 3:00 pm.
CATALOG AVAILABLE: No
MAIL-ORDER AVAILABLE: No
DISPLAY GARDENS: Yes
CLASSES: Yes

CONTACT
16 W658 Frontage Road
Hinsdale, IL 60521
PHONE: (630) 655-8283
WEB ADDRESS: www.hiddengarden.net
EMAIL: None

DIRECTIONS
FROM THE INTERSECTION OF INTERSTATE I-55 AND RT. 83 (KINGERY HIGHWAY): From Rt. 83 and I-55, proceed south on Rt. 83 to the first light, Central Avenue. Turn right (west) on Central Avenue and drive two blocks to Sunrise Avenue. (You will be traveling through a subdivision to get to Frontage Road.) Make a right turn (north) on Sunrise Ave. and continue to Bonnie Brae Lane, which is the fourth intersection. Turn left (west) on Bonnie Brae Lane, which after a bend in the road, becomes Frontage Road. Hidden Gardens is located on the left side of the road, a short distance down.

GPS: N 41° 44.32', W 87° 57.07'

Fine ornamental shrubs include: **bottlebrush buckeye**, **witchhazel**, **serviceberry**, **barberry**, **butterfly bush**, **bluebeard**, **redbud**, **flowering quince**, **smoke bush**, **lilac**, **rose mallow**, and **St. John's wort**. Other shrubs, not as readily available elsewhere, include **Carolina allspice** (*Calycanthus floridus*), **pea tree** (*Caragana arborescens*), **fringe tree** (*Chionanthus virginicus*), **cornelian cherry** (*Cornus mas*), **deutzia** (*Deutzia*), **silver bell** (*Halesia carolina*), **seven sons flower** (*Heptacodium miconioides*), and **beauty bush** (*Kolkwitzia amabilis*). **Hydrangeas**, **viburnum**, and **spirea** are well represented here, and there are excellent choices of **boxwood**, **azalea**, **summersweet**, and **rhododendron**.

> *"More than anything, I must have flowers...always, always."*
> —CLAUDE MONET

The nursery has a notable selection of ornamental trees brought in from outside sources. Most trees are large, specimen-sized plants of impressive health, available in all manner of prices and sizes. Stock supplies fluctuate and some plants sell out quickly, so if there is something you cannot live without, it might be wise to secure it at once. Hidden Gardens offers **katsura** (*Cercidiphyllum japonicum*), exciting cultivars of **Chinese dogwood** (*Cornus kousa*), and a beguiling range of **Japanese maples**—green, red, variegated, weeping, and upright. Of special interest is the wealth of conifers: **false cypress**, **juniper**, **yew**, **spruce**, **pine**, **fir**, and **hemlock**.

Grouped according to category—sun, shade, vine, rose, ornamental grasses, etc., all plants are attractively displayed alphabetically by scientific nomenclature on long tables or in neat, long rows on the ground. Informative and descriptive, plant tags are clear and easy to read. The nursery grows superior varieties of **aster**, **lady's mantle**, **columbine**, **astilbe**, **phlox**, **daylily**, **beebalm**, **sedum**, **bluestar**, **aster**, **bellflower**, **tickseed**, and **cranesbill**. Among the handsome shade perennials are numerous **hosta**, **coral bells**, **ferns**, **astilbe**, **lamium**, and **toadlily**.

★ SIDE TRIPS ★

OAK BROOK SHOPPING CENTER, Oak Brook, IL (northeast corner of 22nd St. and Rt. 83), is a premier, upscale outdoor shopping mall renowned not only for the quality of its tenants but also for its incredibly landscaped grounds.

ILLINOIS

Woodlanders include **bleeding heart, jack-in-the-pulpit,** delicate **corydalis, columbine, Solomon's seal, trillium, wild ginger, barrenwort, hellebore, heucherella,** and **bluebells.**

For gardeners with a yen for the pouffy look of English gardens, the nursery has a great collection of cottage garden plants such as **foxglove, delphinium, boltonia, valerian, poppy, pinks,** and **catmint.** Hidden Gardens carries extensive collections of **peonies, garden phlox, iris,** and a prodigious **lily** collection.

Besides perennials, Hidden Gardens sells spirited **pansies** early in the spring, attractive hanging baskets, and a sizeable collection of interesting annuals. The nursery's annual plant stock is best early in the season; after mid-July, the lot is depleted and prices slashed. Perennial vines include **porcelainberry,** several varieties of **honeysuckle,** the tree-hugging and shade-tolerant **hydrangea** (*Schizophragma hydrangeoides*), and a number of gorgeous, large- and small-flowered **clematis.** If ponds are your passion, the nursery carries a complete range of water plants, marginals, and oxygenators. One hoop house is filled with an extensive collection of bonsai. Bonsai, the English translation of which is "tree in a tray," is the name for the centuries-old art of growing a paradox in a pot.

ILLINOIS

HORNBAKER GARDENS

❧ ❧

Located approximately 5 miles southeast of Princeton, Hornbaker Gardens is a popular premier nursery renowned for its vast collections of hosta, daylily, and iris. This nursery attracts collectors, connoisseurs, and everyday gardeners from the Midwest and much of the rest of the country. With its extensive display gardens (worth seeing in their own right) Hornbaker is justifiably a favorite destination for numerous horticultural society and garden club day trips. An annual open house in June features wonderful specials, garden tours, and refreshments.

This cutting-edge nursery has its roots in fruit trees and berries, not ornamental plants. In 1976, Rich Hornbaker, a lawyer, and Kathy, a teacher, purchased 14 acres of isolated farmland with the intent of making a living by marketing organically grown fruits and veggies. Horn's Berry Farm, a small pick-your-own fruit farm, turned out to be a great learning experience, if not a financial success. In July of 1986, Rich attended a weeklong symposium of the then newly formed Perennial Plant Association (PPA), and the rest is history. Enthused about the future of perennials in general, but totally smitten by hosta, Rich came home a changed man. That fall the berries were plowed under, the practice of law forsaken, and a new business—Hornbaker Gardens—was born.

OWNERS: Rich and Kathy Hornbaker
TYPE: Large specialty and retail nursery
SPECIALTIES: Hosta; daylilies; iris; perennials; trees, shrubs, dwarf conifers; grasses; aquatic plants; ponds and pond supplies.
OPEN: mid-April through mid-Oct.: Mon.-Sat. 8:00 am to 5:00 pm, Sun. Noon to 5:00 pm. Closed Easter, July 4th, and Labor Day.
CATALOG AVAILABLE: Printed price sheets and online listing
MAIL-ORDER AVAILABLE: Yes
DISPLAY GARDENS: Yes
CLASSES: No

CONTACT

22937 1140 North Avenue
Princeton, IL 61356-8545
PHONE: (815) 659-3282
FAX: (815) 659-3159
WEB ADDRESS: www.hornbakergardens.com
EMAIL: mail@hornbakergardens.com

DIRECTIONS

FROM I-80: At exit 61 (4 miles east of Princeton) go south on I-180 about 5 miles, and exit at Route 26. Go west, toward Princeton only about 1/4 of a mile, and take the first left. Then go 2 miles up the steep hill. Hornbaker Gardens is at the top of the hill on the right. Look for the sign. **FROM PRINCETON:** Follow Route 26 as it winds through the town, and continue south on Route 26 from the east edge of town. About a mile or so south of town watch for a blue "tourist attraction" sign for Hornbaker Gardens. Turn right at the blue sign and go about a half-mile. Take the first left, and then proceed for 2 miles until you see the Hornbaker sign.

GPS: N 41° 18.72', W 89° 24.77'

ILLINOIS

Hornbaker Gardens sells more than 600 varieties of daylilies, 500 of irises, 70 of ornamental grasses, 700 of sun and shade perennials, 150 of tree, shrub, and dwarf conifers, and 35 of aquatic plants. However, there is no question that hosta—with well over 550 varieties—is the big boy here.

In the dappled shade of a woody section of the farmstead, Rich transformed a bramble-infested ravine into a "botanical garden" fantasyland full of mature, robust, specimen-sized hosta plants. Visitors flock to this site in droves! These astonishing arrays of well-labeled hostas are planted out throughout the ravine, in containers, ringed around trees, combined with other shade loving perennials, and lined along the numerous pathways and steps. They are ingeniously fantastic salesmen in their own right.

Besides the great plants, there is an extensive selection of interesting containers scattered around a rather minimal gift shop that carries a small selection of tools, books, and garden accessories. The emphasis in garden sculpture is on ornamental value—unique, interesting, but not outlandish. On my last visit, I was particularly intrigued by an absolutely realistic 6-foot metallic praying mantis. However, if car space or budget restraints prevent you from considering the 6-footer, there are some adorable 18-inchers to choose from.

WHAT YOU'LL FIND

The one-of-a-kind **hosta** display showcases such selections as cute dwarf and mini 'Baby Bunting' and 'Baby Kim'; the somewhat larger, shiny leafed 'Don Stevens'; the blunt-tipped 'Decorata'; and the semi-upright, impressive clump, 'Flower Power'. There is the extraordinarily huge 'Vim and Vigor' (a green sport of 'Sum and Substance'—my favorite); and hundreds more. The seduction of these plants is impossible to resist. As Rich's interests have grown, he has enhanced the display with the addition of a large pond, a gazebo, and a diamond-dusted stream cascading down several sparkling waterfalls. Across the drive in the shade greenhouses, all the hosta plants currently available are conveniently arranged in alphabetical order.

Several other display gardens showcasing sun perennials are threaded liberally throughout the nursery. Visitors are encouraged to stroll through the impressive displays featuring mixed perennial borders, grasses, and a growing collection of unusual trees and shrubs. Kathy Hornbaker is fully committed to trialing as many plants as possible; consequently, each repeat visit to the nursery reveals ever-expanding gardens. I was particularly taken with the vast selection of **phlox**—26 varieties at last count (garden, tall, woodland, and creeping). In addition, I noted 14 varieties of **buddleia**, 12 of **campanula**, 17 of **cranesbill**, 36 of **coral bells**, 9 of **persicaria**, 20 of **lungwort**, 14 of **yarrow**, and 18 of **columbine**, to name a few. The most recent development has been in the area of ponds and aquatic plants. Rich has added 2 more water gardens, opening up a whole new world of gardening pleasures. The largest pond is 40 feet in diameter with 150 feet of streams and waterfalls.

If you have a soft spot in your horticultural heart for **bearded iris**—then prepare yourself for major temptation! Bloom season for iris starts around the first of May when the shorter varieties start flowering, but peak bloom for the tall bearded iris is generally mid- to late May. Guests are invited to stroll through the iris growing-fields—a dazzling tapestry of glorious hues—to pick whichever varieties pluck at their heartstrings. All varieties of iris (sold only bare root) are dug in July, when they are shipped; however, a great many of Hornbaker' customers opt to pick up their orders in person, when the daylily fields are in full bloom. The prolific bloomers generally are at their peak from July 5 through July 25. Hornbaker Gardens carries all six classes of iris: miniature dwarf bearded, standard dwarf bearded, intermediate bearded, border bearded, miniature tall bearded, and tall bearded. In addition to bearded Iris, they also offer potted irises such as: *Iris cristata, I. ensata, I. pallida, I. pseudacorus,* and *I. sibirica.*

In Greek mythology, Iris, messenger of the gods, bridged heaven and earth with her magnificently colored rainbows. However, it's the comforting thought that Iris also escorts women's souls to heaven that prompted me to plant a rhizome . . . or three.

For the weekend gardener or the experienced pro, there simply isn't a better perennial than the daylily (*Hemerocallis*). They are virtually disease and pest free, come in a myriad of colors and shapes, and are able to withstand drought, poor soil, and shade. At Hornbaker Gardens, daylilies are sold in three different ways: potted, bare root, and clumps. Each spring, the staff digs up and pots a couple of thousand pots of their best selling varieties, which are then available throughout the season.

Daylily enthusiasts on the lookout for different and unusual variations prefer walking the colorful fields during peak bloom. Orders are taken at this time, and

ILLINOIS

after the season ends (usually in early August), the plants are dug up, cut back, and shipped to customers. Gardeners seeking a bigger plant, the uncommon variant, or big splashes of instant gratification usually elect to purchase the entire clump. Generally ranging in price between $15 and $50—depending on variety and number of fans—these are dug up right on the spot, dropped in a plastic bag, and sent home with the customer to be successfully planted into the landscape.

Of the daylily selections, I found 'Artic Snow' (a large flowered crème-white) totally irresistible. And then there was the show-stopper 'Chance Encounter'; the cream with lavender edged 'Chicago Petite Lace'; super colorful 'Hasty Albert'; the fragrant, iridescent, coral beauty, 'South Seas'; the unusual spider-like, crimped, and ruffled yellow 'Techny Spider'; and still another near-white, 'Heidi Edelweiss'.

Although the focus of Hornbaker Gardens is still on perennials, interesting conifers and woodies (deciduous trees and shrubs) are making some remarkable inroads, as well as aquatic plants (hardy marginals, tropical marginals, **water lilies**, hardy **lotus**, floaters, and oxygenators). When it comes to ponds, Rich and Kathy are so fully convinced that Aquascape ponds are the best ponds on the market that they offer no other. If you are interested in ponds, installed or in kit form, talk to the very friendly and helpful Mike Sayler.

★ **SIDE TRIPS** ★

Princeton is popular for its wide array of antique shops. An original old-time **RED COVERED BRIDGE** (one of six in the state), built in 1863, is a popular attraction—located off Rt. 26 just north of I-80. History buffs will enjoy **THE LOVEJOY HOMESTEAD** complex, one of the most important stations on the Underground Railroad in Illinois, (815) 879-9151. Annual **CIVIL WAR RE-ENACTMENTS** are held annually in October in City-County Park just north of Princeton, (815) 875-2616.

ILLINOIS

JONES COUNTRY GARDEN

❧ ❧

Okay, I admit it. I stumbled upon this horticultural gem purely by chance. But to say it made my day is an understatement. It made my summer! Jones Country Garden embodies everything that a gardener searches for in a nursery.

Jones Country Garden specializes in cutting-edge ornamental container plants and luscious hanging baskets. This innovative horticultural enterprise is rooted in its owners' rural farming heritage, and this nursery is just one example of the innovative spirit exhibited by farming families bent on finding ways to retain and use their rural legacy.

The nursery got its start in the early 1980s as a strawberry farm. Today, there are 20 greenhouses (more than an acre under glass) attached to the old family barn, filled to their glass rafters with the latest horticultural gems. Owners Linda and Robert Jones, tired of the ubiquitous annuals that were readily available at every nursery and garden center, flexed their adventurous horticultural inclinations by searching endlessly for unsurpassed plant varieties for container gardening. Their specialty is to focus on unusual ornamental annuals and tender perennials, propagated and grown in the farm's greenhouses. The result-

OWNERS: Linda and Robert Jones, Chad Jones
TYPE: Specialty nursery.
SPECIALTIES: Annuals; tender perennials; hanging baskets; herbs; perennials.
HOURS: April: Mon.-Sat. 8:00 am to 6:00 pm; May and June: Mon.-Sat. 8:00 am to 6:30 pm, Sun. Noon to 4:00 pm; July and Aug.: Mon.-Sat. 8:00 am to 2:00 pm; Mid-Sept. thru Oct.: Mon.-Sat. 10:00 am to 6:00 pm. (Times can vary at beginning and end of season. If coming from a distance, call to confirm hours.)
CATALOG AVAILABLE: No
MAIL-ORDER AVAILABLE: No
DISPLAY GARDENS: No
CLASSES: No

CONTACT
22055 N. 800 East Road
Pontiac, IL 61764
PHONE: (815) 358-2585
WEB ADDRESS: None
EMAIL: None

DIRECTIONS
FROM I-55: I-55 to IL-116 (Exit 197) toward Pontiac/Flanagan. Turn west (right) onto IL-116/E 1700 Rd and drive 5.4 miles to 800 Rd E. Turn north (right) onto 800 Rd. E and drive for 5.1 miles to nursery on your left. Turn onto the long curving driveway and drive to the barn. Entry to the greenhouses is through the barn. **FROM I-39:** Take I-39 to IL-116 (Exit # 22) toward Pontiac. Turn east (left) onto IL-116 (Follow IL-116 to IL-251 for 0.4 miles where you will turn north (left) driving for 1 mile to IL-116/900 Rd. Make a right turn onto IL-116/1900 Rd. Take IL-116/900 Rd. for 13.2 miles to 800 Rd. Turn north (left) and drive for 5.1 miles to nursery. (see above for entry.)

GPS: N 40° 56.72', W 88° 46.68'

ing stock, a kaleidoscope of colors, tones, and textures, ranges from the uncommon but well-known, to exotics lacking common names.

What You'll Find

"What a pity flowers can utter no sound. A singing rose, a whispering violet, a murmuring honeysuckle— oh, what a rare and exquisite miracle would these be!"
—Henry Ward Beecher

Traditional choices include scads of **abutilon**, **impatiens**, **fuchsias**, **ivy geranium**, **begonias**, and **lantanas**, augmented by **ageratum**, **arctotis**, **cobbity daisy**, **brachyscome**, **osteospermum**, **licorice plant** (*Helichrysum*), and **vinca vine**. Extraordinary finds include **cat's whiskers**, *Orthosiphon stamineus* (a frisky member of the mint family); several varieties of **angel's trumpet**, *Brugmansia* (broad leaves and amazing, perfumed flowers); **blue butterfly flower**, *Clerodendrum ugandense* (small blossoms, mini butterflies in flight, in a beautiful combination of sky blue and very dark blue; and **lion's ear**, *Leonotis leonurus* (whorls of rust-orange, fuzzy flowers).

Being a pushover for anything new with an interesting leaf, I was attracted to dozens of intriguingly handsome foliage plants. There's flashy **coleus**, *Solenostemon* (bringing playful fun and colorful creativity to any container); and selections of *Acalypha* (always unusual, outrageously colorful, and texturally exciting copperleaf). You'll find a mix of *Alternanthera* (colorful leaves cloaked in jazzy colors of bloodleaf); **false dracaena**, *Cordyline* (spiky phormiuim look-alike); *Graptophyllum pictum* (regal, upright caricature plant); and **sweet potato vine**, *Ipomoea batatas* (heat-loving tender perennial producing a vigorous carpet of colorful foliage). Look for **bloodleaf**, *Iresine* (smoldering beauty); and tropical **mint**, *Plectranthus* (fuzzy yet colorful foliage).

A container garden's beauty is created with a concentration of glowing color transformed into a showstopping focal point. To that end, Jones Country Garden carries a universe of **petunias**: Superbells™, Supertunia™, Surfina™, Wave™, Double Wave™, and Million Bells®. They offer their customers a world of *Torenia*, *Scaevola*, *Osteospermum*, *Verbena*, *Lobelia*, *Bacopa*, and *Angelonia*, along with an ocean of *Nemesia*, *Diascia*, *Lotus*, *Monopsis*, *Strobilanthes*, and *Turnera*. I planted some of the nursery's *Agastache* 'Blue Fortune' in a container in my garden, and watched in sheer delight as bumblebees and butterflies engaged in a feeding frenzy.

Jones Country creates its own extra-sumptuous hanging baskets—more than 8,000 every spring. Ranging in size from 10-inch wire baskets to impressive 24-inchers, these luscious creations dripping gorgeous blossoms fly out the door by the car-load, especially the two weeks leading up to Mother's Day. In the fall, they grow more than 10,000 pots of mums in a rainbow of colors planted out in numerous container and basket sizes.

The nursery's perennial collection, though exemplary, is rather small, accounting for a relatively small portion of their business. However, I did note good choices of **coral bells**, **cranesbill**, **bellflower**, some **daylilies** and **hosta**, and ornamental vines. The Jones' son Chad is instrumental in steering the nursery towards incorporating ornamental shrubs—old and new—into its stock, and spring visitors find thriving flats of herbs and vegetables.

This nursery was an exciting discovery. Here was a place that had exceptionally well-grown, cutting-edge plants at reasonable prices and staff that was friendly and helpful. What more could I possibly ask for? So like any "great explorer," big smile plastered on my tired face, I quietly limped home with my hoard of plants crammed into every nook and cranny of the car's trunk and interior. I heartily recommend you follow my example.

ILLINOIS

KLEISS FARM & NURSERY

Linda and Jerry Kleiss have created a bit of paradise I'll bet many of their customers only dream about. Tucked back into a peaceful rural setting, Kleiss Farm & Nursery is a popular plant nursery overlooking an open family farm that closely resembles a private estate. The nursery is approached by way of an eye-catching street-side planting, rich in ornamental grasses, asters, rudbeckia, and other exemplary perennials and bulbs. A graceful entry framed by soaring trees leads the way into seductive display gardens around the Kleiss private residence, rich in a variety of foliage, flowers, and shrubs. A pond is home to goldfish and koi and a broad range of well-selected plants including structural foliage that provides a living architecture to the garden. It is a place of understated serenity, where foliage and texture flow like a restful river. The staff is friendly and knowledgeable.

Although aquatics are a specialty, intriguing perennials, charming annuals, captivating vines, attractive hanging baskets, adorable topiary, and some interesting trees and shrubs are also available. The Kleiss' invite customers to tour the gardens, view the trees, shrubs, and perennials in maturity, and to take notes. There are trellises, arbors, and fences placed throughout the gardens to create vertical elements and to show off the plants. The gardens are picturesque, and Kleiss urges visitors to take pictures of the lusty plant combinations that demonstrate luscious color combinations, ornamental forms, and tantalizing textures.

The extra-sumptuous wire and moss hanging baskets in various sizes,

OWNERS: Linda and Jerry Kleiss
TYPE: Retail and wholesale nursery
SPECIALTIES: Aquatics; perennials— sun and shade; annuals; specialty topiary; herbs; planters
HOURS: End of April through end of May: Mon.-Sat. 8:30 am to 5:30 pm, Sun. Noon-4:00 pm; June 1 through end of Oct.: Mon.-Sat. 8:00 am to 3:00 pm.
CATALOG AVAILABLE: Yes.
MAIL-ORDER AVAILABLE: No
DISPLAY GARDENS: Yes
CLASSES: Yes

CONTACT
349 CR 1500 E
Tolono, IL 61880
PHONE: (217) 867-2364
FAX: (217) 867-2365
WEB ADDRESS: www.kleissnursery.com
EMAIL: ldkleiss@hotmail.com

DIRECTIONS
FROM ROUTE 130 (CHAMPAIGN/URBANA):
Take IL Rt-130 south to 300 N St., approximately 12 miles south of Champaign/Urbana. (Watch for the sign on the southwest corner of the intersection). Turn west (right) onto 300 N St., driving 1.1 miles to 1500 E Rd. (Watch for the sign on the northeast corner of the intersection). Turn north (right) onto 1500 E and drive 0.4 miles to the nursery on your left.

GPS: N 39° 55.77', W 88° 10.83'

some quite large (and in quantities in the hundreds), are also a specialty of the nursery. During the winter months, customers bring back baskets, containers, and urns for repotting, choosing from an excellent range of greenhouse-grown bodacious plants of superior flower-power.

WHAT YOU'LL FIND

Kleiss Farm grows zesty mounds of **nemesia**, **lobelia**, **trailing snapdragrons** (Luminaire™), **black-eyed susan vines**, **verbena**, **bacopa**, **lantana**, **plectranthus**, **double portulaca**, **scaevola**, **licorice plant**, **angelonia**, **impatiens** (double, mini, New Guinea), and **diascia**. There are yards of **petunias** including Wave™, Double Wave™, Trailing Suncatcher®, and Million Bells®. You'll find an array of **coleus** in every shape, size, and vibrant color; and scintillating selections of annual **salvias**, **fuchsias**, **geraniums** (*Pelargonium*), **pentas**, **cuphea**, **gaura**, **osteospermum**, **sweet potato vine**, and **colocasia**.

> *"To cultivate a garden is ... to go hand in hand with Nature in some of her most beautiful processes, to learn something of her choicest secrets, and to have a more intelligent interest awakened in the beautiful order of her works elsewhere."*
> —CHRISTIAN BOVEE

On my visit, I found upscale garden perennials, wonderful ornamental grasses, excellent fresh herbs, and winsome shrubs. What makes Kleiss Farm & Nursery special is the inventive plant selections, which include ravishing old favorites, handsome new cultivars, and cool plants that you may not have heard of before. Kleiss tries to offer perennials not readily available elsewhere and provides pertinent advice and timely suggestions for its customers. The site is populated with well-grown, well-labeled plants attractively arranged in long rows backed with landscape plastic. Flats of vegetables are available in the spring, **mums** and spring-blooming bulbs in the fall. Additionally, the nursery is gaining a following for its animal topiary, my favorite being a

EXTRAS

Kleiss Farm & Nursery offers a Plant of the Week Sale, basically a different perennial selected each week. Additionally, each month on its website, Kleiss notes "$'s Off Coupons" that can be downloaded and used multiple times per month at the nursery.

monkey with an outstretched arm that can be hung from tree branches to swing freely from limb to limb.

Pond and pool owners can find pond-ready **water lily** hybrids worthy of Monet's masterly strokes and all the hardy **lotus**, floating plants, oxygenating plants, surface plants, and marginals needed for a naturalistic landscape. All container planted aquatic plants are grown in custom made, specialized pools, organized by plant maturity sizes within a greenhouse built specifically for that purpose. Plumbing supplies include liners, fountains, tubs, pumps, filters, and ancillary items.

Kleiss Farm is a custom grower for homeowners, landscaping professionals, and institutions, including a number of the local park districts. Environmentally conscious, the Kleiss' heat one greenhouse with an ingeniously designed heating system run on used motor oil collected from the neighboring farms.

★ SIDE TRIPS ★

ALLERTON PARK, (217) 762-2721, 515 Old Timber Rd., Monticello, IL. Allerton is 1,500 acres of formal gardens, sculptured hedges, a nature area with over 20 miles of hiking trails, and the manor house of Robert Henry Allerton. MABERY GELVIN BOTANICAL GARDEN, (217) 586-3360, N. Route 47, Mahomet, IL features peonies, iris, perennials, and herbs. PHILO TAVERN on Rt. 130, a couple of miles north of the nursery, is a restaurant with an outstanding dining area, great burgers, daily specials, and a gorgeous hanging basket décor.

ILLINOIS

LEE'S GARDENS

❧ ❧

Lee's Gardens, located in a scenic, woodsy area of central Illinois, is a family owned and operated perennial plant garden and nursery, specializing in landscape plants that grow well in the gardens of its proprietor, Janis Lee. Most of the plants offered at the nursery can be seen growing throughout various impressive display gardens surrounding the residence and winding their way down a shady ravine. A mulched path (lit at dusk) twists and weaves through the woodland gardens of hosta, ferns, and wildflowers to a secluded deck, a peaceful place providing visitors a quiet retreat to reflect on the intrinsic beauty of shade gardens. Visitors are encouraged to view these gardens for subtle combinations of leaf sizes, shapes, and colors throughout the seasons.

What makes Lee's special is its extensive yet innovative plant selections, which include handsome old classics as well as gorgeous new cultivars, and woodland plants that you may not be all that familiar with.

All mail-order plants are field grown and shipped bare root as soon as they can be dug in the spring; consequently, the nursery ships plants somewhat later than nurseries that raise plants in containers in hoop houses. The small gift shop carries an interesting array of garden related ornamentation. Given the country location of this nursery, the plant selection is bold and far-reaching.

OWNERS: Janis Lee
TYPE: Specialty nursery.
SPECIALTIES: Hosta; daylilies; perennials—shade and sun; wildflowers
HOURS: April 12 through June 1, Mon.-Fri. 8:00 am to 6:00 pm, Sat. 8:00 am to 3:00 pm, Sun. Noon-3:00 pm. Closed Memorial Day. June 2 through Aug. 31: Mon.-Fri. 9:00 am to 4:00 pm, Sat. 9:00 to 3:00 pm. Closed Sundays and Holidays. Sept. 1 through Oct. 15 or Frost (whichever comes first): Mon.-Fri. 9:00 am to 5:00 pm, Sat. 9:00 am to Noon. Closed Sundays and Holidays. Other times open by appointment.
CATALOG AVAILABLE: Yes
MAIL-ORDER AVAILABLE: Yes
DISPLAY GARDENS: Yes
CLASSES: No

CONTACT
25986 Saunder Road
Tremont, IL 61568
PHONE: (309) 925-5262
FAX: (309) 925-5010
WEB ADDRESS: www.leesgardens.com
EMAIL: jiboshi@aol.com

DIRECTIONS
From I-155: Take I-155 to IL Rt. 9, driving east on IL. Rt. 9 for 1.6 miles to Ropp Rd. Turn south (right) onto Ropp Rd. for 1 mile to Sauder Rd. Turn east (left) onto Sauder Rd., drive 0.5 miles to the nursery on the left. Take the long driveway to the nursery.

GPS: N 40° 30.29', W 89° 26.34'

ILLINOIS

Ferns, once the rage during Victorian times, were practically forgotten for decades, but today the trend toward natural landscaping is helping these wild beauties make a dramatic comeback. Good ferns for beginners available at the nursery include **autumn fern** (*Dryopteris erythrosora*), **lady fern** (*Athyrium filix-femina*), **leatherwood fern** (*Dryopteris marginalis*), **maidenhair fern** (*Adiantum pedatum*), **ostrich fern** (*Matteuccia struthiopteris*), and **soft shield fern** (*Polystichum setiferum*).

> *"A morning-glory at my window satisfies me more than the metaphysics of books."*
> —WALT WHITMAN

A few of my all-time favorite shade-loving plants offered at Lee's include: **bellflower, bleeding heart, lamium, toad lily**, and **cardinal flower**. Garden worthy woodland plants include: **baneberry, monkshood, rue anemone, jack-in-the-pulpit, spring beauty, lily of the valley, variegated fairy bells, shooting star, dog toothed violet**, and **wax bells**.

Lee's Gardens carries more than 500 varieties of **hostas**—a large collection by any standard—including species in all shapes, sizes, and colors: blue, gold, green, striped, variegated, edged, crinkled, pie-crusted, cupped, corrugated, puckered, and diamond dusted, from dainty dwarfs to stately giants. Is there a better house-warming gift for newlywed gardeners than a trunkful of 'Everlasting Love', 'Chantilly Lace', 'Formal Attire', 'Heart's Content', 'Heart and Soul', and 'Sweetie' hostas for their first shade garden? There are many spectacular fall blooming perennials including: *Aconitum, Buddleia, Cimicifuga, Echinacea, Verbascum,* **agastache, Japanese anemone, aster**, and grasses. Fall foliage plants include *Bergenia, Ceratostigma,* evergreen ferns, and vinca.

The nursery's field-grown **daylilies** offer sizzling colors in a range of shapes from all major breeders. Among the more impressive cultivars are 'Little Missy' (purple-red flowers with tiny white edges), 'Caprician Fiesta' (honey apricot with russet eye and good pie-crusting), 'Sunday Gloves' (very fragrant, near white with ruffled edges), and 'Spider Miracle' (large deep gold exotic looking blossoms).

I was especially taken with *Asarum* 'Takaoi Galaxy' (a **ginger** from Japan); *Astilbe japonica* 'Rock and Roll' (white plumes on red stems); *Baptisia* 'Carolina Moonlight' (a soft yellow **false indigo**); *Delphinium* 'Blushing Brides' (deep mulberry pink with white bees **delphinium**); and *Paeonia suffruticosa* 'Hanakisoi' (apricot-pink tree **peony**).

There is always a good selection of healthy, container-grown plants available under a shade lath by the gift shop, but the majority of plants are field-grown plants with massive roots, potted up as needed.

★ SIDE TRIPS ★

MACKINAW VALLEY VINEYARD, (309) 359-9463, 33633 IL Rt. 9, Mackinaw, IL 61755. **TEAROOM AT THE DEPOT,** 301 North Main St., Mackinaw, IL 61756, is a restaurant serving good sandwiches and salads in a historic train depot in the heart of Mackinaw.

ILLINOIS

LONG'S GARDEN

❧ ❧

"It has become increasingly popular to incorporate more and more ornamental grasses into perennial borders, garden beds, and mixed plantings," says Amy Long. Amy, along with her husband, Jason, and partner, Rick Sherry, are the new owners of Long's Garden, the former Bald Eagle Nursery. According to Amy, ornamental grasses "are reliable perennials tolerant of drought, are disease resistant, and deer and other wildlife don't like them." In addition, these plants always look like they are having a good hair day. They come in different shades of green, some sport horizontal striations or vertical stripes, and all display a diversity of plume shapes and colors.

Long's Garden is one of the first nurseries in the Midwest devoted exclusively to ornamental grasses. Started approximately twenty years ago, it changed hands for the third time in August of 2003. Thus far, except for the name change, all remains the same. Quietly growing all summer long, the 2-acre display garden is at its most impressive in fall, when it dazzles in the autumn sunshine. Be sure to stop, really look, and listen! Watch how the sunlight dances from stem to stem, glinting off slender blades, glowing in pinks, russets, or golds. Grasses delight the ear as well as the eye. It takes only a light breeze to start these beautiful garden accents gently swaying. Listen to them whisper as they shiver in the breeze or roar when stiff winds blow.

OWNERS: Amy & Jason Long, Rick Sherry
TYPE: Specialty nursery
SPECIALTIES: Ornamental grasses; perennials; trees; shrubs
HOURS: Mid-April thru Thanksgiving: Mon.-Sat. 8:00 am to 5:00 pm, Sun. Noon to 5:00 pm.
CATALOG AVAILABLE: Handout sheets at nursery and online information
MAIL-ORDER AVAILABLE: No
DISPLAY GARDENS: Yes
CLASSES: No

CONTACT

18510 Sand Road
Fulton, IL 61252
PHONE: (815) 589-4121
FAX: (815) –589-4120
WEB ADDRESS: http:/www.longsgarden.com
EMAIL: info@longsgarden.com

DIRECTIONS

FROM QUAD CITIES: take IL-84 North to US-30. Go East on US-30 for approx. 2 miles. Nursery is on the right side, turn at the sign. From Chicago: Take I-88 (East-West Tollway) to US-30 exit to Clinton. Proceed on US-30 for 20 miles. Nursery is on the left side of the road, turn at sign. (If you cross the river, you've gone too far.) **FROM PEORIA:** take I-74 to IL-78 North. Turn left at US-30 at the stoplight in Morrison, IL. Proceed 12 miles to nursery sign.

GPS: N 41° 51.54', W 90° 07.13'

ILLINOIS

Locals in the know stop by often to wander the grounds, pausing to spend a few minutes or a couple of hours in quiet contemplation at the wooden benches scattered throughout. Many eat their picnic lunches under the two tents located next to the Sales Barn. Customers are encouraged to do the same. As always, remember that the nursery is also the private residence of the owners, so please respect their privacy.

WHAT YOU'LL FIND

Amy notes that 4-foot tall *Miscanthus* 'Bitsey Ben' is their biggest seller. 'Bitsy Ben', M. 'Bodacious Ben', M. 'Jailbird Ben', and others having "Ben" in their names were all hybridized at the former Bald Eagle Nursery (BEN). Though the present owners have no plans to continue the hybridization program, with over 100 mature varieties of grasses producing seeds in the dis-

> *"I lean and loafe at my ease observing a spear of summer grass."*
> —WALT WHITMAN

play gardens, it would surprise nobody if Mother Nature lent a helping hand and a new BEN was born.

Long's Garden offers its customers more than 150 varieties of grasses in 1-gallon containers (transplanted into 2-gallon containers come July), and also larger field-grown clumps in containers. Mature 1- to 5-year-old specimens are field grown and dug for the customer that same day. Additionally, Long's carries some perennials, shrubs, and small trees, all of which consort well with ornamental grasses. Customers are handed a flyer listing all varieties of ornamental grasses, and are then sent out to view the clearly labeled mature plantings.

Some of the scrappy little guys that caught my attention, perfect for the front of the border or windowbox, were **Japanese blood grass** (*Imperata cylindrica* 'Red Baron'), **blue oat grass** (*Helictotrichon sempervirens* 'Sapphire'), **sedge** (*Carex morrowii* 'Silver Scepter'), **Japanese silver grass** (*Miscanthus sinensis* 'Dixieland'), and purple **love grass** (*Eragrostis spectabilis*). Those in the middle range of grasses, large enough to be specimen plants yet small enough to mass, include **maiden grass** (*Miscanthus sinensis* 'November Sunset' and 'National Arboretum'), **dwarf pampas grass** (*Cortaderia selloana* 'Pumila'), and **feather reed grass** (*Calamagrostis acutiflora* 'Karl Foerster'). A couple of the gentle giants, whether used as impressive specimens or convenient screens,

ILLINOIS

were giant silver grass (*Miscanthus sinensis* 'Giganteus') and switch grass (*Panicum virgatum* 'Cloud Nine').

Flowing and spontaneous, big and dramatic, spiky and puffy, full of motion, color, and sound, grasses are as carefree as they are hardworking. Their fresh new growth heralds the arrival of spring. In summer, their lushness adds a soothing green frame around colorful perennials. But it is in the fall, when perennials fade, that a garden of swaying grasses comes into its own. For one of the best, most extravagant, mature ornamental grass collections, head straight to Long's Garden.

ILLINOIS

The Natural Garden, Inc.

❧ ❧

Former owner Walter Stephens, a St. Charles plant collector with a passion for wildflowers and herbs, established the Natural Garden in 1953. At first, he shared potted divisions grown in old coffee cans with friends and then grew perennials in beds, digging up plants for customers on site. However, as interest in perennials and woodland wildflowers brought in more and more customers, the nursery expanded its selection and started growing plants in pots. What began as a great place to swap plants quickly grew into a large retail operation producing more than 1,000 varieties of container-grown perennials on 25 acres for both the retail and wholesale trades. According to current owner, Jan Sorensen, "We still have older customers who tell us that everything they know about gardening, they learned from Walter."

A cutting edge nursery, The Natural Garden operates out of a tiny, shingled cottage nestled at the base of majestic old oaks. Visitors are encouraged to tour the 4-acre display garden (some of which are themed garden beds) and gather ideas on the many ways plants can be integrated into the landscape.

The Natural Garden propagates and grows from seed, cuttings, or divisions, approximately 65 percent of its herbaceous perennial plants. The remainder is brought in as bare root or plugs. The garden shop offers quality

OWNERS: Jan V. Sorensen
TYPE: Specialty nursery; retail and wholesale
SPECIALTIES: Perennials—sun and shade; annuals and tender perennials; ferns; grasses; herbs; vegetables; trees and shrubs
HOURS: Jan. through mid-April: Mon.-Fri. 9:00 am to 5:00 pm; mid-April through June: Mon.-Fri. 9:00 am to 7:00 pm, Sat. and Sun. 9:00 am to 5:00 pm; July through Dec. 23: Mon.-Sat. 9:00 am to 5:00 pm, Sun. 11:00 am to 5:00 pm; Dec. through Jan 1: Closed.
CATALOG AVAILABLE: Yes
MAIL-ORDER AVAILABLE: No
DISPLAY GARDENS: Yes
CLASSES: Yes

CONTACT
38W443 Highway 64 (North Avenue)
St. Charles, IL 60175
PHONE: (630) 584-0150
FAX: (630) 584-0185
WEB ADDRESS:
www.thenaturalgardeninc.com
EMAIL: gardeninfo@thenaturalgardeninc.com

DIRECTIONS
FROM I-90: I-90 (in Elgin) to Randall Road exit south. Drive approximately 12 miles south on Randall Rd. to Hwy. 64 (North Ave.), turn west (right) and drive 1.5 miles to the nursery on your left. **FROM I-88:** Take I-88 to Orchard Road exit north, drive to Randall Rd. Turn north (left) onto Randall Rd. and drive approx. 9 miles to Hwy 64 (North Ave.). Turn west (left) onto Hwy 64 (North Ave.) and drive to the nursery, approx. 1.5 miles on your left.

GPS: N 41° 55.31', W 88° 21.91'

ILLINOIS

tools, a diverse selection of garden books, unique containers, trellises, garden benches, birdbaths, garden fairies, birdhouses, and numerous other gardening gifts.

WHAT YOU'LL FIND

The Natural Garden has become one of the largest suppliers of native prairie plants in Illinois. Initially, these plants were propagated from seed collected within a 90-mile radius of St. Charles; now, however, the nursery's primary seed source is from well-established on-site stock beds. Additional seed is acquired from reliable suppliers who have either

> *"Spring unlocks the flowers to paint the laughing soil."*
> —REGINALD HEBER

gathered seed from their own stock plants or, with permission, from restorations or wild populations. While native "forbs" (in this case, herbaceous perennials or biennials that are not grasses) are grown in containers and sold at the nursery as plants, The Natural Garden also sells native forb seed in $^1/8$-ounce packages.

The Natural Garden exceeds the norms of most nurseries by carrying an interesting array of classic native plants generally not available elsewhere, including: **prairie dandelion, wingstem, prairie milkweek, upland white aster, silky aster, hairy wood mint, Indian plantain, prairie Indian plantain**, and **Illinois sensitive plant**. Other rare finds include **Kankakee mallow, false dandelion, seed box, glade mallow, cowbane, wild quinine, smooth prairie lettuce, swamp goldenrod**, and **meadow parsnip**.

The Natural Garden built its reputation by growing good quality, healthy ornamental plant material in various sized containers. The nursery offers large and unusual collections of **yarrow, columbine, astilbe, delphinium, barrenwort, cranesbill, daylilies, coral bells, beebalm, poppy**, and **phlox**. True to its roots, it carries a vast assortment of wildflowers: **jack-in-the-pulpit, ginger, spring beauty, lily of the valley, trout lily, liverleaf, Virginia bluebells, trillium**, and **merrybells**. On a recent spring visit, I was especially taken with the dark foliage of *Astilbe* 'Eden's Odysseys'; the sparkling flower heads of the too-seldom-seen *Astrantia major* 'Primadonna'; the purple-bronze foliage of the woodlander *Corydalis flexuosa* 'Purple Leaf'; the delightful and charming *Geranium pratense* 'Splish-Splash' (white with blue streaks); and the jazzy leaves of *Heuchera* 'Regina'.

ILLINOIS

The Natural Garden carries a galaxy of **iris**, **hibiscus**, **hosta**, **veronica**, and **peony**. Its collection of **lilies** is outstanding (Asiatic, Oriental, LA Hybrid, and Trumpet), including the gorgeous, but almost impossible to find elsewhere, native lily, *Lilium michiganense*. They also carry landscape **roses**, spectacular vines, native grasses and **sedges**, and an excellent selection of ornamental trees and shrubs.

The Natural Garden focuses on growing a variety of uncommon plants covering many categories, the current emphasis being on popular and unusual annuals and tender perennials. These plants of superior flower-power delight savvy gardeners from spring or early summer until their demise at the icy fingers of the first heavy frost. The nursery grows scads of **ageratum**, **begonia**, **calibrachoa**, **cleome**, **gazania**, **lantana**, **ivy**, **zonal geranium**, and **petunia** (Wave™, Double Wave™, Tidal Wave™ series). It has yards of annual **salvias**, an amazing array of colorful **coleus**, profuse bundles of cascading **verbena**, awesome **sweet potato vine**, and exciting and dainty **diascia**.

The herb section has traditionally been excellent, combining common culinary herbs with such exotics as **caper bush**, **cardoon**, **Aztec sweet herb**, **costmary**, **cumin**, **perilla**, **lemongrass**, **epazote**, **Jerusalem sage**, and scented **mints**. Best of all are the ornamental herbs that not only hold their own in the perennial bed but also add a fragrant scent, especially the many-colored **thymes** and all the **lavenders**—French, variegated, fringed, early, and fern-leaf.

ILLINOIS

ORCHIDS BY HAUSERMANN, INC.

❧ ❧

O rchids by Hausermann, located in the heart of America with close to $4^1/_2$ acres under "glass," is one of the world's largest orchid growers. The number of orchids they grow for the cut-flower industry is staggering—400,000 *Cattleya* blossoms alone are produced annually in the greenhouses.

Orchids by Hausermann was started in 1920 by Carl Hausermann. The first plants grown were sweet peas, roses, and, somewhat later, gardenias. Orchids, once thought suited only to the controlled environment of a greenhouse, have moved into modern horticultural prominence in spite of various widespread misconceptions about growing them. Edwin Hausermann, son of the founder, began raising orchids in 1935 and amassed what was to become the nursery's stockpile of plants. Orchids eventually replaced all of the previous plants they were growing for the cut-flower industry.

In 1959, with their introduction of the sale of whole orchid plants, demand for exquisite and unusual orchids increased dramatically, permitting steady growth and several expansions of the business. Today, orchids at the nursery are grown exclusively by means of highly automated and specialized methods. The owners have also been in the forefront of hybridization efforts, creating many notable hybrids.

Hybrid orchid varieties are grown from seed or acquired from many growers throughout the world. Superior plants of jungle origin or hybrid creation are multiplied in the

OWNER: Carl Hausermann
TYPE: Large specialty nursery.
SPECIALTIES: Orchids
HOURS: Mon.-Sat. 9:00 am to 5:00 am, Sun. 11 am to 3:00 pm.
CATALOG AVAILABLE: Yes
MAIL-ORDER AVAILABLE: Yes
DISPLAY GARDENS: No
CLASSES: No

CONTACT
2N134 Addison Road
Villa Park, IL 60181-1191
PHONE: (630) 543-6855
FAX: (630) 543-9842
WEB ADDRESS:
www.orchidsbyhausermann.com
EMAIL: info@orchidsbyhausermann.com

DIRECTIONS
FROM SOUTHBOUND I-294 (TRI-STATE): Take I-294 to Route 64 (North Avenue) exit, west on North Ave to Addison Rd., turn north (right) and drive to the nursery on your left, less than 2 blocks down. **FROM NORTHBOUND ON I-294:** Take exit marked I-290/Rt.20/Rt. 64, then proceed on Route 64 as noted above. **FROM CHICAGO AREA:** I-290 west, to North Avenue (Exit # 13B). Take North Avenue west 4 miles to Addison Rd., turn north (right) and drive to the nursery on the left side of the road less than 2 blocks down. **FROM I-355:** Exit I-355 on North Ave (Rt. 64), drive east 2 miles to Addison toad, turn north (left) and drive to the nursery less than 2 blocks on your left.

GPS: N 41° 54.33', W 87° 59.31'

ILLINOIS

nursery's own laboratory facilities by means of the meristem tissue culture method. This process steadily improves quality, increases available variety, and makes those orchid plants considered rare and unusual more readily available. Orchids by Hausermann presently serves local, mail-order, and overseas customers. They sell books, pots, bark, plant stands, and other ancillary supplies. The full-color catalog, available at the office, is standard fare.

WHAT YOU'LL FIND

There is almost nothing as enchanting as a greenhouse full of **orchids**. Being able to walk through 30 or more greenhouses full of blooming orchids is pure heaven. But even when not in bloom, orchids carry a majestic and mysterious presence unparalled by any other plant. Vanda orchids, for example, are art-deco perfections as foliage plants even when not in flower. At Orchids by Hausermann, there are hundreds of plants in every greenhouse, some hanging from the ceilings and walls, others sitting placidly on low tables, and epiphytic varieties tucked into driftwood and bark.

Orchids by Hausermann offers species orchids and hybrids by the thousands from these groups: *Aerides, Ascocenda* hybrids, *Cattleya, Dendrobium nobile* hybrids, *Laelia, Lycaste, Miltoniopsis* hybrids and mericlones, *Odontoglossum/Oncidium* hybrids and mericlones, *Phaius, Phalaenopsis, Rhyncostylis, Vanda* hybrids, and *Zygopetalum* hybrids.

Cattleya, such as the striking orange-red *Slc.* Jewel Box 'Dark Waters', are prized for their large, flamboyant flowers. Despite their exotic looks, *Phalaenopsis* (moth orchid) hybrids are surprisingly easy to grow, and fly out of the nursery in numbers too great to count. The nursery holds an incredibly well-attended annual Open House the last weekend in February, where these orchids enjoy an extremely high profile. During the many years that I have attended this open house, I have yet to see a customer, any customer, leave without at least one phaly plant (but more likely 2 or 3) for his or her collection.

My favorites have always been the pure white phalys with lovely markings only on the lip, such as *Phalaenopsis* 'Catalina' and *P.* 'Happy Girl'. My gardener friend, on the other hand, is definitely partial to phalys with intricate pink veinings, such as *P.* 'Fajan's Fireworks', or *P.* 'Flare Spots' and *P.* 'Hawaiian Darling' with specklings and pepperings in the center of the bloom.

One group of orchids, *Miltoniopsis,* has evolved to look like giant pansies, fresh-faced and perky. They are often beautifully patterned in "waterfall" markings, such as the scarlet with white waterfalls *Miltonia* 'Celle'. (Many *Miltonia* hybrids are actually made using species from the genus *Miltoniopsis* but are usually referred to as *Miltonia.*) These exceptionally colorful orchids range from shades of dazzling white, delicate pinks, purples, and yellows to the deepest of reds and almost black.

> *"What is a weed?*
> *A plant whose virtues have*
> *not yet been discovered."*
> —RALPH WALDO EMERSON

They are always adorned with a "mask," a butterfly-shaped design at the center of the bloom on the base of the lip. *Miltonia* 'Butterfly' is a gorgeous confection in shimmering pastel shades of pink, gold, and purple on pristine white. M. 'Jersey' is a vibrant red and white pansy, and M. Zorro 'Yellow Delight' is a soft yellow blossom with red markings.

Novices contemplating their first plunge into the sweet addiction of orchid growing, and gardeners looking for a good bargain, should check out the "sale" table for good deals. E-savvy orchid enthusiasts can take advantage of specials regularly offered on the nursery's website.

ILLINOIS

PLANTER'S PALETTE

֍

Planter's Palette is situated on a 39-acre plot of land on the edges of Winfield, a quaint, western suburb of Chicago. Planter's Palette is a stylish, upscale retail nursery that caters to the needs of savvy gardeners with serious interests in gardening. Customers converge on the nursery throughout the gardening season to select from an exceptional array of perennials, annuals, grasses, vegetables, and shrubs. The highly knowledgeable staff, many of whom are popular contributors to the gardening sections of local newspapers, are quite adept at assisting gardeners of all levels.

A series of graceful wooden arbors guides customers from the parking lot to the sales areas where the riveting displays of jazzy plant combinations await. Their display gardens are minimal, but Planter's Palette prides itself on showcasing tantalizing new ornamental plant cultivars. You'll find a prodigious number of updated varieties of tried-and-true garden workhorses. This trend-setting establishment also manages to locate a few unexpected patrician surprises guaranteed to generate the "wow!" factor—and greatly expand the customer's horticultural boundaries.

Planter's Palette also offers iron

OWNERS: David Tyznik, President
TYPE: Large retail nursery. Wholesale.
SPECIALTIES: Perennials—sun and shade; annuals—tender perennials; tropicals, summer bulbs; trees; ornamental grasses; shrubs; hanging baskets; vines; aquatics; garden art; containers; roses; vegetables
HOURS: Jan. thru April 15 (winter office hours): Mon.-Fri. 10:00 am to 4:00 pm; April 16 thru June: Mon.-Thurs. 9:00 am to 6:00 pm, Fri. 9:00 am to 8:00 pm, Sat. 8:00 am to 6:00 pm, Sun. 10:00 am to 5:00 pm; July-mid-Nov.: Mon.-Fri. 9:00 am to 6:00 pm, Sat. 9:00 am to 5:00 pm, Sun. 10:00 am to 5:00 pm, Sun. 10:00 am to 5:00 pm; mid-Nov. thru Dec.: Mon.-Fri. 10:00 am to 4:00 pm.
CATALOG AVAILABLE: Printed
MAIL-ORDER AVAILABLE: No
DISPLAY GARDENS: Yes
CLASSES: Yes

CONTACT

28W571 Roosevelt Road
Winfield, IL 60190
PHONE: (630) 293-1040
FAX: (630) 293-1588
WEB ADDRESS: www.planterspalette.com

DIRECTIONS

FROM I-88 (EAST-WEST TOLLWAY): Exit Rt. I-88 at Winfield Road Exit. Proceed north 4 miles to Roosevelt Road (RT. 38). Turn west (left) onto Roosevelt Rd. and drive 1 mile to the nursery which is located on the south (left) side of the street. **FROM NORTHWESTERN SUBURBS:** Take Rt-59 south to Roosevelt Road (Rt. 38). Turn east (half/cloverleaf exit, watch for signs). Proceed east on Roosevelt Rd. (Rt. 38) for 1 mile, the nursery is on the south side (right side) of the street.

GPS: N 41° 51.44', W 88° 10.71'

ILLINOIS

and wooden furniture, an impressive selection of large pottery, containers, tools, statuary, and botanical themed gifts. They have an impressive arbor full of hanging baskets, and a willing staff to load your car. Checkout, using an ingenious computerized pad, is nothing short of a breeze.

WHAT YOU'LL FIND

Currently, more than 2,500 varieties of plants are listed in their catalog, *Plants for Garden Artistry*. Its offerings include dapper denizens of the shade such as heart-shaped **epimedium**, **coral bells**, **foamy bells**, **foamflowers**, **forget-me-nots**, **ferns**, **astilbe**, **trillium**, and **toad lily**. Look for a range of colorful sun worshippers including **peonies**, **campanulas**, **cranesbills** (hardy geraniums), **coneflowers**, **phlox**, **poppies**, **pinks**, **yarrows**, **asters**, and **mums**. Native woodlanders include: **rue anemone**, **snakeroot**, **sharp-lobed hepatica**, **fairy bells**, **shooting stars**, and **mayapple**. You'll also find perennial ground covers such as **bugleweed**, **wild ginger**, **snow-in-summer**, **spotted deadnettle**, **yellow archangel**, and **pachysandra**.

"Some people like to make a little garden out of life."
—JEAN ANOUILH

Planter's Palette has a bewildering **hosta** collection; extensive numbers of **daylilies**; good assortments of **hardy geraniums**, **sedum**, **beebalm**, **lungwort**, and **coreopsis**. There are interesting compilations of **artemisia**, **allium**, **monkshood**, and **spurge**. Its bevy of bodacious lilies includes Asiatic, LA, and Oriental hybrids, and the seldom seen but much beloved martagon and turk's cap.

Perennial vines include the colorful **honeysuckle**; a vigorous but non-invasive **trumpet vine**; the showy, shade-tolerant climbing **hydrangea** (*Hydrangea anomala* ssp. *petiolaris*); and those coy climbers, elegant **clematis**. The nursery's herb collection is legendary, its veggie list all encompassing, and the ornamental grasses extensive.

Turn to this nursery for ideas in container gardening. Scattered throughout the grounds, a wide variety of pre-planted arrangements in pots, windowboxes, and baskets (all composed in eye-catching and elegant vignettes) are created with a touch of whimsy and tended with tons of love and dedication.

The range of annuals at Planter's Palette is exemplary. A sparkling array of white, pink, red, orange, lavender, and multicolored blossoms highlight the green, gold, white, and bronze hues of the foliage. Traditional choices include charming **petunias**, **impatiens**, **fuschias**, **geranium**, **lantanas**, **verbenas**, and **begonias**—supplemented by selections of *Abutilon, Diascia, Nemesia, Scaevola,* and *Torenia.* The nursery stocks recent introductions such as *Dichondra,* and dozens of exciting **coleus** and **dragon wing begonias**.

There are colorful climbers such as **hyacinth bean**, **cardinal climber**, **moon flower**, and **morning glories**. There is a world of unusual foliage plants for container gardeners: *Alternanthera purpurea* (with striking purple leaves), *Acalypha* (variegated and splotched), *Colocasia* (**elephant ear**), *Glechoma* (skirt plants of green and white), *Helichrysum* (**licorice** plants), and *Ipomoea batatas* (**potato vine**).

The nursery's flats contain 18 to 24 plants in a deep tray, allowing the Planter's Palette to produce a larger plant that is ready to make an immediate impact in the landscape. Many are also available in 4-inch or 6-inch pots, or in hanging baskets. An incredible gardener and savvy horticulturist from my neighborhood observed that, "vigorous, well-branched plants [are] sold with pride—and prices to match." Though she grumbles about overspending, she continues to buy them each year. (I try to attend the big fall sale, with great prices designed to ease plants off their tables and into my car.)

You will find plants resistant to deer, attractive to butterflies and hummers, and tolerant of salt or foot traffic. Some have interesting seed heads, and are just plain long blooming. Most of the plants—annuals, marginals, and perennials—are grown out in the nursery's rather extensive greenhouses, Quonsets, growing pads, and cold frames.

EXTRAS

The Planter's Palette hosts interesting classes and demonstrations. Star studded early spring symposiums feature the likes of John Elsley, Tracy DiSabato-Aust, and Dan Hinkley. Call and ask about their impressive, month-long summer festival.

ILLINOIS

RICH'S FOXWILLOW PINES NURSERY, INC.

∼❧ ❧∼

About an hour west of Chicago lies a nursery like no other. Here, at Rich's Foxwillow Pines Nursery, rare and unusual trees and garden conifers are the norm rather than the exception, and Richard Eyre is somewhat of an enigma himself. He is a whiz at grafting and travels the country seeking and collecting bud mutations (a local genetic alteration producing permanent changes that can be retained by grafting) and bud variations (deviations from ordinary growth producing a sport). From these he starts new plants, adding them to his ever-growing collection at the nursery.

On 36 acres (the nursery consists of 6 acres plus 30 acres of production fields close by), Eyre cultivates more than 100,000 trees, including more than 2,500 cultivars from the conifer family and 1,000 of woodies. Almost all of these trees exhibit some exemplary quality—be it exceptional color, singular texture, or extremely slow growth.

The nursery has, according to Eyre,

OWNERS: Susan and Richard Eyre
TYPE: Specialty nursery.
SPECIALTIES: Trees; conifers; shrubs; hosta
HOURS: March 1 through Nov. 30: Mon.-Sat. 8:00 am to 4:30 pm; Dec. 1 through Feb. 28: By appointment. Closed Sundays.
CATALOG AVAILABLE: Printed and online
MAIL-ORDER AVAILABLE: No
DISPLAY GARDENS: Yes
CLASSES: Yes

CONTACT
11618 McConnell Road
Woodstock, IL 60098
PHONE: (815) 338-7443
FAX: (815) 338-7446
WEB ADDRESS: www.richsfoxwillowpines.com
EMAIL: coniflora@richsfoxwillowpines.com

DIRECTIONS
FROM CHICAGO AREA OR I-90: Take I-90 to Rt. 47 exit northbound. Take Rt. 47 north for 13 miles to McConnell Rd. Turn east (right) on McConnell and drive 0.4 miles to nursery on your left. **FROM NORTH (WI):** Take WI Rt.20 south, which becomes Rt. 47 in IL. Right after the Jewel Grocery Store in Woodstock, turn east (left) on McConnell Rd., driving 0.4 miles to the nursery on left.

GPS: N 42° 18.37', W 88° 25.45'

"the largest collection of conifers together in one place in this climate in the world." It is located in his backyard, and the plants he sells are from the collection of conifers he has been nurturing since the early '70s. As a peace corps volunteer in the late '60s, Eyre came across a book on dwarf conifers and right then and there decided to start collecting them as soon as he returned to the States. In 1983,

ILLINOIS

he and his wife, Susan, moved to the present location, bringing with them thousands of trees. They continued amassing trees, until finally in 1988, when the hobby outgrew its bounds, the only thing left was to open a nursery. And they've never looked back.

Garden conifers, considered by Eyre to be the bones of any garden, come in a range of shapes and display a virtual rainbow of colors. Weeping, pendulous, prostrate, narrow upright (fasigate), broad upright, irregular, globose (rounded), spreading, mounding, and pyramidal shapes come in shades of green, yellow, and blue—sometimes highlighted by orange bark, red new growth, and lavender or purple cones. Some have bicolor needles or stripes; others offer patches or spots. Some conifers have stiff needles; others are soft and feathery. And except for yews and junipers which produce berries, all conifers bear cones in a wondrous array of colors and shapes. "Garden conifers differ from small plants" by their short growth between nodes," says Eyre. "For a four-season garden of color, add a number of these conifers to your landscape," he notes. According to Eyre, in the spring new conifer growth adds an interesting dimension to the garden. During the summer months, they fade into a background for splashy bloomers, and in autumn their colors contrast beautifully with fall's colorful leaves. Finally, fluffy winter snows enhance the conifer's golden yellow and green branches.

> "The sky is the daily bread of the eyes."
> —RALPH WALDO EMERSON

WHAT YOU'LL FIND

Yellow cultivars such as the lacy threadleaf false cypress, (*Chamaecyparis pisifera* 'Filifera Aurea Nana' or 'Lemon Thread'), can brighten any garden. The dwarf **Alberta spruce**, (*Picea glauca* 'Rainbow's End'™), sports creamy-yellow foliage on its second flush of growth in late spring (the first push of growth is green). The awesome dwarf **Scots pine**, (*Pinus sylvestris* 'Watereri') is a slow growing, dense pyramidal form with steel blue-green needles, and dynamite orange bark).

Variegated conifers can tie plant colors together, provide the necessary transition from one section of the garden to the next, or stand as high interest specimens on their own. Electric yellow-green variegation is found on both the **Japanese red pine** (*Pinus densiflora* 'Oculus-draconis') and the **Serbian spruce** (*Picea*

ILLINOIS

omoríka 'Expanse'). A slender spire with drooping branches and upturned tips, the weeping Serbian spruce (*Picea omoríka* 'Pendula') adds drama to the landscape with the addition of stunning purple cones in early spring. The show-stopping **Korean fir** (*Abies koreana* 'Silberlocke') with its stupendous curving needles of blue and showing pristine white undersides is virtually guaranteed to attract attention.

Eyre is partial to Asian plants, and his collection of more than 100 **Japanese white pine** (*Pinus parviflora*) cultivars reflects this interest. Behind the white clapboard farmhouse is a garden (possibly planted by munchkins), filled with some of his best Asian miniature plants as well as miniature perennials and other alpine plants. These are his specialties. "Slow growth translates into low maintenance," he notes. "We like to call them the husband's delight, since they grow less than 6 inches per year," Eyre says of these trees.

For diminutive accents, common **juniper** (*Juniperus communis* 'Effusa') shows off cinnamon growth in early spring, and **creeping juniper** (*Juniperus horizontalis* 'Mother Lode' P.P. #5948) sports attractive bright golden-yellow color that turns pink in winter. A group of conifers that provides more winter interest than most includes the dwarf **globe white cedar** (*Chamaecyparis thyroides* 'Heatherbun') with soft blue-green foliage that turns to stunning plum in winter. Typically, new growth on conifers is a lighter shade of green, but then there is nothing typical about this nursery or its trees. New growth on the **Norway spruce** (*Picea abies* 'Rubra Spicata') emerges fire-engine red in spring but turns to green in warmer temperatures.

From the parking area, customers catch sight of the old willow (once home to a fox), which gives the nursery its name. Beyond the willow, past a bed of colorful perennials, is the rock and water garden where a thirty-year-old weeping

> ## EXTRAS
>
> The sale of hosta, dwarf daylilies, and dwarf iris directly benefits Heifer International, based in Little Rock, Arkansas. The Heifer Project gives impoverished families income-producing animals and the necessary instructions for caring for them. In turn, these families share the animal offspring and their newfound knowledge with their neighbors. This is the Eyre's personal fight against world hunger. Richard's mother, Margaret, handles the perennial sales that support the project.

ILLINOIS

gingko (1 of only 3 or 4 of its kind in the world) holds court over a waterfall and two pools that feed into the main pond.

"Where other nurseries carry a lot of common trees and a few rare ones, we carry just the opposite," says Eyre. The list of slow-growing deciduous trees is mind-boggling: **dwarf river birch** (*Betula nigra* 'Little King'); **weeping katsura tree** (*Cercidiphpyllum japonicum* 'Pendula'); **weeping European hornbeam** (*Carpinus betulus* 'Pendula'); a dwarf bushy form of **maidenhair tree** (*Ginkgo biloba* 'Chi Chi'); a purple leafed **smoketree** (*Cotinus coggygria* 'Pop's Pink Champagne'), and **weeping goat willow** (*Salix caprea* 'Pendula'), to name a few. Customers must keep in mind that anything this rare and unusual will come with higher prices, but then none of these plants is your typical store bought plant.

In addition to an exciting collection of trees, the Eyres also carry amazing selections of **hosta**, **dwarf daylilies**, and **dwarf iris**.

ILLINOIS

ROSES & ROSES & ROSES

᯾

Once a well-kept secret of the local garden community, Roses & Roses & Roses now has a far-flung base of loyal customers. Started twenty-two years ago as a rose garden service enterprise, Roses & Roses & Roses' primary thrust is the full-season care of rose gardens up and down Chicago's North Shore. Laurie and Mike Dolan, sophisticated landscape designers who still keep their hands in the dirt, design, plant, and maintain 120 rose gardens yearly. These range in size and scope from the single rose in the middle of a border (that according to Laurie "sulks and pouts and does not share fertilizer with its fellow perennials") to gardens where the rose count is in the hundreds.

Let's face it. Sooner or later, every gardener wants to grow roses. They can be short or tall, grown as specimen plants or massed for hedges. Roses can carpet the ground or they can climb arbors and trees. They can grow as a lone standard or a jungle riot over a trellis. It really doesn't matter—we want them. They seduce us, delight our senses, speak to our hearts, celebrate events, symbolize emotions, and mark our passages through life. And even though roses may have a simple beauty, selecting the right rose for the gardener and the garden can sometimes be anything but simple.

At this wonderful nursery, rose fanciers have the incredible opportunity

OWNERS: Laurie and Mike Dolan
TYPE: Small specialty nursery and rose garden service enterprise.
SPECIALTIES: Roses
HOURS: Last Saturday of April to (approx) June 10: Mon. - Sat., 10:00 am to 3:30 pm, or by appointment. (Call for exact start and end dates as they vary somewhat.)
CATALOG AVAILABLE: Printed brochure and online information
MAIL-ORDER AVAILABLE: No
DISPLAY GARDENS: No
CLASSES: No

CONTACT
14985 W. Wadsworth Rd.
Wadsworth, IL 60083-9659
PHONE: (847) 336-1086
FAX: (847(360-1070
WEB ADDRESS:
http://www.roses-roses-roses.com
EMAIL: roses@avenew.com

DIRECTIONS
BOTH NORTH- AND SOUTH-BOUND FROM I-94 (TRI-STATE): Exit I-94 at Grand Avenue (Rt. 132) Eastbound. Proceed on Grand Avenue for 1.4 miles to Milwaukee Avenue (SR-21). Turn north (left) on Milwaukee and drive 1.1 miles to Skokie Hwy (Rt. 41). Turn north (left) onto Skokie, driving 2.9 miles to Wadsworth Road. Turn east (right) on Wadsworth, the nursery is located approx. 0.7 miles down on the north side (left side) of the street. Look for the nursery sign on the yellow farmhouse located across the street from the white clapboard church. Note: If the driveway is full, you can park in the church parking lot.

GPS: N 42° 25.72', W 87° 55.67'

to purchase exceptional quality roses at reasonable prices. They also have the chance to tap into the knowledge, expertise, and wisdom of two individ-

uals who have spent close to a quarter of a century observing and working exclusively with roses. From spring cleanup and planting, through fertilization, pruning, spraying, weeding, and winter protection, Lori and Mike Dolan know roses.

Laurie heads up the retail location of the business, and Mike manages the service end. The family owned business carries approximately 170 varieties and sells more than 3,500 of them every year. Purchased bare root from three major growers, the Dolans pot up the plants, keeping them in greenhouses until ready for sale in spring. Roses & Roses & Roses sells its plants regionally, focusing primarily on those roses that perform well throughout the northern suburbs of Chicago. All plants are grade #1, two-year old specimens, available in $2^1/_2$- or 3-gallon peat pots, which are somewhat narrower but taller than the traditional plastic.

Though Roses & Roses & Roses do not ship, it is possible to reserve your roses in advance simply by emailing your selections to the nursery. So while this list changes from year to year, it's a good idea to check the offerings on a yearly basis. All orders placed prior to the opening date must be picked up within one week of opening; orders placed after opening day will be held for one week. All payment is by check or cash, only.

WHAT YOU'LL FIND

Roses & Roses & Roses' list includes hybrid teas, grandiflora, David Austin™, Romantica, floribunda, shrub, climber, and tree **roses**. Hybrid teas, sometimes known as everblooming roses, grow from 2 to 6 feet tall, have single or double blossoms with varying degrees of fragrance, and vary in winter hardiness and disease resistance. At Roses, I found the popular 'Double Delight' (very fragrant, creamy white brushed with strawberry-red); 'Fragrant Cloud' (fragrant, unusual yet stunning, coral-orange); 'Pink Peace' (heavenly scented, heavy blooming, vivid pink); and everyone's favorite 'Tropicana' (award-winning, intensely fragrant, salmon-orange rose).

Shrub roses are a large group of roses that include, among others, hybrid rugosa, hybrid musk, hardy Canadian Explore™, David Austin™, Meilland, and Buck. Among the Buck roses, for example, are clear pink 'Carefree Beauty'™, deep

ILLINOIS

pink 'Country Dancer', and the unusually colored 'Distant Drums'. The Canadian Explorer series included a good red 'Champlain' and the deep pink pillar 'William Baffin'. Hybrid rugosas are known for their disease resistance, winter hardiness, and easy care. Some excellent rugosas include the clear white 'Blanc Double de Coubert', silvery pink 'Frau Dagmar Hartopp', and another great white 'Alba'. One of my favorites, the bright pink with cream reverse 'Carefree Wonder'™, a Meilland introduction, needs no pruning, no winter protection, is lightly fragrant, has large cupped blossoms, and re-blooms so enthusiastically that one might say it "blooms its brains out" when happy.

While this isn't exactly a "destination" nursery, it's a place to get some great roses, and gives you an excuse to take some interesting side trips when picking up your order.

ILLINOIS

SHADY HILL GARDENS

❧ ❧

Shady Hill Gardens is a family owned, two-generation wholesale and retail business that has gained an exemplary reputation as a geranium specialty nursery. Long before Chuck Heidgen, along with his wife, Mary Ellen, started Shady Hill Gardens, Chuck's growing fascination with geraniums had already sparked the beginning of a life-long interest in the species. They started the nursery by purchasing the empty, run-down 1900s greenhouses in Batavia in 1974. What started out as a small collection of novelty geraniums from a nursery in Maine now numbers around 1,000 species and varieties.

Ten years ago, Shady Hill built some production greenhouses on property acquired in Elburn, IL, a town roughly 10 miles northwest of Batavia. But in 1998, right next to the utilitarian production greenhouses, three interconnected, Victorian, atrium-style greenhouses were built, majestically rising out of the surrounding cornfields. These state-of-the-art Dutch greenhouses provide Shady Hill with a much needed second retail location (and more space!).

OWNERS: Chuck and Mary Ellen Heidgen
TYPE: Large specialty nursery
SPECIALTIES: Geraniums (Pelargoniums); annuals; hanging baskets; mums; poinsettias; perennials
HOURS: (Both Locations) April, May, June, and Monday before Thanksgiving thru Christmas Holidays: Mon.-Sat. 9:00 am to 5:00 pm, Sun. 11:00 am to 4:00 pm; July, Aug., and Nov. thru Thanksgiving: Closed.
CATALOG AVAILABLE: No
MAIL-ORDER AVAILABLE: Limited mainly to collections
DISPLAY GARDENS: No
CLASSES: No

CONTACT
821 Walnut Street
Batavia, IL 60510
PHONE: (618) 879-5665
WEB ADDRESS: www.shadyhill.com

DIRECTIONS
FROM I-88 (EAST-WEST TOLLWAY): Exit Rt. I-88 at Rt. 31. Travel North on Rt. 31 for 3.6 miles to Walnut Street. Turn west (left) on Walnut (look for a small sign at the intersection) and proceed for 3½ blocks (approx. 0.4 miles) through residential streets. Greenhouses are on right side. Parking is next to the greenhouses or on the street.

GPS: N 41° 50.63', W 88° 19.18'

WHAT YOU'LL FIND

As houses have gotten bigger and gardens smaller, the pleasures of fresh-cut flowers and homemade floral bouquets have fallen by the wayside. Cutting gardens, as they were known, have become a rarity. However, cutting gardens of truly grand proportions are located at the Elburn facility. Over twenty 3-foot- by 40-foot- beds of **zinnias**, **sunflowers**, **asters**, **celosia**, **dahlia**, **cosmos**, and **snapdragons** are yours for the cutting during September and October. Shady Hill provides a cutting basket, clippers, and an umbrella (should one be needed in either rain or shine). Prices are reasonable, the beds are planted out in succession for prolonged harvest, and next to those incredible greenhouses anyone can feel like a lord or lady of the manor.

Much of Shady Hill's **geranium** stock is propagated by cuttings and sold well-labeled with substantial roots. Plant selection varies annually yet always wildly exceeds all expectations. There is no catalog; therefore, it is recommended that geranium fanciers, beginners and connoisseurs alike, plan on visiting Shady Hill to find out what is available that year. Formerly of the genus *Geranium*—now *Pelargonium*—geraniums are arranged by groupings. There are sprawling stellars (named for their star-shaped leaves and flowers); captivatingly fragrant scented-leaf geraniums (grown for their aromatic leaves); tulip-flowered, cactus-flowered, and rosebud geraniums (with flowers resembling those of their namesakes); pendulous cascade, floribunda, and ivy geraniums (that trail seductively down the sides of containers); and the ever so curiously handsome species geranium. What greets the eye upon entering the greenhouses is a sparkling array of white, pink, red, orange, lavender, and multicolored blossoms. Additionally, they are highlighted by the startling variety of gold, tricolor, silver, bronze, variegated, cut, scented, serrated, edged, ruffled, and veined fancy-leaf selections.

SATELLITE LOCATION

Shady Hills' Elburn, IL location also includes a cutting garden.

FALL EXPANDED HOURS AT ELBURN LOCATION ONLY: Labor Day to Late October: Mon-Sat. 9:00 am to 5:00 pm, Sun. 11:00 am to 4:00 pm.

CONTACT

42W075 Route 38
Elburn, IL 60119
(630) 365-5665

DIRECTIONS

FROM THE INTERSECTION OF RANDALL ROAD AND RT. 38 (ROOSEVELT ROAD): Drive west on Rt. 38 for 5.5 miles. Greenhouses on left. **FROM THE SOUTH I-88 (EAST-WEST TOLLWAY):** Exit I-88 at Rt. 31. Drive North on Rt. 31 to Oak Street, turn west (left) on Oak St. to Randall Road, turn north (right) on Randall driving approx. 7.5 miles to Rt. 38 (Roosevelt Road), turn west (left) on Rt. 38 for 5.5 miles. Greenhouses on left. **FROM THE NORTH I-90 (NORTHWEST TOLLWAY):** Exit I-90 at Randall Road. Drive South on Randall Road for 12 miles to. Rt. 38 (Roosevelt Road), turn west (right) on Rt. 38 for 5.5 miles. Greenhouses on left.

GPS: N 41° 54.36', W 88° 26.76'

Most popular are the foolproof zonal geraniums, named for the dark red, horseshoe-shaped band on their leaves. One of the major problems with the "mass produced" zonals is that the flower heads are so tightly grouped that, when a single flower dies, there is no place for the petals to drop. So the withering flowers clump together in a brown blob while other flowers continue to open, a characteristic needlessly exacerbated by our typically hot and humid summers. Some of the noteworthy zonals available at Shady Hill, however, have more open flowering, thus giving every bloom the room needed to die gracefully.

> *"Flowers are the sweetest things God ever made and forgot to put a soul into."*
> —HENRY WARD BEECHER

The blooms themselves are sensational, especially in the stellars. I was particularly taken with 'Staccato' (showcasing star-shaped flowers in light pink, tipped in red); 'Red Witch' (deep scarlet, semi-double); and 'Arctic Star' (displaying shredded edges on pristine white petals). And who can resist of pot of the bewitching geranium, 'Pandora' dotted by the very free blooming, compact, deep pink clusters of "mini-tulip blossom" nosegays? For gardeners whose tastes run toward the sizzling hot, on a recent visit I noted the ever popular 'Vancouver Centennial' (a gaudy confection of bright yellow-lime leaves with a broad zone of chocolate brown topped by a head of searing orange-red blossoms).

At the Elburn location, it is a pure delight to wander the beds of the cutting garden, picking out the absolutely perfect blossoms and placing them in the ribbon-bedecked baskets. The friendly and knowledgeable staff then wraps the entire collection, presentation style, in colorful tissue and satin ribbons. (See "Satellite Location" box on facing page.)

EXTRAS

If you've ever wanted to get lost in a field of poinsettias, and would also like to have that memory preserved, now's your chance. In early December, Shady Hill sets aside a couple of hours at each location, where a professional photographer will gladly take a wonderful holiday picture "in the poinsettias." There is no charge, and if you cannot return to pick up the picture in a couple of days, Shady Hill will gladly mail it to you.

ILLINOIS

(Note: What many gardeners still know and refer to as a geranium, typically grown as a houseplant, annual container plant, or for bedding out, is actually a **pelargonium**. The pelargonium was originally in the genus *Geranium* then, due to distinct botanical differences, was given its own genus. However, this fact hasn't stopped the name "geranium" from becoming the common name for this plant, thus confusing many people. Shady Hill specializes in the genus *Pelargonium*, though everyone—customers and staff alike—still refer to the plants as geraniums. For the purposes of this nursery description, and to avoid further confusion, I have followed suit.)

Though geraniums are still the largest and main crop, Shady Hill also sells a wide variety of annuals, herbs, hanging baskets, vegetables, and perennials—plus **mums** and **poinsettias** during the fall and winter holiday seasons. As with geraniums, the selection is geared to offering customers different, unusual, rare, and uncommon plants. Several years ago, way before the Wave™ petunia became available at every nursery, garden center, and box store, Shady Hill offered a colorful and exciting 'Purple Wave'™ hanging basket. It was so gloriously full and bloom laden that just three baskets, hanging near a front entry, achieved dramatic impact and sophistication. Thanks to those baskets, I was able to live every gardener's dream—that of being the first within my friendly competitive gardening circle to display a voluptuously colorful new plant.

TED'S GREENHOUSE, INC.

ᵉᵍ⪫ ⪪ᵍ

Ted's Greenhouse, a family-owned, two-generation business, is a well-known Chicagoland institution. Established as a nursery in 1948 by owner Ted Biernacki, a trained horticulturist, Ted's Greenhouse moved to its present location in 1957. What was once merely 1 greenhouse in the middle of the cornfields, is today a nursery sited on 5 acres, and a business composed of 30 greenhouses (75,000 sq. ft) totally surrounded by a network of residential subdivisions. The nursery's specialty, according to co-owner Dan Biernicki, is "nothing." However, in running this cutting-edge nursery, the Biernickis built their reputation by being perpetually on the hunt for new plants; those flower and foliage annuals and perennials generally unavailable at most typical garden centers.

WHAT YOU'LL FIND

Ted's Greenhouse offers more than 800 varieties of perennials, 1,200 annuals and tender perennials, plus cactus, succulents and carnivorous plants, hanging baskets, hardy bamboo, ferns, ornamental grasses, herbs, shrubs, water plants, seasonal, holiday and specialty plants.

This is an energetic nursery advancing ornamentals that are interesting and provocative: **salvia**, **lungwort**, **peonies**, **poppies**, **coral bells**, **cranesbill**, **bellflower**, **spurge**, **daylilies** and **hosta**. Urban gardeners rarely encounter such characteristic perennials as **crosswort** (*Phluopsis stylosa* 'Purple Glow'), **horned poppy** (*Glaucium flavum*), **candy lily** (*Pardancanda*), variegated

OWNERS: Ted Biernacki, Daniel Biernacki
TYPE: Retail nursery
SPECIALTIES: Cactus; succulents; perennials—sun and shade; annuals and tender perennials; herbs; bamboo; fern; ornamental grasses; shrubs; aquatics
HOURS: Year-round: Mon.-Fri. 9:00 am to 5:00 pm, Sat. 9:00 am to 3:00 pm, Sun. 10:00 am to 3:00 pm. Closed Sundays from November 1 to March 31.
CATALOG AVAILABLE: Price list and online listing
MAIL-ORDER AVAILABLE: No
DISPLAY GARDENS: No
CLASSES: No

CONTACT
16930 S. 84th Avenue
Tinley Park, IL 60477
PHONE: (708) 532-3575
FAX: (708) 532-3585
WEB ADDRESS: www.tedsgreenhouse.com
EMAIL: biernackid@sbcglobal.net

DIRECTIONS
FROM I-80: Take I-80 to Rt. 45 (LaGrange Rd.) north (Exit 145). Drive north for 1.4 miles to 175 th Street. Turn east (right) onto 175th. St. and drive 1.5 miles to 84th Ave. Turn north (left) onto 84th and drive 0.6 miles to the nursery on your left.

GPS: N 41° 34.94', W 87° 49.36'

horseradish (*Amoracia rusticana* 'Variegata'), **blue eyed grass** (*Sisyrinchium*) and ornamental **Chinese rhubarb** (*Rheum palmatum*). The nursery has good holdings of, **yarrow**, **hyssop**, **columbine**, **hibiscus**, **iris**, **phlox**, **ballonflower**, **tickseed**, **primula**, **toad lily**, **spiderwort**, and **pinks**.

> *"I have never had so many good ideas, day after day, as when I worked in the garden."*
> —JOHN ERSKIN

Wonderful as its perennial holdings are, the nursery is also famed for its houseplants and hanging baskets. For container gardeners, an intoxicating range of colorful annuals and jazzy tender perennials is stocked early in the season. Ted's Greenhouse grows scads of **coleus** (94 varieties), yards of **abutilon**, **bacopa**, **elephant ear**, scented and tender **geranium** (actually **pelargonium**), **plectranthus**, **sweet potato vine**, **diascia**, **nemesia**; and some attractive trailers and vines. It has an interesting array of **calibracoa**, **canna**, **impatiens**, **begonia**, **fuchsia**, **ginger**, **pentas**, **nasturtium**, **mandevilla**, **dahlia**, **verbena**, and **passion vine**. Vegetables include **tomatoes**, **peppers**, **squash**, **melons**, **okra**, and **lettuce**.

The nursery has a terrific flock of herbs, both culinary and medicinal, including **lavender** (11 varieties), **stevia** (used as a sweetener), **tarragon** (French), **basil** (11 varieties), **chives**, **rosemary**, **oregano**, and **thyme**. They grow **chamomile** (Roman & German) and **mint** for tea, **catnip** for our feline friends, **fennel**, **nasturtium**, and **mesclun** for salads, **patchouli** for potpourri, and **gotu kola** for "brain power."

Ted's Greenhouse offers noteworthy houseplants and desert plants, and is favored by collectors for the cactus and succulent collections that are among the most extensive in northern Illinois. In 2003, Ted's Greenhouse won the Silver Award (Second Place) at the Chicago Flower and Garden Show for its cleverly designed cactus display, "All the World's a Stage." This was a theatre in the round concept where the succulents were "dressed" as the audience, and the flower show attendees ended up "onstage" inside a circular display.

Gardeners with ponds can find hardy **water lilies** in ravishing shades of red, pink, yellow and white, enhanced by mottled foliage and striking fragrance. Water gardeners can also find hardy tropicals, hardy marginals, shallow water marginal plants such as **pickerel weed**, and various floating and oxygenating aquatic plants.

Seasonal plants, such as **Easter lilies**, **tulips**, **daffodils**, **mums**, and **poinsettias** are sold at holidays. If there is one complaint, it is the lack of pricing on all containers, necessitating constant forays in search of salespeople.

SEARCHING INDIANA

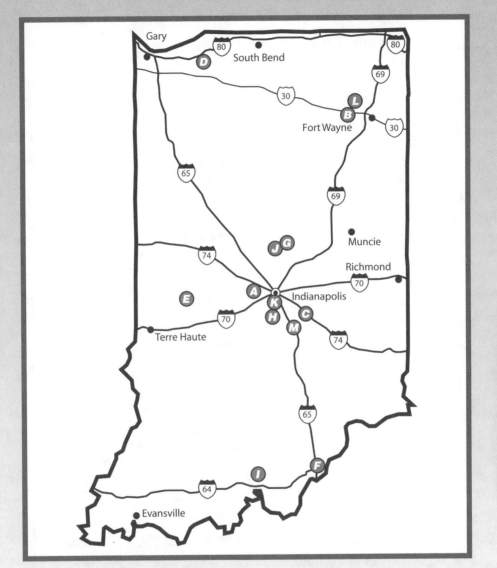

AVON PERENNIAL GARDENS

❧ ❧

Located about fifteen minutes west of Indianapolis, Avon Perennial Gardens is a popular nursery and garden center that boasts of being "Indy's best selection of quality plants and garden accessories." The nursery specializes in outstanding perennials, trees, and shrubs that grow and prosper in northern climes.

Early May is a magical time in these gardens. The 3-acre display gardens full of woodlanders, spring perennials, and ephemerals welcome gardeners to this seductive rural setting. Display gardens (which are the Robbins private gardens as well as on-going trial beds) are awash in color, offering customers a delightful opportunity to view the nursery plantings in action. These include shady woodland borders, imposing mixed beds, shimmering pond gardens, a handsome hosta glade nestled in a majestic ravine highlighted by a stream running through it, container gardens, an interesting pergola, and a deck for resting.

Avon Perennial Gardens' gift shop offers interior décor items, pretty candles, scented potpourri, handsome bird feeders, a variety of birdbaths, different statuary, melodic wind chimes, artificial flower arrangements, trellises, obelisks, arbors and other whimsies. The beautiful display gardens are available for outdoor weddings, receptions, luncheons, group meetings, baby and bridal showers, rehearsal dinners, and any other outdoor event one can conjure up.

One word of caution for the camera bugs out there: Before you go whipping out your cameras for a floral photo fest, be advised that there is a charge for taking pictures in the gardens. To be sure, the gardens are gorgeous in their own

OWNERS: Karen Robbins
TYPE: Specialty nursery.
SPECIALTIES: Perennials—sun and shade; daylilies; grasses; annuals; aquatics; shrubs; trees; standards; conifers
HOURS: Wed.-Sat.: 10:00 am to 4:00 pm, Sun. noon to 4:00 pm.
CATALOG AVAILABLE: No
MAIL-ORDER AVAILABLE: No
DISPLAY GARDENS: Yes
CLASSES: No

CONTACT
6259 E. County Road 91 N
Avon, IN 46123
PHONE: (317) 272-6264
WEB ADDRESS: www.avongardens.com
EMAIL: karen@avongardens.com

DIRECTIONS
FROM I-465 (IN INDIANAPOLIS): I-465 to 10th Street (100 N) westbound. Take 10th Street for 6.8 miles to SR-267, cross SR-267 and in exactly 0.5 miles you will see CR 91 branch off to your left. Take CR-91 for 0.4 miles to the nursery on your left. (It's easy to miss the entrance the first time; however, once you've been there, you'll never miss the driveway again.)

GPS: N 39° 46.53', W 86° 25.00'

right; however, considering the numerous other floral photo ops available in the area for a lesser amount—or free—one really needs to weigh this unusual option carefully.

WHAT YOU'LL FIND

This is an intriguing, cutting-edge plant source offering horticulturally interesting varieties of such outstanding newcomers as the drought tolerant, dark rosy-red flowers of **yarrow** (*Achillea millefolium* 'Red Velvet'), charcoal stems and grey-green foliage of **false indigo** (*Baptisia* × 'Purple Smoke'), and the Blooms of Bressingham introduction, the two-tone pink **tickseed** (*Coreopsis rosea* 'Sweet Dreams').

> *The sun and air are the lungs and hearts of flowers."*
> —LOUISA JOHNSON

The perennial list is uncommonly interesting; new plants are forever being brought out, so repeat trips are advised. On random visits during the growing season, I found winsome collections of what can only be called the "in crowd"— old plants with a new lease on life (and fame) or genuinely new cultivars, plants deemed "of the moment." These included yarrow (*Achillea*), **Japanese anemone** (*Anemone*), **goat's beard** (*Aruncus dioicus*), and selections of *Astilbe*. I also saw **masterwort** (*Astrantia*), false indigo (*Baptisia*), **bellflower** (*Campanula*), **bugbane** (*Cimicifuga*), and **bleeding heart** (*Dicentra*). You'll also find **barrenwort** (*Epimedium*), **cranesbill** (*Geranium*), **coral bells** (*Heuchera*), (*Monarda*), **peony** (*Paeonia*), and **beard tongue** (*Penstemon*).

EXTRAS

Late summer customers are rewarded with an outrageous sale on some perennials. (I picked up hostas for $1 and cranesbill and corydalis for a paltry $2 each.) Even late in the season, these were healthy, well-grown, and cared for plants. If planted early enough for the roots to get established, fall-planted perennials are a frugal way to get a jump on next season's floral bounty.

INDIANA

Area gardeners rarely encounter such distinguished plants as **toadlily** (*Tricyrtis formosa* 'Samurai'), **comfrey** (*Symphytum* 'Axminster Gold'), and **dragonshead** (*Dracocephalum grandiflorum*). They have **foam** flower (*Tiarella* 'Pink Brushes'), *Heucherella* 'Viking Ship', and **campion** (*Silene* 'Clifford More'). Avon's impressive **daylily** collection (more than 500 varieties) grows in stature on a yearly basis, with **hostas** (more than 100 varieties) coming into their own stride. Perennials are set out alphabetically on long tables interspersed throughout the nursery, with the occasional specials snapped up at an incredible rate.

Avon Perennial Gardens, a "Best in Indy" garden center award-winner, is known for its superior tree and shrub cultivars, particularly standards and conifers. The shrub yard contains **lilac** (*Syringa*), **bottlebrush buckeye** (*Aesculus parviflora*), *Viburnum*, *Spirea*, *Deutzia*, variegated **willow** (*Salix*), *Weigelas*, *Magnolias*, and *Hydrangea*. The ornamental tree section offers weeping **redbuds** (*Cercis*), variegated **dogwoods** (*Cornus*), **Japanese tree lilac** (*Syringa reticulata*), tricolor **beech** (*Fagus*), **weeping cherries** (*Prunus*), and **serviceberries** (*Amelanchier*). A sampling of shrubs grafted onto standards include **viburnum**, **lilac**, **blue spruce**, **hydrangea**, and **pea shrub** (*Caragana arborescens*).

In late spring, Avon Perennial Gardens breaks old man winter's grip by offering dazzling hanging baskets jam packed with the latest annual creations: **fuschia**, **diascia**, **impatiens**, "mini petunias", daisy-like flowers of every shape and color (from *Argyranthemum* and *Bracyscome* to *Osteospermum*), **bacopa**, **geranium**, **nemesia**, **verbena**, and **torenia**.

An Open House is held the last weekend in June and first weekend in July, during the peak daylily bloom period. Once a well-kept secret of local gardeners, Avon Perennial Gardens now attracts customers from greater distances for its 3 annual garden tours of the nursery beds and borders, plus a spring wildflower walk. This nursery offers a great opportunity to indulge your senses amidst beautifully landscaped gardens and state-of-the-art water features.

★ SIDE TRIPS ★

WHITE RIVER GARDENS, (317) 630-2001, 1200 West Washington St., Indianapolis, IN. This is a 3.3-acre landmark botanical attraction, and sister institution to the Indianapolis Zoo, combining the best of gardening ideas, plant information, and inspirational design. www.whiterivergardens.com. **GARFIELD PARK CONSERVATORY & SUNKEN GARDENS**, (317) 327-7184, 2450 Shelby Street, Indianapolis, IN. Garfield Park has one of Indiana's most significant landscapes, with graceful fountains, formal gardens, and a 7,500 square foot conservatory. www.indygov.org.

INDIANA

BLUE RIVER NURSERY

❦ ❧

Located on 40 beautiful acres in the scenic rural countryside west of Fort Wayne, Blue River Nursery is the country nursery, imposing perennial gardens, and spacious horticultural playground of owner Shawn Locker. Initially started as a wholesale business growing conifers, ornamental grasses, and hosta, the first greenhouse went up in 1998, morphing Blue River into its present day reincarnation of a cutting-edge nursery offering a massive collection of uniquely distinctive plants for the home gardener.

The emphasis at Blue River is on ornamental plants of superior value suited to the growing conditions of the local climate. Whether you are creating an English style cottage garden, an alpine or rock garden, a shade garden, or a sun border, the nursery is tailored to assist both the novice and expert gardeners alike. It's also a great resource when creating an area to attract critters such as butterflies, birds, and other wildlife.

Blue River is a bit out of the way, yet this secluded nursery's exemplary list of well-grown, well-tended plants makes it worth the extra effort. On my visit late in the season, I saw many healthy, well-tended plants—a sure litmus test indicator of a good nursery. In fact, Blue River prides itself on never running out of a particular plant, as it is in a constant state of propagating new ones.

WHAT YOU'LL FIND

Blue River grows scads of rare and hard to find plants, with an emphasis on unique, noteworthy perennials, handsome dwarf conifers, singular

OWNERS: Shawn Locker
TYPE: Specialty nursery
SPECIALTIES: Perennials—sun and shade; shrubs; trees; grasses; vines; alpines; conifers, dwarf; herbs
HOURS: Everyday, including Sundays and holidays. Mon.-Sun.: 9:00 am to 6:00 pm.
CATALOG AVAILABLE: Yes
MAIL-ORDER AVAILABLE: No
DISPLAY GARDENS: Yes
CLASSES: No

CONTACT
4484 E. Hartman Road
Columbia City, IN 46725
PHONE AND FAX: (260) 244-7420
WEB ADDRESS: www.bluerivernursery.com
EMAIL: shawn@bluerivernursery.com

DIRECTIONS
FROM I-30 TO EAST OF COLUMBIA CITY: I-30 east of Columbia City to 300 E Road, turn north at 300 E to Hartman Rd. (A good landmark for 300 E is Paige's Crossing & Thompson Chevy on the south side of US 30, there is a stop light at the intersection.) Turn right (east) onto Hartman Road and drive 1.7 miles to the nursery on your right. (Locally Hartman Road is known as 13 curve road, because though it's only 2 miles long it has 13 curves.)

GPS: N 41° 09.47', W 85° 24.46'

INDIANA

Japanese maples, and remarkable weeping trees. This 7-acre nursery is dense with well-labeled plants that are seamlessly integrated into the nursery sales areas and the ever-expanding, always imposing display gardens.

> *"The love of gardening is a seed that once sown never dies."*
> —GERTRUDE JEKYLL

Along with the traditional or classic perennials, there are many recent introductions from Europe and Asia on the nursery's plant list. Blue River Nursery specializes in what it calls "perennials with personality," explaining that "while we grow most of the more common perennials, our fancy really is the newly released and newly imported species." Locker aims to keep the nursery on the cutting edge of new introductions. He consistently introduces and grows improved cultivars sporting either larger flowers, greater color blossoms, longer lasting blooms, enhanced color, new or more attractive foliage, or greater compactness to fit better within today's smaller landscapes and the ever increasingly popular trough, rock, and railroad gardens.

Uncommon finds include *Hibiscus* 'Sweet Caroline' (whose lovely light pink flower buds open to resemble roses), *Hemerocallis* 'Penny's Worth' (a mini lemon-yellow **daylily**), and *Platycodon* 'Sentimental Blue' (extra-dwarf **balloon flower**). You'll also see *Monarda* 'Gardenview Scarlet' (a scarlet red **beebalm**), *Echinacea* 'Baby White Swan' (compact, white **coneflower**), and *Trifolium repens* 'Dragon's Blood' (a stunning **clover** with shimmering red stains over mint green leaves). Blue River's repertoire contains two interesting **daisies**, *Leucanthemum* 'Northern Lights' and dwarf *L.* 'Shady Lady', as well as **sun daisy** *Osteospermum barberiae* var. *compactum* (hardy, pink to purple-flowered, from South Africa). Pink *Dianthus* 'Shawn's Tough Guy' (a spectacular chance seedling found by Locker to have "survived untold abuse and neglect") joins another heart-throb pink, *D.* 'Heart Attack'.

For container gardeners, a wonderful selection of temperennials (tender perennials used for container gardens) is stocked in early spring. Blue River does not, however, stock any annuals. Some examples of the available tender plants include *Dahlia* 'Bishop of Llandaff', *Canna* 'Black Knight', *Begonia* 'Angel Wing', and hardy banana *Musa* 'Basjoo'. You'll also find **angel's trumpet** *Brugmansia*, *Perilla* 'Autropurpurea', and *Tweedia caerulea*.

Of special interest are the many unusual shade perennials such as the drooping racemes of pink- and white-flowered **hardy begonia** (*Begonia grandis*), glossy **foam flower** (*Tiarella* 'Lacquer Leaf'), and **coral bells** (*Heuchera sanguinea* 'Green

Spice'). Exemplary plants enriched with dark leaves include several cultivars of bronze-black fairy candles (*Cimicifuga* 'Brunette', *C.* 'Hillside Black Beauty', and *C.* 'Black Negligee'), the low-growing purple leafed clover (*Trifolium repens* 'Purpurescens'), and the near-black leaves and rich red-purple flowers of **sedum** (*Sedum* 'Purple Emperor').

Blue River pots thousands of perennials annually, most sold in gallon containers at very reasonable prices. Specimen trees are grown in containers because they are easier for the staff to handle and have a more fibrous root system, which translates into the plant's ability to establish itself quicker in the landscape.

In the tree category, Blue River is an incredible source for weeping trees: **cherry**, **cherry contorted**, **crab**, **mulberry**, **pussy willow**, **willow**, and **corkscrew willow**. One of the many desirable maples, the **paperbark maple** (*Acer griseum*), is available with its flamboyant, peeling red bark. But the nursery's list also includes **ash**, **quaking aspen**, **bald cypress**, **beech**, **birch**, **dawn redwood**, **elm**, **lilac**, **oak**, **redbud**, **serviceberry**, **sweetgum**, **sourwood**, and **yellowwood**. Blue River offers more than 100 typically hard-to-come-by cultivars of **Japanese maple**, of which my favorites were two dwarfs awash in small leaves that come out pink in early spring—*Acer palmatum* 'Corallinum' and *A.p.* 'In the Pink'.

Blue River has an excellent range of flowering shrubs including **bottlebrush buckeye** (*Aesculus parviflora*), **scotch broom** (*Cytisus scoparius* 'Lena'); and a large pink-flowered, hardy **hydrangea** (*Hydrangea macrophylla* 'Sadie Ray') found growing at a north Indiana farmhouse for over fifty years. You'll also find a new, true dwarf **butterfly bush** (*Buddleia davidii* 'White Ball') and the variegated **kerria** (*Kerria* 'Japanese Rose').

★ SIDE TRIPS ★

FRELLINGER-FREIMANN BOTANICAL CONSERVATORY, (260) 427-6440, 1100 S. Calhoun Street, Fort Wayne, IN 46802. Frellinger-Freimann has 25,000 square feet of indoor gardens featuring imaginative floral gardens, a tropical garden and a Sonoran Desert. Website address is: www.botanicalconservatory.org.

FOX ISLAND COUNTY PARK & NATURE PRESERVE, (260) 449-3180, 7234 Yohne Road, Fort Wayne, IN 4680. Fox Island is 605 acres of woods, fields, marshes, and ancient forested sand dunes offering 6 miles of hiking, birding, picnicing, swimming, and cross country skiiing.

INDIANA

The nursery carries a tribe of bamboo including variegated (*Pleioblastus fortunei* 'Variegata'), **yellow groove** (*Phyllostachys aureosulcata*), **stone** (*Phyllostachys nuda*), and **fountain bamboo** (*Fargesia nitida*). The selection of ornamental grasses runs the gamut of **maiden grass**, **blood grass**, **fountain grass**, **switchgrass**, **oat grass**, and **sedge** in sizes from only a few inches high to an architectural giant topping out at more than 9 feet tall.

Blue River has several resident dogs, a sort of unofficial greeting committee, of which the chief greeter is lovable "Stoney," referred to by the staff as the "real boss." Because of the friendly critters roaming the nursery, Blue River requests that you leave your dogs in the car. Additionally, they reserve the right to "become downright irritated when people let their kids run wild, mistreat the dogs, throw stones, and exhibit other less than polite behavior." Considering the outstanding display gardens available for the visitor's viewing, the enormous healthy plant selection, the old-fashioned genuinely friendly service, the knowledgeable staff, and the very reasonable prices offered gardeners at the nursery, the request appears exceedingly reasonable to me.

CEDARTHORN GARDENS

❧ ❧

Cedarthorn Gardens, located on 2 acres of land in the quaint town of Shelbyville, is a registered American Hemerocallis Display (AHS) display garden. It's also the residence of Louise and Bobby James, and home to their prolific hybridization program. As an AHS garden, the James's garden features more than 500 well-marked, registered cultivar daylilies amid the many other complementary perennials in a variety of garden designs.

While the emphasis is always on daylilies, they do not stand alone. Two rather interesting beds amidst the various landscape designs are the "Showcase Garden," which features all of the registered daylily introductions bred at Cedarthorn Gardens, and "The Medalist Bed," which is planted only with those significant daylilies that have achieved the prominent AHS Medalist award.

WHAT YOU'LL FIND

OWNER: Louise and Bobby James
TYPE: Small specialty nursery
SPECIALTIES: Daylilies
HOURS: Daily, by appointment: 10:00 am to 7:00 pm (during season).
CATALOG AVAILABLE: Color catalog and internet listing
MAIL-ORDER AVAILABLE: Yes
DISPLAY GARDENS: Yes (AHS Display Garden)
CLASSES: None

CONTACT

1487 E. Cedarthorn Drive
(P. O. Box 869)
Shelbyville, IN   46176-0869
PHONE: (317) 392-0264
FAX: (317) 392-4604
WEB ADDRESS: www.cedarthorn.com
EMAIL: Lbjames@Lightbound.com

DIRECTIONS

FROM INDIANAPOLIS: Take I-74 East to the 1st Shelbyville exit (Exit # 113), drive to the circle in downtown Shelbyville, Take East Washington until it T's at Vine Street, turn left on Vine which will curve around, you will pass a cemetery. After you pass the cemetery, turn left onto Knightstown Road, and drive for approx. 2 miles to Cedarthorn Drive. Turn left onto Cedarthorn Drive, nursery is at the first stop sign. You can't miss them. Park in the driveway, but if driveway is full, park on the other side of Cedarthorn Drive.

GPS: N 39° 32.93', W 85° 45.24'

Cedarthorn Gardens is a specialty grower of more than 600 varieties of named **daylily** hybrids and 3,000 or so of the James' own seedlings. Hybridizers generally concentrate all their efforts on one specific trait. It could be cold-hardiness, a certain form such as spiders, miniatures, or doubles, reblooming capabilities, different colors (thus far blue is still elusive), tetraploids, or extended periods of bloom. Louise describes their hybridization goals as "somewhat mixed, but with the overall direction of different." Intrigued by the challenge of the color blue, specific color traits (one such trait being a contrasting edge color with no eye pattern), and new breakthroughs in texture, James sums up her hybridizing as an effort towards achieving a "pretty face", good performance, and something "different." To that end, she trials close to 750 brand new daylily seedlings each season and maintains seedling beds containing several thousand hybrids from her previous efforts, all carefully watched and studied throughout their two-year trial period.

Currently James has 33 registered daylilies that comprise the Cedarthorn Garden Daylily Collections. These consist of the Camelot Collection (intended to be grown together as a group, each complementing one another in color, height, and bloom time), the Shelby Series (honoring garden visitors from Shelbyville), Melodies in Bloom (song titles), and the Cedarthorn Classics (exceptional in overall beauty and performance). Each plant has showy, prizewinning characteristics that are unusual, spectacular, and (voila!) different.

With my zany penchant for striking or incongruous names, I was instantly drawn to what turned out to be James' first introduction, 'Seven Come Eleven.' The striking coral cream with rose eye hybrid "so heavily veined that the texture appears to be corduroy" is the surprising product of Louise James's naïve and haphazard "first summer of dabbling pollen." She compares it to "throwing a pair of dice onto a crap table." Another favorite, 'Behold Gwenevere' (a gorgeous frosted pink with a high bud count

EXTRAS

Cedarthorn offers a unique opportunity to purchase select two-year-old seedling clumps (unregistered plants) from its hybridization program, drawn from the gene pools of some of the newest daylilies available today and proven to be outstanding. These seedlings, limited in quantity, produce some enchanting bargains and tend to be snapped up rather quickly. Cedarthorn also offers exciting deals on large clumps of overstocked (some are just vigorous growers) registered daylilies and occasionally runs a "buy 2 get 1 free" sale (perfect for sharing with friends).

INDIANA

and good branching habits) is the perfect foil to 'Hail King Arthur' (pink with rose band and lovely cream edge—always a visitor magnet). Don't miss the vibrant rose-red 'Lancelot of France' (which, of course, will always complement Gwenevere yet forever compete with Arthur).

Cedarthorn Gardens' field-grown plants are sold primarily by mail-order, but visitors will always find a good selection of mature, quality, field-grown, freshly potted, container plants to choose from. Peak daylily bloom at Cedarthorn is early July, but visitors are welcome anytime during bloom season. Please note that as this is the James's residence, so it is always advisable to call ahead and respect their privacy.

INDIANA

COBURG PLANTING FIELDS

❦

A true rural gem for daylily enthusiasts and a surprising treat for gardeners in general, Coburg's Planting Fields is a picturesque, charming, rural destination nursery that grows, among other things, more than 750 named varieties of daylilies. Owners, Philipp Brockington, a retired Valparaiso University law school professor, and Howard Reeve, Jr., a daylily hybridizer and antique enthusiast, are passionate, knowledgeable plant people. They are always ready and available to talk with gardeners about their two favorite subjects—daylilies and hosta.

Like many obsessions, Brockington's infatuation with daylilies began innocently enough. As he relates it, a local hybridizer in Dyer, the man responsible for the 'Stella d'Oro' phenomenon, shared a few plant starts. "You know how gardeners are; they tend to share." He notes with a chuckle, "I had already started collecting a few daylily plants—I don't know how it happened. One day you have a few plants; suddenly, the next thing you know, you're a collector of daylilies."

The next step was inevitable. Growing and hybridizing daylilies became a passion. And as with other daylily connoisseurs, collecting daylilies naturally evolved into collecting hosta. By 1998, the owners had hybridized 5 unusual forms of daylilies with good branching and high bud counts, plants that should be available to their customers by the summer of 2004.

WHAT YOU'LL FIND

Coburg's production fields consist of more than 100 rows in 3 separate

OWNERS: Phillipp Brockington, Howard H. Reeve, Jr.
TYPE: Specialty nursery
SPECIALTIES: Daylilies; hosta
HOURS: No set hours or days. If you must be sure of availability, call ahead. It's recommended that you get to the fields before 3 pm. Appointments appreciated, but not necessary.
CATALOG AVAILABLE: Printed
MAIL-ORDER AVAILABLE: Yes
DISPLAY GARDENS: Yes
CLASSES: No

CONTACT
573 E 600 N
Valparaiso, IN 46383
PHONE: (219) 462-4288
EMAIL: phil.brockington@valpo.edu

DIRECTIONS
FROM I-80: Take I-80 to IN-49 (Calumet Ave.) south. Take IN-49 (Calumet Ave.) for 3.9 miles to 600 N, turn east (left) onto 600 N and drive for 4.0 miles to the nursery on your left, right before IN-2. **NOTE:** CR 600 N (an east-west road) is one road away from CR 600 E (a north-south road), both of which intersect IN-2 which runs diagonally. Be sure you're headed in the right direction on CR 600.

GPS: N 41° 31.18', W 86° 57.31'

fields of lined out **daylilies**. Available plants come in a rainbow of colors from off-white and cream to an ocean of reds, pinks, lilacs, purples, burgundies, oranges, yellows, and all shades in between. Second only to color are the incredible shapes and patterns of the blossoms—an array of ruffled, bicolored, and watermarked, and eyezones flecked with glitter called "diamond dust."

The nursery's catalog offers approximately 200 daylilies by mail-order and lists the breeder, year of introduction, height of plants, diam-

"A garden is a delight to the eye and a solace to the soul."
—SADI

eter of blossom, and bloom habit of each plant. The list showcases hardy hybrids (capable of surviving Indiana's weather extremes), including a gorgeous bur-gundy-purple spider 'Morticia', a rose-peach spider with rose eyezone 'Parade of Peacocks', and a striking white with shimmering pink tint 'Indy Seductress'. The list also highlights the handsome yellow with wide black eyezone 'Bold Black Eyes' and a pale cream rainbow polychrome spider 'Tylwyth Teg' (both can be seen at the nursery). Although the new hybrids can cost upwards of $100, Coburg Planting Fields offers wonderful cultivars for $6, and many plants in between. For on-site customers, the nursery carries daylilies not listed in the catalog, both container grown and freshly dug. All plants are shipped, freshly dug, well-rooted, double fan divisions that have lived through at least one Indiana winter without protection. On orders of $50 or more, the nursery includes bonus plants.

For inexperienced gardeners, few challenges are more intimidating than trying to grow plants in the shade, but for the owners of Coburg Planting Fields, it comes naturally. The nursery offers more than 100 **hosta** cultivars, both field grown and pre-potted. The hosta herd has a good selection of the crinkled, blue, gold, creamy, streaked, smeared, cupped, puckered, waffled, corrugated, frosted, and edged varieties. The plants are tough, too, having survived at least one full winter outdoors before being offered to customers. Visitors are invited to stroll through the shady areas of the nursery display gardens to view mature hostas in their element.

Like reliable old friends, hostas come back bigger and more beautiful, reaching their peak in the fourth or fifth year. There's everyone's favorite, 'Sum & Substance' (thick, oval chartreuse leaves spreading to 5 feet or more), 'Sweet Expectations' (margins of blue-green forming a contrast to the creamy, yellow center), and golden yellow 'Sun Power' (to brighten dark corners). Though slow

INDIANA

to get established, the strutting 'Gold Standard' (variegated gold edged with dark green) shows visitors it's worth the wait. Other visitor favorites include 'Blue Wedgewood' (chalky blue heart-shaped leaves), 'Daybreak' (large, bright gold), 'Fire and Ice' (white centered, heart shaped leaves) and 'Pineapple Poll' (heavily rippled, green foliage).

INDIANA

DOGWOOD FARM

❧ ☙

Dogwood Farm, located in Brazil, 40 miles southwest of Indianapolis, is a 30-acre farm turned commercial hosta grower. This nursery grows more than 300 kinds of hosta and a goodly variety of high-quality, shade-loving perennials. Here you can find many of the newly developed hybrids or difficult to find cultivars typically attractive to collectors and connoisseurs. The nursery specializes in hardy perennials of a robust nature that are field grown in typical Midwest weather conditions.

Visitors are invited to stroll through the extensive display gardens which offer hosta glades, a pond garden, a shade garden, and benches and chairs for introspection and quiet enjoyment.

WHAT YOU'LL FIND

The **hosta** swarm has all the gold, blue, green, cupped, crinkled, variegated, waffled, wavy, twisted, furrowed, furled, corrugated, margined, mottled, misted, streaked, splashed, speckled, and folded varieties any gardener could ever hope for. Notable in the variegated list are the dwarf *Hosta* 'Green Eyes' (yellow turning cream with narrow green margins), *H.* 'Rascal' (light yellow leaves with variable dark green margin), *H.* 'Five O'Clock Shadow' (gold and white variegated), and *H.* 'Mixed Nuts' (a streaked sport of *H.* 'Krossa Regal').

OWNERS: Bob Whitmore
TYPE: Specialty nursery
SPECIALTIES: Hosta; perennials— shade
HOURS: Late April through July, and Early Sept.: Thurs.-Sat.: 10:00 am to 5:00 pm, Sun. noon to 5:00 pm. Other times by appointment. Call for exact opening dates.
CATALOG AVAILABLE: No
MAIL-ORDER AVAILABLE: Yes
DISPLAY GARDENS: Yes
CLASSES: No

CONTACT
6070 S 1000 E
Brazil, IN 47834
PHONE: (765) 344-0103
FAX: (765) 344-0133
WEB ADDRESS: www.hostagarden.com
EMAIL: dogwoodfarm@hostagarden.com

DIRECTIONS
FROM I-465 (IN INDIANAPOLIS): I-465 to US-36 west to SR-59. Turn south (left) onto SR-59, drive to Rt. 325 (also called New Discovery Rd.) , turn east (left) and drive to 1000 E (also called CR-161 on some maps). Turn right (south) onto 1000 E, and drive to the nursery on the right side of the road.
FROM I-70: I-70 to US-231 northbound (Exit 41). Take US-231 to US-40, turn west (left) onto US-40 and drive for 10.8 miles to N 500 E, and drive about 7.2 miles to Greencastle Rd. (also called CR-720 S) N 500 E becomes CR-61 about 4 miles down. Turn west (left) on Greencastle Rd. and drive 3 miles to 1000 E (also called CR-161 on some maps). Turn north (right) and drive 2 miles to the nursery on your right.

GPS: N 39° 40.90', W 87° 02.99'

Gold-leafed hostas of merit include *H.* 'Grey Ghost' (a sport of *H.* 'Blue Angel', emerges nearly white, turns butter yellow, then blue), *H.* 'Center of Attention' (golden yellow medium hosta), *H* 'Centerfold' (intensely corrugated, puckered with slightly rippled margins, available at only two nurseries nationwide), and the medium *H.* 'Super Bowl' (deeply cupped with thick round leaves).

> "*Gardeners, I think, dream bigger dreams than emperors.*"
> —MARY CANTWELL

Since my personal preference always runs to *H.* 'Sum & Substance', I couldn't leave without picking up *H.* 'Parhelion' (a white edged *H.* 'Sum & Substance'), *H.* 'Winter Snow' (another white edged *H.* 'Sum & Substance'), and my favorite of this trip, *H.* 'Chinese Dragon' (a streaked *H.* 'Komodo Dragon') to join all the other giant hostas currently cavorting happily in my yard.

The nursery's own introductions, *Hosta* 'Bodacious Blue' (giant blue, available in limited numbers), *H.* 'Goldie' (yellow), and *H.* 'White Bikini' (a sport of *H.* 'Striptease' with a bright white center among rich green leaves) more than hold their own against such robust stalwarts as 'Sum & Substance', 'Great Expectations', 'Guacamole', 'Patriot', 'Regal Splendor', 'Elegans', and 'Fire and Ice'.

As companions to your hosta, there are shade plants to found such as, **coral bells** *Heuchera* 'Magic Wand' (small scalloped dark green leaves and cerise red flowers) and *H.* 'Veil of Passion' (mahogany colored foliage and bright red flowers). Another plant available here for the hosta border is **lungwort** (*Pulmonaria*). Additional noteworthy hosta companions include *P.* 'Ice Ballet' (white bloomer) and *P.* 'Coral Spring' (mahogany colored foliage and bright red flowers).

Dogwood Farm's policy is to sell good, healthy tissue cultures of plants at least one year old or divisions of mature plants that have been grown on "the farm" for at least one winter. On-site sales are potted plants, whereas mail-order plants are shipped bare root.

HIDDEN HILL NURSERY

❧ ❧

For more than twenty-five years, Bob Hill has been a columnist and feature writer for the *Louisville Courier-Journal*, including several years spent wandering Kentucky and Southern Indiana in search of interesting people, fun, fact, and whimsy. Additionally, he's published eight books on subjects ranging from gardening to basketball history to two collections of his newspaper columns. He is also co-host of the "Home-grown" radio show with fellow garden expert Jeneen Wiche.

Behind the scenes, Hill and his wife, Janet, are co-owners of Hidden Hill Nursery, located a mere 8 miles northeast of Louisville (KY) in southern Indiana. The nursery specializes in a zesty selection of rare shrubs, trees, and unusual perennials, supplemented by exotic landscaping ideas and large works of garden art that can't be found in any typical garden nursery, garden center, or gallery.

The overriding attribute of Hidden Hill Nursery is the exhilarating manner in which it exhibits its charm and innocent sense of fun. A main attraction at the nursery is the 8-acre plant nursery and sculpture garden built around the Hill's old farmhouse. Here you'll encounter fountains, arbors, benches, containers, garden whimsy, and a newly expanded outdoor electric train—in addition to the unique plants.

As seen on HGTV's "Secret Gardens," this one-of-a-kind site of

OWNERS: Janet and Bob Hill
TYPE: Specialty nursery
SPECIALTIES: Trees; shrubs; perennials
HOURS: April through Oct.: Fri. 10:00 am to 7:00 pm, Sat. 9:00 am to 7:00 pm, Sun. Noon to 5:00 pm. Other times by appointment.
CATALOG AVAILABLE: No
MAIL-ORDER AVAILABLE: No
DISPLAY GARDENS: Yes
CLASSES: No

CONTACT
1011 Utica-Charlestown Road
Utica, IN 47130
PHONE: (812) 280-0347
FAX: (812) 923-7464
WEB ADDRESS: www.hiddenhilnursery.com
EMAIL: bobjanhill@aol.com

DIRECTIONS
FROM LOUISVILLE (I-65): I-65 North across Ohio River (Kennedy Bridge), to Court Ave. (Exit 0). Take Court Ave. to Spring St. Turn south (right) to Market St., turn northeast (left) on Market St. which turns into Utica Pike and drive 5.6 miles where Utica Pike becomes 4th St., continue through Utica to Utica-Charlestown Rd. (log cabin community hall on left at intersection). Turn northwest (left) and drive 0.5 miles to nursery on your left. Look for nursery sign. **FROM THE NORTH (I-65):** Take I-65 southbound to I-265 east to the Clark Maritime Centre on Utica Pike Rd. Turn northeast (left) onto Utica Pike Rd. and travel through the town of Utica to Utica-Charlestown Rd. (log cabin community hall on left at intersection). Turn northwest (left) and drive 0.5 miles to the nursery on your left. Look for the sign.

GPS: N 38° 20.59', W 85° 39.34'

carefully landscaped beds and borders also includes woods, meadows, stone and wooden fences, ponds, and a restored barn that now serves as a gift shop. On my visit, one customer described the garden as "a monument to passionate eccentricity." While peering through an oversized door at the edge of the lawn, opening onto a meandering path through pasture grasses, I experienced an "Alice in Wonderland" moment. This is a garden for leisurely walks, reflective strolling, and introspection.

What You'll Find

Hill propagates and grows high quality plants—as he has done for the past twenty years—traveling around the country and abroad in pursuit of his gardening hobby. Of special interest are the many interesting shrubs, including fragrant **abelia** (*Abelia mosanensis*), white **forsythia** (*Abeliophyllum distichum*), a variegated forsythia (*Forsythia viridissima* 'Kumson'), and **blue bean** (*Decaisnea fargesii*). You'll also find C**hinese fringetree** (*Chionanthus retusus*), native **fringetree** (*Chionanthus virginicus*), **the devil's walking stick** (*Aralia spinosa*), and **dwarf birch** (*Betula nigra* 'Little King')

> "He who would have beautiful roses in his garden must have beautiful roses in his heart."
> —S. R. Hole
> ❧❧

along with some gorgeous **Japanese witchhazel** (*Hamamelis intermedia* 'Angelly' and 'Barmstead Gold').

The list continues with *Hydrangea petiolaris* 'Miranda' (a green and white variegated climbing hydrangea), and *Cotinus coggygria* 'Young Lady' (a smokebush which blooms when very young with fluffy blossoms covering every inch of the plant). Don't overlook the variegatead five-leaf **aralia** *Acanthopanax sieboldianus* (aka *Eleutherococcus sieboldianus*), and *Itea virginica* 'Little Henry' (compact sweetspire shooting off white flowers like so many fireworks).

When challenged with a burdensome site, I know a viburnum shrub will be my salvation; consequently, I am constantly on the look-out for new additions to my collection. At Hidden Hill, a number of viburnum stopped me in my tracks, including *Viburnum* 'Michael Dodge' (a Winterthur Gardens' introduction, glistening white flowers followed by a multitude of large golden berries); *V. dilatatum* 'Erie' (a confection whose overwhelming abundance of creamy, white fuzzy flowers produces enormous numbers of striking coral red fruit); and *V. dilatatum*

'Cardinal Candy' (floriferous, eye candy of a shrub, tons of creamy white flowers in early spring bringing forth a myriad of brilliant, bright red fruit in late summer).

Hidden Hill Nursery offers a full spectrum of garden perennials: graceful shade plants, colorful sun perennials, native woodlanders, personable ground covers, comely vines, and architectural grasses. Hill has a predilection for airy blue **star flower** (*Amsonia hubrectii*) which is teamed with **allium** puffballs and blue **salvia** in various parts of the garden. The nursery has a prodigious selection of updated classics such as red **valerian** (*Centranthus ruber* 'Pretty Betsy'), **dragonshead** (*Dracocephalum argunense* 'Fiji Blue'), **bush clover** (*Lespedeza* 'Summer Beauty' and 'Pink Cascade'), **aster** (*Aster* 'Raydon's Favorite'), and **speedwell** (*Veronica* 'Goodness Grows').

A recent phenomenon, the Scott County Heritage Garden Weekend held on the nursery grounds includes lectures by Bob Hill and Janeen Wiche. There is also a garden market, soil testing, garden and nature related gallery exhibitions, a children's tent, and children's nature walk. Other events, offered for a nominal fee, include a reception, silent auction, dinner, and a gardening symposium.

★ SIDE TRIPS ★

HOWARD STEAMBOAT MUSEUM, (812) 283-3728, 1101 E. Market Street, Jeffersonville, IN, Tues.-Sun. 10:00 am to 4:00 pm. This museum is inside a 22-room Victorian mansion, featuring stained glass windows, intricate hand carved furniture, artifacts, and models of famous boats. **FALLS OF THE OHIO STATE PARK,** (812) 280-9970, 201 Riverside Dr., Clarksville, IN, Mon.-Sat. 9:00 am to 5:00 pm, Sun. 1:00 pm to 5:00 pm. At this park you'll have 220 acres of exposed Devonian fossil beds to explore, plus an interpretive center. **JOE HUBER FAMILY FARM AND RESTAURANT,** (812) 923-5255, 2421 Scottsville, Star- light, IN. They offer good eats, fields of daylilies, apple orchards, and a farm market.

INDIANA

MILLER'S MANOR GARDENS

୧ଓ ଓ୨

This family-run nursery, sited on land adjoining the Miller residence, is known for its diverse yet imaginative selection of healthy container- and field-grown plants. Linda Miller, affable co-owner of this cutting-edge enterprise, is continually on the prowl for the best of the newest plants, offering them to her customers long before they are available elsewhere. Miller's Manor was the first nursery at which I found *Campanula* 'Beautiful Trust' (stunning with lacy, thread-like white flowers), *Achillea* 'Red Velvet' (non-fading, deep red), and *Persicaria microcephala* 'Red Dragon' (non-running, sterile).

When purchasing, keep in mind that "extras" (of the nursery's choosing) are included with each iris and daylily order over $15.

WHAT YOU'LL FIND

One of the home-based nursery's specialties is **iris**: miniature bearded, standard dwarf bearded, intermediate bearded, bordered bearded, miniature tall bearded, aril & aril medians, tall bearded, beardless iris species, and Siberian iris. Miller's Manor offers more than 1,000 iris varieties in all

OWNERS: Linda and Roger Miller
TYPE: Specialty nursery
SPECIALTIES: Iris; daylilies; hosta; dwarf conifers; peonies; trees; shrubs; perennials—sun and shade
HOURS: Mid-April thru Mid-Oct.: Mon., Tue., Thurs., Fri. 9:00 am to 6 pm, Sat. 9:00 am to 4:00 pm. (closed Wednesdays); Apr. thru June: Sun. 11:00 am to 4:00 pm (if coming from a distance, check for exact season opening and closing dates).
CATALOG AVAILABLE: Online for iris, daylilies, and hosta only
MAIL-ORDER AVAILABLE: Yes
DISPLAY GARDENS: Yes
CLASSES: No

CONTACT
12788 East 191st St.
Noblesville, IN 46060
PHONE: (219) 462-4288
WEB ADDRESS: www.millersmanorgardens.com
EMAIL: Lindamiller@iquest.net

DIRECTIONS
FROM INDIANAPOLIS: Take I-465 to north I-69/IN-37 (Exit 37B) toward Ft. Wayne, driving 5.5 miles to I-37 north (exit #5) toward Fisher/Noblesville driving for 7.2 miles to E 191st St. Turn east (right) onto E 191's and drive 2.6 miles to the nursery on your left.
FROM THE EAST (I-70): Take I-70 to north IN-9 (Exit # 104) toward Maxwell. Drive on IN-9 for 12.8 miles towards Maxwell, turn west (left) onto IN-38, driving for 8.0 miles to Cyntheanne Rd. Turn north (right) onto Cyntheanne Rd. (small jog at 176th St.) driving 2.8 miles to 191st Street. Turn west (left) on 191st Street, driving 3 miles to the nursery.

GPS: N 40° 04.00', W 85° 56.46'

imaginable states of color, ornamentation—in amazing patterns, ruffles, frills, and edges—and repeat blooms, all on plants proven reliably hardy in the north. Linda

Miller, winner of numerous prestigious iris awards, developed a hybridizer's passion for the plant when she married her husband, Roger, who comes from a family of

hybridizers. The Millers hybridize, propagate, and grow iris hybrids not only from their own successful program but also from gorgeous plants from various well-known hybridizers across the country.

Of the 12 imposing new cultivars introduced in 2003, my favorites were the gorgeous, tall bearded 'Time Goes By' (with its light lemonade standards and rich purple falls); another superb, tall bearded iris, 'Teen Star' (with a shimmering pink and orchid pink combination); and the showy, standard dwarf bearded iris, 'Sweet Cheeks' (light neon orange accented by a halo of plum brush marks). The colorful iris bloom season starts with the miniature dwarf bearded iris in late April and concludes with the Siberian blooms, which end in early June.

The Miller garden is home to a capacious daylily collection with more than 400 named daylily cultivars; its catalog notes breeder, bloom habit and size, and general plant characteristics of each plant. A few daylilies are priced upwards of $50, such as the coral self, 'Da 'Boss'; and purple with chalky purple watermark, 'Forbidden Desires'. But the majority of what the nursery offers are endearing daylily classics such as 'Evening Bell' (light yellow), 'Mask of Time' (rose with plum eyezone), and 'Honey Dew' (soft yellow with red eye). You'll also find 'Mauna Loa' (bright deep orange), 'Purple Rain' (purple with black eyezone), and 'Penny's Worth' (micro-mini yellow). All of these are bargains at $7 or less. Peak daylily bloom period is during the month of July.

Miller's Manor grows a bevy of **hosta**, with all the wavy, corrugated, waffled, crinkled, streaked, and edged new hybrids in blue, gold, and green that any gardener could ever hope for. What I like best about this nursery's hosta was the vigor and enduring characteristics of the plants, all sold at reasonable prices. Gazing over the impressive plant selection, it was not long before my gardening friend and I pulled together the beginnings of a new theme border—Famous Melodies—for her woodland garden. These included 'Achy Breaky Heart', 'Afternoon Delight', 'Band of Gold', 'Bette Davis Eyes', 'Blue Danube', 'Blue Velvet', 'Ebb Tide', 'Jimmy Crack Corn', 'Moon River', and 'Showboat'.

The nursery is also a treasure trove of dwarf conifers and unusual trees and shrubs, especially variegated cultivars, that attract collectors and connoisseurs by

INDIANA

the car load. Rare dwarf conifers, cavorting in an array of unusual shapes, stand cheek to jowl with handsome tribes of **pine** (*Pinus*), **elm** (*Ulmus*), **hemlock** (*Tsuga*), **false cypress** (*Chamaecyparis obtusa*), **spruce** (*Picea*), and **holly** (*Ilex*), along with selections of **hydrangea**, and **viburnum**. Miller's Manor offers ornamental trees, such as **Eastern redbud**, **dogwood**, and **hazelnut**, alongside memorable cultivars of **beech** (*Fagus*), **redvein enkianthus** (*Enkianthus*), **maidenhair tree** (*Ginkgo biloba*), and **Japanese maple** (*Acer*).

The annual Open House (call for specific dates), and "open garden" days, timed to coincide with a breathtaking bloom display, are well attended. The open garden days present a wonderful opportunity to stroll through the nursery's growing beds and examine the extensive iris and daylily holdings.

INDIANA

MORNINGSIDE GARDENS

❦

Amidst the tangle of cornfields in central Indiana, Debra Henricks, an undisputed gardening dynamo, has created what can only be called the horticultural "Field of Dreams." Arguably the most beautiful nursery in Indiana, it is a little slice of heaven—a gardener's Nirvana.

With thirteen floral acres, more than 100 beds and borders, nearly 300,000 blooms of more than 3,000 varieties of registered and unregistered daylily cultivars, more than 1,800 types of hosta, and the seemingly endless varieties of countless companion plants, this place is mindboggling. Still, these are only numbers. Seeing this acreage in bloom for the first time, however, is like looking into a netherworld of endless blinding blossoms shimmering in open fields. It's a garden that explodes with intense color, flaunting a bountiful exuberance of blooming fireworks. Edna St. Vincent Millay said it best in one of her poems, "Lord, I do fear Thou'st made the world too beautiful this year."

OWNERS: Debra and Walt Henricks.
SPECIALTIES: Daylilies; hosta
HOURS: Open May 1 to approximately Sept.: Tue.-Sun. 10:00 am to 5:00 pm, or by appointment.
CATALOG AVAILABLE: Yes
MAIL-ORDER AVAILABLE: No
DISPLAY GARDENS: Yes
CLASSES: No

CONTACT
7201 West SR - 44
Morgantown, IN 46160
PHONE: (317) 422-9969
FAX: (317) 422-5593
WEB ADDRESS: www.morningsidegardens.com
EMAIL: perennials@morningsidegardens.com

DIRECTIONS
FROM INDIANAPOLIS: Take SR-135 (South Meridian) to SR-44 (5 miles south of Bargersville). Turn west (right) onto SR-44 and drive for 4.5 miles to the nursery on the left. (Look for the sign).

GPS: N39° 26.73', W 86°14.41

Daylilies are the plants that gardeners' dreams are made of. Morningside Gardens offers these glorious flowers in every shape and shade imaginable (except blue). The nursery and display gardens twine and intermesh, as plants are grown out in the fields not in production lines but in harmoniously laid out beds and borders. The nursery is a "digging garden," says Walt Henricks. "We sell right from the gardens, so you know exactly what you are buying." The well-labeled plants are garden worthy, unpampered, well-grown perennials that survive and thrive in this climate.

These gorgeous polytechnic gardens are the shining result of a very tragic accident. In 1978, Henricks was in a head-on collision that left her with a broken back and crushed right leg. (She has suffered through five surgeries on her leg and one on her knee.) Henricks, an artist, worked on her drawings as a means of recuperation; however, her doctor suggested gardening as a better form of therapy. She took him at his word, turning all that pain and agony into a flooding mass of vibrant color. "It got a bit out of hand," she says with a shrug. So fifteen years ago, the couple decided to open their gardens to the public, and the hobby morphed into a thriving enterprise. Henricks emphasizes that, although it is a business, visitors are always welcome to drop by just to look.

WHAT YOU'LL FIND

Within the 70-acre site that includes the Henrick's residence, farmland, and woodland, the gardens are ever expanding. What began as small beds around the house now include butterfly gardens, an Oriental garden, **daylily** gardens, perennial beds, and a wedding garden. There's even a healing garden in memory of her dad, who died of heart disease, and her aunt, who died of breast cancer.

The themed gardens, though primarily planted in daylilies, also include an assortment of perennials and hardscaping chosen specifically to fit within each design concept. The butterfly gardens includes a buffet of nectar-bearing flowers such as **hardy hibiscus**, **sedum**, **crocosmia**, **coneflower**, **salvia** and **buddleia**. In the Oriental garden, statuary, concrete Japanese lanterns, and impressive Oriental fountains augment the serenity of **Japanese iris**, ornamental grasses and hosta. The daylily gardens are vast sweeping masses of colorful daylily blooms, sometimes grouped by color, sometimes arranged in a kaleidoscope of multicolored beds spread out to-and-fro throughout the fields. In the wedding garden, a long, grassy pathway through a field of brilliant daylilies ends at an imposing white trellised pergola nestled at the base of majestic trees. The healing garden is a secluded site at the back edge of the property, and is dedicated to cancer and heart patients, as well as anyone else in need of healing (physical or mental). The garden, accessed through an impressive pergola built by Walt, is open to all who just want to sit, relax, reflect, and enjoy the peace, beauty, and tranquility of the garden.

INDIANA

Morningside sells only perennials, primarily daylilies and **hostas**, along with a few vines and roses. The catalog includes the latest cultivars, which can sell upwards of $75, but it also offers good, classic old-timers for $5 and many reasonably priced plants in between. One of the all-time favorites, hybridized by her uncle and always a hit with Purdue fans everywhere, is deep gold *Hemerocallis* 'Boilermaker'. However, the ones that caught my attention were *H.* 'Pink Flamingo', *H.* 'Poetry in Pink', *H.* 'Ruffled Lassie', *H.* 'Solomon's Treasure', and *H.* 'Atlanta Royalty'.

Morningside Gardens is bit out of the way, "in the middle of nowhere," but whatever extra time is needed to get there is time truly well spent. Peak bloom is typically from the middle of June through the end of July.

MUNCHKIN NURSERY & GARDENS, LLC

⊱⊰

Munchkin Nursery & Gardens is a small, family-owned nursery, located in rural southern Indiana. The origin of Munchkin Nursery & Gardens is best described by Gene Bush himself. "The garden began literally by accident in 1984. I was riding a lawn tractor, attempting to mow on a steep hillside, when the tractor began sliding sideways. An old cedar stump stopped the tractor from continuing over the cliff edge, preventing serious injury. Mountain goats refused to go up [the cliffs] to nibble grass without a parachute, so I decided to plant the area in trees and shrubs. I made the mistake of requesting gardening catalogs. . .the rest is history as they say."

My addiction to garden catalogs and gardening only grows stronger with each passing year. My first attempt at garden design was creating an English cottage garden. Plants were ordered by looks only, with no knowledge of their needs. I killed more plants than I kept alive through my initial ignorance. Those disappointments led me to read gardening books while looking around to see what grew naturally in my area. An interest in native species became a passion. Once I reached the point where more plants were surviving than dying, I looked around for related species from other parts of the world." And the nursery was born!

Munchkin Nursery & Gardens is a small, family-owned nursery, located

OWNERS: Gene E. Bush
TYPE: Small specialty nursery
SPECIALTIES: Shade perennials; woodland wildflowers
HOURS: By appointment only
CATALOG AVAILABLE: Online
MAIL-ORDER AVAILABLE: Yes
DISPLAY GARDENS: Yes
CLASSES: Yes

CONTACT
323 Woodside Drive, N.W.
Depauw, IN 47115-9039
PHONE/FAX : (812) 633-4858
WEB ADDRESS:
http://www.munchkinnursery.com
EMAIL: genebush@munchkinnursery.com

DIRECTIONS
(**NOTE:** Munchkin Nursery is located in Milltown. Depauw is purely a mailing address.) **FROM LOUISVILLE, KY:** I-64 (to St. Louis, MO) to Georgetown (exit #118) State Road 64. Drive on SR-64 (west) to Milltown, across railroad tracks to Main Street. Turn South (left) onto Main following the right fork to Spencer. Turn south (left) on Spencer, drive 2 city blocks to fork, take left fork (Woodside Drive) and proceed 0.2 miles. Nursery is on left. **FROM INDIANAPOLIS:** Take I-65 to I-265. Then I-265 to I-64 to SR-64 west. From this point follow instruction above. **FROM BLOOMINGTON AREA:** Take I-65 to I-265. Then I-265 to SR-64 West. From this point follow instructions above. (Since all visits to the nursery are by appointment, it is best to confirm driving directions for your first visit.)

INDIANA

in rural southern Indiana. Gene, noted author and lecturer, and his wife, JoAn , do it all, from planting and propagation to shipping. They're "a two-person band. . .hoping to sound like a symphony." Their goal is to offer top-notch service for all shade garden needs.

Munchkin Nursery surrounds the Bush's private residence. Visits to the nursery are by appointment only (calm down—it's worth it!). All visitors enjoy a personally guided tour of the fascinating display gardens and interesting nursery offerings. Gene's policy is to treat you more like a guest than a customer, and as such he devotes his entire attention to you and your needs.

WHAT YOU'LL FIND

The plants at Munchkin Nursery & Gardens reflect Gene's passion for bloom in a shade garden. He contends that an extended bloom period is neither an impossible, nor difficult goal for the midwestern gardener. He firmly believes that there is no shortage of color out there, if you're willing to educate yourself on perennial choices.

At the Bush's nursery, you will find a sophisticated and stimulating selection of well-grown plants that leaves you delirious with indecision. I seriously pondered the seldom-seen **fairy wand** (*Chamaelirium luteum*), the native **larkspur** (*Delphinium tricorne*), and the yellow **star grass** (*Hypoxis hirsuta*), a plant resembling grass in need of a shave. I also saw **plum iris** (*Iris graminea*) with its blossoms of lavender, red-violet, violet, and purple—think "oil slick on water." I was most fired up by the **Chinese sacred lily** (*Rohdea japonica*), a plant generally listed as Zone 7 in most books but now surviving happily in my Zone 5 garden.

Considering my predilection for unusual names, how could I pass up **colic root**, *Aletris farinosa* (used as an herbal remedy for colic in babies); *Erigenia bulbosa* (the tiny harbinger of spring also known as **salt and pepper**); or *Streptopus roseus* (with a **rose twisted stalk**). I found **stinking Benjamin**, *Trillim erectum* (one of the larger trilliums); and creeping **wood phlox**, *Phlox stolonifera* 'Home Fires' (bright pink and gorgeous). Being a pushover for anything new with interesting foliage, I was attracted to a **downy wood-mint**, *Blephilia ciliata* (green leaves on top, purple

INDIANA

underneath) and **ginger** (a type new to me) *Asarum naniflorum* 'Eco Décor', sporting mini, dark-green leaves with silver veins. I also wavered over *Carex conica* 'Snowline' (a miniature variegated **sedge**) and **Indian cucumber root**, *Medeola virginica*, (foliage resembling a tall trillium with insignificant flowers but purple berries come fall). Addtionally, Munchkin offers interesting collections of **anemone**, more **ginger**, **shooting stars**, **barrenwort**, **ferns**, **phlox**, **Solomon's seal**, **primula**, **foam flower**, **trillium**, and **toad lily**.

SHIELDS GARDENS LTD.

❧ ❧

Shields Gardens is a small, family-run nursery located on 5 acres at the edge of a subdivision, approximately 25 miles north of downtown Indianapolis. Shields, a former research scientist (Ph.D. in biochemistry) and adjunct professor of chemistry at Indiana-Purdue University, started gardening for fun and relaxation. Today, his nursery offers adventurous plant collections of daylilies, geophytes, clivias, and rare and unusual bulbs.

WHAT YOU'LL FIND

Shields Gardens grows more than 500 named varieties of **daylilies**, including approximately 30 of its own introductions. Measures of his success in breeding dazzling daylily cultivars for northern climates include 'Hoosier August Flame' (very late blooming, burnt-orange), 'Westfield New Day' (pink petals edged in shimmering gold), 'Westfield Lavender Simplicity' (creamy lavender), and 'Baroque Brocade' (lush, ruffled pink). Imposing selections of major hybridizers' cultivars, such as 'Alien Encounter' and 'Bela Lugosi', are available at the nursery and can run upwards of $175. However, Shields Gardens also carries a striking array of highly ornamental, richly colored, competitive daylilies in the $10 to $15 range.

Shields Gardens also offers *Clivia* (pronounced Clive-ee-a), one of the more primitive genera of the Amaryllidaceae family. These are neither bulbs nor rhizomes but possess an abundance of thick, rope-like roots. *Clivia*, native to southern Africa and now at the height of their popularity, have predominantly orange, bright red, salmon, or cream colored flowers. However, according to Shields, **clivias** have

OWNERS: Jim Shields
TYPE: Small specialty nursery.
SPECIALTIES: Daylilies; geophytes; bulbs; clivia
HOURS: By appointment only.
CATALOG AVAILABLE: Online
MAIL-ORDER AVAILABLE: Yes
DISPLAY GARDENS: Yes
CLASSES: No

CONTACT
17808 Grassy Branch Road
P.O. Box 92
Westfield, IN 46074
PHONE: (317) 867-3344; (866) 449-3344 (Toll free, orders only)
FAX: (317) 506-4726
WEB ADDRESS: www.shieldsgardens.com
EMAIL: jim@shieldsgardens.com

DIRECTIONS
DIRECTIONS FROM INDIANAPOLIS: Take I-31 north to SR-32. Turn east (right) onto SR-32, drive for 1.5 miles to Grassy Branch Road. Turn north (left) onto Grassy Branch Road, nursery is 0.2 miles down, on west side of the road. **PLEASE NOTE:** Shields residence is what's visible from the road, so look for address only.

GPS: N 40° 02.75', W 86° 06.55'

INDIANA

a "future that includes a greater selection of variegation." He goes on to note that "already there are dozens of types of stripes and even horizontal bands on leaves." Shields says there is a strong trend towards miniaturized plants, picotee-edged blooms, white throats, deep reds, pure pinks, and pure whites. To that end, Shields, currently the Director and President of the North American Clivia Society, breeds, propagates, and grows an incredible variety of Clivia in a number of exciting color variations and leaf variegations—from seedlings to bloomed, mature plants. Additionally, for those adventurous souls with unlimited patience—or limited funds—the nursery offers fresh Clivia seeds. Most seeds offered are in the $1 to $2 (per seed) range; however, the rarer, more unusual colorations can easily run upwards of $20 per seed.

> "A lawn is nature under culture's boot."
> —MICHAEL POLLAN

Shields Gardens is also a source for rare, unusual, and hard to come by **geophytes**. (Geophytes are herbaceous plants with an underground storage organ and may be classed as bulbs, corms, tubers, rhizomes, or tuberous roots.) The geophytes offered by Shields Gardens are typically not for beginning gardeners, as most of what is offered are tender collector's bulbs and seedlings. The nursery categorizes them as summer growing and winter growing bulbs; however, a good number of what they sell are seedlings that have been grown for a number of years.

These are not of the tulip, daffodil, dahlia, or garden variety gladiolus **bulb** category; rather these are collectors' plants, most without common names, plants that take years under exacting growing conditions to grow from seed to floral fruition. For example, the nursery offers the following: six-year-old, near-bloom-size seedlings of *Crinum macowanii;* an uncommon (in cultivation at least) white *Galtonia regalis* from the Drakensberg of the Eastern Cape Province of South Africa; and *Cyrtanthus sanguineus* with vermillion red trumpets. It also offers a jumbo-sized bulb of *Hymenocallis eucharidifolia.* This plant, last found in the wild 150 years ago, is native to the rain forest in Mexico and is currently priced at $100 per bulb. The winter growing category includes more than 20 very rare varieties of *Lachenalia* as well as good selections of *Massonia.*

For those seriously interested in expanding their horizons by growing uncommon plants, a visit to Shields Gardens and some serious discussions with affable Jim Shields can be the first steps toward a new, healthy addiction.

SOULES GARDEN

ᕫᕯ ᕭᕬ

Soules Garden is a charming, popular, and picturesque country destination nursery located in an urban environment a tad southwest of Indianapolis proper. It specializes in superior varieties of daylilies, hosta, and perennials that flourish in the vagaries of the Midwest's hot, humid summers and unpredictable winters. The nursery has always been on the cutting edge of interesting plant varieties, and it stays in vogue by offering its customers stylish newcomers alongside numerous choices of trusty classics.

The nursery's previous owners, well-known hybridizers Marge and Clarence Soules, brought a wealth of experience to Soules Garden's daylily and hosta collections. Marge, a recipient of the Howard Hite achievement award for daylily hybridizing excellence, has well over 100 daylily introductions to her credit, including her best-known daylily creation 'Pastel Classic' (Award of Merit 93). Clarence's expertise ran to hostas, having 12 introductions himself. Together, they created a nursery with a national reputation as the place for hard-to-find, rare, and exotic varieties of daylilies and hosta.

The current owners, Cynthia and Chris Wilhoite, purchased the nursery in 2002 from the Soules and are passionate, knowledgeable plant people. In fact, these self-professed "plantaholics" are the third owners of the nursery started in 1957 by plantsman Earl Roberts. They were already long time customers of Soules Garden long before taking over the reins and responsibilities of guiding the nursery on its new path. At Soules, you'll always find a friendly staff, and interesting folk.

OWNERS: Cynthia and Chris Wilhoite
TYPE: Specialty nursery
SPECIALTIES: Hosta; daylily; perennials—sun and shade
HOURS: April (around the 10th) thru Oct.: Wed., Fri., Sat. 9:30 am to 5:00 pm, Thurs. 9:30 am to 6:00 pm. (Times may change somewhat at the beginning and end of season. If coming from a distance, call and check.)
CATALOG AVAILABLE: Online
MAIL-ORDER AVAILABLE: Yes
DISPLAY GARDENS: Yes
CLASSES: No

CONTACT
5809 Rahke Road
Indianapolis, IN 46217
PHONE: (317) 786-7839
WEB ADDRESS: www.soulesgarden.com
EMAIL: info@soulesgarden.com

DIRECTIONS
FROM INDIANAPOLIS: I-465 to US-31 south (Exit 2B) to Epler Avenue. Turn west (right) onto Epler Ave. for 1 miles to Rahke Road. Turn south (left) on Rahke Rd. and drive to the nursery which is 0.3 miles down on your left. Turn into the paved driveway for parking.

GPS: N 39° 40.87', W 86°10.05'

INDIANA

Soules Garden, nestled on 4½ beautiful acres of production beds and display gardens, sells a majority of its field-grown daylily and hosta plants by mail from the nursery's catalog. They can also be purchased, potted out in containers or freshly dug at the nursery. Hostas, shipped bare root, are priced in the catalog for single crown divisions, except for the miniatures, for which the nursery digs at least a double crown. Daylilies are typically sold as two-fan divisions.

The display gardens, comprised of a series of sweeping beds and borders surrounding the old house, greenhouses, and sheds, are lavishly landscaped and a wonderful destination in their own right. There are grassy paths for meandering, jazzy combinations of plants to look at, and benches on which to sit, rest, and reflect. The tranquil, shady sections of the display garden are a cool respite from the summer heat, a place to relax and be comfortable, where plants with dramatic foliage and interesting shapes and textures entice and cajole. Furthermore, there are numerous venerable specimens of notable hosta cultivars scattered throughout, giving customers the rare opportunity to view a mature clump, some as old as ten years. Visitors are always invited to leisurely stroll through these gardens, admire the plants, and plan their own ingenious combinations.

WHAT YOU'LL FIND

It is generally accepted that daylilies and hosta are two of the most popular perennials available today. Ranging in size from miniatures less than 6 inches tall to monsters more than a yard in height, hostas are the mainstay in most shade gardens. Soules Garden offers more than 800 **hostas** running the gamut from the tiny (mini's) to the very large. In the mini's category, you'll find 'Baby Bunting' (little blue-green fellow), 'Blue Ice' (slow growing but darling), and 'Cat's Eye' (charming trough miniature). Medium sized hosta I saw included 'Brenda's Beauty' (light yellow with green streaky margins), 'Garnet Prince' (green with bright cherry red petioles), 'Permanent Wave' (long narrow wavy leaves, appropriately named), 'Rainforest Sunrise' (gorgeous cupped bright gold leaves with a dark green border), and 'Sweet Home Chicago' (beautifully colorful). Some interesting giants included 'Big-John-os' (huge dark green upright beautifully colorful), 'Bold Ruffles' (large, blue-gray with ruffled edges) 'Butter Yellow' (very large, bright yellow), and 'Witches Brew-os' (heavily textured green foil for colored plants).

The nursery carries a goodly number of Soules hosta introductions such as 'Sunami' (medium large, glossy green) and 'Quilted Skies' (large, textured silvery blue). You'll also find 'Quilted Hearts' (another large hosta with dark, pebble grained surface), glossy 'Placemat', and 'Crinoline Petticoats' (large, extremely dense-leafed deep blue-green).

At this time, Soules Garden grows more than 1,000 varieties of **daylilies** (*Hemerocallis*), having added more than 100 new varieties just last year. Though Cynthia won't name a personal favorite, she is extremely partial to the late blooming, gorgeous, large sculptured, pale yellow Millikan-Soules daylily introduction 'Sarah Christine', and the unusual rebloomer 'Brian Millikan'. The nursery also offers the latest in the Soules introductions—such as the heavily ruffled, pink and light-rose blend with an ivory cream watermark, 'A Maiden's Innocence'. Other Soules introductions include 'Acclamation', 'Afternoon Blues', 'Alicia Rene', 'Angel Artistry' (Honorable Mention 1986), 'Apple Core', 'Banana Boat', 'Classic Accent', 'Glamour Star', 'Gypsy Skirt', and 'Lemon Showers', to name but a few.

> *"In joy or sadness, flowers are our constant friends."*
> —KOKUZO OKAKURA

Knowing my zany penchant and subsequent weakness for plants with uncommon names, my Indianapolis gardening friend happily steered me to the daylilies 'Nebuchadnezzar's Furnace' (a gorgeous double, fiery red with black eye), 'Eye on America' (a showy yellow with bold dark plum eye and edge), and 'Tippy Tippy Tin' (red with yellow edge).

Soules Open House, usually held the second weekend in June for hostas and the second weekend in July for daylilies (when plants are at their peak) is filled with lots of fun, some exciting door prizes, and wonderful specials.

INDIANA

TAYLOR'S ORNAMENTAL GRASSES

༺ ༻

Situated on the outskirts of the pleasant town of Churubusco, northwest of Fort Wayne, Taylor's Ornamental Grasses is a specialty nursery renowned for its fine collection of (what else?) ornamental grasses. Owner Dave Taylor is a self-confessed ornamental grass "nut" whose love affair with these plants got so out of hand that starting a nursery was the only sane solution. Taylor's Ornamental Grasses offers more than 45 varieties of cool and warm season grasses and, just recently, the addition of daylilies and hosta.

For a small nursery, Taylor's grows an impressive array of grasses. Prices are reasonable at $7.50 for a 1-gallon container and $12 for a 2-gallon container. Customers entering the sales area can pick up a grass list conveniently located at the entrance, which notes the plant's location number. All plants are ingeniously housed in a set of buried containers in the ground. This method serves many purposes: plants do not topple in the wind, they can be left in the ground to winter over, they are easy to maintain, and removal by customers is simple and efficient.

Visitors are invited to stroll the 10 acres of display gardens, a destination in their own right. Featured are hundreds of grasses, a springtime daffodil glen, streams, a pond, walking trails, an observation deck, an 8-foot water wheel, a birdhouse tree, a 24-foot covered bridge, a 12-foot by 24-foot gazebo, an 18-foot windmill, and a 28-foot footbridge over a dry pond. (Note: If you're coming strictly for the gardens with no intention of purchasing grasses, there is a $2.50 admission charge.)

OWNERS: Dave Taylor
TYPE: Small Specialty nursery
SPECIALTIES: Grasses; daylilies; hosta
HOURS: April thru Oct.: Tues.-Fri. 1:30 pm to dark, Sat. 8:30 am to dark, Sun. 1:30 pm to dark. Other times by appointment. (If coming from a distance, I recommend a quick call to assure that the nursery will be open.)
CATALOG AVAILABLE: Yes
MAIL-ORDER AVAILABLE: No
DISPLAY GARDENS: Yes
CLASSES: No

CONTACT
15528 McDuffee Road
Churubusco, IN 46723
PHONE: (260) 693-6284

DIRECTIONS
FROM FORT WAYNE: I-69 to US-30/US-33 to US-33 toward Elkhart. Drive on US-33 for 8 miles to McDuffee Rd. Turn north (right) on McDuffee Rd. (jogs at Hyndman Rd.). Nursery is 0.5 miles north past the jog, located on your right.

GPS: N 41° 13.66', W 85° 18.13'

Dave Taylor describes **cool-season grasses** as grasses that grow and thrive in cool, moist weather when the temperature hits about 65 degrees Fahrenheit.

These grasses flower from late winter to early summer and go dormant for the summer before sending out new foliage in the fall. Grasses in this category include **feather reed grass** (*Calamagrostis* 'Overdam' and 'Karl Foerster'), **blue lyme grass** (*Leymus* 'Blue Dune'), **fescue grass**

> *"The shooting of the snowdrop leaves is my particular signal that spring, even if far away, will come in time."*
> —H.L.V. FLETCHER
> ⸰◈◈

(*Festuca* 'Elijah Blue'), **blue oats grass** (*Helictotrichon* 'Saphirsprudel'), **ribbon grass** (*Phalaris* 'Feesey's Variety'), **moor grass** (*Sesleria*), and **sedge** (*Carex*).

Warm-season grasses, according to Taylor, sprout up in the spring, flourish through the heat of summer, flower in the summer and fall, and go dormant in the winter. Grasses included in this category are **bluestem** (*Andropogon*), **gramma grass** (*Bouteloua*), **sea oats** (*Chasmanthium*), **blood grass** (*Imperata*), **pampas grass** (*Erianthus ravennae*), **silver grass** (*Miscanthus*), **switch grass** (*Panicum virgatum*), **fountain grass** (*Pennisetum alopecuroides*), **Indian grass** (*Sorghastrum nutans*), and **cord grass** (*Spartina pectinata*).

The nursery has acquired a good selection of **ornamental grasses**. From the bold *Miscanthus giganteus* (topping out at 8 to 12 feet and prized for its huge column of robust foliage and tall silver plumes) to *Carex morrowii* 'Ice Dance' (a short but definitely not demure sedge), grasses are some of the most interesting plants in the fall and winter gardens. *Miscanthus*, always the showy diva in any landscape production, is well represented at Taylor's Ornamental Grasses. Some particularly noteworthy cultivars include 'Morning Light', 'Gracillimus', 'Sarabande', and 'Silberpfeil'. You'll also find 'Autumn Light', 'Bluttenwunder', and 'Graziella'. One of the more interesting and unusual grasses is Dave's **eyebrow grass** (*Bouteloua gracilis*), a fine-textured, warm-season, clumping grass with tiny "combs" attached to the stems, looking convincingly like eyebrows.

All structures in the display gardens have been hand-built by Dave, progressing from paper drawings to scale models to full-sized structures. The intricate, scale models are displayed in a small office structure close to the house.

INDIANA

WINTON'S IRIS HILL

୬ଌ ଌ୬

First time visitors strolling through the display gardens at Winton's Iris Hill nursery on a fine late spring or early summer day are often left breathless. What speeds the pulse and dilates the pupils are the dazzling fields of color. From the colorful splashes of potted daylilies, iris, and perennials lined up along the gravel driveway to the vivid strokes of richly hued flowers planted out over 5 acres, owner Doris Winton's display gardens are true works of art. Her love affair with the genus *Iris* began more than twenty years ago, and today's nursery is the by-product of a hobby gone wild.

Located a short distance south of Indianapolis, Winton's Iris Hill is a magical place where the sight of thousands of irises, daylilies, and blooming perennials in full, vivid flower pulls many a passersby off the road. Business and blossoms bloom from early spring to the end of summer.

Paths draw visitors in and around different beds surrounding the Winton's A-frame house and growing fields, and demonstration beds and borders highlight the use of shade-loving plants as well as plants for sunny or wet areas of the landscape. The beds, interspersed with strategically placed shrubs, draw visitors to explore the view around the next bend. Doris Winton encourages customers to relax and take in the spectacular sights. She provides fresh ice water and lemonade to cool off with while relaxing on strategically placed benches and chairs throughout the gardens.

The artist Monet was an enthusiastic grower of irises. Inspired by their beauty, he used them as subjects in a great many of his paintings. Visitors compare Winton's gardens to the

OWNERS: Doris & Charles Winton
TYPE: Specialty nursery
SPECIALTIES: Daylilies; iris; hosta; perennials
HOURS: April 24 thru August 28: Mon.-Sat. 8:00 am to sunset, Sun. 10:30 am to sunset.
CATALOG AVAILABLE: Price lists by specialty
MAIL-ORDER AVAILABLE: Yes
DISPLAY GARDENS: Yes
CLASSES: No

CONTACT
7131 E. 550S
Franklin, IN 46131-8012
PHONE & FAX: (812) 526-9237
EMAIL: dwinton@hsonline.net

DIRECTIONS
FROM I-65: Take I-65 to SR-252, Edinburgh Exit. Drive West on SR-252 to 800E Rd (first intersection), turn north (right) on 800E and drive approx. 3 miles to 550S. (trailer park at intersection). Turn west (left) on 550S and drive 0.75 miles. The nursery is on the left hand side, look for the sign.

GPS: N 39° 23.88', W 85° 58.05'

vibrant color harmonies of Monet's garden or the free-flowering romanticism of English borders.

What You'll Find

Doris Winton grows more than 900 varieties of bearded iris, 2,000 varieties of daylilies, 400 varieties of hosta, and hundreds of the latest perennials. One of the pleasures of my visit to Winton's Iris Hill was seeing *Iris* 'Dreamcake' (a tall, bearded, luminous salmon pink iris with coral beards). Also, I cannot think of any better additions to my sunny borders than **irises** 'Dark Treasure' (a deep, shimmering reddish purple iris with tangerine beards), 'Goodnight Kiss' (a hot pink self with shrimp beards), 'Ruby Morn' (an oxblood red wine self of intricate detail), or 'Ladies Only' (bright pink flower with red beards). Although Winton's carries hybrids costing $25 or

> *"The love of flowers is really the best teacher of how to grow and understand them."*
> —Max Schling

more, the majority of the iris cultivars are very reasonably priced, and some are downright inexpensive. Typically, peak bloom for iris is the last two weeks of May; however, as spring weather is unpredictable, it is best to call ahead.

Few flowers pack as much visual punch as the seductive **daylily**, which has such extravagant colors, forms, bloom varieties, and length of blooming times. Daylily beds are scattered all over the property at Winton's. There's a bed by the wood fence, in the pasture, down by the blacktop and driveway, and next to the garage. For visitors, the daylily price list orients guests to each plant's location in the growing beds, wherein each plant is well labeled for selection and display.

A bevy of beautiful daylilies with fanciful names call the nursery home: *Hemerocallis* 'Belle Isle Bandit' (creamy yellow with a purple eye), 'Fat Lady Sings' (a large reblooming magenta blend), and 'Mighty Highty Tighty' (a large red bloom with burgundy halo). You'll also find 'Small Town Girl' (short, pink with red eye) and Winton's own, 'Do You Know Doris?' (cantaloupe color, reblooming). Some enduring daylily standbys such as the Siloam series, the Jedi series, and the Indy series are modestly priced; others such as 'Early April', 'Ed Kirchoff', and 'Joy Ride' are outright bargains. Can you think of a nicer wedding gift for newlyweds than 'Wedding Band' and 'Wedding Vow' to mark the momentous occasion? Peak bloom for daylily plants is the first two weeks of July.

INDIANA

Winton's offers more than 400 varieties of **hosta**, both field grown and pre-potted. For inexperienced gardeners, few gardening challenges are more intimidating than trying to grow plants in the shade; for Winton, it's a blissful adventure. The A-frame house and trees on the hill were the fixed points around which Winton built her shady gardens.

Today, the hillside garden unfolds like a stage. The hosta herd has all the crinkled, blue, gold, creamy, streaked, smeared, cupped, puckered, waffled, corrugated, frosted, or edged varieties a gardener could ever wish for. Newer *Hosta* cultivars such as 'Stained Glass', 'Quilted Hearts', and 'Spilt Milk' hold their own against the reasonably priced stalwarts such as 'Invincible', ''Loyalist', 'Montana Aureomarginata', and 'Pearl Lake'. Every nursery has one or two gems hidden within its collections, and Winton's Iris Hill is no exception. Available nowhere else that I've seen was 'Groo Bloo' (with puckered blue leaves), 'Beauty Substance' (a natural sport of 'Sum and Substance' imported from England for display only—until the stock is built up), and 'Frances Williams Squaw Edge'. The plants are tough, too, having survived one full winter (or more) outdoors before being offered to its customers. Hosta plants are shipped early in the spring (May 1 through May 15) and then again during the month of August. Visitors to the nursery, however, have the sometimes hard choice of picking pre-potted hosta plants or freshly dug ones.

Winton's digs and pots hundreds of **perennials** every year; most are sold in gallon containers at very reasonable prices. Here, also, are many unique and lovely perennials such as **astilbe, brunnera, anemone, sweet woodruff, hardy geranium**, and **ajuga**. Whole areas of outdoor space are devoted to **phlox, peony, campanula, penstemon, monarda**, and **toad lily**.

Winton is nearly always on hand to provide assistance with plant selection or horticultural advice. Though the nursery is well equipped to pack the freshly dug plants, it is advisable to bring a few extra plastic bags as a security measure.

★ SIDE TRIPS ★

CONNER PRAIRIE, (317) 776-6000, 13400 Allisonville Rd., Fishers, IN 46038. Experience the past for yourself at one of the nation's finest living history museums. Conner Prairie is a large, open air living history museum made up of five distinct historic areas (all circa 1886), a modern museum, and more than 1,400 acres of natural beauty. Experience how life has changed over the years as costumed interpreters greet you and make you feel right at home.

INDIANA

Searching Michigan

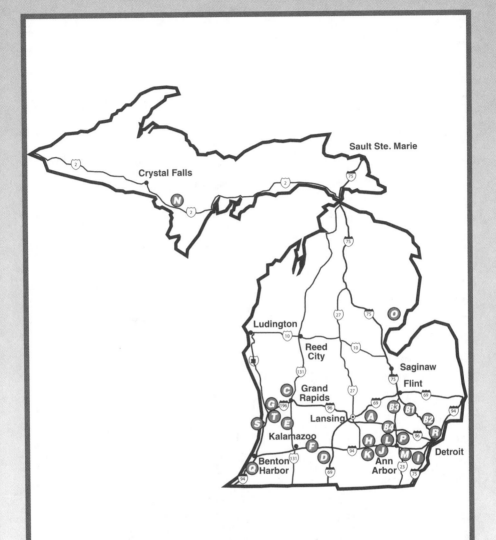

MICHIGAN

ARROWHEAD ALPINES

❧ ❧

Arrowhead Alpines is the plant connoisseur's treasure trove of elusive botanical gems! To visit the nursery is to experience the die-hard plantaholic's nirvana.

Founded by Bob and Brigitta Stewart, this family-owned nursery came about partly through a fascination with the rare, the beautiful, the unusual, and the bizarre, and partly out of a sense of desperation with the overflow of too many cuttings, too many seedlings, and too many plants. The Stewarts are exuberant, yet serious, "plant-people," who have their hands full running twenty-eight greenhouses, an outdoor retail area, wholesale operations, and attractive display gardens. These busy folks have little time for ambiguous questions. If you don't get the answers you need—seek out some of the friendly staff.

Open only in summer, Arrowhead is open from the time they are done shipping in mid- to late May through mid-fall, when the plants are put away. As a general rule in spring and fall, call ahead before venturing out to visit them.

Located on 68 acres of virgin woodland near the town of Fowlerville in southeastern Michigan, Arrowhead Alpines specializes in rare and specialty plants. They have a mind-boggling 10,000 cultivars and

OWNERS: Bob and Brigitta Stewart
TYPE: Large retail and wholesale nursery
SPECIALTIES: Perennials; woodland wildflowers; rare alpines; ferns; dwarf conifers; shrubs; vines; bulbs; lilies
HOURS: Summer hours only (call ahead to be sure they are open for retail), Wed.-Sat. 11:00 am to 7:00 pm, Sun. 11:00 am to 5:00 pm.
CATALOG AVAILABLE: Printed and online (botanical names only)
MAIL-ORDER AVAILABLE: Yes
DISPLAY GARDENS: Yes
CLASSES: No

CONTACT
P.O. Box 857
1310 N. Gregory Road
Fowlerville, MI 48836
PHONE: (517) 223-3581
FAX: (517) 223-8750
WEB ADDRESS:
www.arrowheadalpines.com

DIRECTIONS
FROM I-96: Exit I-96 at Fowlerville (Exit 129). Proceed south (toward the Mobil Gas Station). Drive approx. 100 yards to Van Buren Road. Turn west (right) on Van Buren and go 1 mile to Gregory Road (first intersection). Turn south (left) on Gregory. Drive 1.75 miles to 1310 Gregory (at the third intersection, Mason Road, jog left to pick up Gregory Road, 50 or so feet down). Turn east (left) onto the long dirt driveway and proceed with caution to the nursery (delivery trucks drive up and down this one lane driveway at rip-roaring speed).

GPS: N 42° 36.01', W 84° 05.42'

species of woody and herbaceous plants. The collection is continually enhanced and fine-tuned by additions from remarkable collectors and growers around the world. The fact that a major portion of these plants are propagated, either from seed or vegetatively, and grown out at the nursery is a remarkable feat in itself.

The nursery's eclectic display gardens are scattered throughout the premises and are open to all. But as the Stewart's home and private gardens are also located on the premises, it is a wise move to respect the privacy of the gardens surrounding the house.

This is a dynamic nursery where large numbers of orders are filled every week. Customers should keep their minds open to the endless possibilities but accept the reality that there are no assurances that particular plants will be in stock. Although acquiring plants by mail-order is surely easier, on-site shoppers experience the thrill of the hunt and the warm glow of satisfaction associated with a choice well made.

WHAT YOU'LL FIND

Arranged by botanical names, plants are grouped by type, and a species can exist in more than one category. Before you visit this nursery, I suggest you do your homework and come prepared to deal with the seemingly endless choice of plant material. As the diversity of the plants available can be a bit overwhelming, bringing a reference book or two is highly recommended. (Note: not every plant available at Arrowhead is hardy in the Midwest; nevertheless, they are worthy treasures for microclimate locations, container plantings, greenhouses, or scattered about the garden and treated as annuals.) Though support in locating plants is sometimes minimal, the busy staff at this destination nursery is always friendly, cheerful, and approachable.

As its name implies, the backbone of Arrowhead Alpines is its superb collection of alpines and rock garden plants. Specialty alpines, such as *Dionysias*, *Saxifrage*, and *Androsaces*, belong to a niche market in which only a few nurseries specialize. Arrowhead stocks a vastly eclectic selection, many of them native to remote mountain regions of the world, such as Turkey, India, Bulgaria, China, Spain, and Tibet. Diminutive **dionysias**, for instance, a minute rosette of leaves no more than $1/2$ inch across, are regarded even by alpine enthusiasts as a specialty plant. One of the unusual alpine collections at Arrowhead is **draba**, an Arctic alpine perennial comprised of either a tight, hard dome of bristly rosettes or of tufted

> *"The tiniest garden is often the loveliest."*
> —VITA SACKVILLE-WEST
> ❧ ❧

fuzz-balls, smothered with blossoms on the slenderest of thread-like stalks. These minis (2 to 4 inches high) are handsome plants in rock gardens, troughs, or shallow pots. More favorites, best grown in an alpine house for optimum results, are the various cultivars of *Primula allionii*.

I am somewhat at a loss to summarize these incredible and unusual holdings. Some rarities: the coolest new **epimediums** available today, *Epimedium lishihchenii* (sporting blossoms like alien, yellow spiders tip-toeing after prey); *Gypsophila aretioides*, (a **babies breath** that almost never flowers); *Paeonia mlokosewitschii*, the coveted "Molly the Witch", (a shade-loving **peony** with big, translucent yellow blossoms); the yellow pasque flower *Pulsatilla lutea*; *Asarum caudatum* forma *alba*, (a "white" flowered form of our native **ginger** with curious, creamy-green flowers, each with three spidery tails); and one of the mountain **mints**, *Pycnanthemum muticum*,(soft, hairy leaves topped by odd, velvety starfish flowers that look like little, dainty, silvery poinsettias).

In this era of proliferating store garden centers and ho-hum nurseries, it's rare to see a cultivar list so tantalizing and exceptionally deep. In no time at all, I found splashy and charming, but seldom seen, varieties such as *Buddleja (Buddleia) hemsleyana*, a Japanese species, with showy clusters of two-tone, light and dark purple flowers), *Caryopteris clandonensis* 'Snow Fairy' (an unusually bold variegated blue mist shrub), *Kalopanax pictus* (a hardy, tropical-looking shade tree with huge, maple-like leaves), and *Schizophragma hydrangioides* 'Iwa-Garami' (Japanese climbing **hydrangea**). I also found *Sollya heterophylla* (an Australian climber, excellent container vine with dainty blue, pink, or white bell-shaped flowers from spring through fall); the unique and seldom seen *Dianella tasmanica* (tender Tasmanian beauty loaded with hundreds of one-inch, sky blue flowers on graceful yard-high stems); and *Aster* 'Tiny Tot' (one of the smallest asters, brandishing bright purple blossoms, late summer and fall).

I confess to an affinity for plants with unusual names, buying them on the spot and only later fretting about their proper siting. So it was inevitable that the irresistible hair **sedge**, *Carex comans* 'Nuke-Em Till They Glow—Then Shoot-em in the Dark' would win me over. It has stiff, upright leaves, "glowing" in the oddest shade of green, which, according to Bob, looked "radioactive."

MICHIGAN

Woodland wildflowers, according to the current catalog, are either nursery propagated or wild, collected under state or federal permit from land scheduled to be clear-cut or otherwise destroyed. The choices at Arrowhead are beautiful and inventive: **wake robin**, (*Trillium*); **bellwort** (*Uvularia*); an American **lily of the valley** (*Convallaria montana*); and pink and yellow **lady's slippers** (*Cypripedium*). There is an assortment of **orchids:**

fringed (*Platanthera*), cranefly (*Tipularia*), showy (*Orchis spectabilis*), and Adam and Eve (*Aplectrum hyemale*); and the crème de la crème of American woodland plants, **oconee bells** (*Shortia galacifolia*), to name but a few.

Arrowhead Alpines carries many desirable fern species—wild things that grow in our gardens yet are never truly domesticated. One of the most curious is the **walking fern**, *Camptosorus rhizophyttus*. Though it can reproduce by spores, this fern forms tiny new plants at the ends of the long fronds wherever it touches the ground, thus gradually "walking" or "strolling" throughout the garden.

Arrowhead Alpines is strong on conifers, broadleaf evergreens, and deciduous shrubs. Grafted conifers (1- to 6-year-old grafts), mostly in 2-gallon or larger pots, are priced to reflect rarity, not size, so it's not surprising that some of the least expensive specimens can be some of the largest. And while Arrowhead never set out to be a woody plant nursery, Bob and Brigitta, being hopeless collectors, have over the years amassed quite an astounding collection. The diversity of their unusual shrub collections is enchanting: **azalea, barberry, buddleia, cotoneaster, hydrangea, holly** (*Ilex*), **mockorange** (*Philadelphus*), **potentilla, rhododendron, willow** (*Salix*), **elderberry** (*Sambucus*), **viburnum**, and **weigela** are robustly represented here. The nursery offers one of the largest collections of **daphne** that I have ever seen. Yet, fragrant daphne is a high maintenance little stinker whose demanding relationships with gardeners are generally doomed from the very start. For daphne "phreaks," the catalog offers sage advice for achieving success. (If you wondering, "phreaks" is a catalog term!)

MICHIGAN

BORDINE'S NURSERY, LTD

❧ ❧

Bordine's Nursery is a family-owned, second generation business that caters to upscale gardeners in Detroit's suburbia. Started as a roadside stand in 1939, today it is one of the largest family-owned production and retail garden centers in Michigan. According to the brochure, Marian and Darrell Bordine "had a vision to build the area's best nursery by growing their own plants." Today Bordine's Nursery follows the standards set by its founders by growing major portions of their own annuals, perennials, trees, shrubs, and roses.

Bordine's four locations carry more than 2,000 varieties of container-grown perennials, as well as a vast selection of hanging baskets, grasses, vines, trees, shrubs, annuals, and other ornamental garden plants. All Bordine's locations are easily reached and perpetually crowded, especially so on weekends. The weeks leading up to Mother's Day are an exciting form of bedlam with hanging baskets (too many to count), in all forms of plant and color combinations, being whisked out the door in one continuous, floriferous stream.

OWNERS: Corey Bordine, President
TYPE: Large garden center
SPECIALTIES: Perennials—sun and shade; herbs; annuals; shrubs; trees; grasses; vines; aquatics; garden art; plant containers; houseplants
HOURS: Rochester & Clarkston: Mon.-Sat. 9:00 am to 5:00 pm, Sun. 11:00 am to 5:00 am. Grand Blanc & Brighton: closed Nov. thru April. Hours are the same.
CATALOG AVAILABLE: Printed and online
MAIL ORDER AVAILABLE: No
DISPLAY GARDENS: No
CLASSES: Yes

CONTACT
9100 Torrey Road
Grand Blanc, MI 48439
PHONE: (810) 655-5588
WEB ADDRESS: www.bordine.com

DIRECTIONS
GRAND BLANC: FROM THE SOUTH: Take I-75 north to the M-54/Dort Hwy exit (Exit 109). Merge onto Dort Hwy, turn left onto E. Grand Blanc Road. Take E. Grand Blanc Road to Torrey Road (just as you cross over US-23), turn left. Nursery is 1.5 miles down on right.

GPS: N 42° 44.66, W 83° 27.69'

A landmark garden center, this full service nursery provides just about any type of plant material or ancillary supplies a gardener might need, from soil and fertilizer amendments to an assortment of indoor plants, decorative containers, statuary, and aquatics. Bordine's is a resource for containers, garden furniture, outdoor structures, garden supplies and accoutrements, and all manner of seasonal and holiday items, including Christmas trees and decorations.

On the whole, I found Bordine's stock unusually well-grown, well-stocked, and well-kept for an organization of this magnitude. All plants are well labeled with appropriate cultural information that is easy to read and understand. The friendly, smiling staff, surprisingly easy to find, is adept at assisting novices as well as expert gardeners in selecting the right plant for the right site or container.

WHAT YOU'LL FIND

Bordine's is known for its superior tree and shrub cultivars, particularly flowering **crabapples, dogwood, hydrangea**, and **magnolia**. On a recent visit, there were offerings of **parrotia, yellowwood, Kentucky coffee tree, katsura, ginkgo, stewartia**, and **golden chain trees**, along with good selections of **rose-of-Sharon, birch, elm, maple, oak**, and **mountain ash**. It is unusual, to say the least, to find a **wisteria tree**, cascading **peashrub** tree (*Caragana*), or a **fringe tree** (*Chionanthus*) at a garden center; typically, these can only be found at specialized nurseries. The nursery also carries an extensive line of evergreens, including **arborvitae, fir, hemlock, juniper, pine, spruce**, and **yew**. Sculptural evergreens can be had in weeping, top grafted, pompon, poodle, and spiral forms.

In recent years, Bordine's has developed a good line of **roses**: climbing, English, floribunda, carpet, grandiflora, tea, Meidiland, miniature, National Parks series, and shrub. Some interesting new roses that caught my eye were 'Red Eden' (a deep burgundy climber); 'Chihuly' (apricot yellow, orange, and red floribunda); 'Candelabra' (bright coral orange grandi- flora), and 'Blushing Knockout'™ (light pink sister to the sensational 'Knockout'™).

Its healthy annual stock, extensive selection, and reasonable prices have made this a favorite resource for area gardeners. Bordine's can be counted on to stock something special and unusual alongside the mainstays of ornamental gardening. Some genial old favorites noted on my last visit were: **abutilon, ageratum, anagallis, angelonia, cobbity daisy, bidens, fuschia, heliotrope, nemesia, lobelia, impatiens, petunia**, and **verbena.** New creations, the best examples of sought-after varieties, included: *Arctotis*, (the **renaissance daisy), petunias** in bells galore from Million Bells™ to Superbells™ and **diascias (***Diascias***)** in a diversity of intense colors.

The nursery is a reliable source of annual **geraniums**. They are arranged by group—sprawling stellars with their star-shaped leaves and flowers, the wonderfully fragrant scented-leaf geraniums, the tightly clustered blossoms of the rosebud-flowered geraniums, the curiously beautiful species pelargoniums, and the startling

MICHIGAN

> *"Flowers and fruits are always fit presents—flowers, because they are a proud assertion that a ray of beauty outvalues all the utilities of the world."*
> —RALPH WALDO EMERSON

variety of gold, silver, and bronze fancy-leaf selections.

Bordine's carefully orchestrates immense end groupings showcasing plants at their peak. These groupings can change dramatically or evolve a bit with a fresh infusion of a totally new or somewhat bolder color.

Transporting that combination into one's garden, a customer can have a delicious blend of plants and colors by the pond, artistically grounding the edge of a bed, or a classic punch incorporated into the landscape.

Some groupings showcase plants by cultural requirements. For example, dry shade: **lady's mantle** (*Alchemilla mollis*), **goatsbeard** (*Aruncus* spp.), **astilbe** (*Astilbe* spp. and hybrids), **bergenia (***Bergenia* spp. and hybrids), **bugloss** (*Brunnera macrophylla*), **bellflower** (*Campanula* 'Birch Hybrid'), **sweet woodruff** (*Galium odoratum*), and **hardy geranium** (*Geranium macrorrhizum*).

On random visits to Bordine's, I found an excellent selection, including **coral bells**, *Heuchera* 'Lime Rickey', *H.* 'Petite Marbled Burgundy', and *H.* 'Amber Waves'. There was light blue **bellflower,** *Campanula* 'Samantha'; **blue-eyed grass**, *Sisyrinchium* 'Lucerne'; the largest **coneflower**, *Echinacea* 'Ruby Giant'; the **gaillardia** currently on everyone's radar, *Gaillardia* 'Fanfare'; and dark purple *Sedum* 'Purple Emperor'. There were ornamental grasses, more than 75 varieties of daylilies, healthy, well-grown herbs, winsome sedum, heat- and sun-loving coleus, and almost 100 varieties of hosta. The perennials are supplemented with green and tropical houseplants, engaging annuals and vegetable flats in the spring and seasonal plants spring and fall.

SATELLITE LOCATIONS

CONTACT

Clarkston, MI:
8600 Dixie Highway 48307
PHONE: (248) 625-9100
Rochester Hills, MI:
1835 S. Rochester Road 48307
PHONE: (248) 651-9009)
Brighton, MI:
6347 Grand River Avenue 48114
PHONE: (810) 655-5588

DIRECTIONS

If additional instructions are needed, please call individual locations: **CLARKSTON: FROM I-75:** Take I-75 to Exit 93 north, nursery on right hand side. **ROCHESTER HILLS: FROM I-75:** Take I-75 to Rochester Road, exit north. Drive north on Rochester for approx. 6 miles, nursery on right side, just north of Hamlin Road. **BRIGHTON: FROM US-23N:** Take US-23N to I-96 exit (Exit 60B) towards Brighton/Lansing. Merge onto I-96 west, drive to the Grand River Avenue exit (Exit 145). Turn right onto Grand River Avenue and drive about 3 miles. Nursery will be on your right.

MICHIGAN

Carol Kerr Perennials

❧ ❧

Carol Kerr Perennials is a picturesque and charming small country destination nursery that grows, amongst other things, more than 800 named varieties of daylilies. An accomplished Advanced Master Gardener, owner Carol Kerr is a passionate, knowledgeable plantswoman—a self-professed plant collector—who founded Carol Kerr Perennials when her ever-expanding tribe of plants outgrew their intended boundaries. "Plants thrive and multiply in ever increasing numbers," says Kerr with a laugh, "and there are only so many plants you can share with friends before they've had enough." Unwilling to throw the excess on the compost pile, she took her surplus plants to a celebrated farmer's market, where much to her amazement and delight, she found novice gardeners in search of interesting and unusual plants as well as sage collectors willing to commiserate about their mutual passions.

OWNER: Carol Kerr
TYPE: Specialty nursery
SPECIALTIES: Daylilies
HOURS: Vary, call ahead.
CATALOG AVAILABLE: Printed list of daylilies only
MAIL-ORDER AVAILABLE: Yes
DISPLAY GARDENS: Yes
CLASSES: No

CONTACT

13015 Crinnion
Cedar Springs, MI 49319
PHONE: (616) 696-9366
WEB ADDRESS: No
EMAIL: ckerr@netpenny.net

DIRECTIONS

FROM THE GRAND RAPIDS AREA: Take US-131 north to M-57 (Exit 101) east toward Greenville/Sparta. Proceed east on M-57 for 1.0 mile to Northland Drive NE. Turn north (left) on Northland Drive driving 0.8 miles to 15-Mile Road. Drive on 15-Mile Road for 4.0 miles where 15-Mile Road becomes Pine Lake Avenue. Continue on Pine Lake Avenue for 0.5 miles to Benham, turn right onto Benham, 1.4 miles down turn left onto Crinnion Avenue NE. (portions of Crinnion are unpaved) driving 0.3 miles to 13015, take the long driveway to house. (Nursery located on property.)

GPS: N 43° 12.07', W 85° 26.46'

Carol Kerr's daylily selections reflect the owner's interest, continually mixing old classics with exciting and new introductions. The 1-acre propagation field is a joyous array filled with a bevy of beautiful treasures. Kerr sells carefully selected, beautifully grown, field-hardy daylilies, shipped bare root, with two-or greater fan plants. This is a one-person nursery, and on-site customers should not rely on having their plants dug on the spot; instead, plan on returning for them in a day or two.

Visitors to Carol Kerr Perennials can see first-hand the results of Kerr's enthusiastic perseverance as a self professed "collector." Lavishly planted beds surrounding the residence are very much a reflection of the owner. "There's

MICHIGAN

> *"Flowers are nature's jewels,*
> *with whose wealth she decks*
> *her summer beauty."*
> —GEORGE CROLY

something about woodland gardening that I simply adore," she said as we walked past the shade loving ephemerals in full bloom. The breadth of her knowledge astounded me. She collects just about every intriguing, novel, or just plain beautiful plant that crosses her path. Some beds and borders are the result of good planning, others pure happenstance—her rock garden came into being purely by accident when she found herself stepping on low-growing plants. Her display gardens are a work in progress, as a gardener's garden is never really finished. The nursery also maintains an official American Hemerocallis Society (AHS) display garden. All plants are clearly labeled, with unobtrusive but easy-to-read signage.

WHAT YOU'LL FIND

Carol Kerr Perennials digs and pots hundreds of perennials every year. Many are divisions of her extensive plant collections (2,000 perennial varieties, 200 **hosta** cultivars), others were started from seeds obtained from varying sources, and all are sold at very reasonable prices. Knowledgeable gardeners sign up on her "wishlist," to be notified when certain plants become available.

Over the years, Kerr has plunged into a good number of horticultural romances, but none has been as rewarding as her love affair with the genus *Hemerocallis*. Like many obsessions, Kerr's infatuation with **daylilies** began innocently enough. A friend moved and, not wanting to leave the divided daylilies behind, gave them to Kerr. Shortly after, another friend moved, leaving more boxed-up clumps for Kerr, igniting a passion that still shines. Divisions of those original clumps still thrive in her garden. In honor of her two wonderful friends, in 1998 Kerr registered a "hose-in-hose" double grape daylily with a deep grape (almost black) eye—a sugary confection for the eyes—named 'For Two Friends'.

One of Kerr's early passions was the species *Iris*. If you've already been successful with bearded, Siberian, Japanese, or Louisiana **iris**, it may be time to look into some of the more unusual iris offered here. *Iris cristata* (dwarf crested iris), *Iris verna* (vernal iris), and *Iris lacustris* (lake iris) are all rare, typically hard-to-find, dwarf, woodland plants. Major universities have come to Kerr seeking the elusive white lake iris, which seems to thrive in her gardens.

MICHIGAN

Visitors to the nursery can see for themselves the results of Kerr's philosophy of nourishing the soil. Once a year, she and a friend make a 10-hour round trip drive to Illinois, trailer in tow, to pick up bags of shredded oak leaves destined for the landfill, which she spreads over her borders and propagation beds. The nursery's soil has that rich, friable feel most of us can only wish for.

Carol Kerr Perennials is a bit out of the way, but Kerr is always on hand to provide some horticultural tips, warmly welcome visitors to the AHS display gardens, show her luxuriant borders and propagation beds, and encourage fellow plant lovers to feel at home.

MICHIGAN

CLIVIA CREATIONS

❧ ❧

Owner Michael Morri has been growing and enjoying clivias for close to ten years and has just completed his first "official" year (2003) in the nursery business. Currently he stocks more than 200 new and unique clivia cultivars from growers around the world. A majority of these plants are in short supply and are aimed at the loyal plant collector; however, for those like myself who only recently started romancing these beautiful plants, Michael offers quite a vast selection at reasonable prices.

The majority of sales of clivia at Clivia Creations are mail-order; however, it is possible to pick out a blooming plant on site by making a weekend appointment with Mike Morri. (Keep in mind, though, these tender plants bloom primarily from February through April, and Union City can experience tough winter conditions.) Shipping of clivia plants begins around the first of April, weather permitting.

WHAT YOU'LL FIND

Initially accessible only to the wealthy, today stunningly beautiful **clivia** cultivars, though not inexpensive, are definitely affordable. (Initially, yellow forms were highly prized—and priced. In early 1994, a limited number of yellow flowered clivias could be purchased for the extravagant price of $950.00 each. Today, blooming size plants can be had for $100 or less. Part of the fascination with *Clivia* is breeding, both among the four species (*C. nobilis*, *C. gardenii*, *C. caulescens*, and *C. miniata*) and

OWNER: Michael Morri
TYPE: Small specialty nursery
SPECIALTIES: Clivias; oriental tree peonies; (polytepal) daylilies
HOURS: Weekends only, June thru July: Sat.-Sun. 9:00 am to 5:00 pm; also by appointment.
CATALOG AVAILABLE: Online, and printed flyer
MAIL-ORDER AVAILABLE: Yes
DISPLAY GARDENS: No
CLASSES: No

CONTACT
625 Tuttle Road
P.O. Box 192
Union city, MI 49094
PHONE AND FAX: (517) 741-4769
WEB ADDRESS: www.CliviaCreations.com
EMAIL: info@cliviacreations.com

DIRECTIONS
FROM I-94 AND M-66: Take M-66 south for 14.5 miles to M-60 (Mendon Road). Turn east (left) on Mendon for 2.0 miles to Blossom Road. Turn right onto Blossom Road, proceed for 0.5 miles where Tuttle comes in. Proceed straight ahead into Tuttle and drive for 0.6 miles to nursery. **FROM I-69:** Exit I-69 at Exit 25 (M-60) westbound. Take M-60 for 9.3 miles to Arbogast Road. Turn left onto Arbogast Road and immediately (0.2 miles down) turn right onto Tuttle Road. Proceed 1.4 miles to nursery.

GPS: N 42° 03.50', W 85° 09.52'

MICHIGAN

between forms and colors within the species. Breeders select for specific traits in each generation, producing striking qualities.

Clivia Creations offers a dazzling assortment of the rare, the unusual, the curious, and the unexpected. Noteworthy cultivars abound, from seedlings in quart containers to blooming size plants in 1- and 2-gallon pots. Clivia Creations offers different forms of variegation: 'Light of Buddha' (wide, horizontal-banded leaf variegation, insignificant flowers, regarded as living sculptures); and Akebono (Japanese wide leaf with horizontal bands of cream-yellow markings). They offer diverse colors including:

> *"The habit and flower of amaryllis demand everyone in their path stop and take notice."*
> —DIANNE BENSON

'Aussie Sunset × self' (red-orange and white bicolored blooms); 'Near-White' (very pale cream); 'Rydal Pink' (pinkish-yellow); 'Alice' (stop-light-red); 'Ngome Gardenii' (cream-yellow with green); and 'Pink Perfection' (palest pastel pink). Plus, there are various shapes including: 'Yellow Showers' (long, semi-pendulous blooms); 'Pastel' *Cyrtanthiflora* (pendulous blooms); 'Tessa' (flaring, tulip-shaped); 'Yellow Spider' (thin florets); 'Anna' (multipetal, overlapping blooms); and finally, a few differences in leaf textures such as Monk (dark green leaves with protruding veins).

On 3 acres of production fields surrounding the Clivia Creations greenhouses and Morri residence, Mike is growing 50 varieties of **Oriental tree peonies**, primarily polytepals (multipetal). The Chinese have always prized the lush "thousand-petal" varieties of tree peonies, an aesthetic quality probably better known to Westerners through Chinese art and pottery than through garden plants. Clivia Creations thus far has not succumbed to our American habit of attempting to decipher Chinese names (for which I am grateful). Bursting with color, the sheer exuberance of these plants makes it hard to choose a favorite, for they are all spectacular. However, two with "knock your socks off" potential (the colors alone are infectious) were stylish 'Heihuakui' (semidouble maroon-black flowers) and 'Huaerqiao' (multicolored double in magenta and pink). Hardy, well grown, woody tree peonies are available in sizes ranging from 1- to 6-year-old plants with at least 2 to 3 branches each.

Horticulturally hungry gardeners are welcome to view (and purchase) tree peonies from the vast production fields during Clivia Creations' Open House. Held every weekend during the month of June, with Mother Nature's help, this event ideally coincides with the peak bloom period of these magnificent plants.

MICHIGAN

ENGLERTH GARDENS

❧ ❧

E nglerth Gardens is a picturesque farm growing hosta and daylilies, plus a few companion shade plants, on 75 acres of fertile farmland in southwest Michigan. After seventy years of providing exceptional plants to the wholesale market and retail trade, the nursery business, which was founded in 1931 by Mary Herrema's parents, is being scaled back to a more manageable size. Today, the husband and wife team sell their plants directly to the public from the charming nursery surrounding their 100-year-old farmhouse. Ken works the fields; Mary takes care of the paperwork.

Daylilies and hostas can be ordered by mail from Englerth's price list or purchased, freshly dug, at the nursery. Keep in mind, however, that at present this is a two-person operation, and things can sometimes back up during prime planting season. Though every attempt is made by the nursery to fresh dig your plants while you wait; visitors should maintain an adventurous spirit, recognize the fact that this may not be feasible and, instead, plan on returning for them in a day or two. Plants can be shipped too, if you can't make a second trip right away. If you are coming from a distance, I suggest you arrive early and make arrangements to pick up your plants later in the day.

WHAT YOU'LL FIND

Englerth Gardens offers more than 750 varieties of **hosta** cultivars, including big-name stalwarts and Englerth Gardens introductions. The late Larry Englerth, Ken's father-in-law and one of the founding fathers of the American Hosta Society, had some amazing introductions such as 'Mary

OWNERS: Mary and Ken Herrema
TYPE: Specialty nursery
SPECIALTIES: Hosta; daylilies
HOURS: May thru Sept. (call for exact dates): Thurs.-Fri. 9:00 am to 5:00 pm, Sat. 9:00 am to 2:00 pm.
CATALOG AVAILABLE: Printed price list
MAIL-ORDER AVAILABLE: Yes
DISPLAY GARDENS: Yes
CLASSES: No

CONTACT
2461 22nd Street. Route 2
Hopkins, MI 49328-9639
PHONE: (269) 793-7196

DIRECTIONS
FROM US-131: Take US-131 to MI-222/116th Avenue (Exit 55) towards Martin (eastbound). Take MI-222/116th Avenue for 4 miles to 20th Street. Turn north (right) onto 20th Street and drive for 4 miles to 124th Avenue. Turn west (left) onto 124th Avenue (portions are unpaved) and drive 1.0 miles to 22nd Street. Turn north (right) onto 22nd Street, nursery is 0.3 miles down the road.

GPS: N 42° 35.95', W 85° 45.66'

Marie Ann' (1982), which has intrigued collectors for many years because of the way its twisted, wavy foliage seems to be constantly changing color; 'Wrinkles and Crinkles' (1985) is heavily corrugated but also unruly and cupped. 'Ryan's Big One' (1982) has impressive heavily corrugated, blue-green foliage; Blue Horizon' (1985), has outstanding deep blue-green leaves; and 'Little Blue' (1976), is a hosta with shiny, dark green leaves.

Ken has adopted the charming practice, typically common to **daylily** hybridizers, of naming his introductions after his native landscape—in this case, Allegon County. 'Allegon Fog', a green leaf hosta with a wide center of creamy white dotted liberally with green flecks, turned out to be a sur-prise hit at the 1999 American Hosta Society (AHS) convention.

At this time, Englerth Gardens grows more than 500 named cultivars of daylilies (*Hemerocallis*), including a good number of exciting new hybrids. Winifred Englerth, Mary Harrema's mother, was well known for introducing daylilies with a high bud count. She had the delightful habit of using the same letter of the alphabet when naming her plants. Many of her exemplary creations, such as 'Mini Minx', 'Skippy Skeezix', and 'Pinky Pinkerton' can still be found in gardens of the area. The nursery also grows a smattering of companion plants, which are planted up early in the spring and "when they are gone, they're gone."

Englerth's display gardens are lavishly landscaped, comprised of a series of sweeping beds and borders surrounding the farmhouse. The beauty continues underneath the butternut tree, next to the chicken coop turned

MICHIGAN

> *"That which we call a rose
> by any other name would
> smell as sweet."*
> —FROM *Romeo and Juliet*

packing shed, near the hoop houses and production fields, and under the pear trees out back.

The tranquil gardens promote shade as a place to relax and be comfortable, demonstrating that plants with dramatic foliage and interesting shapes and textures can be used to advantage. Among all the jazzy combinations of plants, there is at least one mature specimen of every hosta and daylily being sold at the nursery today. Visitors are invited to stroll these gardens leisurely, admire the plants, and plan their own intriguing compositions.

MICHIGAN

ENSATA GARDENS

❦

Located in the country on a quiet out-of-the-way road, Ensata Gardens is an in-ground nursery that houses some true horticultural treasures including Japanese, Siberian, and species iris. Started in 1985 by Bob Bauer and John Coble, today Ensata boasts that they have "the largest collection of Japanese iris varieties outside of Japan." Additionally, John notes that they also have a historical group of Japanese varieties from the 1800s and early 1900s.

Ensata Gardens is strictly mail-order; however, all are invited to visit the gardens (not to be missed at peak bloom) for a wonderful opportunity to stroll the growing beds, examine the extensive and well-labeled holdings, and with luck, meet the amazing hybridizing duo. No reservations required! Really. However, if you are considering some of their wonderful plants, such as their richly colored, textural irises for your garden, you must access their incredible website or order a copy of the catalog.

OWNERS: Bob Bauer and John Coble
TYPE: Mail-order only
SPECIALTIES: Iris—Siberian, Japanese, species; hostas; daylilies
HOURS: Call ahead.
CATALOG AVAILABLE: Printed and online
MAIL-ORDER AVAILABLE: Yes
DISPLAY GARDENS: Yes
CLASSES: No

CONTACT
9823 East Michigan Avenue
Galesburg, MI 49053
PHONE AND FAX: (269) 665-7500
WEB ADDRESS: www.ensata.com

DIRECTIONS
FROM I-94: I-94 (East of Kalamazoo) to 35th Street (Exit 85). Proceed north on 35th Street for a mile to Michigan Avenue (SR-96). Turn west (left) on Michigan (SR-96). The nursery is 0.5 miles down.

GPS: N 42° 17.30', W 85° 26.19'

WHAT YOU'LL FIND

Strolling the breathtaking display gardens with my friend, a die-hard Siberian devotee, we were dizzy like kids in a candy store. At the peak of bloom, the 450 varieties of Japanese and 200 of Siberian **iris** totaling more than 5,000 plants, is pure ambrosia for the eyes.

Discussions with iris fanciers usually lead to discussions of Ensata's hybridizing prowess. The Bauer and Coble introductions of both Siberian and Japanese iris will inspire an instant need to expand your horticultural family.

MICHIGAN

> *"All my heart became a tear.*
> *All my soul became a tower,*
> *Never loved I anything*
> *As I loved that tall blue flower!"*
>
> —EDNA ST. VINCENT MILLAY

Over the past ten years, Bauer and Coble have released hybrids that venture into exciting new colors and fascinating, multihued blends. The choices left me salivating: Siberian 'Kabluey', a multipetalled blue so dazzling that it could shame a delphinium, the tetraploid 'Kaboom', with unbelievably velvety, navy-blue petals etched in fine lines of gold; and 'Rambunctious', with blue petals furled to resemble a rose. Last year's Bauer-Coble introduction, the knockout 'Pink Pepper', a shimmering lavender pink iris, heavily peppered with dark lavender dots and dashes, may just have started a new genetic line! Three incredibly voluptuous introductions in 2000—Japanese 'Dragon Mane', 'Eileen's Dream', and 'Muffington'—are so crammed with petals that it takes 'Dragon Mane' three full days to unfurl.

And then there are the **daylilies**! A collector's ardor runs deep, so it was inevitable that Ensata Gardens' interests would expand to include other species. A couple of years ago, they embraced daylilies, and their collection often goes hand in glove with their **hosta** devotion. More than 300 daylily cultivars make Ensata Gardens a breathtaking vista of exuberant color for most of the summer. A mature clump of daylilies boasting ten or twelve scapes, each bearing dozens of flowers, is a wonderful sight. Rivaling the colors are the incredible shapes, sizes, and patterns of the flowers. Some are ruffled; others have bicolored or even reverse bicolored effects. There is a tremendous variety of patterns in shades that are darker, lighter, or different from the base color. One of the more memorable pleasures of an outing to Ensata Gardens is witnessing a hybridizing effort in progress.

EXTRAS

All plants freshly (and personally) dug by Bob or John, at least two eyes or fans, are shipped bare-root in mid-April to June in spring, and August to October in fall. The best bargains are the "Iris Collections of Ten," named and labeled plants in quantities of ten. Though the actual varieties are Ensata's selection, customers are given incredible leeway in the choice of color, type, and form (single, double, etc). Also, a sliding scale based on purchase amount presents an interesting opportunity to pick up some incredible buys.

MICHIGAN

GARDEN CROSSINGS L.L.C.

❧ ❧

Garden Crossings is a specialty merchandiser of interesting plants, with the biggest emphasis on rare clematis and unique perennials. Though the actual greenhouses are located in Hudsonville, Michigan, Garden Crossings is a virtual nursery geared to gardeners comfortable surfing the web. The internet catalog, generously sprinkled with vibrant color photographs and searchable both by common and botanical names, is simple to navigate and use.

As an added bonus, the nursery's cultural sheets go way beyond what is usual. For clematis, the nursery lists the plants' pruning group as well as growing and maintenance tips. It gives height and spread, cultural requirements, hardiness zones, "critter resistance," notable attributes (such as cut flower, foliage, etc), design use (trellis, container, etc); and "nature attraction" (hummingbirds, butterflies, etc). For perennials, it also includes "good companions."

OWNERS: Chad Walters and Rod Grasman
TYPE: Mail-order nursery; not open to the public
SPECIALTIES: Clematis; perennials— sun and shade; hostas; daylilies
HOURS: Not open to the public.
CATALOG AVAILABLE: Online
MAIL-ORDER AVAILABLE: Yes
DISPLAY GARDENS: No
CLASSES: No

CONTACT
3676 Black Creek Drive
Hudsonville, MI 49426
PHONE: (616) 550-7501
FAX: (914) 931-5336
WEB ADDRESS: www.gardencrossings.com
EMAIL: sales@gardencrossings.com

Chad Walters and Rod Grasman have over twenty years experience growing perennials, and have established special relationships with some of the nation's best perennial wholesalers—giving them access to some of the latest introductions (sometimes long before these plants become available at local garden centers and nurseries). Granted, not every plant offered here is a new introduction; some are classics worthy of continued interest. But certainly there are cutting edge plants in the mix, available in few other places.

Garden Crossings' stated goal is to "provide home gardeners with exceptional quality plants." It meets that goal by providing its customers with exceptionally well-grown, well-rooted, two-year-old plants, sold for the most part in 2-quart pots rather than the more typical mail-order sizes of 2-inch, 3-inch, or 4-inch containers.

MICHIGAN

The range of plants offered at Garden Crossings is diverse. New introductions include a stately **hollyhock** *Alcea rosea* 'Crème de Cassis', (white blooms with scrumptious raspberry centers); *Athyrium nipponicum;* 'Burgundy Lace', (graceful painted **fern** with silvery-green fronds with purple midribs); a handsome **sedge**, *Carex hachijoensis* 'Evergold', (creamy yellow-green variegated); **hosta** *Hosta* 'Eternal Flame', (white center sport of *Hosta* 'Whirlwind'); and the graceful ornamental grass **miscanthus** *Miscanthus sinensis* 'Huron Sunrise', (blooming more profusely than any other *Miscanthus*). In addition, the nursery fills their website with a wide selection of **phlox, dianthus, heuchera, butterfly bush, salvia, astilbe, daylilies, sedum,** and **hardy hibiscus**.

The website confirms that black is where it's at this year. Check out *Sedum* × *hybrida* 'Purple Emperor', (almost black foliage, reddish pink flower); *Polemonium yezoense* 'Purple Rain', (brown-black foliage with blue flowers); *Cimicifuga* 'Hillside Black Beauty', (dark purple-black foliage); and *Iris* 'Before the Storm', (black, mysterious blossom).

There are intriguing white variegated plants, such as *Caryopteris divaricata* 'Snow Fairy', the new **blue mist spirea** from Japan with clean, crisp white and green variegated leaves; also *Miscanthus sinensis* 'Dixieland', a variegated creamy white and green grass. Look for yellow variegated plants such as the **reed grass** *Calamagrostis acutiflora* 'El Dorado'; and shade-illuminating plants such as *Carex siderosticta* 'Lemon Zest', with sword-like lemon yellow leaves forming neat clumps.

Classic vines available that have withstood the test of time in gardens include, **trumpet vine** (*Campsis radicans*); variegated **porcelain vine** (*Ampelopsis* 'Elegans'); and updated classics, such as the ever popular, but now improved, *Clematis* 'Jackmanii'.

Garden Crossings specializes in **clematis** vines, currently offering more than 50 cultivars. Many of these are award winning plants, such as *Clematis* 'Blue Angel', (6 feet, sky-blue ruffled petals); C. 'Barbara', (8 feet, vivid purplish-pink blossoms fading to purplish-red); C. 'Hania', (8 feet, bicolor with velvety purple-red petals and light pink margins); and C. 'Julka', (8 feet, velvety violet with deep purple-red bar). The nursery carries doubles, such as *Clematis* 'Blue Light', (5 feet, unique, fully double violet-blue); C. 'Countess of Lovelace', (7 feet, lavender-mauve flowers); C. 'Florida Sieboldii', (4 feet, unusual creamy white flowers with large centers of purple stamens); and C. 'Josephine', (6 feet, lilac with pink bar inner petals and bronzy outer petals). The nursery carries one of my favorites, soft pink flowered *Clematis* 'Piilu', an exceptional, compact variety suitable for a small trellis or for climbing through a small shrub. It has the

> *"If I could put my words in song*
> *And tell what's there enjoyed,*
> *All men would to my gardens throng,*
> *And leave the cities void.*
> —RALPH WALDO EMERSON

charming capacity to throw off double flowers in the first flush of early spring, only to rebloom again in late summer with bold, single blossoms, looking completely like a different flower.

For those of us open to new ideas and suggestions (or just plain "companion-challenged" individuals), the recommendations on the cultural sheets are invaluable. As an example, for the extremely hyped new **gaillardia** of 2004, *Gaillardia grandiflora* 'Fanfare'®, "good companions" include *Coreopsis verticillata* 'Moonbeam' (tickseed); *Calamagrostis acutiflora* 'Karl Foerster' (feather reed grass); *Echinacea purpurea* 'Ruby Giant'); *Geranium* 'Rozanne' (cranesbill); and *Panicum virgatum* 'Heavy Metal'. All these plants have colors that harmonize, accentuate, or complement one another and exhibit similar cultural requirements. Whether combined with only one of the suggestions or with all of them, they will give the gardener an irrepressibly jazzy grouping in the landscape.

MICHIGAN

GEE FARMS

❧ ❧

Located in rural south-central Michigan, Gee should be the number one choice on everyone's list for conifers or deciduous trees for landscaping needs. You may have to sidestep a motorized forklift or two, duck an errant sprinkler, or even concede defeat and hitch a ride on a golf-cart with one of the friendly staff, but you will eventually find almost any tree, shrub, bush, or ornamental plant available today.

Gee Farms started as a small family-owned business. Established in 1849 by Gary Gee as a fruit and vegetable stand, today with 20 greenhouses, 10 acres of potted nursery stock, and 75 acres of large field-grown trees, it is a major player in the horticultural industry. Justifiably billing itself as "the largest retail nursery in Michigan," their motto "from the usual to the unusual, Gee Farms has it all" is dead on. Though specializing primarily in unique and unusual evergreens, one would be hard pressed to come up with a tree, shrub, or vine that isn't available at Gee. Favored by busy, no-nonsense professional designers and landscapers for its immense and varied selection of landscape-grade shrubs and trees; Gee still manages to maintain its "aw shucks" friendly, customer-oriented attitude.

OWNERS: Gary, Kaye, and Kary Gee
TYPE: Large retail and wholesale nursery
SPECIALTIES: Evergreens; shrubs; trees; perennials—hostas; ornamental grasses; annuals; hanging baskets; vines; roses; aquatics; statuary
HOURS: Year-round: Mon.-Sun. 8:00 am until dark.
CATALOG AVAILABLE: Online for trees, shrubs, vines only
MAIL-ORDER AVAILABLE: No
DISPLAY GARDENS: Yes
CLASSES: No

CONTACT

14928 Bunkerhill Road
Stockbridge, MI 49285
PHONE: (517) 769-6772
TOLL FREE: (800) 860-BUSH
FAX: (517) 769-6204
WEB ADDRESS: www.geefarms.com
EMAIL: geetrees@modempool.com

DIRECTIONS

FROM ANN ARBOR: I-94 to Chelsea exit (M-52) to Stockbridge. Take M-106 to the left until you come to Territorial Road that forks to your right. Take the right fork and follow Territorial to Bunkerhill Road. Go right 1 mile. **FROM JACKSON** Take I-94 to Exit 139 (Cooper Street/M-106). Go north on Cooper/M-106 until Bunkerhill Road forks off to your left (approx. 8 miles past the state prison). Continue on Bunkerhill Road for 3 miles. **FROM (I-96)** Take I-96 to the Williamston Exit. Turn south on Williamston Road to Howell/ Mason Road, turn right on Howell/Mason Road and proceed approx. 0.1 miles, to first road on left (Williamston Road again). Turn left. Follow Williamston Road for approx. 5.7 miles through the sharp 90 degree turn; Williamston Road turns into Baseline Road. Continue to first intersection on your right—Bunkerhill Road. Nursery entrance on right side.

GPS: N 42° 25.48', W 84° 18.73'

Though browsing is encouraged, with the myriad of choices before you, this is not a place for a slow, leisurely stroll. I suggest coming prepared with a game plan, shopping

list in hand (all plants are cataloged by botanical names), and striding forth in comfortable walking shoes. If this is your first visit, I heartily suggest you stop by the sales area and acquaint yourself with the lay of the land. The friendly and knowledgeable office staff can answer questions, offer suggestions, or direct you to the right area.

WHAT YOU'LL FIND

Gee Farms has an acre or so of display gardens surrounding the old farmstead and an interesting 5-acre arboretum where you can find row after row of interesting trees in various stages of maturation. Depending on your energy level, Gee Farms can be totally grueling or incredibly inspiring. If you are physically up for it, this is one terrific place to look over a huge range of ornamental trees and shrubs. From the standpoint of physical endurance, I recommend bringing water and treating this nursery as a destination day hike with all appropriate preparations.

True to their roots, the Gee's still maintain a fruit and veggie stand but have embellished it with a small refreshment section with the "most delicious" hand-dipped ice cream around. It is incredibly good in the cool comfort of the store but pure ecstasy on a hot and humid summer's day while you amble up and down the countless rows lusting after all that horticultural candy spread out before your eyes.

Adjoining the main sales area, an acre of heated greenhouses offers up a variety of potted plants, including bedding and seed **geraniums**, an overwhelming selection of annuals—both tried and true staples and newer introductions—perennials, hanging baskets, and a complete line of vegetable plants. Gardeners flock here in spring, when Gee Farms also sells colorful annual vines such as **scarlet runner bean**, **moonflower**, and **morning glory**, along with **mandevilla** and anything else that thrives in a pot. Across the path, in the safety of shaded greenhouses, Gee Farms carries garden mainstays such as **hosta** (200 varieties), spring ephemerals for the woodland, ground covers, and numerous other denizens of the shade. In the sunny sections, Gee Farms delights with

MICHIGAN

ornamental grasses, aquatics, and comely container-grown perennial plants. In recent years, Gee Farms has added a good stock of **roses**: hybrid, bush, shrub, and tea. The stars, however, on a stage of 10 acres, remain the potted up deciduous trees, shrubs, and conifers of all shapes and sizes.

★ **SIDE TRIPS** ★

Good place for a meal: **HANKERD GOLF COURSE**, (517) 769-2507 in Pleasant Lake, (ask staff at Gee for driving directions). Restaurant open year round for breakfast, lunch, and dinner.

Gee Farms' container and field-grown stock is wide-ranging and incredibly hard to summarize. I inquired about **magnolia** trees, for instance, and was confronted with the following cultivars: 'Butterfly', 'Elizabeth', 'Gold Glow', 'Heaven Scent', 'Ivory Chalice', 'Leonard Messell', 'Ballerina', 'Waterlily', 'Nigra', 'O'Neill', 'Marilyn', 'Meogidon', 'Royal Star', 'Vulcan', 'Galaxy', 'Golden Gala', 'Alexandrina', 'Rustica Rubra', 'Spectrum', 'Star Wars', and 'Yellow Bird', in various sizes and levels of growth. The shrub selection embraces **maples, boxwood, clethra, smokebush, barberry, butterfly bush, spirea, quince, witchhazel, mockorange, azalea, rhododendron,** and more **dogwood, viburnum,** and **hydrangea** than should be legal. The nursery's collection of evergreen trees and shrubs is even more expansive.

The choices are endless. The flowering **Bradford pear**, as an example, is probably the most well-known of all the ornamental pears. It is a fairly large-growing tree that has considerable ornamental value in the landscape. However, in recent years, problems surfaced; its tight-crotch branching has resulted in the loss of limbs and even the splitting of the entire tree. Gee Farms offers smaller cultivars that are superior in strength such as 'Trinity' and 'Chanticleer'. Everyone loves a towering **bur oak** or a spreading **sugar maple**, but when space is limited, small scale trees like **amur maple** or **flowering crabapple** are a better fit. Other uncommonly beautiful trees include **yellowwood, yellowhorn,** and the **American hornbeam**.

Most plants are sizable and priced accordingly, yet remain incredibly reasonable. Many are available in multiple sizes, ranging from gallon containers to huge, mature trees. For those in need of instant gratification, throw on your hiking boots and head out into the 75 acres of large field-grown trees. Most professionals personally inspect specimen trees before they tag them, and you should too.

GRASS ROOTS NURSERY

❧ ❧

Grass Roots Nursery has been propagating, growing, and selling water lilies, bog plants, lotus, floaters and fish for twenty-two years, well before the current infatuation with water gardening got its start. Located on a boggy pocket next to the expressway, surrounded by a patch of farmland beyond the edges of an industrial park, Grass Roots Nursery is a family-run operation owned and operated by Gary and Rosemary Bates and their son, Scott. A place of few pretensions, what it lacks in glitzy ambiance it more than makes up for in a broad range of spectacular pond and water plants. Included are hardy water lilies, water iris, and marginals. They also sell pond supplies. Started some thirty years ago as a landscaping enterprise, the nursery also stocks incredible finds in perennials, annuals, shrubs, and trees.

WHAT YOU'LL FIND

This slightly cluttered nursery, soft and spongy underfoot, is especially lively with butterflies and birds. Numerous ponds, full of aquatics, are scattered about. Dragonflies dance over fragrant waterlily blossoms and goldfish bubble up from below. Yet, it's the water that draws me in.

"Water is irresistible." says Scott. "It adds a new, distinct dimension to the garden." And so it does. The splash of a fountain or the murmur of a stream lures us, the shimmering pool seduces us, and the dazzling

OWNERS: Gary and Rosemary Bates, Scott Bates
TYPE: Specialty nursery
SPECIALTIES: Aquatic plants—water lilies and lotus; pond supplies; fish; perennials; annuals
HOURS: (Days and times can vary; call ahead) Winter hours: Tues.-Sat. 9:00 am to 4:00 pm; end of March through Fall: Tues.-Fri 9:00 am to 6:00 pm, Sat. 9:00 am to 5:00 pm, Sun. Noon to 5:00 pm.
CATALOG AVAILABLE: Online, and printed handouts
MAIL-ORDER AVAILABLE: Yes
DISPLAY GARDENS: Yes
CLASSES: Yes

CONTACT
24765 Bell Road
New Boston, MI 48164
PHONE: (734) 753-9200
FAX: (734) 654-2405
WEB ADDRESS: www.grassrootsnursery.com

DIRECTIONS
FROM THE NORTH: I-275 south to South Huron Road (Exit 11B).Turn right onto South Huron Road. Make a quick left (south) on Bell Road (Burger King is on the corner). Drive approx. 1.5 miles to nursery on the left.
FROM THE SOUTH: I-275 north to South Huron Road (Exit 11) Turn west (left) onto South Huron Road, driving over the expressway, then turn south (left) onto Bell Road. Proceed on Bell Road for approximately 1.5 miles to the nursery on the left.

GPS: N 42° 07.44', W 83° 22.90'

MICHIGAN

flashes of colorful fish mesmerize us. Casting its spell, the shrouded beauty of a waterlily rising from the deep, leaves floating serenely on the surface and exquisite blossoms appearing as if by magic, enchants us completely.

> "... iris, fair among the fairest,
> Who, armed with golden rod,
> And winged with celestial
> azure, bearest,
> The message of some God."
> —HENRY WADSWORTH LONGFELLOW

Grass Roots Nursery propagates and grows all its hardy aquatic plants, inside and outside the greenhouses. **Hardy water lilies** and **lotus** undergo several years of growth before truly mature specimens are offered for sale in 2-, 3- and 5-gallon pots. (Bare-root plants are available for mail-order and at the nursery with a seventy-two hour notice.) The nursery has an extensive collection of perennial water lilies (*Nymphaea* spp.), segregated in growing ponds by color group in warm shades of yellow, pink, white, red, and peach. For a quick show in a new water garden, rosy-pink *Nymphaea* 'Hollandia' (sometimes called 'Darwin') is a good choice, though Grass Roots Nursery also offers a number of other great choices, too.

Arresting at every stage of the development, hauntingly aromatic lotuses (*Nelumbo* spp.) are not at all hard to grow, and gardeners with even the slightest sense of adventure should include a tub (or two) of the smaller ones in their ponds. Arguably, it is difficult to surpass the pristine beauty of a white lotus. My favorites, available here, are two excellent choices: *Nelumbo* 'Alba Grandiflora', (huge, free-flowering, and notably fragrant); and for smaller ponds or large containers, the dwarf, tulip-shaped flowers of white 'Shirokunshi' fits the bill. The nursery also carries one of the smallest of the lotuses, deep pink 'Momo Botan', which translates loosely to "like a double peony," something it mimics quite gracefully.

In addition to hardy aquatics, Grass Roots grows some truly spectacular, fragrant, and free flowering tropical **water lilies**. Available in both day and night blooming varieties, they come in scintillating shades of white, yellow, pink, red, blue, and purple. The nursery also carries shallow water marginal plants such as **four leaf clover, floating heart, pickerel rush**, and **parrot's feather.** In the tropical bog plant category, Grass Roots carries interesting plants such as **canna, papyrus, taro, umbrella palm, sensitive plant, melon sword, water hyacinth,** and **water poppy.** The list of hardy bog plants is just as extensive, including **rush, water mint, arrowhead, horsetail, sweet flag,**

lizards tail, thalia, water celery, water bamboo, and **water plaintain**. All plants at Grass Roots are available as jumbo potted plants (for pick up only) or bare root.

This nursery offers an extensive list of ponds and pond-related products such as pumps, fountain heads, test strips, biological filters, and underwater lighting. Pond care products include netting, heaters, bubblers, vacuums, rakes, poles, skimmers, thermometers, and two types of tape. There is an exceptional collection of "no hole" pots and containers running the gamut from a 1-gallon squat pot to a 110-gallon toter.

And the Bates add: "If it's fish and critters you are looking for we have over thirty high-density tanks that hold 200 or more gallons each," filled to capacity with all sorts of swimming, darting, and trailing forms of life.

GREAT LAKES ROSES

❧ ❧

Great Lakes Roses is devoted exclusively to growing winter-hardy modern and antique roses. Because of their toughness and beauty, all the roses offered here are species, heirlooms, and rugosas. To that end, Nancy and Roger Lindley, passionate rose growers and unlucky casualties of corporate downsizing, have transformed an 1890s farmstead into a charming country destination for lovers of old garden roses and modern varieties especially suited for the Midwest.

Over the years, the Lindley's have developed the grounds around the house into a large, residential display garden with an eclectic landscape that includes more than 700 clearly marked rose bushes. Customers are encouraged to stroll the paths, scrutinizing each plant's unique characteristics: flower color and shape, leaf shape and color, shrub shape and size, and in autumn, its hips—characteristics impossible to appreciate from a catalog or photo. At peak bloom, the place is awesome!

On-site amenities include a rose-clad screened-in summer cottage where you may rest, eat a snack or picnic lunch, or browse the plethora of rose reference books scattered about. Consider planning your visit around a workshop or talk, and come prepared to spend some very enjoyable and educational time wandering the gardens.

OWNERS: Nancy and Roger Lindley
TYPE: Specialty nursery
SPECIALTIES: Roses
HOURS: April 10 thru Oct 13 (dates vary, call ahead): Thurs.-Mon. 10:00 am to 6:00 pm (during the months of July and Aug, open only Fri. and Sat.). Also, by special appointment
CATALOG AVAILABLE: Online, and printed flyer
MAIL-ORDER AVAILABLE: No
DISPLAY GARDENS: Yes
CLASSES: Yes

CONTACT
49875 Willow Rd. (P.O. Box 54)
Belleville, MI 48112-0065
PHONE: (734) 461-1230
FAX: (734) 461-0360
WEB ADDRESS: www.GreatLakesRoses.com
EMAIL: Info@GreatLakesRoses.com

DIRECTIONS
FROM SUMPTER TOWNSHIP, SOUTH OF BELLEVILLE: Take I-94 to Exit 187 (Rawsonville), drive south for 7 miles, turn east (left) on Willow Road and proceed for 0.7 miles to nursery on right.

GPS: N 42° 06.90', W 83° 31.60'

WHAT YOU'LL FIND

Great Lakes Roses carries the gamut of hardy, northern grown **roses**. There are more than 500 varieties available, on their own roots, including varieties of albas, centifolias, damasks, portlands, gallicas, moss, species, antique, bourbons, hybrid perpetuals, hybrid musks, polyanthas, rugosas, shrub, floribundas, climbers, and miniature roses. You'll also find popular series, including Canadian Morden Parkland™, Canadian Explorer™, Town & Country, and Buck Shrub.

Okay, I confess to a passion for hardy roses requiring no Herculean efforts on my part for their survival. Still, my gardener's heart was unprepared for the sheer beauty of these roses—robust blooms, gracefully arching canes, and sumptuous, colored blossoms that open like teacups filled with fluffy petals. Viewing the gardens on your own is informative and fun; touring

> *"Blossom by blossom the spring begins. . ."*
> —A.C. SWINBURNE

them with its owner is sheer inspiration. Roses are her life's blood, and Nancy, the "Raising Roses" columnist for *Michigan Gardener*, enjoys mixing with rose enthusiasts, sharing information, and dispensing cultural tips along the way.

Since I am not one to primp, pamper, or coddle my roses, I was immediately drawn to the immense collections of Buck, Explorer, and rugosa. Buck roses are the result of the work of Dr. Griffith Buck at Iowa State University in Ames, Iowa. The result of his breeding program is a beautiful collection of hardy and fragrant roses, with a flower quality that is comparable to those of floribundas and hybrid teas. Sturdy enough to withstand the disease pressures of a hot and humid summer and cold-hardy enough to shrug off the rigors of nightmarish winters. Though most were created in the 1970s, Dr. Buck's exquisite roses only recently captured gardeners' attentions and captivated their hearts. The Great Lakes Roses collection includes as complete a collection as I've ever seen. Some have charmingly Midwestern names, such as 'Hi Neighbor', 'Wandering Wind', 'Barn Dance', and his most ravishing creation, 'Hawkeye Belle' (officially listed as white, in reality white blushed with a pale shell pink finish that deepens within the center). Others were named for acquaintances, such as 'Aunt Honey' and 'Pearlie Mae', while still others, such as 'Malaguena' and 'Paloma Blanca', are named in honor of his mentor.

The Explorer series, named for Canadian explorers, offers a combination of disease resistance, extreme hardiness, repeat-bloom, and tolerance of heat and humidity. 'Champlain' and 'J.P. Connell' are prolific bloomers and mid-sized shrubs; 'George Vancouver', is a short bush that explodes with an extraordinary number of vivid red blooms; 'William Baffin' is vigorous enough to cover a trellis in a year; and 'John Davis' and 'John Cabot' are excellent candidates for pillars. Clearly, there are enough winter-hardy antique and modern roses at Great Lakes Roses to keep any gardener happy incorporating roses for a long, long time.

Roses are propagated and grown on site. Most roses are available as strong-rooted, two-year-olds in 2¹/₂-gallon pots; some varieties are one-year-olds in quart containers, while minis are grown out in 1-gallon pots. Own-root roses may initially appear smaller than grafted ones; however, in the garden they are more vigorous and outperform grafted ones even with one cane tied behind their collective clumps.

EXTRAS

Weekly lecture programs are well attended. All events are free and reservations are not required. Topics are varied, but, consistently, the most popular remains "Winter Preparation for Roses." Great Lakes Roses offers quantity discounts, a great excuse for shopping with a friend. For visionary gardeners, an end-of-season sale produces great early October bargains.

The sales staff, consulting Rosarians and master gardeners, are friendly, knowledgeable, and eager to help. Visitors are met by the nursery's official canine greeter, Josephine, who does not want to share her home and nursery with other dogs. Therefore, it is requested that all pets be left in the car.

Additionally, since the historic barn (used primarily for classes) with its exposed beams and balcony can be very attractive but potentially dangerous to unsupervised children, the otherwise easy-going Lindleys are adamant that children be closely supervised. If your kids are rambunctious, it is better to leave them at home than face the potential request to leave the premises.

MICHIGAN

HALLSON GARDENS

❦

Discover this rural gem! Come to Hallson Gardens prepared to spend some very enjoyable and educational time wandering the many growing beds, mixed borders, display beds, and a very neat and tidy sales area. There is a small but cheery gift shop carrying a few accessories, tools, gifts, and books.

One would be hard pressed to meet two nicer people in the nursery trade than Chris Wilson and Brian Hall. It is obvious from the very first moment you meet them, Chris and Brian just plain LOVE plants. They enjoy growing them, take pleasure in discussing them with their customers, and are more than happy to share any and all information. Additionally, they are never too busy, too tired, or too pressured to grace customers with a smile, a helping hand, or good advice.

Although plants are available by mail-order, visitors to Hallson can select plants right out in the growing beds on all but the busiest of weekends and have them freshly dug on the spot. If you have not had the opportunity to meet these fine nursery owners, I highly recommend you make the effort to seek them out, even if they are outside your immediate nursery-exploration range.

OWNERS: Chris Wilson and Brian Hall
TYPE: Specialty nursery
SPECIALTIES: Hosta; daylilies; perennials—sun and shade; vines; bulbs
HOURS: April 1 thru July 31: Wed.-Thurs. 9:00 am to 7:00 pm, Fri.-Sat. 9:00 am to 9:00 pm, Sun. 10:00 am to 6:00 pm; Aug. 1 thru Sept. 30: Wed.-Sat. 9:00 am to 7:00 pm, Sun. 10:00 am to 5:00 pm; Oct: by appointment only.
CATALOG AVAILABLE: Online
MAIL-ORDER AVAILABLE: Yes
DISPLAY GARDENS: Yes
CLASSES: No

CONTACT
411 Wolf Lake Drive (P.O. Box 220)
Brooklyn, MI 49230
After approx. 9/1/04:
14280 S. Meridian Road (P.O. Box 220)
Cement City, MI 49233
PHONE/FAX: (517) 467-7955
WEB ADDRESS: www.perennialnursery.com
EMAIL: hallsons@perennialnursery.com

DIRECTIONS
(BROOKLYN) FROM JACKSON: Take US-127 south to US-12. Turn east (left) and drive 8 miles to Onsted Hwy. Turn south (right) and drive 0.5 miles to Wolf Lake Drive. Turn east (left) on Wolf Lake, nursery is the gray house on left on small hill. From Ann Arbor/Detroit: (US-12 & US-23) Drive west on US-12 for 32 miles to Onsted Hwy. Turn south (left) proceeding 0.5 miles to Wolf Lake Drive. Turn east (left) on Wolf Lake, nursery is the gray house on left on a small hill.

BROOKLYN GPS:
N 42° 03.27', W 84° 11.79'

After approx. 9/1/04:
(CEMENT CITY) FROM JACKSON: Take US-127 (Meridian Road) south to 0.5 miles north of US-12. Turn right at nursery on west side of road. From Ann Arbor/Detroit (US-12 & US-23) drive west on US-12 for 39 miles to US-127 (Meridian Road). Turn north (right) on US-127 and drive for 0.5 miles. Nursery is located on the left.

MICHIGAN

WHAT YOU'LL FIND

The choice of plants at this small nursery is limited, however the sophistication of the plants available is both intriguing and satisfying. The longer I poked around, the more excited I became. I even ran into a customer who proclaimed this to be his favorite nursery, while deftly loading up his cart with what looked like every imaginable **hosta**.

"The butterfly is a flying flower,
The flower a tethered butterfly."
—ECHOUCHARD LE BRUN
(FRENCH POET)

In the ground in tidy rows, Hallson grows most of their exceptional collection of hardy and incredibly well-rooted plants in well thought-out display beds scattered throughout the property. Here you will find a selection of perennials, shrubs, daylilies, and of course, hostas.

The main thrust of the stock is in the hostas, of which Hallson carries well over 300 varieties. While my feelings about the flowers of *Hosta* species and cultivars are somewhat lukewarm, my admiration for the foliage knows no bounds. The variety of sizes, shapes, and shades of green—as well as the cupping, puckering, edging, and coloration of the leaves—is truly mind-boggling. Hallson's hostas, for the most part, are sold as container plants. Selections include gentle giants, scrappy dwarfs, striped, variegated, edged, stitched, cupped, puckered, crinkled, and corrugated, with blue, gold, chartreuse, and emerald colors. I am particularly enamored of the huge yellow-green leaves of *Hosta* 'Sum and Substance', so naturally I gravitated immediately to 'Bottom Line', 'Parhelion', 'Sum of All', and 'Vim and Vigor', all sports of 'Sum and Substance'. Being partial to "cutesy" names, as well as feeling the effects of a missed lunch, I couldn't pass up 'Fried Bananas', 'Fried Green Tomatoes', 'Guacamole', 'Maraschino Cherry', 'Pineapple Juice', and for dessert, 'Pineapple Upsidedown Cake' with 'Spilt Milk'.

The perennial list is uncommonly interesting and deep. New plants are forever being brought in, so repeat trips are advised. On random visits during the growing season, I found winsome collections of summer blooming **astilbe, bleeding heart, coral bells, iris, phlox, pulmonaria, sedum, toad lily**, and **veronica**. Sure, many nurseries carry the tried and true varieties of those listed above, but I had to pull out my reference book to learn about *Astilbe* 'Bumalda', *A.* 'Pink Lightning',

A. 'Sister Teresa', *Phlox paniculata* 'Rubymine', and *P. p.* 'Red Riding Hood'. Hallson Gardens has many plants for shady sites and offers a nice selection of Midwestern natives, "bold plants," sun-loving companions, some ornamental grasses, and butterfly bushes.

April is a magical time in the gardens at Hallson. Spring perennials, bulbs, and ephemerals welcome customers in this seductive rural setting. Hallson's collection of **daylilies** (*Hemerocallis*) is limited by space constraints. But the field-grown plants, adapted to Midwestern conditions, are huge, robust beauties with excellent prices. Consequently, it was rather easy to add more goodies to my pile: *H.* 'Exotic Love', (vibrant golden-yellow that pops and has a dark maroon eye); *H.* 'Big Smile', (the colors of sunrise); and *H.* 'Happy Returns', (an improved 'Stella de Oro').

After eight prosperous years at this location, Hallson Gardens is obviously stretched to capacity and bursting at its seams. Last summer, Chris and Bob purchased a choice parcel of land they describe as having "rolling hills, mature trees, open fields, marshland, a creek, a pine forest, and an incredible sunset view." From that moment, besides running their business at its present location, they have been busy cleaning out new fields and starting display borders and propagation beds. With luck, all will fall into place at their new location by September, 2004.

★ **SIDE TRIPS** ★

HIDDEN LAKE GARDENS, Tipton, MI (517) 431-2060, located in southern Michigan. Hidden Lake Gardens is a 670-acre park surrounding Hidden Lake and owned by Michigan State University. A landscape arboretum "for the benefit and education of the public," it has both driving routes and hiking trails and some outstanding plant collections. Hosta Hillside, for example, is a collection of about 500 hosta cultivars.

Chris and Brian always keep their finger on the heartbeat of the serious gardener. On their website, besides the requisite catalog listing of plant selections, Chris writes a monthly "Wolf Creek Journal," lists specials, answers questions, and moderates an incredible array of forums.

MICHIGAN

MICHIGAN MINI ROSES

❧ ❧

Michigan Mini Roses is a family venture, founded by Judy and Doug Bell in 1981. Judy runs the business end, Doug builds the greenhouses and propagating benches, daughters Casey and Veronica help out, and Grandma Betty answers the phone (please speak up when you call).

Michigan Mini Roses is the largest nursery in the Midwest devoted exclusively to miniature roses. It carries more than 200 varieties, including micro-minis, minis, mini-floras, climbers, moss, single, striped, bicolor, and cascading. The nursery propagates all of its own roses and ships them year-round to most U.S. destinations.

If you've thought of miniatures as frail or fragile, the vigorous, hardy, own-root varieties of minis available at Michigan Mini Roses will forever put that misconception to bed. Their offerings will flower in the garden from spring until late fall, survive the harshest of winters, and bounce right back with flowers the following spring.

The nursery is the product of serendipity. Rose fanciers for more than thirty years, the Bells won a pint-sized rosebush as a door prize in 1967. Not sure what to do with the little rascal, they planted it behind some tea roses—and promptly forgot about it. That winter's exceptionally brutal weather killed close to 30 of their prized rose specimens, but the neglected spunky miniature was green with promise. "Here was this little guy we'd totally neglected, all leafed out," Judy recalls fondly. And the rest, as they say, is history. A fledging backyard business was born. Today the backyard venture that began in a lean-to shed fills eight greenhouses.

OWNERS: Judy and Doug Bell
TYPE: Wholesale and retail nursery
SPECIALTIES: Miniature roses
HOURS: (Retail) May: Mon-Fri 8:00 am to 2:00 pm; June 1-15: 8:00 am to 1:00 pm. Other days and times by appointment.
CATALOG AVAILABLE: Printed and online
MAIL-ORDER AVAILABLE: Yes
DISPLAY GARDENS: No
CLASSES: No

CONTACT
45951 Hull Rd.
Belleville, MI 48111-3507
PHONE: (734) 699-6698
FAX: (734) 699-5814
WEB ADDRESS: www.michiganminiroses.com
EMAIL: BellMMR@earthlink.net

DIRECTIONS
FROM I-94: Exit I-94 at Belleville Road (Exit 190). Proceed south on Belleville for about 0.7 miles. Belleville Road merges into Main Street. Stay on Main for 0.6 miles to South Street. Turn south (right) onto South Street (road name changes to Sumpter) for 1 mile to Hull Road. Turn west (right) on Hull. Nursery is located 0.3 miles down.

GPS: N 42° 11.39', W 83° 29.32'

Entering the greenhouse, seeing a verdant sea of color lavishly blooming before me was like finding the end of a rainbow. **Miniature roses** in blazing yellows, soft purples, brilliant reds, pristine whites, rich pinks, and some rather startling pigment combinations greeted me. (The catalog and website provide color photographs of most of the hybrids.) At peak, Michigan Mini Roses stocks more than 50,000 miniature roses, including some new varieties, rare older ones, and their own magical creations. The medium red 'Betty's Baby'; light red 'Here's Ian'

> *"O thou beautiful Rose!...*
> *so fair and sweet..."*
> —JULIA C. R. DORR,
> "THE CLAY TO THE ROSE"

(named after the Bells youngest grandchild); white with dark pink edges 'PJ's Pride'; and the multi-colored 'Firedance' are just some of the Bells' creations. I love yellow blossoms, so naturally I was immediately smitten with the tall, elegant, 'Arizona Sunset' (light yellow flushed with orange); the bright yellow 'Behold'; and 'Cal Poly', one of the most intense yellows I have ever seen (also available as a 96-inch climber). According to Judy, the most popular color is lavender, followed by yellow, red, blends, and pink. A Bell introduction, lavender 'Folkdance', has unusual, frilly blossoms.

For the most part, miniature roses have no fragrance; however, some hybridizers, including the Bells, have been concentrating their efforts on changing that. For their part, the Bells have introduced a highly fragrant, light-yellow mini, 'Diamond Doll'. For the cat lovers out there, there's 'Little Tiger', a miniature version of the ever so popular yellow and orange 'Oranges and Lemons' rose. Can't you just picture this little cutie crouching in the garden?

Michigan Mini Roses specializes in climbing miniature roses. The long stems of the gorgeous 'Red Cascade' can be trained to climb a trellis, drape over a wall, or scramble horizontally, ground cover style. 'Orchid Jubilee' a vigorous and hardy climber (6 feet) with vibrant purple blooms bursts to life early, blooming continuously throughout the season. 'Jeanne Lajoie' is a vigorous and very hardy pillar climber (6 to 8 feet) with blossoms of a lovely pink, kissed with coral.

Minis are usually sold in $2^1/_2$-inch pots; however Michigan Mini Roses' standard pot is $3^1/_2$ inches (with a soil volume of a 4-inch pot), and most containers have two stems. Hanging baskets as well as larger size containers—1-gallon and $2^1/_2$ gallon—are also available. Most sales are mail-order, and for obvious reasons, a shipping frenzy occurs just before Mother's Day.

MICHIGAN

OLD HOUSE GARDENS

Old House Gardens, a specialty merchandiser, operates from the garage of a charming, two-story Queen Anne house in Ann Arbor. A landscape historian, Scott Kunst is the enthusiastic owner of this, the country's only mail-order source devoted exclusively to heirloom bulbs (some call them antique bulbs). According to Scott, "heirloom bulbs are often tougher, generally fragrant, posses unusual characteristics, display ethereal gracefulness, thrive in vastly different climates, and, where needed in garden restorations, are period appropriate. In a word, they are simply gorgeous! But they are also rare and endangered, and in need of help for their preservation."

The popularity of today's bulbs can be traced directly to the world-wide distribution of their ancestors, paralleling the evolution of world trade routes. As people started valuing bulbs for their culinary, medicinal, and ornamental properties, the exploration, collection, and propagation greatly expanded their variety and availability. But as new varieties became more readily available, many others became more difficult or impossible to find. "Ninety-nine percent of all the old bulbs have disappeared from the known trade," says Scott. For those trying to recreate period gardens, such as Monticello, finding period bulbs has become a real challenge.

Back in the late 1980s, this accomplished landscape designer and hands-on gardener decided to do something about the rapidly disappearing bulb choices. In fact, it was the tulip 'Prince of Austria' that launched him into the bulb mail-order business. At first glance, the red tulip seems like any other red tulip, but Kunst says, "It is incredibly fragrant."

WHAT YOU'LL FIND

Through close collaboration with collectors across the globe, Scott is able to find and acquire dozens of

OWNER: Scott Kunst
TYPE: Small specialty mail-order; not open to the public
SPECIALTIES: Heirloom/antique bulbs
HOURS: Office Hours: Mon-Fri 9:00 am to 5:00 pm; order pickup by appointment only.
CATALOG AVAILABLE: Printed and online
MAIL-ORDER AVAILABLE: Yes
DISPLAY GARDENS: No
CLASSES: No

CONTACT
536 Third Street
Ann Arbor, MI 48103
PHONE: (734) 995-1486
FAX: (734) 995-1687
WEB ADDRESS: www.oldhousegardens.com
EMAIL: charlie@oldhousegardens.com

MICHIGAN

varieties of **antique bulbs**. Choices include **crocus, tulips, narcissus, hyacinths, dahlias, cannas, glads, lilies, elephant ears, rain lilies**, and **tuberose** (which today is extinct in the wild). Though some of his sources include growers in the Netherlands, France, Latvia, and Australia, a majority of his bulbs are propagated and grown on various farms right here in the United States.

Scott's aim is to be a premiere source of rare antique bulb varieties, verifying their authenticity through research, and their reliability by growing them out in beds for a few years. According to Scott, a bulb's unique merits, the reason for its longevity, are just not that obvious. Take *Crocus vernus* 'Grand Maitre' (1920s). It may seem like just another purple crocus, until one realizes that it blooms later in the season—exactly when the first daffodils blossom. Then it's easy to understand why it was planted and replanted over the years, helping it to survive. Part history, part gardening, and part anthropology, interest in these early forms of bulbs is relatively new. But the trend isn't going unnoticed, as more and more companies are starting to list them in their catalogs.

> "It is impossible to have too much love or too many daffodils."
> —KATHERINE WHITESIDE

The unique qualities that make heirlooms so captivating are not necessarily the qualities that nurseries and garden-centers value. Most heirloom bulbs have a soft, graceful, willowy look about them. "Older daffodils are a good example," says Scott. "Their flowers sway in the breeze like butterflies in a garden," so unlike today's ramrod straight daffs.

Old House Gardens' annual catalog describes its noteworthy collection of approximately 250 varieties of heirloom bulbs, including their history, descriptions, tips, and ordering information. Most are aimed for fall plantings. One of the oldest bulbs in cultivation, *Crocus* 'Mammoth Yellow', first cataloged in 1665, appears in the catalog whenever the supplies are adequate, along with the nearly 400-year-old white and pink tulip, *Tulipa* 'Zomerschoon'. At the height of Dutch Tulipmania (called the greatest flower craze of all times), this cultivar traded for fortunes and bankrupted hundreds.

Old House Gardens is aware of fashion's vagaries. Scott understands that what is popular today may not be so tomorrow. Certainly cannas, so popular in landscapes and container gardening today, yo-yo'd back and forth in popularity for decades. The nursery's current, intriguing collection includes the rare (1920s) 'Assaut', (voluptuous blossoms of pure dark crimson); 'Ehemannii' (1863)

For the beginner, Scott has put together starter samplers. These are collections of some of his favorite bulbs within each category. Also, sometimes Scott finds bulbs too late for inclusion in the catalog. Gardeners in the know, subscribe to his free email newsletter "The Friends of Old Bulbs Gazette" which offers tips, news, history, and special offers—such as these bulbs—which are snapped up almost immediately. To receive this email, just send Scott an email with "subscribe" in the subject line to newsletter@old-housegardens.com.

Then there's the famous "Scott's Garage Sale" sampler. Inevitably, in one category or another, Old House Gardens ends up with a few too many bulbs. For the consumer willing to wait until April, Scott will put together a $30 sampler (his choice of bulbs) of wonderful, top-quality, and diverse bulbs—all labeled—with a catalog value of $35. And finally, Old House Gardens offers T-shirts ("Bury some antiques in your garden"), books, interesting thermometers, reprints of antique catalogs, and a couple of heirloom flower calendars. The friendly staff truly enjoy meeting their customers, so if you want to pick up your order personally, just add a note to your order and they'll notify you when it's ready.

(topped by "arching sprays of dangling, bell-shaped, deep rose colored flowers, like over-sized fuschias"); and the best selling flamboyant beauty; 'Florence Vaughan' (1893) (vibrant yellow blossoms are splashed in orange). You can also find the impressive architectural giant, **banana canna**, *Canna musifolia* (1858, 8- to 14-feet tall with huge, green, maroon-trimmed leaves and tiny red flowers).

As with other plants from the Victorian gardens, dahlia cultivation underwent neglectful breaks before its current resurgence in popularity. Brought into gardens by the Aztecs, the plant arrived in Europe in 1789, and by the 1840s was the rage in American landscapes. Exciting new forms were introduced in the 1870s; however, of the 10,000 or so dahlias introduced during the 1800s, only 4 survive today—'Kaiser Wilhelm' (1892, preserved by the German Dahlia, Fuchsia, and Gladiolus Society); 'Nellie Broomhead' (1897, from a Japanese source); 'Tommy Keith' (1892, British National Collection of Dahlias); and

MICHIGAN

'Union Jack, Star of Denmark' (1882, the oldest known surviving dahlia). Old House Gardens lists these, plus 23 other extraordinary dahlias in an astonishing array of flower blossoms that are small and large, in shapes resembling cactus, water lily, ball, pompom or dinner plate; in growth from 12 inches to 7 feet. They are available in just about every color of the rainbow, (except blue). The colors alone are infectious.

Dahlia fever can do strange things to a gardener. Want impact? My fixation was officially underway as soon as I saw the burgundy foliaged, glowing scarlet 'Bishop of Llandaff'. A soft look? Go with buttery yellow 'Glorie van Heemstede'. Prefer to mix and match? Try 'Princess Louise de Suede'—a tantalizing color scheme that is neither pink, nor red, nor orange, but a misty blend of the three.

Old House Gardens also offers fragrant Mexican tuberose bulbs; 5 to 8 feet tall (depending on where and how it's grown) violet-stemmed **taro**; **St. Joseph's lily** (1799), the hardiest amaryllis ever introduced; an orange **fire lily**; and a wonderful assortment of glads, whose colors, patterns, texture and size defy description.

MICHIGAN

REATH'S NURSERY

～⚮ ⚮～

Someone once said of the peony, "Peonies have a feeling of place." And that place in the Midwest is the upper Michigan peninsula, or more exactly, Reath's Nursery, in Vulcan. Founded by the late Dr. David Reath who began hybridizing peonies in 1961, today, the 50-acre nursery is a reflection of the Doctor's interests. Today, his son Scott continues to uphold Dr. Reath's principle of providing customers with top quality plants.

Reath's Nursery offers a rotating group of peony hybrids selected from its collection of 150 varieties, depending on availability. Many of these plants are not available anywhere else. Spring collections and the occasional special are posted online. Reath's catalogs ($3) are sumptuously illustrated with color photographs and are well worth the price.

For years the large double-flowered hybrids dominated the cutflower market and were the most popular choices for garden planting. However, around the turn of the last century, A.P. Saunders began a breeding program that would bring about dramatic changes in color and form. Unfortunately, despite the creativity of his work, his hybrids, mostly single or semi-double, failed to be accepted by the public.

Though he eventually created 15,000 hybrids, many have been lost. Fortunately, for the peony lover in particular and the gardener in general, Dr. David Reath, a veterinarian, managed to acquire a number of the Saunders hybrids. Not only did he preserve them from extinction but he also continued the hybridization efforts started by Saunders, producing beautiful garden plants with durable, strong stems, bright or unusual pastel flower colors, and attractive finely-textured foliage.

OWNERS: Scott Reath
TYPE: Large specialty nursery; open to the public only during open house
SPECIALTIES: Herbaceous and tree peonies; iris
HOURS: No retail hours. Call for open house dates and hours.
CATALOG AVAILABLE: Online
MAIL-ORDER AVAILABLE: Yes
DISPLAY GARDENS: Yes, accessible during open house
CLASSES: No

CONTACT
N 195 County Road 577
Vulcan, MI 49892
PHONE: (906) 563-9777
FAX: (906) 563-9777
WEB ADDRESS: www.reathsnursery.com
EMAIL: reathnur@up.net

DIRECTIONS
The nursery is located approximately 3 miles northwest of the town of Faithorn, on County Road 577.

GPS: N 45° 42.80', W 87° 47.95'

MICHIGAN

WHAT YOU'LL FIND

Although Reath's nursery operates exclusively by mail-order, for one glorious weekend in June, when **peonies** and **iris** are at peak bloom, the nursery throws open its doors and invites one and all to tour the colorful fields, view mature plants, pick their favorites, and place their orders. Admittedly, considering that the nursery is located on a rustic county road vir-

> *"If you truly love nature, you will find beauty everywhere."*
> —Vincent van Gogh

tually in the middle of nowhere, one might think it's not worth the trip. However, that would be a grave error, as the open house attracts eager, knowledgeable gardeners by the busload. Peak bloom time (typically mid- to late-June) is dependent on Mother Nature's whims; therefore, it's best to call ahead for the exact dates. Sweeping acres of peonies in full bloom is a sight worth spending a few quality hours in a car any day.

Included in their catalog on a regular basis are some of my favorites: 'Windchimes', (luminous single, pink); 'Blushing Princess', (sly, semi-double, blush blooms); 'May Music', (apricot buff single with crimson flares); and 'White Frost', (pristine white, double). Another peony that caught my attention was 'Elizabeth Ann', a peachy blend introduced by Scott Reath.

When my gardening friend decided to put in a rock garden, one of the first plants she purchased was Dr. Reath's cute-as-a-button, 'Little Red Gem'. The short (12 to 18 inches) rock garden peony bears single, light red blossoms early on in the season.

Unlike herbaceous peonies, which die back to the ground each year, **tree peonies** (*Peonia suffruticosa*) grow into 3-to 4-foot shrubs, which merely lose their leaves while their woody stems and branches remain intact. Tree peony flowers, sporting huge, tissue-paper blossoms, are especially exquisite and striking. Not only do they come in a rainbow of colors, but

EXTRAS

Reath's Nursery, unlike many others, offers its customers various "sizes" of roots (shipped in the fall): a "double size" root for the gardener wishing instant gratification, the traditional 3- to 5-eye root, and a smaller, more economical size for those with time and patience.

MICHIGAN

petals can be silky smooth, shiny, or crinkled. Two outstanding cultivars at Reath's: 'Exotic Era' (a blend of apricot and rose) and 'Golden Era' (a yellow with reddish flares) are outstanding additions to any landscape.

Tree peonies offered through the catalog at Reath's Nursery, just like the herbaceous peonies, come in three sizes: 2-year, 3- to 4-year, and 6-year plants. They are selected on a rotating basis from their collection encompassing 80 varieties.

Though known primarily for peonies, Reath's Nursery also carries a comfortable collection of Siberian irises, such as 'Dear Delight', (a light blue); 'Waucedah Peace', (an upright, white); 'Shirley Pope', (deep velvety purple); and spuria iris such as 'Blue Spiderweb', (exceptionally showy medium blue blooms with deep blue and yellow veining). Perfect companions, these plants share their bloom period with mid- or late-blooming peonies adding grace and beauty to the landscape.

MICHIGAN

RENAISSANCE ACRES
ORGANIC HERBS

❧❧ ❧❧

Renaissance Acres Organic Herb Farm propagates more than 500 varieties of culinary, medicinal, scented, native, dye, and ceremonial herb plants and seeds. Propagation is from seeds, cuttings, and root divisions, all done locally at the farm, located in historic Webster Township in Whitmore Lake, approximately 10 miles north of Ann Arbor.

All of the plants Renaissance Acres grows are raised with the strictest organic growing methods. According to owners Kristina and Peter Stark, no pesticides, herbicides, fungicides, or synthetic fertilizers are used.

WHAT YOU'LL FIND

According to Stark the use of plants to cure disease is as old as the human race. Man has been dependent on the plant world for existence in a nutritional sense throughout much of his history; it was therefore inevitable that knowledge of herbal medicine would evolve. Medicinal herbs, (herbs that most of us grow for their ornamental value, not medicinal), include **butterfly weed** (expectorant), **calendula** (skin irritations), **gotu kola** (brain function), and **skullcap** also known as **mad dog** (diuretic). The Starks also raise numerous Chinese medicinals, herbs that are for the most part totally unknown to me. **Schisandra** (Wu-wei-zu), also referred to as "Chinese Prozac" has adaptogenic and immune-enhancing properties similar to ginseng. **Tibetan Gentian**, a rare medicinal species from

OWNERS: Kristina and Peter Stark
TYPE: Specialty nursery
SPECIALTIES: Herbs; organic vegetables; organic plants; and seeds
HOURS: May thru Aug.: Thurs.-Sat. 10:00 am to 4:00 pm, closed Sundays and holidays. Sept. thru Apr.: by appointment only.
CATALOG AVAILABLE: Online
MAIL-ORDER AVAILABLE: Yes
DISPLAY GARDENS: Yes
CLASSES: Yes

CONTACT
4450 Valentine Road
Whitmore Lake, MI 48189-9691
PHONE: (734) 449-8336
WEB ADDRESS:
http://www.provide.net~raohf
EMAIL: raohf@provide.net

DIRECTIONS
FROM ANN ARBOR: Take US-23 north for 8 miles to Territorial Road. Drive west on Territorial Road for 2.1 miles to Jennings Road. Turn north (right) on Jennings toward Valentine Rd. Turn west (left) on Valentine and drive 1.0 miles to the nursery on your right. The owners request all parking be in front of the greenhouse.

GPS: N 42° 24.17', W 83° 49.33'

MICHIGAN

> *"Die when I may, I want it said of me by those who knew me best, that I always plucked a thistle and planted a flower where I thought a flower would grow."*
>
> —ABRAHAM LINCOLN

Tibet, is used to expel wind dampness, jaundice, and "dry constipation," perhaps the answer to those who find their laxative just doesn't do the trick.

Still figuring out the difference between an herb and a spice? "For the most part, the difference between herbs and spices can be easily defined," says Kris. "Herbs are the leaves of fresh or dried plants, and spices are the aromatic parts: fruits, berries, buds, roots, and bark that have been dried." Sometimes a plant can supply both an herb and a spice. For example, take **cilantro**. We call the fresh leaves cilantro, but the aromatic seeds are known as **coriander**.

Renaissance Acres offers well-rooted plants, mostly grown in 3-inch containers. For the most part, these are starter plants and as such, need to be transplanted into larger containers—or the ground—as soon as possible. At the greenhouse and gift shop, Renaissance Acres offers live plants lined out in larger containers, heirloom **tomato** plants, potted and freshly harvested veggies such as **kale, swiss chard**, and fresh tomatoes (in season). The gift shop stocks hand-rolled pure beeswax candles, rustic furniture, pottery, and beneficial insects. The nursery also sells seed, which is harvested from their own plants, gathered from wild plants, or bought from other seed companies; however, all seed is guaranteed to be untreated.

The nursery carries 25 varieties of **hot peppers**, some with such intriguing names as 'Rat Tail', 'Rat Turd' (small, orange, and shaped just like your imagination paints them) and 'Pretty Purple Pepper' (purple plants, red peppers). They also sell a delightful 150 recipe collection cookbook, entitled *In the Herb Garden*, showcasing new culinary delights. Their display gardens are planted alphabetically in rectangular beds and are open to the public during regular business hours.

The herbs offered here cover a range of uses. The majority of herbs raised at Renaissance Acres are culinary, but medicinal herbs are slowly gaining ground. Common culinary herbs grown at the nursery includes **basil** (20 varieties), **tarragon, chives** (3 varieties, including a rare Chinese chive), **fennel** (3 varieties), **oregano** (2 varieties), **rosemary** (7 varieties), and **dill**. Ornamental herbs include **angelica, bugloss, cardoon, feverfew, peppergrass, unicorn plant,** and **vitex**. Herbs used for the extraction of dyes include **agrimony** (yellow, gold, and green dye), amaranth (red), bloodroot (red), elecampane (blue), and loosestrife (yellow). There is chamomile, ephedra, and mint for tea; catnip for cats; echinacea and St. John's wort for all that ails us. A half-acre production field is just for fresh cut herbs.

What a selection! I had to crack open books for explanations of asafoetida (far-eastern condiment), madder (dye plant), mugwort (tea), shungiku (culinary), tea ree (antibacterial, antifungal and antiviral), weld (dye), and withiana (sedative). Insect repellent herbs, which release their scent only when brushed or bruised, include santolina (reputed to be the most effective natural insecticide) and lemon thyme.

For you lavender lovers, Renaissance Acres carries 20 varieties of lavender— named 1999 Herb of the Year by the International Herb Association. The Starks note that lavender is usually thought of as a fragrant garden plant only, but in reality it can also be used in cooking. What most people may not be aware of is that lavender is often included in the seasoning mix Herbes de Provence. Lavender makes good herbal oils and colorful vinegars. Lavender oil relieves burns, and pain and stiffness. Vinegar infused with lavender is an antidote for tension headaches.

Saguaro Nursery & Gardens

⊷⊷

S aguaro offers a broad selection of more than 2,000 varieties of hardy plants and 1,000 varieties of tender plants. This nursery specializes in rare desert, house, tropical, and hardy plants but also sells unusual annuals, herbs, and temperennials (temperate perennials). Some, like hoyas, begonias, orchids, succulents, cacti, bromeliads, and the newer varieties of jade plants, are popular greenhouse subjects; others are newer, alien creatures.

Richard Tuttle was a graduate student in botany in the early 1970s when he opened a plant boutique inside a laundromat near the campus. Several moves and thirty years later, Saguaro Nursery & Gardens is anybody's definition of a horticultural gem. A far cry from the cramped quarters of the laundromat, the present reincarnation of the nursery sits on 22 acres, providing elbow room for greenhouses, display gardens, a sales area, and a gift shop.

In a trellissed sales area by the parking lot, in what looks like a display garden but is instead an ingenious sales lot, Saguaro Nursery offers its collection of hardy perennials, woody shrubs, dwarf conifers, and bamboo and ornamental grasses, including some stunning, imported, Chinese tree peonies from Cricket Hill. Between the intricacies associated with importation, propagation, and time spent in the fields, mature Chinese tree

OWNERS: Richard Ford and Raven Tuttle
TYPE: Large retail nursery
SPECIALTIES: Perennials—sun and shade; annuals; alpines; shrubs—rare; grasses; aquatics; temperennials; houseplants; tropical plants; succulents; containers; bamboo
HOURS: April thru Christmas: Tues.-Sun. 10:00 am to 6:00 pm; Jan. 1 thru Mar. 31: by appointment only.
CATALOG AVAILABLE: No
MAIL-ORDER AVAILABLE: No
DISPLAY GARDENS: Yes
CLASSES: Yes

CONTACT

470 W. Five Mile Road
Whitmore Lake, MI 48189
PHONE: (734) 449-4237
FAX: (734) 449-2114
WEB ADDRESS: www.saguaroplants.com
EMAIL: saguaro@earthlink.net

DIRECTIONS

FROM THE BRIGHTON AREA: Take US-23 south to Six Mile Road (Exit 50) head west over the overpass to Whitmore Lake Road. Turn left (south) onto Whitmore Lake Road, and drive 1 mile to Five Mile Road. Turn (right) onto Five Mile Road. The nursery is ¹/₂ mile down on your right (at this point it is called W. Five Mile Road). **FROM ANN ARBOR AREA:** Take US-23 north to N. Territorial (Exit 49). Turn west (left) a short distance and drive to Whitmore Lake Road (first intersection), turn north (right) onto Whitmore Lake Road to Five Mile Road. Turn west (left) onto Five Mile Road WATCH FOR SIGN. Nursery is ¹/₂ mile down Five Mile Road on your right.

GPS: N 42° 23.16', W 83° 46.86'

MICHIGAN

peonies can be expensive. However, when properly planted and cared for, a Chinese tree peony can live for upwards of 300 years; a perfect living legacy for your heirs.

WHAT YOU'LL FIND

The best selection and freshest plants are, of course, in spring and early summer, yet Saguaro manages excellent stock throughout the entire season. On my last visit late in the growing season, I noted healthy, well-grown *Caryopteris* 'Blue Knight', *Acer japonicum,* 'Aconitifolium', blooming **seven son flower** (*Heptacodium miconioides*), healthy **serviceberries** (*Amelanchier*), and graceful **fountain bamboo** (*Fargesii nitida*).

If on the trees the leaves still hold,
the coming winter will be cold."
—ANONYMOUS

The nursery carries some hard-to-find wildflowers such as **toad lily** (*Tricyrtis dilatata*); **dwarf Solomon seal** (*Polygonatum humile*); a non-ephemeral **bluebell** (*Mertensia asiatica*); **Celandine poppy** (*Stylophorum diphyllum*), the native **astilbe** (*Astilbe biternata*), **iris** (*Iris cristata*), and **oconee bells** (*Shortia galacifolia*). I found it heartening to see prairie plants such as the gray-headed **coneflower**, purple **prairie clover**, darling **prairie skullcap**, a profusion of wine-red **poppy mallow, Indian grass,** Willa Cather's beloved "reed grass," **little bluestem,** the feathery plumes of **prairie smoke,** and imposing **prairie dock.** "A lot of these plants can take both drought and heavy rain," says Tuttle. "They're adapted for both and, as such, are a good recommendation for global warming gardening." One of the primary advantages of many native prairie plants is that their root systems go down deeper, reaching long term water sources that make regular watering virtually unnecessary.

Saguaro's desert plants are just as captivating. A bewildering array of armed cacti and succulents, a specialty of Tuttle and well beyond my skills, left me dumbfounded. I noted alien **ant plants**, such as *Hydnophytum formicarium* and *Myrmecodia tuberosa*—bulbous "condos" above ground where ants love to live; an aerial **yam** (*Dioscorea elephantipes*), whose most striking feature is an enormous, cracked, gray tuber growing on the ground; 'Baby Ears' (*Fenestraria rhopalophylla*). and 'Tiger Jaws' (*Faucaria tigrina*). They also had choices of *Lithops*, or **living stones.** I saw variegated and striped **dwarf aloe**; a group of clump-forming succulents (*Haworthia*) banded, tentacled, or fringed with long silver hairs; and the

MICHIGAN

almost perfectly spherical **baseball plant** (*Euphorbia obesa*). For other cacti-challenged gardeners like myself, there are delightful hypertufa's already crammed with these small plants. For those with individualized tastes, Saguaro will gladly assemble customized mixes.

The nursery offers a vast assortment of tropical and container plants, one of which is the seductive **angel's trumpet** (*Brugmansia*). In their **jade** collection, I noted two newer cultivars, *Crassula ovata* 'Hobbit' and 'Gollum', named for characters from the trilogy and blockbuster, *The Lord of the Rings*.

Impressive display gardens, at once educational and aesthetically pleasing, surround and wrap the property in colorful, ever bolder waves. Floriferous beds, peaty bogs, and stunning ornamental woodlands showcase plants available at the nursery, leading one to postulate whether the nursery exists to support the landscaping or the mere presence of the stunning gardens sustains the business.

The nursery's healthy plant stock comes from in-house propagation; some are grown from seed or plugs, and some are brought in from reputable growers. Handsome Italian terracotta containers, pots from additional regional sources, garden art, and organic supplies can be found alongside the barn. The gift shop carries candles, antique-look jewelry, and plant related gifts.

As their sign warns, the resident pooches, territorial critters that they are, do not throw out welcome mats for other canines. Better to leave your dogs in the car.

SUNSHINE PERENNIAL NURSERY

❧ ❧

Shrubs and vines give function and form to the landscape, but it's the perennials that give it pizzaz. Sunshine Perennial Nursery specializes in a limited line of field grown perennials that are intriguing, colorful, and hardy. It appears rather nondescript from curb-side, but inside Sunshine Perennial Nursery turns out to be quite the appealing place. It's not big, but Sunshine is the kind of nursery worth spending quality time in for rummaging through all the potted containers. It is a friendly place where the nursery staff knows the customers by name and in turn the customers feel appreciated enough to share their unusual plants with the nursery.

One such plant, brought in by a customer, is the hardy begonia, *Begonia grandis*. The customer's variety, much taller than typical, has established quite a large, respectable clump in the display garden, but more importantly, it can now be purchased.

A quaint, small greenhouse, perhaps more decorative than functional, is the heart of the sales area. Home to a variety of herbs early in the spring, it is where all cultural requirement placards are stored, sales are rung up, and the easy confidences of plant mishaps and triumphs are exchanged.

The display gardens at Sunshine Perennial Nursery are surprisingly large, innovative, and well designed. For the most part, plants are well labeled, but the few varieties missing placards are quickly identified by the helpful and attentive staff.

OWNERS: Shirley and Sam Somora
TYPE: Small specialty nursery
SPECIALTIES: Peonies; daylilies; hosta; perennials—shade and sun
HOURS: April thru Oct 30: Mon.-Sun. 10:00 am to 6:00 pm.
CATALOG: No
MAIL ORDER AVAILABLE: No
DISPLAY GARDENS: Yes
CLASSES: No

CONTACT
1251 W. Hinchman Road
Baroda, MI 49101
PHONE: (269) 422-2126

DIRECTIONS
FROM I-94: Take I-94 to Red Arrow Hwy (Exit 16) towards, Bridgman. Proceed northeast on the Red Arrow Hwy for 0.1 miles to Lake Street. Turn east (right) onto Lake Street (Lake becomes W. Shawnee Road) and drive for 3.4 miles to Cleveland Avenue. Turn north (left) onto Cleveland, drive 2.0 miles to Hinchman Road. Turn east (right) onto W. Hinchman; the nursery is 0.5 miles down on your left. **FROM US-31:** Take US-31 to Hinchman. Turn East (left) onto Hinchman and drive 5.1 miles to the nursery on your right.

GPS: N 41° 58.29', W 86° 29.01'

MICHIGAN

WHAT YOU'LL FIND

Sunshine's policy is that they "grow each and every plant three full years" before offering it to the public. Plants are first field-tested in the display gardens, then if worthy are grown out in the fields behind the nursery. A limited number of peonies and daylilies, are field-grown right on the nursery grounds, and customers interested in these can reserve them with a deposit.

> *"Flowers are nature's jewels, with whose wealth she decks her summer beauty."*
> —GEORGE CROLY

Sunshine offers more than 400 varieties of lush, pre-potted, well-grown, well-rooted perennials in good sized containers. The nursery also offers more than 400 **daylilies** available field grown or in containers. For a small nursery, the **peony** selections are quite extensive—45 different cultivars, including the gorgeous, yellow Itoh peony 'Yellow Heaven', an outstanding plant resulting from a cross between herbaceous and tree peonies. The plants are big, reasonably priced specimens.

Sunshine Perennial Nursery offers a treasure trove of woodland plants: popular **Jack-in-the-pulpit**, **ginger**, fiery **columbine**, pristine **snowdrops**, heart-shaped **epimedium**, and **tiarella**. You'll also find silvered **lungwort**, **lenten rose**, dainty **bleeding heart**, **creeping phlox**, and **Virginia bluebells**. There are decorative plants such as blue **amsonia**, white **rock cress**, different colored **poppy**, tall **bearded iris**, **penstemon**, and **malva**. Indispensable classics include **campanula**, **coral bells**, and **hosta**. Also available are exceptional cottage garden plants such as **hollyhock**, **perennial phlox**, **fern leaf yarrow**,

★ SIDE TRIPS ★

FERNWOOD BOTANICAL GARDEN AND NATURE PRESERVE, (616) 695-6491, 13988 Range Line Road, Niles, Michigan. This is a public garden with acres of themed gardens, a conservatory, art displays, a 40-acre arboretum, and a 50-acre wooded nature preserve. Knot, herb, rock, fragrance, children's and English cottage gardens are included. There is also a gift shop and cafeteria. From I-80/90 take US 31 north to Walton Road (Exit 7), follow signs.

dianthus, and **clematis**; enhanced varieties of cottage-garden classics such as **campanula**, **veronica**, **delphinium**, and **cranesbill geranium** are screened for both durability and usefulness.

There is a little pocket in the shady sales area, a wee region appropriately called "The Connoisseur's Corner," where treasures, such as an incredibly robust *Kirengeshoma palmata,* abound. The nursery also offers woody shrubs— *Caryopteris* 'First Choice', **Korean lilac**, and burgundy **smokebush**, among others—perfectly suited for double duty as singular specimen plants or complimentary perennial companions.

Although Sunshine Perennial Nursery sells no annuals and has no catalog or mail-order, visitors can count on finding well-chosen ornamental perennials, vines, shrubs, and trees throughout the season. Given the countrified location of this nursery, its plant selection has a keen, up-to-date edge to it.

TELLY'S GREENHOUSE

❧ ❧

This is one of a handful of garden centers that I heard about over and over again. There was always a common refrain, "This place has some of the newest and greatest plants at good prices." You know what? They were right! Telly's Greenhouse is a popular nursery and garden center on the northern fringes of Detroit that could, if it wanted to, boast of being a destination garden center. It has built its reputation on specializing in rare, unusual, and remarkable plants that are hard to find in the normal horticultural channels, as well as offering their customers hundreds of new perennial introductions annually. The nursery carries more than 4,000 varieties of perennials (1,000 varieties under $5), 2,000 varieties of annuals, 200 roses, and 300 herb and vegetable plants.

Back in 1978, young George set up a roadside stand in front of his parents home to sell to passing motorists the tiny plants that he had started himself. The venture proved profitable and productive, growing in size throughout each successive summer until George decided to return with his biology degree to the original farmstand. With a lot of support from his parents and wife, Kellie, George says he has "parlayed a table full of homegrown flowers into acres of healthy blossoms."

WHAT YOU'LL FIND

Telly's has amassed unsurpassed holdings of **coral bells** (a passion of mine), **coreopsis, daylily, phlox, hardy geranium, iris, toad lily, peony, epimedium, bleeding heart, foxglove, hellebore, aster, columbine**, and **mum**.

OWNER: George Papadelis
TYPE: Large garden center
SPECIALTIES: Perennials—shade and sun; annuals; tender perennials; tropicals; and summer bulbs; hanging baskets; roses; herbs; aquatics; vines; grasses; garden art; containers; topiary
HOURS: Mon.-Sat. 9:00 am to 6:00 pm, Sun. 10:00 am to 6:00 pm.
CATALOG AVAILABLE: No
MAIL-ORDER AVALABLE: No
DISPLAY GARDENS: Yes
CLASSES: Yes

CONTACT
3301 John R Road
Troy, MI 48083
PHONE: (248) 689-8735
FAX: (248) 689-8730
WEB ADDRESS: www.tellysgreenhouse.com
EMAIL: tellysghs@aol.com

DIRECTIONS
FROM I-696 (WALTER P. REUTHER FWY): Take I-696 to I-75. Drive north on I-75 for 6.5 miles to Rochester Road, Exit 67. Proceed North (right) on Rochester for 0.2 miles to Big Beaver Road. Turn east (right) on Big Beaver Road for 1.2 miles to John R. Road. The nursery is 0.3 miles down. Look for plantings by the street.

GPS: N 42° 34.19', W 83° 06.51'

MICHIGAN

One of the "holy grail" of plants for the Midwest, a plant all of us lust for but few can grow, is the blue **Himalayan poppy**. For the discerning gardener, or the hortiholic willing to push boundaries, Telly's can supply both *Meconopsis* × *sheldonii* and *Meconopsis betonicifolia*. On my visit, a collection of oriental poppies preened like contestants in a beauty pageant. While there is no such thing as an ugly oriental poppy, cultivars exhibit wide differences in height, habit, and color—which can range from the familiar scarlet and crimson to orange, pink, white, peach, and even a shade of purple.

> *"Flowers are love's truest language."*
> —PARK BENJAMIN

Whoever said "less is more," has never seen Telly's peony selection. Any astute plant hunter knows that "more is more" when encountering this incredible selection: fernleaf peony *Paeonia* 'Smouthii' (crimson-red); P. 'Dia-Jo-Kuhan' (semi-double Japanese-style peony with blossoms in a rare bright lemon-yellow) or P. 'Dancing Butterflies' (bright lipstick-pink).

Telly's was an early promoter of **hostas**, and today maintains a collection of 300 worthy cultivars. They are a major source of topiaries, offering spiral, mop-head, and globe shapes in evergreens, herbs, and ivies. For the patio or container layouts, Telly's offers enchanting flower standards of **coleus**, blooming tropicals, and **poinsettia** (early winter) clipped into the standard lollipop shapes. They have an extensive selection of spring blooming woodland plants such as **trillium, bloodroot, Virginia bluebells**, and **Jack-in-the-pulpit**. I should mention that the selection of aquatic plants and all things "pond-y" is extensive. Most of Telly's choice **roses**, selected for Michigan hardiness and hardy root stock, come from Bellarose in Ontario, Canada, and cover the gamut of roses: hybrid teas, floribundas, miniatures, carpet, climbers, shrub, grandifloras, antique, English, Canadian Explorer™, and Canadian Morden Parkland™.

Display borders grace the property curbside and surround the gray farmhouse located on nursery land. Here Tom Guibord, Perennial Manager, trials new and exciting stock—a spin around the premises to view his efforts is highly recommended.

There are tables filled with ground covers, perennial vines, alpines, and ornamental grasses. The golden wood **millet**, *Milium effusum* 'Aureum' (a dense mound of beautiful chartreuse-yellow foliage) is a superb companion intermingling with hostas or ferns, and definitely caught my attention.

The shop carries more than 2,000 varieties of annuals, 100-plus selections of coleus, and does a brisk business in very special hanging baskets featuring riveting and jazzy plant combinations. They also promote hundreds of old, new, underused, and rare annuals that look great planted out in perennial beds. Stock is replenished weekly. Consequently, even late in the season, plants look fresh.

Telly's offers an impressive selection of large pottery containers, moss baskets, grapevine wreaths, posey pouches, patio planters, window boxes, tools, statuary, garden benches, arbors, and botanically themed gifts. Come fall, the nursery stocks more than 100,000 traditional and specialty bulbs for, according to the catalog, "one of the largest selections of bulbs available in Southeast Michigan." They also offer mums in bewitching colors, and frost-tolerant annuals such as **pansies**, **stock**, and **flowering kale**. According to the National Gardening Survey conducted by the non-profit National Gardening Association, Midwestern gardeners plant more flower bulbs than gardeners in any other region.

Holiday magic is available with Christmas trees, Christmas cactus, flowering plants, wreaths, roping, and poinsettias. Check their website for more information and sign up for their excellent newsletter.

EXTRAS

In August and October, savvy plant hunters descend in droves to partake of their enticing sales. Free lectures and workshops (registration required) are offered to experienced as well as novice gardeners on such subjects as gardening with hostas, spring wood gardening, annual and perennial vines, rose selection and care, spring bulbs, and ornamental grasses. A popular annual event is the container gardening workshop. (My sources tell me this fills up early, so, if you're interested, don't dawdle in registering.) Bring your own container (or purchase one), and let Telly's staff guide you through successful plant combinations for either sun or shade.

WAVECREST NURSERY

❧ ❧

Wavecrest Nursery is a family owned second-generation business that caters to the needs of upscale gardeners throughout southwestern Michigan. It was founded in 1960 by Robert Louis Tomayer, who had a keen interest in plants and a desire to collect and sell many rare and unusual varieties. Today, the nursery is in the capable hands of his daughter, Carol. Wavecrest is treasured by serious gardeners for its noteworthy collections of trees and shrubs, rare conifers, choice ornamental grasses, and stalwart perennials. The nursery backs up to the Hop residence, whose garden holds a true rarity—a mature, blooming (in season) *Davidia involucrata*, the dove tree. The tree's most distinctive feature, and the reason for its name, is the pair of eye-catching papery white bracts giving the impression that flocks of white doves are roosting in the tree's branches. The nursery offers an incredible cultivar of this tree, 'Vilmoriniana', available both at the nursery and by mail-order.

In the Barn Owl Gift Shop, Wavecrest Nursery offers a wide selection of bird feeders, a unique collection of birdbaths, interesting statuary and art forms, a good selection of sundials, and an array of stone benches and fountains. Additionally, the gift shop offers some fine gardening tools, books, and gifts.

WHAT YOU'LL FIND

Wavecrest carries an exceptional range of enticing rare plant material—more than 1,400 varieties—not readily available elsewhere. Deciduous trees

OWNER: Carol T. Hop
TYPE: Specialty nursery
SPECIALTIES: Trees and shrubs; conifers; perennials; ornamental grasses
HOURS: Mid-March thru October: Mon.-Sat. 10:00 am to 5:00 pm, Sun. Noon to 5:00 pm.
CATALOG AVAILABLE: Online
MAIL-ORDER AVAILABLE: Yes
DISPLAY GARDENS: Yes
CLASSES: No

CONTACT
2509 Lakeshore Drive
Fennville, MI 49408
PHONE: (616) 543-4175
FAX: (616) 543-4100
(888) 869-4159 Order Dept.
WEB ADDRESS: www.wavecrestnursery.com
EMAIL: wavecrest@i2k.com

DIRECTIONS
DIRECTIONS FROM I-196 DIRECTLY WEST OF FENNVILLE: Exit I-196 at M-89 (Exit 34). Proceed west on M-89 over the expressway to Lakeshore Drive, 0.25 miles west (Road ends in a T). Turn north (right) and drive 0.5 miles to the nursery which is on your right. (Lakeshore Drive is a narrow lane road through scenic woods with residential homes scattered here and there.)

GPS: N 42° 36.01', W 86° 13.37'

MICHIGAN

> *"I think that I shall never see*
> *A poem lovely as a tree.*
> *A tree whose hungry mouth is prest*
> *Against the earth's sweet*
> *flowing breast."*
> —JOYCE KILMER

include the **American yellowwood**, *Cladrastis lutea* (with long fragrant panicles of white flowers in late spring); variegated giant **dogwood**, *Cornus controversa* 'Variegata' (showing horizontal branching and beautiful white and green foliage); and **Korean evodia**, *Evodia daniellii* (sports beech-like bark and masses of white flowers in midsummer, and red to black fruit in late August). Along with these are **castor aralia**, *Kalopanax pictus* (impressive and tropical in appearance, with large clusters of white flowers); **cut-leaf durmast oak**, *Quercus petrea insecta* (almost thread-like, deep-cut leaves); and, though technically a conifer and usually listed as deciduous, the **maindenhair tree**, *Ginkgo biloba* 'Princeton Gold' (a male noted for brilliant gold fall color).

Wavecrest offers a notable selection of **Japanese maples**, **buckeyes**, **service-berries**, **magnolias**, **Japanese dogwood**, and **beech** as well as the large grouping of **quince**, **summersweet**, **deutzia**, **barberry**, **hydrangea**, **clethra**, **viburnum**, and **rose of Sharon**. For the bonsai enthusiast, the nursery carries some incredible **dwarf boxwood** ('Morris Midget' and 'Kingsville Dwarf'), **hornbeam** (*Carpinus coreana*), and **weeping willow** (*Salix repens* 'Boyd's Pendula).

The beauty of small trees is reason enough to include them in your garden. Beyond handsome foliage, colorful blossoms, or striking bark, small trees can bridge the gap between taller trees and shrubs and ground covers. I seriously coveted the weeping **European beech**, *Fagus sylvatica* 'Pendula' (with contorted stems and branches growing in almost any direction), the **seven sons flower**, *Heptacodium miconioides* (small, fragrant white flowers and showy fall color), and the copper beauty **witchhazel**, *Hamamelis* × *intermedia* 'Jelena' (large, outstanding flowers glow like copper when in bloom). I felt most thrilled to bring home a **scotch laburnum**, *Laburnum alpinum,* which will have pendulous racemes, of golden yellow flowers come next May (I hope).

They also offer a wide variety of conifers: dwarf, weeping, and contorted, plus the rare and unusual. Some freaky examples brought forth by nurserymen with a good sense of humor include *Larix* × *eurolepsis* 'Varied Directions', (top grafted on a standard, branches emerging in an octopus arm-like fashion). It is perfectly named. Once described as "Phyllis Diller on a bad hair day", this plant never ceases to attract. Another oddity, *Picea glauca* 'Pendula', is a very narrow spruce whose extremely pendulous branches almost brush the central leader. Tim Boland,

MICHIGAN

Curator of Horticultural Collections at The Morton Arboretum, once said of 'Pendula' "In silhouette the tree appears out of a Dr. Seuss landscape. In fact, maybe it's the tree that was shoved up the chimney when the Grinch stole Christmas."

Other singular conifers—in strange shapes, different forms, and interesting colors—include a number of cypress: *Chamaecyparis obtusa* 'Blue Feathers' (soft blue foliage), *C. o.* 'Cripsii', (bright golden yellow fern-like foliage), *C. o.* 'Kosteri' (cupped and twisted foliage), and *C. o.* 'Nana Lutea', (a dwarf with frosted lemon-yellow tips). I admired a couple of **junipers**, confections of blue-green foliage iced in golden yellow, *Juniperus* × *media* 'Daub's Frosted', and bold, columnar *J. scopulorum* 'Sparkling Skyrocket'. Fun finds include **Japanese white pine** *Pinus parviflora* 'Adcocks Dwarf', once described as a "meatball on a stick." Much used in bonsai, it grows into a feathery globe and *Cryptomeria japonica* 'Cristata', a small evergreen with cockscombed foliage looking for all the world like a alien reject from the local hen house.

Wavecrest's hybridization program has provided some remarkable notables including *Viburnum sieboldii* 'Wavecrest', *Sciadopitys verticillata* 'Wavecrest', *Berberis thunbergii* 'Antares', as well as more than 100 holly introductions. The nursery propagates its own stock, but due to the vast number of varieties the nursery grows, supplies are limited and popular shrubs often sell out fast. Trees and evergreens come in various sizes from 1-gallon containers to large, one-of-a-kind specimens in impressive health with freshly balled-and-burlapped root systems. The sales area is dense with well-labeled plants, the overflow attractively integrated into the ever-expanding display.

★ SIDE TRIPS ★

CRANE'S PIE PANTRY & RESTAURANT is famous for their incredible cakes and pies. 6054 124th Avenue, Fennville, MI, 49408, (269) 561-2297. **STAR OF SAUGATUCK BOAT CRUISES** in Saugatuck let's you paddlewheel down the Kalamazoo River, (269) 857-4261. The **TULIP FESTIVAL** in Holland, MI is a fun event usually held early- to mid-May, (800) 822-2770. **VELDHEER TULIP GARDENS, DEKLOMP WOODEN SHOE,** and **DELFTWARE FACTORY** are located on an 80 acre tulip farm and perennial garden in Holland, MI, where windmills, canals and drawbridges create an atmosphere that is distinctively Dutch, (616) 399-1900. **WINDMILL ISLAND** showcases a 240 year old Dutch windmill that is the centerpiece of this 36 acre complex with gardens—open April to October, (616) 355-1030.

WESTVIEW FARMS

❧ ❧

Westview Farms is a family owned and operated retail nursery located in a picturesque rural setting south of Holland, the Midwest's famous "tulip town." Founded in 1983 by husband and wife, Lee and Kay Ver Schure, the nursery shares space with the historic "Westview School," a 135-year old, two-room schoolhouse which serves as the couple's residence. Backed by display gardens that also act as the nursery's test fields (on what was once the "old ball field") is a 5,000 square foot combination greenhouse and sales area—the heart of the nursery operations. Though relatively small in size, what makes Westview Farms extra special is their genuine desire to help clients succeed with their garden. To that end, the Ver Schures offer exceptional personalized service and expert advice on plant selection and cultivation practices.

WHAT YOU'LL FIND

Westview Farms offers an outstanding selection of classic old favorites, interesting new cultivars, and some rather arresting choices of companion plantings, such as **rhododendrons**, **azaleas**, and **mountain laurel**. The nursery specializes in locally grown, winter-hardy perennial cultivars and species, as well as a very good selection of herbs propagated by seed or vegetatively by the Ver Schures. More importantly, the Ver Schures offer truly personalized service and

OWNERS: Kay and Lee Ver Schure
TYPE: Small garden center/nursery
SPECIALTIES: Perennials—sun and shade; herbs; annuals; shrubs; bulbs
HOURS: First weekend in May thru end of June: Mon.-Sat. 9:00 am to 5:00 pm, Sun. Noon to 5:00 pm, (Opening day is weather dependent. Please check before coming out.) July 1 thru Aug 31: Thurs.-Sat. 9:00 am to 5:00 pm, Sun. Noon to 5:00 pm; Sept: Sat.-Sun. Noon to 5:00 pm; also by special appointment.
CATALOG AVAILABLE: Printed plant list
MAIL-ORDER AVAILABLE: No
DISPLAY GARDENS: Yes (minimal)
CLASSES: Yes

CONTACT
4051 60th Street (Graafschap Road)
Holland, MI 49423-9330
PHONE: (616) 396-8858
FAX: (616) 396-3737
WEB ADDRESS: None
EMAIL: None

DIRECTIONS
FROM HOLLAND: Take 32nd Street west to Graafschap Road. Turn south (left) onto Graafschap Road. (60th St.) and drive 4 miles to nursery. **FROM SAUGATUCK:** Take Blue Star Hwy (Also called Washington Road in places) toward Holland, drive to 60th Street (Graafschap Road), turn north (left) onto 60th Street (Graafschap Road) and continue on for 1.25 miles to the nursery.

GPS: N 42° 42.63', W 86° 08.14'

MICHIGAN

expert advice, doing their best to insure that each plant that leaves their nursery will not only survive, but thrive—big time. Most perennials, acquired from local growers and grown in 1- or 2-gallon containers, are well rooted, robust plants.

Tucked in a corner behind the greenhouses, the nursery has a small gift shop selling a variety of gardening supplies, tools, gift items, bagged soil amendments, organic pest and disease controls, fertilizers, stepping stones, plant supports, and books. Additionally, Westview offers a heady assortment of garden and landscape services: overall consulting services, site analysis and evaluation, design services, installation, maintenance, and custom container plantings.

> *"Beauty is in the eye of the beholder."*
> —OLD PROVERB

On my recent visit to the nursery, I noted plants that would seduce even the more timid gardeners, such as the deep butter-yellow flowered **tickseed**, (*Coreopsis* 'Crème Brulee'); a deeper yellow fluted tickseed (C. 'Zamfir'); two **gaillardia** (*Gaillardia* 'Fanfare' and 'Tokayer'); a couple of interesting **hardy geraniums**: *Geranium* 'Black Beauty' (deep purple foliage and striking dark lilac/blue flowers); and the small G. 'Tiny Monster' (rose-purple). I also saw *Hibiscus* 'Plum Crazy', *Phlox* 'Shortwood', and *Sedum* 'Purple Emperor' (the improved *Sedum* 'Autumn Joy').

For the shade gardener, it would be easy to succumb to the charms of the black-edged **foamflower** *Tiarella* 'Black Snowflake'; **toad lily** *Tricyrtis* 'Gilt Edge' (with leaves of green variegated with gold accents); **lady fern** *Athyrium* 'Lady in Red' (vibrant burgundy running thru green fronds); and the almost black *Heuchera* 'Obsidian'.

Lee Ver Schure has always had a special interest in herbs, offering an outstanding array of perennial, biennial, and annual herbs valued for their culinary, ornamental, medicinal, and aromatic uses. He is instrumental in designing and installing a number of outdoor "herb gardens" on restaurant properties in Holland and Saugatuck for cutting-edge chefs interested in providing diners with the freshest of flavors. I am by no means a chef, but I do love the simple and savory taste of a good herb in a meal.

Specialists from across the country consider 14 basic herbs, called "kitchen herbs," essential garden and cooking ingredients. **Thyme** certainly fits this requirement since fresh, minced leaves make almost any dish more appetizing. (Seven different varieties of thyme can be had at the nursery.) The remaining

MICHIGAN

13, all available at Westview Farm are **basil** (12 varieties, including 'Sweet Dani', 'Magical Michael' and 'Holy Basil'), **sage**, **chives**, **cilantro** (Japanese and Vietnamese), **fennel**, **French tarragon**, **mint**, **oregano**, **parsley**, **rosemary**, **sweet bay**, **sweet marjoram**, and **winter savory**. Other culinary herbs worth noting were **perilla**, **arugula**, and **mitsuba** (Japanese parsley).

Culinary herb gardens are great, but using herbs throughout your landscape means greater possibilities—including more natural diversity and less work. Ver Schure notes that herbs demand little and yield much when allowed to sprawl, crawl, or climb naturally over the landscape.

Although perennials and herbs are definitely the main attraction at the nursery, Westview Farms does manage to carry a bit of everything. I found a good selection of ornamental grasses, ground covers, ferns, vines, native species, bog plants, and ephemeral wildflowers. For the vegetable grower, the nursery carries a number of classic **tomatoes** and **peppers**, interspersed with a fairly good offering of heirloom tomatoes such as Brandywine and Mr. Stripey.

SEARCHING OHIO

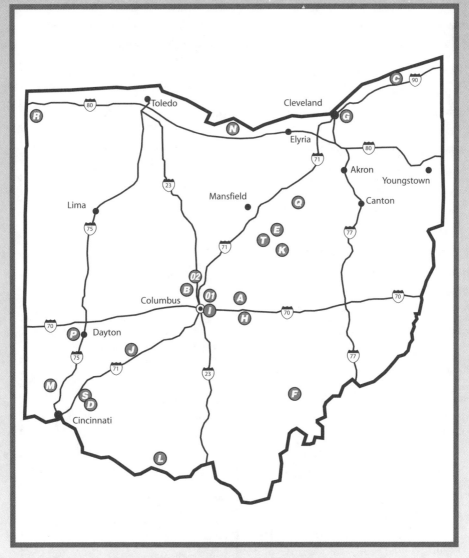

OHIO

BAKER'S ACRES GREENHOUSE

❧ ❧

Known region-wide, Baker's Acres, located a mere 25 miles northeast of Columbus, built its solid reputation on well-grown, high quality annual and perennial plants and exciting container plantings that defy the norm. Long known for its exceptional selections of interesting new, underused, and unusual plants, this "hot" nursery is respected in the gardening community not only as a premier storehouse of the rare and unusual, but also as a "fun" horticultural haven for novices and connoisseurs alike.

Nancy and Chris Baker, owners of Baker's Acres Greenhouse, approach the nursery business with a tongue-in-cheek humor that is not seen often these days. According to the catalog, Nancy, a degreed home economist, and Chris, with a degree in Music Theory and Composition, "ended up in the greenhouse biz" because "Nancy married incorrectly," and "Chris is a lousy composer."

The catalog, referred to as "The Papery Thing with the Words and Stuff," is comprehensive, but it would certainly be helpful to many novice gardeners (probably even accomplished ones) if descriptions accompanied the listings. However, a dear friend of mine and major gardening

OWNERS: Nancy and Chris Baker
TYPE: Large retail nursery
SPECIALTIES: Annuals; perennials—sun and shade; container plants; herbs; vegetables; vines; trees; shrubs
HOURS: April: Mon.-Sat. 9:00 am to 7:00 pm, Sun. 10:00 am to 5:00 pm; May: Mon-Sat. 9:00 am to 8:00 pm, Sun 10:00 am to 5:00 pm; June: Mon.-Sat. 9:00 am to 7:00 pm, Sun. 11:00 am to 5:00 pm; July: Mon.-Sat. 9:00 am to 5:00 pm, Sun. Noon to 4:00 pm; Aug.: Wed.-Sat. 9:00 am to 4:00 pm, Sun. Noon to 4:00 pm; Sept.: Mon.-Sat. 9:00 am to 5:00 pm, Sun. Noon to 4:00 pm; Oct.: closed first week.
NOTE: Baker's Acres "reserves the right to close early when the temperature exceeds 92 F." (On hot days over 90 F., it is advisable to call before heading out to the nursery.)
CATALOG AVAILABLE: Printed and online
MAIL-ORDER AVAILABLE: No
DISPLAY GARDENS: Yes
CLASSES: No

CONTACT
3388 Castle Road
Alexandria, OH 43001
PHONE: (740) 924-6525; (800) 934-6525
FAX: (740) 924-0500
WEB ADDRESS:
www.bakersacresgreenhouse.com
EMAIL: bakrzakrz@voyager.net

DIRECTIONS
FROM THE COLUMBUS AREA: Take OH-62 northeast to Duncan Plains Road. Turn southeast (right) onto Duncan Plains Road continuing toward OH-37. (Duncan Plains Road makes a sharp left turn before OH-37 at which point it becomes Castle Road) Continue on Castle Rd. across (north of) OH-37 for 0.2 miles. Nursery is on the right.

GPS: N 40° 06.53', W 82° 38.39'

maven from Columbus calls the catalog "one major hoot" and spends quality time reading it.

Events worth checking into are the "Not Quite All Night Extravaganza," the "Shop with a Friend" program, the "Feed Me" signup, and of, course, the two very popular (there are waiting lists) "garden parties" held every year. Did I pique your interest?

Pick a sunny morning, invite a friend (Tuesday is best—ask about "Shop with a Friend"), empty the car of all but the rudimentary basics, and make a day trip of it. Don't forget to check out the bathroom—you've never seen anything like it. The line forms over there...

WHAT YOU'LL FIND

Today's hottest horticultural trend is all about tropicals. Wickedly cool, shamanistic *Brugmansia* and *Datura*, red and green **banana trees**, *Phormiums*, and **paddle-leaved cannas**, are all the "darling" showboat annuals of today. And Baker's Acres, a cutting-edge nursery always on the prowl for the new and the exciting, is the place to go for these annuals, tropicals and temperennials (tender perennials) so popular today. Baker's Acres offers a wonderful selection of these exotic plants for use as focal points, as accents, or in grouped vignettes. Plants are trucked in on a more or less regular basis during the early weeks of spring. Obviously, repeat visits early in the season could be quite rewarding.

Although tropical plants are for the most part not hardy in the Midwest, many such as the **jumbo-leaved banana** can grow up to 8 feet tall, in just one season. Sporting burgundy-backed leaves 6 feet or longer, **red-leaf Abyssinian banana** (*Ensete ventricosum* 'Maurellii') makes as bold a statement in the garden or container as any gardener could hope for. Many extraordinary tropicals, still little known among gardeners, appear on the nursery's plant list. I found **copper leaf** (*Acalypha*), 8 varieties of **angel's trumpet** (*Brugmansia*), assorted colors of *Bougainvillea*, 9 different **canna**, **elephant ear** (*Alocasia* and *Colocasia*), **bed of nails** (*Solanum quitoense*), **pigeon berries** (*Duranta erecta*), **Persian shield** (*Strobilanthes dyerianus*), exotic looking annual **sages**, and some really fine *Alternanthera*..

And then there were the **coleus** plants! Though Baker's Acres might not have the largest collection of coleus plant varieties in the state, it has to be an extremely close second, with somewhere around 150 cultivars in a seemingly endless variety of colors, patterns, leaf shapes, and growth habits. Any gardener worth his mettle

OHIO

will have a hard time choosing a favorite from this bevy of outrageous plants, some of which are exclusive to Baker's Acres such as 'Blond Bombshell', 'Kiwi Herman', 'Purple Pumpernickel', 'Copacetic Yellow', and 'Doctor Wu'.

> "I appreciate the misunderstanding I have had with nature over my perennial border. I think it is a flower garden: she thinks it is a meadow lacking grass and tries to correct the error."
>
> —SARA STEIN

The nursery also excels in greenhouse-grown annuals and tender perennials—plants of superior flower power that begin blooming early in spring and continue nonstop until frost cuts them down. Baker's Acres grows scads of **flowering maple**, *Diascia*, and **lantana**. They have an explosion of **petunia** varieties from Wave™, Supertunia™, and Tiny Tunia™, to petunia-like *Calibrachoa* Million Bells™, Minifamous™, and Superbells™. **Tuberous begonias** are there, with evocative names such as 'Antholes', 'Hawaiian Freakout', 'Rhinestone Jeans', 'Streaky Jeans', and 'Wild Fury'. These stand cheek to jowl with **geranium** (zonal, ivy, and scented), **double impatiens**, and **licorice plant**. An interesting panoply of **New Guinea impatiens** bounces off the vivid colorations of **sweet potato vine** 'Marguerite'. There are diverse configurations of **verbena** such as Aztec™, Superbena™, Tapien™, Temari™, Babylon™, and Wildfire™; and an amazing array of **caladium**, **dahlia**, **bacopa**, *Alternanthera* species, and **pentas**.

Springtime visitors will find thriving pots of herbs and vegetables in the greenhouses. Tomato seedlings include uncommon varieties such as the heirloom 'Mortgage Lifter', 'Mr. Stripey', 'Old German', 'Green Zebra', 'Druzba', ' and 'Cherokee Purple'. Dazzling hanging baskets (more than 3,000) fly out the doors Mother's Day weekend teeming with every sort of flower and color combination imaginable.

As wonderful as the annual stock may be, Baker's Acres also built its reputation at the perennial end of the spectrum by offering plants that are hard to find in the horticultural trade. There are other plants, though pedestrian, that are strong, healthy, and very well grown.

Outside the greenhouses, Baker's Acres offers ornamental grasses, hardy perennials, and hardy trees and shrubs. Woodland gardeners will be pleased to see **rue anemone**, **snowdrops**, **Jack-in-the-pulpit**, **spring beauty**, **liverleaf**, **trillium**, **twin leaf**, **Virginia bluebells**, and **mayapple**. Perennial collections include **daylily**,

OHIO

dianthus, some lovely old-fashioned **campanula** and **phlox**, stately **delphinium**, **hosta**, **aster**, **penstemon**, and **heuchera**.

You'll see interesting selections of **dianthus** ('Gran's Favorite', 'Heart Attack'), **cranesbill** (*Geranium* 'Purple Pillow', 'Silver Shadow', 'Terra Franche', 'Jolly Bell'), *Monarda* ('Stone's Throw Pink', 'Snow White', 'Ohio Glow', 'Colrain Red'), **evening primrose** (*Oenothera* 'Comanche Campfire', 'Lemon Sunset', 'Summer Solstice') and more phlox (a variegated 'Silvermine' and 'Rubymine'). Gardeners in central Ohio rarely encounter such distinctive perennials as **desert mallow** (*Sphaeralcea ambigua*), **wooly sunflower** (*Eriophyllum lanatum*), **willow herb** (*Epilobium fleischeri*), **umbrella leaf** (*Diphyllia cymosa*), **dragons head** (*Dracocephalum forrestii*), and **kings spear** (*Asphodeline lutea*).

Bakers carries intriguing items such as **dawn redwood** (*Metasequoia*), **bottle-brush buckeye** (*Aesculus parviflora*), **chocolate vine** (*Akebia quinata*), and **paw paw** (*Asimina triloba*). Popular flowering shrubs include **hydrangea**, **azalea**, **butterfly bush**, **spirea**, **rhododendron**, and **lilac**; and stalwarts of the garden, such as **crabapple**, **magnolia**, and **viburnum**. For vertical interest there is **clematis**, **trumpet vine**, and **wisteria**; but when your garden is full of preening beauties, Baker's Acres has some little charmers in the categories of alpines, ground covers and trough plants.

OHIO

BAKERS VILLAGE GARDEN CENTER

❧ ❧

B akers Village Garden Center is a large, stylish, upscale garden center a few miles northwest of Columbus. Encompassing 5 acres at the garden center location, plus an additional 15 acres nearby, Bakers Village is a Columbus institution specializing in custom containers, excellent container-grown perennials, annuals, grasses, herbs, vines, roses, and other ornamental garden plants.

The nursery's plants, sold in various sized containers, are a vigorous lot. They are sold with tags noting botanical names and a full accounting of their horticultural needs. The staff—active, friendly, and helpful—is attentive and adept at assisting both novice and expert gardeners in selecting the right plant or accessory. A charming shop offers animal statuary, glazed pottery, baskets, butterfly houses, urns, wreaths, innovative floral table toppers, home accessories, furniture, books, spades, trowels, augers, and seasonal gifts.

Halloween, Thanksgiving and Christmas are major decorating events. The nursery offers fall revelers a rich smorgasbord of autumnal decorations and plants; while winter signals a flurry of activity. Every nook and cranny of the shop is transformed into a magical Christmas wonderland of trees, wreaths, swags, tree ornaments, table décor, lights, and seasonal gifts.

Most Bakers Village plants are propagated and grown out on the nearby acreage and in the nursery's greenhouses; some ornamental trees and woody shrubs are brought in from regional sources, mainly from Lake County.

OWNERS: Donna and Doug Baker
TYPE: Garden center/Nursery
SPECIALTIES: Perennials—sun and shade; roses; annuals—tender perennials; tropicals; summer bulbs; hanging baskets; vines; grasses; garden art; containers.
HOURS: Year-round. Mon.-Sat. 9:00 am to 6:00 pm, Sun. 10:00 am to 4:00 pm. Closed two weeks in February—call ahead.
CATALOG AVAILABLE: No
MAIL-ORDER AVAILABLE: No
DISPLAY GARDENS: No
CLASSES: No

CONTACT
9267 Dublin Road
Dublin, OH 43017
PHONE: (614) 889-9407
FAX: (614) 793-9407

DIRECTIONS
FROM I-70: I-70 to I-270 north (Exit 93) to OH-161/US-33 east for 1.2 miles toward Dublin. At High Street, turn north (left), driving for 3.5 miles to nursery on your left. (High Street becomes Dublin Rd.)

GPS: N 40° 09.46', W 83° 08.05'

The Bakers have a knack for knowing what sophisticated gardeners are searching for each year, and without exception their garden center carries many of the choicest plants available to the public. As Doug notes, " gardeners may end up paying 10% more for a specific plant, but in the long run, they know they will be able to get that unusual or rare plant at Bakers Village and it will be a healthy, thriving one."

WHAT YOU'LL FIND

Gardeners sprucing up an existing perennial border, or starting one from scratch, can find superior varieties of **phlox**, **aster**, **bellflower**, **coreopsis**, **astilbe**, **foxglove**, **coral bells**, and **bee balm**. The garden center carries classic varieties of old favorites, such as **daylily** and **hosta**, as well as some of the latest cultivars of these plants. I found a number of uncommon perennials, such as: the fluffy, glowing rose-pink plumed *Astilbe* 'Catherine Deneuve'; the indispensable double, pink

> *"The best rose bush, after all, is not that which has the fewest thorns, but that which bears the finest roses."*
> —HENRY VAN DYKE

sun rose *Helianthemum* 'Annabel'; the pink **foam flower** with prolific and extended bloom periods, *Tiarella* 'Pink Pearls'; the sterile rose campion which won't spread about, *Lychnis* 'Gardener's World'; and the premiere plant for shade gardens, **lungwort** *Pulmonaria* 'Opal', with pale opalescent blue buds maturing to even paler hues.

Bakers Village offers the pink phlox *Phlox paniculata* 'Shortwood', an offspring of the powdery mildew resistant *P. p.* 'David', named for plant maven Stephanie Cohen's private garden. Additionally, the nursery carries the perennial **bachelor button** *Centaurea* 'Gold Bullion'. In Greek mythology, Chiton the Centaur used plants of this genus to heal his wounded foot, and though I have no need of this plant for foot relief, its chartreuse foliage does lend an irresistible soothing quality to the garden.

For container gardeners, a range of colorful annuals, tropicals, and temperennials, in a delirious clash of colors, is stocked in spring and early summer. The nursery carries the shorter, sturdier, pristine white *Agapanthus* 'Bressingham White'; a striking **montbretia** *Crocosmia* 'Irish Sunset' whose red-tipped yellow buds virtually explode from purple sheaf; and the gorgeous **hebe** *Hebe* 'Margret', a

OHIO

most extraordinary carefree container plant throwing off a profusion of long lived flowers.

Early in the spring the nursery undergoes what can only be described as a "potting frenzy" as long time customers bring back numerous containers for custom plantings.

For formal gardens the nursery stocks many "lollipop" shaped topiaries crowning 3-foot clay pots. They also have **pinks**, **bleeding hearts**, **hellebores**, **delphiniums** and **peonies** for cottage gardens. Herbs, **grasses**, reliable **roses**, soothing **ferns**, and woody ornamentals round out the plants of superior horticultural merit available here.

Container plants in captivating end groupings are attractively interspersed throughout the grounds. Some arrangements highlight similar tones, such as the purple **butterfly bush** with tiny, golden eyes behind the rich yellow **daylilies**.

OHIO

Others, white **begonias**, **shasta daisies**, **phlox** and skyrocketing **nicotiana** (*Nicotiana sylvestris*) cool off the sultry, hot tones of reddish-pink **cosmos** and red **monarda**.

Although spring is the best time for buying choice perennials, wonderful, healthy plants can still be had at this nursery well into fall. On my last visit one stifling September morning, I found sprightly climbing **hydrangea**, a thriving population of **roses**, sedate **artemesia**, a remarkable collection of **salvia**, a bevy of **daylilies**, quite a few **rudbeckias**, unusual fall **mums**, and a few choice trees and shrubs.

OHIO

BLUESTONE PERENNIALS

❦

Located in Madison, midway between Cleveland, OH and Erie, PA, Bluestone Perennials is the Midwest's best-known mail-order perennial nursery. Bluestone got its start in 1972 in two small rented greenhouses. Visionary that he was, owner Richard Boonstra felt that the new plastic cell-packs and soil-less potting mediums were the perfect resources in which to successfully ship plants to home gardeners across the country. Bluestone Perennials shipped a mere 400 orders that first year. Today, it has grown to include 50 greenhouses (5 acres under glass), employs a staff of seventy-five during the shipping season, and ships more than 60,000 orders (3 million plants) annually.

A three-generation business, Bluestone specializes in perennials, shrubs, mums, ground covers, and vines. Though its primary focus is on mail-order, the nursery welcomes thousands of customers annually to its Outlet Center, basically the mail-order picking area doubling as a retail store. Within these extensive greenhouses, perennials arranged alphabetically by botanical names are set out on endless tables.

The nursery built its solid reputation by providing inexpensive, good quality starter plants with healthy, well-developed root systems. Bluestone Perennials is a bit out of the way; however, the nursery encourages visitors to visit the greenhouse and walk the production fields.

OWNERS: William Boonstra
TYPE: Nursery/greenhouse. Retail and wholesale
SPECIALTIES: Perennials—sun and shade; shrubs; herbs; vines; mums
HOURS: April-Mid June: Mon.-Sat 8:00 am to 4:00 pm; Late June-Aug.: Mon.-Fri 8:00 am to 4:00 pm; Sept.-Oct.: Mon.-Sat 8 am to 4:00 pm; Oct.-March: Closed.
CATALOG AVAILABLE: Printed and online
MAIL-ORDER AVAILABLE: Yes
DISPLAY GARDENS: No
CLASSES: No

CONTACT
7211 Middle Ridge Rd.
Madison, OH 44057-3009
PHONE: (800) 852-5243
FAX: (440) 428-7635
WEB ADDRESS:
www.bluestoneperennials.com
EMAIL: bluestone@bluestoneperennials.com

DIRECTIONS
IN THE CLEVELAND AREA: I-90 to OH-528 north toward Madison/Thompson for approx 1.0 miles. Take OH-528 to OH-84/WMain Drive east (right) on OH-84/WMain for 1.0 miles to Bates Road, turn north (left). Stay on Bates Rd for 0.9 miles to Middle Ridge Rd. Right on Middle Rd., look for nursery immediately after the turn.

GPS: N 41° 47.38', W 81° 01.95'

WHAT YOU'LL FIND

More than 900 plants and 400 shrubs are listed in the catalog, along with seductive photos, detailed descriptions, and sound cultural instructions. The nursery propagates more than 3 million plants a season; half from seed, the other half vegetatively. For the most part, plants are grown in the nursery's greenhouses and production fields; however, to augment the vast selection of perennials grown inhouse, on-site customers also enjoy limited choices of annuals and hanging baskets brought in from other local wholesale growers. Spring flowering bulbs are available in the fall.

Bluestone carries the classics—plants that are stylish without being faddish. Spring brings a succession of old friends and sweet surprises: **pasque flower** (*Anemone pulsatilla*), **columbine**, **bergenia**, **aubrieta**, old fashioned **bleeding heart**, **hellebore**, **forget-me-nots**, **poppy**, **primula**, **tiarella**, and **sweet violet**. On one spring visit I found prodigious selections of **yarrow**, **dianthus**, **astilbe**, **sedum**, **bee balm**, **salvia**, and **veronica**. Plants with gray foliage included **artemesia**, **snow-in-summer**, **globe thistle**, **lamium**, **rose campion**, and **lambs ears**.

> *"Thus came the lovely spring,*
> *with a rush of blossoms and music,*
> *flooding the earth with flower..."*
> —HENRY WADSWORTH LONGFELLOW

Bluestone Perennials offers a charming assembly of uncommon perennials, such as the yellow **giant hyssop** *Agastache nepetoides*; **shasta daisy** *Chrysanthemum ×superbum* 'Switzerland' (mountains of "hand-sized" single snow white flowers); **Siberian dragon's head** *Dracocephalum ruyshiana* 'Blue Moon' (little known but beautiful with rich blue-purple flowers); *Lewisia × longipetala* 'Little Plum' (small, cute, spring blooming groundcover, covered with intense rose-purple flowers); and the bright yellow thistle-like flowers of the yellow **hard head** *Centaurea macrocephala*.

The diverse **phlox** group shows tall garden phlox and short smooth phlox, woodland phlox and creeping phlox. There's even a short, pink flowering phlox with variegated foliage. There are good **foxglove** choices, excellent **coneflower**, dainty **heronsbill** (*Erodium* 'Charm'), durable, hardy **cranesbill** (*Geranium*), the billowing clouds of **orphanage plant** (*Kalimeris pinnatifida* 'Hortensis'), and perennial **sunflower** (*Helianthus × multiflorus* 'Flore Pleno'). This plant alone has enough heft

OHIO

in its makeup to balance big bruiser grasses like *Miscanthus* 'Variegatus' and *M.* 'Silver Feather' lurking in the background.

Perennials are shipped in deeper than usual, three-cell packs: 2¹/₂-inch × 3-inch standard jumbo packs with plants grown for 6 to 12 months before shipping. They also use the larger 3¹/₂-inch × 5-inch individual cells for plants such as garden phlox, hostas, and daylilies, with plants grown for 12 to 16 months before shipping. Shrubs, reasonably priced starter woodies, are shipped in 4-inch containers.

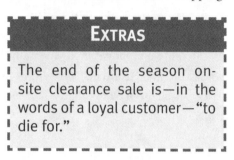

EXTRAS

The end of the season on-site clearance sale is—in the words of a loyal customer—"to die for."

By comparison to other nurseries the propagated shrubs sold at Bluestone Perennials may, at first glance, appear to be rather skimpy plants. They are usually only 6 to 12 inches tall and require a period of two years or more before they reach a size where one can start to consider them "showy." However the inexpensive price points make these shrublets quite attractive. The gardener who enjoys the actual process of watching a sturdy seedling mature into a full size shrub, or those with an abundant amount of patience and a need for larger quantities of plants, will appreciate the benefit of choosing these less-developed options. This is a good place for shoppers with large lists but limited funds.

The nursery is an admirable source of underutilized shrubs such as **elderberry**, **deutzia**, and **fothergilla**; uncommon but wonderful *Leptodermis oblonga*; **seven sons flower** (*Heptacodium miconioides*); and **beauty bush** (*Kolkwitzia* 'Pink Cloud'). It offers its customers a sea of **spirea**, **viburnum**, and **hydrangea**, and a universe of butterfly magnets such as **summer sweet** (*Clethra*), **bluebeard** (*Caryopteris*), and **butterfly bush** (*Buddleia*).

BURTON'S BAMBOO GARDEN

෬ඏ ඏ෬

Dressed in their finest, they stood at attention—the official welcoming committee. I was the only visitor at the moment, and I certainly wasn't expecting anything this grand. Getting out of the car, I wasn't exactly sure how to act. Should I say something? Just walk by? Their presence was absolutely riveting; nothing short of gorgeous! City slicker that I am, I couldn't take my eyes off of them ....male peacocks in full plumage. These birds are surely among the most beautiful and spectacular in the world. And here, in front of me, were four of them. Up close and personal, they were absolutely gorgeous.

Burton's Bamboo Garden, a bamboo specialty nursery on 30 acres, is out in the countryside, close to farms and houses on large lots. Let me tell you right up front—leave your pets at home. This is policy, for there is quite an assortment of critters here: twenty-five peacocks, two emu, mute swans, herons, wood ducks, dogs, cats, and frogs. All friendly and all roaming free.

The grounds, planted out with numerous bamboo, are a sight to behold. The gardens, situated on a large lake, are a pleasure to tour. According to owner, Jerry Burton, bamboos are among Earth's most beautiful and useful plants, providing outstanding texture and form as screens, hedges, ground covers and specimen plants.

Bamboos are nothing more than woody grasses, long grown by Asian cultures for food, building materials, weapons, decoration, landscaping, and

OWNERS: Jerry Burton
TYPE: Specialty nursery
SPECIALTIES: Bamboo
HOURS: Call ahead. Generally open weekends 10:00 am to 5:00 pm. Other times by appointment.
CATALOG AVAILABLE: Online
MAIL-ORDER AVAILABLE: Yes
DISPLAY GARDENS: Yes
CLASSES: Yes

CONTACT
7352 Gheils Carrol Road
Morrow, OH 45152-8558
PHONE: (513) 899-3446
WEB ADDRESS: www.burtonsbamboo garden.com
EMAIL: burton@cinternet.net

DIRECTIONS
FROM CINCINNATI: I-71 north to Columbus. Take Mason Montgomery Rd. (Exit 19) towards Fields Ertel Rd. Turn left onto Mason Road, immediately turn right onto Fields Ertel Rd. Turn slight left onto Montgomery Rd./OH-3/US-22 and drive for 10.6 miles to Front St. (T). Turn right onto Front St. drive for 0.5 miles where Front St. becomes Morrow Woodville Rd./CR-24. Drive for 1.9 miles to Ghiels Carrol Rd. Turn left onto Ghiels Carroll Rd. Look for huge bamboo and ornamental grass clumps near a small nursery sign at the end of a long driveway leading to the Burton residence and bamboo display gardens.

GPS: N 39° 19.94', W 84° 06.61'

OHIO

container plants, including bonsai. Bamboo produces lovely, ethereal, creaking, and rustling sounds caused by breezes blowing through delicate leaves. Bamboo varieties can range in size from the creepers of a few inches to those soaring more than 100 feet tall, and come in a staggering variety of cane color, leaf size and shape.

Burton started growing bamboos back in 1975, when his peaceful and serene lakes bred too many swans. He gave a friend two royal mute swans and in return, the gentleman gave Burton ten clumps of bamboo. After planting them and observing one growth cycle, Burton became intrigued. In time he joined the American Bamboo Society (he is currently the President of the ABS MidStates Chapter), started showing his bamboo at countless garden shows (including the Cincinnati Home and Garden Show), and in 1998 went "high-tech" selling plants through the internet, which now accounts for the majority of his sales.

Today, the nursery is the Midwest's premier source for exceptional, winter-hardy bamboo plants for the collector and novice alike. It has a good selection of bamboo in tall and dwarf sizes, grown for a minimum of two years in #2 or #5 gallon pots. Landscape-sized specimens can also be purchased at the nursery.

Burton explained to me the importance of purchasing pot grown plants for cold climates. "For taller, new shoots, always select a plant that's been growing in a pot for at least two years or longer. A freshly dug plant may have a larger cane but doesn't have enough rhizome and energy to produce large, new shoots for several years. If you're in a cold zone, the odds are high that the field-dug cane will die back the first winter. The small rhizome cannot provide enough moisture during a cold winter and the canes will die back. When culms (stems) emerge in spring the diameter (of the stem) is set. They attain their full height in forty-five to sixty days and never grow another inch taller or larger in diameter." (Apparently, the inner walls of the bamboo will thicken over the next few years, making the stem that much stronger; however, after that initial growth spurt, the stem itself will never get any taller.)

Consider Burton's a destination nursery and a worthwhile learning experience. Visit the gardens, view the free-growing bamboo groves, and see the numerous, priceless granite carvings from the Yangtse River area of China scattered throughout the property. Watch the peacocks, listen to the emu, and enjoy the peace and tranquility of the place. For those really interested in bamboo, I would even recommend coordinating your trip with one of the classes held at the Haiku House on the premises.

WHAT YOU'LL FIND

There are many bamboo choices here. Tall bamboo grows from 12 to 50 feet depending on variety and conditions. One choice, *Phyllostachys Vivax*, the hardiest of the **timber bamboos**, can grow over 50 feet tall under optimum conditions (with 5-inch diameter stems), and has the best shoots for eating. Other tall bamboos include:

> *"Dirt is matter out of place."*
> —OLIVER LODGE

the ebony stemmed **black bamboo** (*Phyllostachys nigra*); *P. nigra* 'Henon', a shade-tolerant cultivar of the black bamboo which attains a ghostly appearance when the mature culms assume a gray-blue cast; and the incredible *P. bissettii* 'David Bisset', which under hot, wet conditions can grow a foot per day. For "living" privacy screens in Zones 4-6, Burton highly recommends *P. aureosulcata*, the tall **yellow groove bamboo**, a fast growing, very cold hardy species with yellow grooves in the stems (and sometimes even zig-zagged stems).

Low growing bamboos—dwarfs—die back each winter and should be treated as deciduous perennials in the Midwest. Excellent for ground cover, these include: **dwarf greenstripe** *Pleioblastus viridistriatus* (golden-chartreuse leaves with green stripes, and fine hairs on the underside that are soft and downy to the touch); *Indocalamus tesselatus* (a shade loving bamboo, whose leaves, the largest of all cultivated bamboos, are used in cooking to wrap food in the same manner as corn husks); and **arrow bamboo** *Pseudo sasa japonica* (one of the best for windy sites, used in ancient Japan to make arrows). My favorite, however, is **Kuma-Zasa bamboo** *Sasa veitchii*, (short with large, dark green, downy leaves which turn cream along the edges at the onset of colder weather).

For the most part, all bamboos sold at Burton's Bamboo Garden are running bamboos. It is important to note that what may be invasive in one part of the country, may be quite manageable in another. Still, bamboo does spread. In short, it tries to become a grove by sending out tentacles of rhizomes to search for nutrients and moisture. By enlarging it's rhizome mass, it acquires the ability to provide for the new stems emerging in the spring.

Some bamboos in Burton's display gardens have expanded very little, others are a bit more aggressive. But Burton notes that none of the bamboos in his gardens are "contained" by the use of a barrier. And some of the groves have been growing for almost 25 years, without any rampant invasion of the landscape. However, for those gardeners with small spaces who want to keep bamboo out of unwanted areas of the garden, Burton's Bamboo Garden sells Deep Root®, a water/bamboo barrier. By inserting this 36-inch barrier for tall bamboos, and the 24-inch barrier for the dwarfs, you will be able to prevent the spread of the rhizomes. Just remember to leave a slight lip of the barrier a few inches above grade to prevent the rhizomes from growing over the edge.

OHIO

CHARLES APPLEGATE GARDENS

Charles Applegate Gardens is a small family-run nursery in central Ohio, which houses true horticultural gems. The Applegates are one of the new breed of hybridizers who strive to create cold hardy plants with gorgeous, award winning characteristics. They specialize exclusively in propagating and growing advanced daylily hybrids with a "hardy reliable bloomer" constitution. These are daylilies able to withstand central Ohio's cold blustery winters and unpredictable springs, and then bloom reliably, be distinctive, and have excellent substance. To this end, they are in the forefront of a push for the development of floriferous semi-evergreen daylilies like those cultivated by southern hybridizers, but hardy enough to flourish reliably in the North. A measure of their success is the cold-hardy 'Reverence', a fragrant, lavender bitone daylily with darker edges and a dark lavender eye. Similarly imposing is their fragrant, double pink daylily with dark rose-coral eye, 'Morning by Morning', and thrilling purple 'Shield of Faith'.

OWNERS: Charles and Linda Applegate
TYPE: Small Specialty nursery
SPECIALTIES: Daylilies—field grown
HOURS: Gardens are at peak and open July 1 through mid Aug.: Mon.-Fri. 10:00 am to 6:00 pm; Saturdays, late-August and other months by appointment only.
MAIL-ORDER AVAILABLE: Yes
DISPLAY GARDENS: Yes
CLASSES: None

CONTACT
3699 Pleasant Hill Road
Perrysville, OH 44864-9672
PHONE: (419) 938-9672
WEB ADDRESS:
www.GardenEureka.com/Charl

DIRECTIONS
FROM I-71 (SOUTH): Take I-71 north to Rt.-13. Drive north on Rt.-13 to Hanely Rd. Turn east (right) on Hanely Rd. and travel to Touby Rd. (about 1.0 mile). You will cross I-71 in the process. Turn south (right) on Touby Rd. where it merges into Possum Run Rd. (approx. 2 miles down) and continue to follow Possum Run Rd. to Hwy-95. Turn left onto Hwy-95 and drive to Pleasant Hill Rd. (about 0.2 miles). Turn right and drive 0.5 miles to nursery.

GPS: N 40° 37.81'; W 82° 22.66'

Charles Applegate Gardens is a specialty grower of more than 400 named daylily hybrids, plus several thousands of his own seedlings, that are stout, robust and vigorous plants. The nursery, consisting of seven beds of various sizes and shapes, is operated out of a very large plot of land, all of it harsh "rocky soil", in front of their home northeast of Columbus.

Charles Applegate, who according to his wife Linda, is a "true hortiholic from way back," cut his teeth as a hybridizer with the genus *Iris*. One of his cultivars,

> *"Let the black flower blossom as it may!"*
> —Nathaniel Hawthorne
> ⚘

Iris 'Royal Summer', a uniquely different, deep purple, reblooming bearded iris, is still wildly popular even today. Though still passionate about bearded iris, Applegate became enthralled with daylilies due to their longer bloom period. Currently, he is senior gardener in charge of both the iris and daylily collections at Kingwood Center, which also has quite a reputation for it's extensive tulip displays. Applegate is in the enviable position of working with both genera.

WHAT YOU'LL FIND

Since 1980, the Applegates have devoted themselves to breeding **daylilies**, with the first Applegate daylily introduction, 'Blessing', registered in 1989. ('Blessing' went on to win the Eureka Beauty Award in 1994, and today enjoys worldwide acclaim.) Unlike breeders who register and introduce numerous new cultivars every season, the Applegates, with twenty-two registrations to their credit, are quite picky in their choices, finding only one or two plants a year distinctive enough for introduction.

One of my favorites from this program, the lemon-yellow semi-spider, 'Guile', looks somewhat like an evocative orchid. Another interesting trait of this daylily is that no two blossoms are quite the same; just when you're sure which characteristics of the flower appeal the most, the succeeding blossom presents a few additional surprises and, therefore, more choices.

Although his field-grown plants are sold primarily by mail order, visitors viewing the gardens in person

★ SIDE TRIPS ★

KINGWOOD CENTER, (419) 522-0211, 900 Park Avenue, W., Mansfield, OH. Located on Park Avenue West, this center covers 47 acres and contains landscaped gardens. Trails meander through woodland settings and two ponds. The gardens have one of the largest displays of tulips in the country. Various gardens: peony, historic, herb, rose, daylily and iris collections; parterre, perennial, terrace, woodland, trial and cutting beds. Free. Apr. thru Oct. 8 am to dusk, Oct. thru Apr. 8 am to 5 pm.

OHIO

have the immense pleasure of inspecting the well-labeled trial beds and growing fields for selections. These beds, containing daylilies from both his breeding program, as well as hardy plants produced by other breeders, include many huge, ruffled, picotee-edged and ornamentally eyed singles, doubles, and spiders. There is a gamut of amazingly delicious colors, such as strawberry, coral, mandarin, apricot, and raspberry. All daylilies are freshly dug, double (or greater) fans or divisions. These are field-grown, mature plants; each plant having survived at least one bitter Ohio winter, un-pampered, in the fields. Peak daylily bloom is usually mid-July, but there are some daylilies in bloom from the last week of June to the first week in August.

Bonus plants are included with each order. Whenever possible, the Applegates will try to dig up plants without prior notice; however, outside circumstances can come into play, so it is always best to call ahead with specific needs.

EXTRAS

Available only at the nursery, Applegate Gardens offers an extremely generous "hybridizer seedling special"—a remarkable bag of once bloomed seedlings for $5 per bag. Such hybridizer sales can produce some bewitching bargains, for the winnowed seedlings of a gifted breeder are often exemplary plants, with more notable traits than some named hybrids.

OHIO

COMPANION PLANTS

❧ ☙

Companion Plants is, without a doubt, the largest volume grower of herbs in the Midwest. With close to sixty pages of text in its catalog, Companion Plants offers more specialty herbs—common and exotic—than you'll ever have space for in your garden or on your table. They boast 2 to 3 acres of mature display gardens, packed with an idyllic sampling of herbs for your culinary garden, fragrance garden, or medieval garden. The nursery invites all customers to see herbs growing in a series of well labeled beds and growing fields (access is weather dependant).

Started in 1982, offering a mere 30 varieties of herbs, today the nursery carries more than 600 herbs plus seeds, mushroom kits, and plugs. Two greenhouses offer on-site customers larger plants and even greater selections. Potted herbs are arranged alphabetically on tables accompanied by placards with interesting descriptives, uses, and tidbits. Did you know *Achillea* was named after Achilles who is said to have used it to heal his soldiers at the siege of Troy? Or that *Inula helenium* is named after Helen of Troy, who was said to be harvesting the herb when she was abducted?

Owner, Peter Borchard, defines an herb as "a plant that has been used somewhere by someone for some reason." Their list of useful plants includes some used for aroma, culinary purposes, dyes, medicine, and shamanistic practices. In short, Borchard has assembled such a vast assortment of plants as to satisfy the herbalist in all of us.

OWNERS: Peter Borchard
TYPE: Specialty nursery. Retail and wholesale
SPECIALTIES: Herbs; perennials; wildflowers; ornamental bulbs; vines; mushrooms
HOURS: March through Thanksgiving: Thurs.-Sun. 10:00 am to 5:00 pm; Thanksgiving to February: Closed. Closed all national holidays.
CATALOG AVAILABLE: Printed
MAIL-ORDER AVAILABLE: Yes
DISPLAY GARDENS: Yes
CLASSES: Yes

CONTACT
7247 North Coolville Ridge
Athens, OH 45701
PHONE: (740) 592-4643
FAX: (740) 593-3092
WEB ADDRESS: www.companionplants.com
EMAIL: complants@frognet.net

DIRECTIONS
FROM US-33: Take US-33 to CR-25/Rock Riffle Road. Follow Rock Riffle Road for about 1.9 miles to an intersection where CR-90/Terrell Rd. veers off to the left and Long Run Rd veers to the right. Take the left fork a short distance to N. Coolville Ridge Road and turn east (right). Proceed about 1.25 miles on N. Coolville Ridge Road to the Nursery.

GPS: N 39° 18.59', W 82° 02.55'

OHIO

Interesting seeds available at the nursery include **hopi red dye amaranth**, and **wormseed** *Epazote*, a coarse, weedy, smelly plant used in Mexican bean dishes, and **horned poppy**.

Their common culinary herbs, popular since pre-Medieval times, include incredible numbers of varieties of **basil**, **thyme**, **parsley**, **fennel**, **rosemary**, and **sage**. They also carry **angelica**, **borage**, **cardamom**, **marjoram**, **cardoon**, **chamomile**, **chervil**, **sugarleaf**, **chives**, **lovage**, **burnet**, **comfrey**, **coriander**, **horseradish**, **oregano**, **savory**, and **lavender**, among others.

> *"And the Spring arose on*
> *the garden fair*
> *Like the Spirit of Love*
> *felt everywhere;*
> *And each flower and herb on*
> *Earth's dark breast*
> *Rose from the dreams of*
> *its wintry rest."*
> —PERCY BYSSHE SHELLEY

Showy ornamentals available at Companion Plants include classics such as **sweet flag**, **wormwood**, **mallow**, **foxglove**, **gayfeather**, **evening primrose**, **feverfew**, **germander**, **lobelia**, **purple coneflower**; and **tansy**. Sophisticated ornamental herbs, seldom seen in local nurseries, include: **mouse-eared hawkweed** *Hieracium pilocella* (with solitary 1-inch-wide yellow flowers); **henbane** *Hyoscyamus niger* (sporting striking greenish-yellow flowers with purple veins); **iboza** *Iboza riparia* (African medicinal plant sold in this country mainly for the showy sprays of winter blooming flowers); and **viper's bugloss** *Echium vulgare* (tall stalks of rosy blossoms). An herb called **Aztec dream** *Calea zacatechichi* (a rare plant from South Mexico), induces sleep with particularly vivid dream episodes; **blessed thistle** *Cnicus benedictus* (commonly grown in European monasteries) is a low growing, red stemmed, yellow flowered ornamental thistle; and **racambole** *Allium sativum* 'Ophioscorodon' (also called **serpent garlic**), throws off curious flower stalks that curl into double loops.

Medicinals include **ginkgo**, **ox-knee**, **cinnamon vine**, **gotu kola**, **creeping violet**, **ginseng**, **St. John's wort**, **goldenseal**, and **echinacea**. **Ayahuasca** (*Banisteriopsis caapi*) is also there; its name loosely translates to "spirit of the dead" and is used as a visionary vine by South American shamans to cure a number of ailments.

Woodland plants available at Companion Plants include **Jack-in-the-pulpit**, **sweet woodruff**, **greater celandine**, **lily-of-the-valley**, **hellebore**, **liverleaf**, **twinleaf**, **mayapple**, and **solomon's seal**. Coffee (*Coffea arabica*) can be found there,

OHIO

along with strongly scented garden **heliotrope** (*Valeriana officinalis*). You can buy some baby **Hawaiian woodrose** *Argyreia nervosa,* a vine with heart shaped leaves, funnel shaped lavender-blue flowers, deep red throats, and seed pods that resemble carved wooden roses when dry.

For cooking you'll find **garden mace** *Achillea decolorans* (scented foliage reminiscent of mace), **licorice flag** *Acorus gramineus* 'Licorice', (used in Thai cooking for it's great licorice scent and taste), and **safflower** *Carthamus tinctorius* (a commercial source of cooking oil and orange dye).

Available at Companion Plants, **bedstraw**, **weld**, **woad**, and **madder** can be used for dyeing. Useful weeds include **lambs quarters** (the most nutritious and delicious of wild greens), **stinging nettle** (the leaves are a good source of vitamins), and **dandelion** (for everything from salads to making wine). **Mushroom** plugs include the legendary "Mushroom of Immortality;" the **dancing mushroom** (in North America known as **hen-of-the-woods**), **lion's mane**, **chicken-of-the-woods**, **shiitake**, and **oyster**.

★ SIDE TRIPS ★

ADENA STATE MEMORIAL (800) 319-7248, 848 Adena Road, Chillicothe, OH 45601. This is a 300-acre memorial with a restored 20-room mansion, 5 outbuildings, and gardens of roses, annuals and perennials. **SUGARLOAF MOUNTAIN AMPHITHEATRE, "TECUMSEH!" OUTDOOR HISTORICAL DRAMA** (800) 413-4118, Chillicothe, OH 45601. Considered to be one of America's best outdoor dramas, this play tells the epic story of the Shawnee leader, Tecumseh, defending his homeland. (There is also a restaurant, museum and gift shop).

OHIO

CRINTONIC GARDENS

❧ ❦

Crintonic Gardens, located above the Chagrin River Valley in northeast Ohio, is "dedicated to creating beautiful and distinctive daylilies rigorously selected for consistency and vigor under typical Zone 5 garden conditions." Owner Curt Hanson is known for his eclectic taste in hybridizing including pleated forms, unusual patterns, and near-black colors. He has won the Bertrand Farr Silver Medal, the lifetime achievement award for outstanding hybridizers, and is known for such award winning cultivars as 'Primal Scream', 'Spiritual Corridor', and 'Supreme Empire'.

Hanson, a prodigious hybridizer and self-described "60's hippie" began breeding daylilies more than 25 years ago, a time when it wasn't "hip" to be a daylily hybridizer, especially a daylily hybridizer in the North. He believes "the daylily is Americas favorite flower because it demands so little." (They are virtually disease and pest free and are able to withstand drought, poor soil, and shade.) He notes that daylilies, originally from Asia, have a long history both in the garden and the kitchen. The tender foliage was eaten as a spring green, the buds and flowers were eaten raw and in soups, and the swollen portions of the root were boiled, then eaten. Today there is a lot less eating of daylilies and substantially more appreciation of the glamorous colors, forms and sizes.

One of the paramount pleasures of visiting Crintonic Gardens is witnessing the master hybridizer in action. During peak bloom time, the pace is frenetic, yet a pleasurable sense of calm continuously wraps the gardens at all times. Visitors can leisurely stroll the incredibly vast gardens (10 acres),

OWNERS: Curt Hanson
TYPE: Specialty nursery
SPECIALTIES: Daylilies
HOURS: No set hours, open July and August. Appointments preferred and recommended.
CATALOG AVAILABLE: Printed and online
MAIL-ORDER AVAILABLE: Yes
DISPLAY GARDENS: Yes
CLASSES: No

CONTACT
11757 County Line Road
Gates Mills, OH 44040
PHONE: (440) 423-3349
WEB ADDRESS: www.crintonicgardens.com
EMAIL: crintonic@core.com

DIRECTIONS
DIRECTIONS FROM I-271: Take I-271 to Rt. 322 (Mayfield Road) eastbound. Continue east down the river valley; at the top of the hill, at the first traffice light turn north (left) onto County Line Road. Continue on County Line Road; after the stop sign, drive 0.5 miles further. Gardens will be on the east (right) side of the road.

GPS: N 41° 32.69', W 81° 23.44'

OHIO

view production fields, and note their favorites. It may come as a surprise to people to discover that Hanson hybridizes more than daylilies; currently one can find

him playing with pollen in the hellebore and epimedium beds.

One could say Hanson supports his breeding with successful sales techniques; but the simple truth of the matter is that his plants are such sumptuous marvels that they sell themselves. Although new Hanson hybrids can easily cost $150, there is an incredible array of his hybrids selling for $20 or less.

WHAT YOU'LL FIND

In 2003, the highly esteemed AHS (American Hemerocallis Society) Stout Silver Medal was awarded to the **daylily** 'Primal Scream', a screaming orange, 1994 introduction. Asked to describe it, Hanson noted: 'Primal Scream' definitely demands attention. The garish and lurid color, combined with the stark simplicity of the form, creates a dramatic, almost overpowering statement in a well-orchestrated garden." That wasn't the only prize awarded to Hanson on that day; Honorable Mention awards were given to 'Women Seeking Men' (lusty rose-pink **"Amazon"** plant), 'Joan Derifield' (raspberry rose), 'Notify Ground Crew' (tall, 72 inches, yellow), 'Wind in the Rigging' (liquid orchid exotic), and 'Stephanie Grappelli'(classy purple).

Crintonic Gardens sells only Hanson cultivars; older varieties are generally double divisions or greater, while the newer and more expensive cultivars are bloom size singles. Mail order plants are all freshly dug, organically grown daylilies, and bonus plants are included with each order. They are also home to thousands of named Hanson hybrids as well as several thousand unnamed seedlings.

Though Hanson's hybridizing goals might take a slight detour here and there, the main focus has always been on unique shapes and saturated colors. To that end, on a 2-acre patch of land protected from Bambi's noshing by an electrified fence, he grows 20,000 to 30,000 seedlings a year; an incredible feat for a single-handed affair.

Hanson breeds his daylilies on his farm in Gates Mills, a lovely town on the far-east side of Cleveland. Using hybrids from his and other hybridizers' programs, he creates cold-hardy plants with awesome, prizewinning characteristics. His aim is for high bud count, good branching habits, cold-hardiness, and rich, saturated colors. The man is supremely humble, "The gift of happenstance plays no small part in a hybridizer's work," he confesses. "While we may smugly assume our intuitive brilliance, nature debunks our arrogance and proves that beauty and popularity cannot be predicted."

Hanson is a pioneer in developing un-pampered daylilies capable of not only surviving but thriving in our harsh winters, and of semi-evergreen lilies that will flourish in the North. Hybridization is approached with a zest for fun—not taking himself too seriously. A tongue-in-cheek attitude is easily detected in his eclectic choice of names: 'Law and Order' (tall, medium lavender), 'As the World Turns', 'Lost in Space' (sunfast black-purple), and 'Sea Hunt' (unusual shade of orchid). For Trekkies he has: 'Photon Torpedo' ("tall cruise missile claret"), 'Romulan Defector' (odd "alien purple" blend), 'Vulcan Logic' (three distinct bands of color), 'Borg Technology'(medium purple with an odd pattern), and 'Spocks Ears' (recurved and pinched petals). A play on words is exhibited with 'Carnival Knowledge' (showy warm shrimp coral), 'Den of Inequity' (small purple), 'Now and Zen' (showy gold with a purple eye), and 'Xon Valdez' (huge, maroon).

Peak daylily bloom here is during the months of July and August. What most people don't realize is that Hanson has countless other plants besides his noted daylilies—including some rather impressive collections of **oaks**, **magnolias** and **hostas**—incorporated into the lavishly landscaped gardens. A phone call prior to visiting Crintonic Gardens is highly appreciated.

DAYLILY LANE

❧ ❧

The colorful gardens of Pat and Dick Henley's Daylily Lane are located about 10 miles east of Columbus. They grow and sell more than 1,500 named daylily cultivars. Additionally, they are one of the officially sanctioned AHS (American Hemerocallis Society) Display Gardens. It's important that a daylily be beautiful, but since beauty can be subjective this is a great place to see if a specific specimen appeals to your senses.

Boasting that Daylily Lane is "home to the largest collection of daylilies in Central Ohio," the nursery contains more than an acre of cold-hardy plants grown on rich, "fudgy" bottomland next to the Henley home near Baltimore. They are known for having well-grown plants at great prices.

Pat (a Ph.D. in Horticulture from Ohio State) and Dick were both avid daylily connoisseurs when happenstance brought them together at a local daylily club. Deciding to combine their mutual interest was easy; finding just the right plot of land on which to plant out their collection was not. After searching in four counties for just the right location, they felt they found it at Daylily Lane. Walking the growing fields with these two genial people is an education in itself.

OWNERS: Patricia and Dick Henley
TYPE: Specialty nursery
SPECIALTIES: Daylilies; hosta
HOURS: End of June to mid August: Mon.-Sat. 10:00 am to 4:00 pm. Other times by appointment.
CATALOG AVAILABLE: Internet listing.
MAIL-ORDER AVAILABLE: Yes
DISPLAY GARDENS: Yes, (including AHS Display Garden)
CLASSES: No

CONTACT
11800 Poplar Creek Lane
Baltimore, OH
PHONE: (740) 862-2406
WEB ADDRESS: www.daylilylane.com
EMAIL: daylilylane@greenapple.com

DIRECTIONS
FROM I-70: Take I-70 to Hazelton-Etno Rd. (Exit # 118). Drive south on Hazelton-Etno Rd. for 1.4 miles to SR-204 (stoplight). Turn east (left) onto SR-204 and then IMMEDIATELY turn right and follow SR-204 for 1.75 miles to Refugee Rd. (stoplight). Continue across Refugee Rd. where SR-204 becomes Poplar Creek Rd. Nursery is the fourth house on the left.

GPS: N39° 54.01', W 82° 40.15'

WHAT YOU'LL FIND

Dick Henley and I discussed the complexities of describing flower colors. According to Dick, "Yellow is not just yellow." He went on to note that the general term "yellow" encompasses many shades: pale yellow, light yellow, sulphur-yellow, cadmium-yellow and orange-yellow. Dick said, "Most of the

OHIO

daylily hybrids are yellow, as is evidenced by the majority of the AHS winners. Daylilies with flowers of this color are generally not too complicated. Typically they open without problems, have longer bloom periods, and often are scented." While at the garden, we looked at 'Yellow Lollipop' (medium yellow) and 'Texan

> *Flowers are the sweetest things that God ever made and forgot to put a soul into.*
> —HENRY WARD BEECHER

Sunlight' (a gold self). Both are gorgeous miniatures, and both are past winners of the Donn Fischer Memorial Cup.

Daylily Lane carries many large, ruffled, picoteed, color throated, diamond dusted, watermarked, and eyed daylilies from notable breeders in a dazzling array

---

★ SIDE TRIPS ★

HISTORIC HOUSES & BUILDINGS OF LANCASTER: As a legacy the city has not one, but four National Register Historic Districts. They are: Lancaster Historic District bound by 5th Ave, Penn Central RR tracks, OH-33, and Tenant St.; Lancaster West Main Street Historic District, West Main bounded by Broad on the East end and Columbus on the West; Lancaster Methodist Episcopal Campground Historic District, bounded by the Hocking River, W. Fair Ave, and Ety Rd.; and Square 13 Historic District at long Broad and High Streets between Mulberry and Chestnut. Historic Square 13 is considered by many architectural historians to be one of the finest collections of 19th century homes in a concentrated area. Check www.visitfairfieldcountyoh.org for a virtual walking tour. **COVERED BRIDGES:** Ohio has one of the largest collections of covered bridges in a concentrated area outside of PA. George Hutchins Bridge, built in 1865 with a 49-foot span, has been reconstructed at Alley Park. South of Lancaster off Rt. 33A, 0.5 miles south of the last traffic light at Lancaster on Rt.33, turn right on Stump Hollow Road. In a few yards there is a stop sign, turn left on Old Logan Rd. and drive about 0.5 miles to the entrance of Alley Park. Walk from the parking lot to the bridge, which is over a narrow part of Lake Loretta.

OHIO

of colors. Strawberry, carrot orange, mustard yellow, apricot, lemon yellow, tomato red, deep persimmon, and butterscotch blend left me yearning for a salad. My favorites include: the tallish yellow spider 'Cat's Cradle' (a must for cat lovers); 'Elegant Candy' (pure manna, pink with a red eye); 'Fairy Frosting' (a confection for the fairy gardens of this world having an ivory and cream blend); flesh pink to yellow polychrome 'Ferengi Gold' (anyone seen Capt. Piccard?); and the near white 'Iditarod' ("mush, mush!").

Dick dabbles in a little hybridization, but very few of his seedlings are for sale. His field-grown plants are sold mainly on-site—freshly dug, double or larger fans or divisions—though he does sell daylilies by mail order. (Shipping is free on $100.00 or more.)

Hostas are sold only on-site. Daylily Lane carries many of the latest hybrids, but the majority are well-grown, winter-hardy (having survived Ohio winters in the ground), and are reasonably priced plants.

Visitors to Daylily Lane can have the fun of reconnoitering well-labeled growing fields and display gardens containing hundreds of blooming plants. Pick up a printed guide to unusual perennials, trees, and shrubs located throughout the beds and borders near the house. You'll find the slow growing, majestic **redbud** *Cercis canadensis* 'Forest Pansy' (wine red to dark-purple leaves); numerous **oaks** (black, red, white) all grown from acorns, and several southern **magnolias**.

Peak daylily bloom at the nursery is usually around the 4th of July (it can get crowded), but the range extends from the last week of June to the end of July.

DeMonye's Greenhouse

❧ ❧

Located on busy Airport Drive in Columbus, a short distance from the Columbus International Airport, DeMonye's Greenhouse is a popular garden center whose close proximity to the airport is definitely no deterrent to avid gardeners. The nursery has managed to connect with all gardeners: beginners sowing their first seeds or planting their first perennials, or advanced gardeners seeking rare and unusual plants. Thrifty consumers buy several seedlings, upscale homeowners seek out sumptuous specimen plants, and crafty gardeners explore new ideas.

DeMonye's Greenhouse specializes in well-rooted, healthy, container-grown perennials in more than 1,300 varieties. They also carry, grasses, vines, geraniums, roses, herbs and other ornamental plants. Hanging baskets dripping luscious blossoms fly out the doors in early spring, and cleverly designed, spiffy plant combinations in planted-out containers make the briefest of stops before being snatched up by customers eager for these prizes.

What You'll Find

This is home to dazzling selections of plants—imaginatively co-mingling

OWNER: Jerome Killilea
TYPE: Garden Center
SPECIALTIES: Perennials—shade and sun; annuals; tender perennials; tropicals; summer bulbs; hanging baskets and containers; roses; herbs; vines; ornamental grasses. aquatics.
HOURS: Jan thru March 15: Mon.-Fri. 8:00 am to 5:00 pm; March 15 thru Dec.: Mon.-Fri. 8:00 am to 7:00 pm, Sat. 8:00 am to 6:00 pm, Sun. 10:00 to 5:00 pm.
CATALOG AVAILABLE: Printed plant list.
MAIL-ORDER AVAILABLE: No
DISPLAY GARDENS: No
CLASSES: No

Contact
2500 Airport Drive
Columbus, OH 43219
PHONE: (614) 252-6046
FAX: (614) 252-6047
EMAIL: killjams@aol.com

Directions
(Unfamiliar? Call the nursery for instructions.) **FROM THE EAST ON I-70:** I-70 west to I-270 north (left ramp Exit #41A). I-270 to I-670 (US-62) (Exit #35) for 1.6 miles to (Exit #9) towards Cassidy Ave/ International Airport. Turn south (left) onto N. Cassady Ave then immediately turn west (right) onto Airport Drive to nursery on right hand side. **FROM THE NORTH:** I-71 south to I-270 west at Exit (# 119A). Continue on I-270 to I-670 (US-62) (Exit 35A) for 1.6 miles to Exit #9 towards Cassady Ave./International Airport. Turn south (left) onto N. Cassady Ave then immediately turn west (right) onto Airport Drive to nursery on right hand side. **FROM THE WEST:** on I-70. Take I-70 east to I-71 north, I-670 east to Exit 7 towards Fifth Ave. Left onto E. 5th Ave to the second stop light, N. Nelson Road. Turn north (right) onto Nelson Rd. to Airport Drive. Turn right onto Airport Drive to nursery.

GPS: N 39° 59.61', N 82° 56.18'

OHIO

annuals, perennials, and tropicals. For gardeners who appreciate the whimsical, deMonye's offers their exclusive, ingeniously designed, 4-foot tall or so, "Topiary People." Imagine, if you will, a lollipop shaped "pot person" dressed in overalls, gardening garb, or a dress, with hair of sedum, flowers, ivy or ornamental grass. Top this with a rakish cap, couture hat or beautiful floral "barrette" all of which rises regally from a lush container garden of perennials, tropicals, or annuals.

The heart of the container garden's beauty is the majestic concentration of artistry and color in one, which becomes the show-stopping focal point. At $165.00 their container gardens are not inexpensive; but for those with sufficient disposable income, a container full of impact, drama, and spectacle, is quite the bargain. For more traditional tastes, deMonye's is a major supplier of topiary, offering mop-head and spiral evergreens, **herbs**, and **ivy**, as

well as charming ivy topiaries clipped into handsome shapes, such as dolphin, flamingo, and rooster.

The greenhouse has good collections of *Achillea* (**yarrow**), *Campanula* (**bellflower**), *Chrysanthemum* (**Shasta daisy**), *Coreopsis* (**tickseed**), *Geranium* (**cranesbill**), *Dianthus*, **sedum** and **phlox**. Special assortments for woodland gardens include *Aquilegia* (**columbine**), **astilbe**, *Cimicifuga* (**bugbane**), **corydalis**, **fern**, *Helleborus* (**lenten rose**), *Pulmonaria* (**lungwort**), *Heucherella*, and *Tiarella* (**foamflower**). The garden center is a superior source of **Japanese tree peony**; dazzling **lupines**, and interesting **salvias**. Groupings of **hosta** and **daylily**, include both classics and newer cultivars. Unusual gleanings include **dragonhead**

OHIO

(*Dracocephalum*), **Japanese aster** (*Kalimeris*), **shooting star** (*Lithodora*), and perennial **dwarf snapdragon** (*Chaenorrhinum*).

Perennials are supplemented with annuals, herbs (annual and perennial), vegetable flats in the spring, and perennial vines throughout the growing season. Without a doubt **petunias** and **geraniums** will always be available at garden centers like this, because they are so well suited to the Midwest's prairie growing conditions. Seasonal plants, such as **Easter lilies,** spring flowering bulbs, **ornamental cabbage** and **kale** (12 varieties), hardy **mums** in clear colors, and **poinsettias** are sold at holidays. A wide assortment of spring blooming bulbs is available in the fall. DeMonye's is also a comprehensive source for varied garden supplies, containers, and ancillary needs.

> *"I'm still devoted to the garden... although an old man, I am but a young gardener."*
> —THOMAS JEFFERSON

ESSENTIALLY ENGLISH GARDENS

༺ঌ৯ঌ৯༻

If you had to pick one place in Ohio that excelled in rare and unusual choice ornamental trees and shrubs, Essentially English Gardens would be it. I think gardeners can probably find nurseries that stock more varieties and definitely larger quantities of shrubs and trees; but few, if any, can parallel the uniqueness, quality, and availability of the uncommon plants offered here.

This is not a large nursery with an immense staff; rather this is a labor of love run by one man. Owner Ralph Jaynes, a trained musician, church organist, and designer of pipe organs, likens designing with plants to designing a pipe organ. According to Ralph, "You pick singular members for their individual characteristics which you then combine into a unified whole; where the 'whole' is better than the sum of the individual parts. The main difference is that pipes do what you want them to."

It all started with a neglected garden at Christ Church (Anglican) in Columbus where Jaynes was employed at the time. A member offered to pay for upgrading the neglected landscaping, if Jaynes would oversee the restoration. When the layout drawn up by the architect was rejected, Jaynes intervened. The garden was

OWNERS: Craig Jaynes
TYPE: Specialty nursery
SPECIALTIES: Trees and shrubs—rare and unusual
HOURS: Variable, in Spring. Starting around the beginning of May: Sat. 10 am to 6:00 pm. (call ahead). Other times by appointment.
CATALOG AVAILABLE: Online
MAIL-ORDER AVAILABLE: Yes
DISPLAY GARDENS: Yes
CLASSES: No

CONTACT

6599 Old US 35 East
Jamestown, OH 45335
PHONE: (877) 232-2751, (937) 675-7055
FAX: (937) 675-7022
WEB ADDRESS: www.eegardens.com
EMAIL: Craig@eegardens.com

DIRECTIONS

FROM I-71 (NORTH AND SOUTH): I-71 to Exit #65 westbound. (Within a hundred yards or so of exiting the interstate, look for the signs that say "Old US 35 West.") Turn left immediately after the sign which has an arrow pointing to the left but before the next one also pointing to the left. The turn point is indeed hard to see clearly. EE Gardens is approximately 4.5 miles down on your left. (If you miss the turn, you will have no choice but to follow the new four-lane expressway and exit at the first opportunity which is Jamestown/Cedarville, Rt. 72). Look for the white barn with the silhouette of horse/buggy/dog on front and greenhouse on one side. **US-35 EXPRESSWAY FROM THE WEST (DAYTON OR XENIA, FOR EXAMPLE):** Take US-35 through Jamestown and turn left (east) onto the Old US-35. There is only one major intersection in Jamestown: You'll know if you are headed in the correct direction if, after you've made the turn, the old church with the large steeple is on your right. EE Gardens is about 3.5 miles east of Jamestown on the right.

GPS: N39° 38.92', W 83° 41.22'

OHIO

successfully renovated and the first seeds of a new nursery were sown.

Jaynes moved to the present nine-acre "farm" a mere three years ago. In planning out his future gardens, he notes that he has firmly practiced what he preaches, which is "Plant the 'bones' of the garden, such as trees and shrubs, first." Thus, the display gardens, located on 2^1/$_2$ acres planted out with more than 200 different trees and shrubs, are rather sparse in ornamental flowers—for they are a work in progress. Repeat trips to the gardens during the coming years are definitely warranted, as the unfolding contrasts between foliage, fruits, and the yet to be planted flowers should lead to fascinating ornamental combinations.

Visitors to the nursery are welcome to browse the growing gardens on their own. But for serious gardeners planning on adding that lone "knock your socks off" specimen, or emptying their wallet for major landscaping, it is highly recommended that you make the standard, uninterrupted, two-hour appointment with Jaynes for a tour of the plantings and a serious consultation of your needs. In his words, "I'm always willing to answer any of your questions about plants and gardens, which is why I encourage folks to call and make an appointment to visit. Then we have uninterrupted time together."

The key word is *uninterrupted*—he won't even answer the phone during those times. Saturdays, are left as first-come, first-serve, non-appointment days.

> *"Every garden-maker should be an artist along his own lines. That is the only possible way to create a garden, irrespective of size or wealth."*
> —VITA SACKVILLE-WEST

WHAT YOU'LL FIND

Essentially, English Gardens distinguishes itself with an eloquent variety of sophisticated but underused shrubs and trees. Interesting ornamental woodies include the variegated wonder shrub, *Acanthopanax sieboldianus* 'Variegatus'; five varieties of **boxwood** including the columnar *Buxus sempervirens* 'Graham Blandy'; both the native (*Chionanthus virginicus*) and Chinese (*C. retusus*) **fringe trees**; the temperamental but heavenly scented *Daphne* 'Somerset'; and the spectacular golden-leaved **Mexican orange** (*Choisya ternata* 'Sundance'). The nursery carries five cultivars of **witch hazel** (the richly scented *Hamamelis* 'Magic Fire' is my favorite); a bevy of **magnolias**, including the incredibly gorgeous *Magnolia sieboldii* 'Michicko Renge'; and a universe of **Japanese maple**, *Acer palmatum* 'Butterfly' (bluish green leaves with cream markings). You'll find 'Trompenburg' (from Holland, with deep purple-red rolled leaves), 'Shaina' (excellent for containers), 'Osakazuki' (the intense crimson colors of this cultivar in the fall are enough to render a person speechless), and 'Aka Shigitatsu Sawa' (dark reddish-green, pink, and white foliage), to name but a few. Jaynes offers **bottlebrush buckeye**, **Carolina allspice**, the yellow foliaged **southern catalpa**, a number of yellow leaved **forsythias**, a white blooming **kerria**, and the magnificent Persian **parrotia**. Essentially English Gardens has managed to acquire true **dwarf lilacs**, a peck of **viburnums**, and numerous **weigela**.

English Gardens carries a selection of **Oriental dogwoods**, including everyone's favorite *Cornus kousa chinensis* 'Wolf Eyes', 'Snowflake' (beautiful, white "snowflake-like" flower bracts), and the weeper 'Elizabeth Lustgarten'. The nursery's tree holdings include the yellow variegated **tulip tree**, the pendulous **Katsura** tree, the pink flowered **yellowwood**, and the variegated **ginkgo**.

The conifer selections are just as fascinating. The nursery carries many weepers: **Norway spruce**, **European larch**, **white spruce**, **Serbian spruce**, **Japanese red pine**, **Canadian hemlock**, and **Alaskan cedar**. Connoisseurs flock to the nursery for one of the most unusual conifers, *Cunninghania lanceolata* 'Glauca', (with curved needles growing in parallel lines on each side of its branches). English Gardens' conifer yard also includes the **Korean fir**, *Abies koreana* 'Silberlocke' (stupendous recurved needles with white undersides); the very narrow **false cypress**, *Chamaecyparis nootkatensis* 'Green Arrow'; *Juniperus communis* 'Gold Cone' (an upright **juniper** with golden juvenile foliage); *Metasequoia glyptostroboides* 'Gold Rush' (the golden variety of dawn redwood); *Pinus flexilis* 'Cesarini Blue' (the intensely blue needled, blue limber pine); and *Pinus koraiensis* 'Silveray' (the dramatic Korean pine with very long blue-green needles). Conifer fanatics will relish the **dwarf Hinoki**, **false cypress** 'Nana Gracilis'; the thread leaf **Sawara cypress** *Chamaecyparis pisifera* 'Lemon Thread' (golden yellow, dwarf thread leaf with drooping branchlets); and the **blue star juniper** *Juniperus squamata* 'Blue Star' (with star shaped foliage).

I found I couldn't live without the unique, deciduous **Japanese larch** *'Larix kaempferi* 'Diana' with contorted curling branches, or the golden, eastern **white pine**, *Pinus strobus* 'Winter Gold', whose light green needles indulge in a bit of dramatics by turning a brilliant bright gold in winter.

Jaynes motto is, "If you can see dirt you have room for another plant." and to that end, he espouses vines for necessary vertical statements in sites too small for trees or shrubs, such as **honeysuckle**, (*Lonicera*), 'Graham Thomas' or 'Harlequin' (both cultivars of *Lonicera periclymenum*), **passion flower** (*Passiflora*), or the slow growing, climbing **hydrangea** *Schizophragma hydrangeoides* 'Moonlight' (incredibly awesome growing up the trunk of a tree.)

The nursery carries hardy **rose** varieties, all on their own roots, including 17 varieties of Dr. Griffith Buck's roses, the Canadian Explorer™ rose 'Quadra', some winter hardy climbers, the **mini-climbing rose** 'Jeanne LaJoie' (tall with small blossoms and leaves), hybrid **musks**, hybrid rugosas, and ramblers including 'Constance Spry'.

The nursery's well tended stock, sold in sizes ranging from 2-gallon containers to balled-and-burlapped specimens, is tested for at least one winter on the nursery's wind-swept grounds before being offered to the public.

OHIO

HOMEWOOD FARM

❧ ❧

Homewood Farm is a wonderful find for the discerning plant lover lusting after the rare and unusual. Tucked into the rolling Amish farm country, the nursery's 170 acres are a peaceful, rural gem; a charming spot offering an excellent range of well-chosen and rather sophisticated small trees, shrubs, rare and unusual perennials, herbs, and ground covers, as well as some tropicals and annuals. From rock garden gems to the newest introductions for the shade garden, from billowy ornamental grasses to strapping vines, the five greenhouses offer an unrivaled selection of unique plants.

Homewood Farm was founded in 1990 by owner Janet Kohr, more by accident than design. The first greenhouse was built with an eye on growing organic vegetables, but that quickly proved to be impractical. With no great master plan in mind, Kohr shifted to ornamentals, brought in plants unavailable elsewhere, grew healthy, good quality stock, and found the business "grew like topsy." Her eclectic collection, now grown to mind-boggling proportions (the plant list runs a hefty 100 pages), is based solely on what interests Kohr.

Most plants are propagated from seed, vegetatively, or by division—on site, with a few brought in from outside sources. Homewood Farm's

OWNERS: Janet Kohr
TYPE: Large specialty nursery
SPECIALTIES: Perennials—Sun and shade; herbs; annuals; alpines; shrubs—rare; grasses; aquatics; conifers—dwarf; vines; garden art
HOURS: March: Tues.-Sat. 9:00 am to 4:00 pm; April: Tues.-Sat. 9:00 am to 4:00 pm, Sun. 11 am to 4:00 pm; May: Mon.-Fri. 9:00 am to 7:00 PM, Sat. 9:00 am to 5:00 pm, Sun. 11:00 am to 4:00 pm; June thru Oct.: Mon. 9:00 am to 4:00 pm, Tues.-Sat. 9:00 am to 5:00 pm, Sun. 11:00 am to 4:00 pm. Also, by special appointment.
CATALOG AVAILABLE: No
MAIL-ORDER AVAILABLE: No
DISPLAY GARDENS: Yes
CLASSES: Yes

CONTACT
19520 Nunda Road Drive
Howard, OH 43028
PHONE: (740) 599-6638
FAX: (749) 599-9337
WEB ADDRESS: www.homewoodfarm.com
EMAIL: info@homewoodfarm.com

DIRECTIONS
FROM MT. VERNON: Take Rt.-3 north for 10 miles. Watch for the blue state tourist direction sign 2 miles north of Amity.
FROM CLEVELAND AREA: Take I-71 south to Rt.-30 east (Exit #176) Travel east on Rt.-30 to CR-603. Turn south (right) on CT-603 and drive to Rt.-95. Turn west (right) onto Rt.-95 for 1 mile to Bunker Hill Rd. Turn south (left) onto Bunker Hill Rd, (Bunker Hill becomes Nunda) continue for 9 miles to nursery.

GPS: N 40° 30.87', W 82° 21.72'

OHIO

perennials are vigorous, well-grown stock, with descriptive labels noting botanical names and horticultural needs.

Gardeners must come to Homewood Farm to buy, for there is no catalog or mail order. Make the most of the trip by browsing the stone art, birdbaths, troughs, and benches, or pay a visit to the Amish bulk food and bakery just down the lane. Take your time meandering through the extensive display gardens, check out the county's fanciest outhouse, or settle back on the decks overlooking the grounds and plan your next destination.

> *"Spring unlocks the flowers to pain the laughing soil."*
> —REGINALD HERBER

WHAT YOU'LL FIND

Many of my favorite treasures were discovered at this wonderful nursery: seldom offered **fringe cups** *Tellima grandiflora* 'Forest Frost' (silver veined leaves turning burgundy in the fall); **foamflower** *Tiarella* 'Skeleton Key' (spring flowering woodland native with captivating leaves); a variegated **sage** *Salvia nipponica* 'Fuji Snow' (variegated eye-catching foliage, looks like snow); *Salvia greggi* 'Desert Blaze' (green and yellow, variegated); silvery sedge *Carex temnolopsis*, (a touchy-feely sort of a plant for the "white garden"); the unusual **columbine** *Aquilegia* 'Chocolate Soldier' (a chocolate color that is absolutely stunning in partial shade); and **wax bells** *Kirengeshoma* 'Yatabe' (the first cultivar of this species I have ever seen).

The nursery offers a dazzling assortment of rock garden plants and fascinating woodland flora, including a good selection of hardy **ferns, hellebores, trilliums, violets, bleeding heart, nodding ladies tresses, bloodroot,** and **Solomon's seal**. To accommodate customers requests, Homewood Farm has added a small but very special collection of vines, dwarf conifers, flowering shrubs and small trees.

Area gardeners rarely encounter such a bevy of distinctive perennials as **Japanese wild ginger** (*Asarum* 'Galaxy'), the rare and somewhat temperamental **woodlander** *Glaucidium palmatum,* or the hardy, terrestrial **orchid,** *Bletilla striata*. If variegated foliage makes you quiver, then you'll be delirious with indecision by the spotted, streaked, mottled, marbled, edged, blotched, or banded offerings, including: *Corydalis leucantha* 'Silver Scepter' (copper-green silver mottled leaves, lavender flowers); *Convallaria majalis* 'Aureovariegata (variegated **lily of the valley**); *Disporum*

OHIO

sessile 'Variegatum' (variegated fairy bells); or the heady, ivory margined, specimen **dogwood**, *Cornus kousa* 'Wolf Eyes'. Banding and pin-striping adds a touch of histrionics to the strap-like foliage of **iris**, **grass**, **yucca**, and **hardy bamboo**. Intrepid gardeners lusting for yellow foliage will revel in lots of tasty surprises, such as **bellflower**, evergreen climbing **euonymous**, **saxifrage**, **toad lily**, **rock cress**, **bleeding heart**, **thyme**, and **forsythia**.

While not always showy, low growers are essential in creating tapestries of form, texture and color. A carpet of mini (4-inch) **lady's mantle** (*Alchemilla saxitelis*), **dwarf Solomon's seal** (*Polygonatum humile*), or **Siberian dragon's head** (*Dracocephalum ruyschiana*) beats a drab dressing of bark mulch any day. Homewood Farm features troughs, and trough gardens are ideal places to display tiny horticultural treasures such as dwarf conifers, alpines, miniature succulents, and other precious little plants, one in particular, a miniature **statice** (*Limonium minutum*), proved to be a cutie.

Have a passion for the color purple? *Aster lateriflorus* 'Prince', a native **aster** improved by the British, sports muted purple foliage and come autumn is smothered in starry white flowers with tiny crowns of raspberry stamens. For three solid weeks every fall, this aster is showstoppingly, heartbreakingly, smack-you-upside-the-head-gorgeous! Mixed with the yellows of rudbeckia, it'll wake you up better than any latte, or, partnered with the cool lavender blue of *Aster* 'Lady in Blue' or purple coneflower, it can set your spirit purring like a kitten with a bottomless bowl of cream.

Herbs abound. The nursery carries an incredible selection of common culinary herbs, but there is a growing selection of medicinal herbs. One such herb is **Gatu Kola**, a Chinese medicinal herb used to rejuvenate brain cells. The culinary herbs include: **oregano**, **sage**, **parsley**, **chives**, **garlic**, **mint**, **thyme**, and **basil**.

It's hard for me to imagine having too much basil. If you get tired of the typical 'Genovese' basil, try a different type such as 'Thai', 'Red Rubin', or

★ SIDE TRIPS ★

THE DAWES ARBORETUM, (740) 323-2355, 7770 Jacksontown, Neward, OH. (35 miles east of Columbus) includes 1,149 acres of plant collections and natural areas that offer unique educational experiences in any season. **OHIO'S OLDEST GENERAL STORE**, (740) 392-0336, 115 S. Main Street., Mt. Vernon, OH 43050. In business since 1897, founded by Civil War Vets, it's an interesting place to browse.

OHIO

'Cinnamon' basil. Mixing the different selections in a border can create a striking accent. To that end, 'Holy Basil' works well as an ornamental. The nursery carries numerous varieties of **lavender**, and a rarity, **samphire**, used fresh in salads for a spicy and salty taste.

Ornamental herbs include fruit-scented **geranium**, **bee balm**, **angelica**, 'African blue' basil, 'Pineapple', and 'Honeydew Melon' **salvia**.

Flowering shrubs include **mockorange**, **dogwood**, **butterfly bush**, **bottlebrush buckeye**, and the ultra-chic, grafted tree **wisteria** in white and lavender. On a personal note, I always find it gratifying to find the spectacular butterfly bush, *Buddleia davidii* 'Ellen's Blue'. It was originally discovered on the property of my dear friend, Ellen Horning, owner of Seneca Nursery, Oswego, New York.

Extensive garden rooms and display gardens showcasing Kohr's elegant designs and landscaping talents surround their residence and nursery, and extend onto the expansive grounds. There are riveting displays of jazzy plant combinations, and ornamental grasses in a bewitching blend of color, form, motion and sound. There are blossoms with colors that roll the warmth of an Indian summer's day into the fire of an early autumn sunset. Along with these you'll find the cooling mantle of green conifers, fragrant shrubs, vines, and roses.

LEWIS MOUNTAIN HERBS & EVERLASTINGS

ᶜᵉ᎐᎐ ᎐᎐ᵉᵒ

Lewis Mountain Herbs & Everlastings is a large, stylish nursery specializing in scented geraniums, herbs, and everlastings (flowers that can be dried). Located on 17 acres on top of a hill, the nursery, which grows more than 600 varieties of plants, includes a barn, a well stocked gift shop, six acres of cutting fields, various display gardens, a kennel, and the most recent endeavor, a Bed and Breakfast. A major attraction of the gardens is the incredible pleached crabapple gazebo, which is used for weddings (and once for a funeral).

The barn's rafters function as the perfect drying area for the everlastings that are cut three times weekly, bundled and hung. It is also pressed into service for the various workshops available throughout the year, such as classes for making everlasting wreaths, swags, topiarys (herb and everlasting), English garden arrangements, moss baskets, potpourri, tussie mussies, windowsill herb gardens, and holiday decorations.

Owner Judy Lewis first started "working" at Lewis Mountain Herbs, when her husband, a biology teacher, decided he wanted to own a nursery. Since he was still teaching, and Judy didn't want to grow plants available at other nurseries, Lewis chose to grow herbs. Throughout the past thirty years, the Lewis philosophy of always providing employees with a job—in good times and lean—led to the additions of other various enterprises. "Once you are employed here," says Lewis with a smile, "you are an employee for life."

OWNERS: Judy Lewis
TYPE: Specialty nursery. Retail and wholesale
SPECIALTIES: Herbs; everlastings; scented geraniums
HOURS: Year-round: Mon.-Sat. 9:00 am to 4:00 pm.
CATALOG AVAILABLE: Printed and online
MAIL-ORDER AVAILABLE: Yes
DISPLAY GARDENS: Yes
CLASSES: Yes

CONTACT
2345 State Road 247
Manchester, OH 45144
PHONE: (800) 714-3727, (937) 549-2484
FAX: (937) 549-2886
WEB ADDRESS: www.bright.net/~mtherbs
EMAIL: mtherbs@bright.net

DIRECTIONS
FROM CINCINATTI AREA: I-71 south towards Louisville, merge onto I-471 south, merge onto I-275 east at Exit 1A (ramp on left) toward Columbus, merge onto OH-32 east (Exit 63B) toward Batavia. Turn right onto Main Street/OH-247, go through the town of Union, nursery is approximately 4.5 miles southeast of Union on OH-247.

GPS: N 38° 44.22', W 83° 31.05'

When you visit, you'll see that time spent with Lewis Mountain Herbs quickly introduces the visitor to the lore and history of herbs, an appreciation for how they are grown, methods of preservation, and their many and varied uses.

WHAT YOU'LL FIND

Common culinary herbs include many kinds of **basil** (12), **thyme** (10), **fennel** (3), and **sage** (6). The nursery carries **cardamon, cardoon, chamomile, chervil, chives, comfrey, coriander, dill, horseradish, marjoram, oregano, parsley, rosemary, savory**, and 10 kinds of **lavender**.

Unusual everlastings include **acroclinium** (flowers that feel dry to the touch even when fresh on the stem), **Chinese lantern, coxcomb** (*Caspia*), **lion's ear, pearly everlasting, bells of Ireland, winged everlasting** (tiny white

> *"Just living is not enough," said the butterfly. "One must have sunshine, freedom, and a little flower."*
> —HANS CHRISTIAN ANDERSON

strawflowers), and **yarrow**. Classic dried flowers, the nursery's stock in trade, include yellow **ageratum, globe amaranth** (in pink, lavender, purple, red, orange, champagne, and white), **sweet Annie, money plant**, blue **salvia**, and **larkspur**.

Medicinals available at Lewis Mountain include **betony, comfrey, evening primrose, feverfew, lamb's ear**, and **purple coneflower**. They have perfume herbs such as **patchouli, valerian**, and **lavender**; showy ornamentals such as **artemesia, butterfly weed, heliotrope, hollyhock, fleabane, foxglove, liatris, lobelia, love-in-a-mist** (or **devil-in-the-bush**, depending on your proclivity), **globe thistle, Mexican marigold**, and **tansy**.

Bedstraw, safflower, woad, and **madder** can be used for dyeing; and worthwhile candidates for hanging baskets include **good herb, licorice plant**, and **Vick's plant** (I wonder, though, does anyone really want or need a hanging basket that eternally smells of "vapor rub?").

The nursery offers interesting notes about the herbs they sell. The flower head of the giant **scotch thistle** is good steamed with butter. **Borage** flowers and **burnet** leaves taste like cucumbers in salads. **Samphire** is a good substitute for salt, while **eucalyptus** can smell of lemon and peppermint. **Job's tears** forms hard pods to make beaded jewelry, and the dried fruits of the **luffa** can be used in bathing.

OHIO

Lewis Mountain Herbs & Everlastings is celebrated for its remarkable hoard (80 varieties) of **scented geraniums**. Emitting sweet-smelling essences such as ginger, apple, rose and coconut, scented geraniums (or scented-leaf geraniums) are the perfect potted plant for brightening a home. According to Lewis, scented geraniums exude strong fragrances when stimulated outdoors by the sun's heat or indoors by a gentle touch. She notes that Victorian women tucked leaves into sachets and dropped them in their baths. And it wasn't long before cooks discovered flavor as well as fragrance in the leaves and found unique and interesting ways to use the plants in teas, cakes, cookies, candies, jams, puddings and wines.

Many scented geraniums are named according to their fragrances, and most appear to be named appropriately—rose, peppermint, cinnamon, and coconut. Others, such as 'French Lace' (fruit scented, strong lemon aroma with cream variegation) rely on the imagination or the power of suggestion to make the connection between the plant's fragrance and its name. Some rely on a combination of sight and scent. 'Chocolate Mint' exudes a strong musty mint scent and has a deep chocolate colored blotch on the leaves. Still others jar the senses with a single sniff. 'Mabel Grey', for instance, smells more lemony than furniture polish and 'Old Spice', exudes a spicy nutmeg-apple aroma. And then there are more surprises, such as 'Gray Lady Plymouth' (rose scented with a touch of mint, deep cream variegation, lavender flowers), 'Pink Champagne' (pungent scented), 'Gooseberry' (fruit scented, cream variegated leaves), and 'Oak Leaf" (pine scented, triangular dark green leaves with chocolate brown centers).

Display gardens at Lewis Mountain contain scented geranium varieties divided into groups that are reminiscent of roses, fruits, spices, pine nuts and even pungent eucalyptus.

★ **SIDE TRIPS** ★

GARDEN ACCENTS, LOGAN CLAY PRODUCTS, 201 S. Walnut St., Logan OH 43138. Known for its clay sewer pipe this historic Hill Country industry has expanded to offer a retail location for its garden planters, birdbaths stepping stones, and garden edging. **SERPENT MOUND,** (937) 587-2796, (call for directions) built by Adena people between 800 BC and 100 AD, is famous worldwide as the largest and finest serpent effigy in the US.

OHIO

MARY'S PLANT FARM

❧ ❧

Ask owner and horticulturist, Mary Harrison, and she'll gladly tell you "every bloomin' thing there is to know" about growing her garden. Her twenty-five-year old gardens, all 6 acres of them, are her passion – and they're all for sale. That's right, the nursery stock is grown right in her own gardens.

Harrison treats the growing season as one big garden party. Mary says, "Folks have an open invitation to tour our gardens, to see how our nursery stock looks in the landscape." If time permits, she will give you a personalized guided tour of the gardens—past the rose pergola, the herb gardens, the daylily fields, the shade gardens, and around the lily pond. Even visitors with no expectations of a purchase are invited to see the gardens.

Their extensive gift shop offers garden tools, gardening supplies, herbs, seed mixes, and information about landscaping and florist services. Well patronized by local area gardeners, the nursery andgarden center offers interesting workshops and classes. Peak bloom periods run from mid-May thru September.

WHAT YOU'LL FIND

The emphasis at Mary's Plant Farm is on high quality, farm-bred, field grown, ornamental plants—both the common as well as the rare and

---

OWNERS: Mary Harrison
TYPE: Specialty nursery/garden center/landscaping business
SPECIALTIES: Perennials—shade and sun; roses; daylilies; hosta; bulbs; grasses; tubers; herbs; shrubs; trees; conifers; wildflowers
HOURS: April through end of June: Tues.-Sat. 9:30 am to 6:30 pm, Sun. 12 pm to 5:00 pm; July through October: Tues.-Sat. 9:30 am to 5:00 pm. Other times by appointment.
CATALOG AVAILABLE: Printed and online
MAIL-ORDER AVAILABLE: Yes
DISPLAY GARDENS: Yes
CLASSES: Yes

CONTACT

2410 Lanes Mill Road
Hamilton, OHIO 45013
PHONE: (513) 894-0022
FAX: (513) 892-0022
WEB ADDRESS: www.marysplantfarm.com
EMAIL: sales@marysplantfarm.com

DIRECTIONS

FROM THE WEST (I-70): Take I-70 to US-27. Take US-27 south to Stillwell Beckett Rd. (approx. 4.0 miles southeast of Oxford). Turn east (left) onto Stillwell Beckett Rd. and drive 0.25 miles to Lanes Mill Rd. Turn south (right) on Lanes Mill Rd. Drive to the nursery about 0.2 miles down. **FROM THE SOUTH AND THE EAST:** Take I-275 to US-27, exiting north bound. Drive north about 15.5 miles to Lanes Mill Rd, located at a 5-way intersection. Turn slightly right (due north) on Lanes Mill Rd. for about 0.25 miles to nursery. Look for the nursery behind the residence, next door to the United Methodist Church.

GPS: N 39° 26.98', W 84° 40.98'

unusual. The perennial list is extensive; it includes many shade plants, native varieties, flowering shrubs, understory trees, roses, vines, daylilies, hosta, wildflowers, ferns, and grasses. Some plants were handed down to her from her parents garden and are probably not readily available anywhere else. So, if the plant to set your heart aflutter isn't listed in the catalog, talk to Mary; she just might have it growing on the farm in quantities too small to list.

Cottage Gardeners can pick from a peck of **delphinium**, **pinks**, **foxglove**, **scabiosa**, **hollyhock**, *Malva*, *Monarda*, **poppy**, *Stokesia*, and **peony**. The nursery offers 185 species and cultivars of *Iris*, including *Iris cristata*, *I. pumila*, *I. germanica*, *I. tectorum*, *I. florentina* (orris root), *I. pseudacorus*, *I. sibirica*, *I. spuria* and *I.* Louisiana hybrids.

Mary's Farm offers many **anemone**, **coral bells**, **rudbeckia**, **monarda**, and **astilbe**; several **artemesia**, **campanula**, **sedum**, and **pulmonaria**; and a universe of **asters**, **coreopsis**, **salvia**, **penstemon**, **shasta daisy**, and tall garden **phlox**.

> "Nothing is more beautiful than the loveliness of the woods before sunrise."
> — GEORGE WASHINGTON CARVER

Harrison focuses her efforts on growing more than 1,600 named varieties of **daylilies**: diploids, tetraploids, spiders, trumpets, reflexed or twisted sepals, curled or ruffled petals in colors ranging from near white thru black-red, and every thing in between (except blue). The nursery carries more than 300 varieties of **hosta** sold per crown in blue, green, variegated, gold, and margined.

Mary's Plant Farm grows superior varieties of wildflowers (all are nursery propagated): **spring beauty**, **merry bells**, **marsh marigold**, **snakeroot**, **squirrel corn**, **spiderwort**, **trillium** (11 varieties), **violet**, **yellow root**, **mayapple**, **ironweed**, **liverleaf**, **dutchman's breeches**, and **toad lily**. Harrison collects hardy **geranium** along with **bleeding heart**, **hellebore**, *Pulmonaria*, *Primula*, and **celandine poppy**. The nursery's wide collection of ferns and grasses includes **maidenhair fern**, **royal fern**, **Japanese painted fern**, **leatherwood**, **northern sea oats**, **sedge**, **reed grass**, **love grass**, **switchgrass**, and **miscanthus**.

In the shrub category, the nursery carries **bottlebrush buckeye**, **butterfly bush**, **sweet shrub**, **flowering quince**, and **clove bush**; 20 varieties of **boxwood**, 18 of **witch hazel**, 6 of **mockorange**, and 20 of **spirea**; countless **viburnum**, **hydrangea**, and **lilac**; and a healthy dose of **deutzia**, **smoke tree**, **spice bush** and **ural false spirea** (*Sorbaria sorbifolia*).

OHIO

Mary's Plant Farm's **rose** collection embraces climbers, Buck roses, English (Austin) roses, rugosa roses, shrub roses, old roses, and mini roses. All are superb plants—beautiful, colorful, fragrant, and winter-hardy to the area.

In the fall, Mary's Plant Farm sells a multitude of specialty bulbs, with the emphasis placed on spring bulbs: **hyacinths**, **windflower**, **bluebells**, **crocus**, and **grape hyacinth** are joined by **fritillaria**, **shooting star**, **daffodils** and **tulips**. For summer and fall blooms, Harrison has **camassia**, fall blooming **colchicum**, **allium**, *Cyclamen hederifolium* (white and pink), and various **lilies**.

EXTRAS

Some iris are priced up to $6 per plant at the nursery, but they have a catalog special of $1 per plant for mixed colors, nursery's choice.

MULBERRY CREEK HERB FARM

❧ ❧

Mulberry Creek Herb Farm is a small, certified organic herb and flower farm and nursery, located in the delightfully rural town of Huron, in northeastern Ohio. Owners Karen and Mark Langon, (both with degrees in the field of horticulture) are accomplished gardeners and highly respected educators. The Langon's founded Mulberry Creek Herb Farm ten years ago and now grow well over 400 varieties of herbs, annuals, perennials, miniatures, tender perennials, tomato, and pepper plants. Seed production is achieved on an acre of beds behind the greenhouses adjacent to their country abode.

Attractively planted display gardens, in a bewitching country setting surround their nursery, greenhouses, and home, afford customers the opportunity to experience the sensual flavor, fragrance, and beauty of herbs. The emphasis is on a wide variety of robust herb plants, rather than just vast quantities of the same plant. It is advisable to place your orders early since popular varieties do sell out. Shipping is done from March 1st through the end of May, and though you may order any combination of plants, all orders must be in multiples of six.

OWNERS: Karen and Mark Langon
TYPE: Small specialty nursery
SPECIALTIES: Certifield organic herbs; perennials; annuals; tomato and pepper plants
HOURS: April 1-July: Tues.-Sat. 10:00 am to 5:00 pm; May (only) Sun. Noon to 5:00 pm. Other times by appointment. Shipping: March 1 through June only.
CATALOG AVAILABLE: Printed and online
MAIL-ORDER AVAILABLE: Yes
DISPLAY GARDENS: Yes
CLASSES: Yes

CONTACT
3312 Bogart Road
Huron, OH 44839
PHONE: (419) 433-6126
FAX: (419) 433-44839
WEB ADDRESS: www.mulberrycreek.com
E-MAIL: herbs@mulberrycreek.com

DIRECTIONS
FROM THE TOLEDO AREA: Take I-80 east approx. 38 miles to SR-4 (Hayes Ave.). Proceed north on SR-4 for 4.5 miles to SR-2. Turn east (right) on SR-2 for 4 miles to US-250 (Milan Rd.). Turn southeast (right) onto US-250 (Milan Rd.) for 0.4 miles. Turn east (left) onto Bogart Rd.and proceed l.8 miles to farm.

GPS: N 41° 23.42', W 82° 37.13'

The nursery's memorable plant list, along with the impressive credentials of the erudite owners, offers gardeners information from the Langons' vast experiences with medicinal, culinary, and ornamental herbs. In addition there is information about other quality plants and products.

OHIO

Winter weary cooks beat a path to the annual Open House held the first two week-ends in December; where culinary herbs for windowsills reign supreme.

For the past ten years, they've been providing the largest selection of well grown, certified organic herbs in 3½-inch pots, at reasonable prices.

WHAT YOU'LL FIND

Intriguing herbs include showy ornamentals such as **bee balm** (*Monarda*), **butterfly bush** (*Buddleia davidii*), **foxglove** (*Digitalis*), **nasturtium**, **dwarf delphinium**, **purple coneflower** (*Echinacea*), **elderberry** (*Sambucus*), **foxglove** (*Digitalis*), **lavender** and **lavandin** (*Lavandula*), **sweet flag** (*Acorus*), and **violet** (*Viola*). Unusual ornamentals include the world's smallest **violet** *Viola verecunda* var. *yakusimana*, (a hearthrob that's a mere 0.5-inch tall), a **dwarf ladies mantle** *Alchemilla faroensis* 'Pumila (a 3-inch miniature wearing morning dew as if it was a necklace of fairy diamonds); and the unusual and hard to find **creeping wire vine** *Muehlenbeckia axillaris* (a non-hardy ground cover with ladybug sized leaves on scrawny, wiry stems, whose tiny white flowers morph into mini-pearls). There are good culinary herbs such as **chives**, **sorrel**, **sage**, **oregano**, **parsley** and "hard neck music" **garlic** (*Allium sativum*). You'll find useful medicinals with unfamiliar names such as **gotu kola** (*Centella asiatica*) (improves brain function); **Chinese arum** *Pinellia ternata* (a Chinese medicine for a variety of ailments); and **epazote** *Chenopodiuiim ambrosioides* (useful with bean dishes to "forego the fireworks").

> "That beautiful season the Summer! Filled was the air with a dreamy and magical light; and the landscape Lay as if new created in all the freshness of childhood."
> —HENRY WADSWORTH LONGFELLOW

There are fruit-scented **geraniums**, and interesting **lavenders**, **thymes**, **rosemaries**, and **mints**, including Kentucky Colonel mint *Mentha spicata* 'Kentucky Colonel' (the official mint of the Kentucky Derby's mint julep); and **Amsterdam celery** *Apium graveolens* (a celery substitute with hollow stalks that is also known as "love straw," perfect for sipping tomato juice drinks or tomato based libations.)

Organically grown **pepper** and **tomato** plants in 2½-foot biodegradable fiber pots combine the mundane with jazzy and stylish varieties (not easily found), such as the "damn hot!" 'Thai Dragon', Italian heirloom 'Corno di Toro Red', 'Buldog Hungarian Spice' peppers, and the sought-after 'Arkansas Traveller', 'Mister Stripey', 'Prudens Purple', and 'Mortgage Lifter' tomatoes.

OHIO

Mulberry Creek offers diminutive "Mulberry Miniatures" suitable for small containers, troughs, outdoor railroaders, miniature landscapes, stepping stones, rock gardens, and faerie domains.

The nursery's printed and internet catalogs are, according to the Langon's, "bursting with growing and using tips." They guarantee that after you've finished browsing their website, you'll be qualified to tell Martha Stewart what she can do with her herb garden.

EXTRAS

Gardeners of every experience level are invited to the annual Herb Fair held every June. This event is full of speakers, workshops, demonstrations, entertainment, plant sales, tours, an herb buffet, and herb related vendors showcasing everything from dried flowers and essential oils, to honey, tussiemussies, and soaps. It draws good crowds and even better reviews.

OHIO

OAKLAND NURSERY

⊰⊱

Founded in 1940, Oakland Nursery has grown to become one of the largest garden centers in Central Ohio, offering its customers 17 acres (10 acres in Columbus and 7 in Delaware) of plants, gifts and plant maintenance products. Located in a residential area, the large garden center is popular with landscapers, designers, and gardeners for its outstanding selection of quality plants. Oakland Nursery offers many innovative, rare and unusual shrubs and trees. According to co-owner John Reiner, "If they grow it in North America, Oakland Nurseries sells it." (That might not be an overstatement!) Specials are listed on the internet.

Although Oakland Nursery boasts of its specialized services (see "Extras"), it is, first and foremost, a prodigious source of perennials, roses, trees and shrubs. Priding itself on the saying "If you haven't been to Oakland Nursery, you simply haven't been to a nursery!" the highly trained horticultural staff creates a series of prominent, bold and colorful displays comprised entirely of container grown, beautiful flowering plants. Colors blaze and swirl; there are plenty of pristine whites, sparking yellows, radiant pinks, deep, smoldering reds, rich, warm oranges, and effervescent blues. The new hybrids will get your gardening juices flowing.

OWNERS: Gus Paul, and John Reiner
TYPE: Large garden center
SPECIALTIES: Perennials—sun and shade; herbs; annuals; alpines; shrubs; trees; grasses; aquatics; vines; roses; garden art; containers
HOURS: Year-round: Mon.-Sat. 8:00 am to 8:00 pm, Sun. 9:00 am to 6:00 pm.
CATALOG AVAILABLE: Rose price sheets
MAIL-ORDER AVAILABLE: No
DISPLAY GARDENS: No
CLASSES: Yes

CONTACT
1156 Oakland Park
Columbus, OH 43223
PHONE: (614) 268-3511
FAX: (614) 268-3003
WEB ADDRESS: www.oaklandnursery.com
EMAIL: info@homewoodfarm.com

DIRECTIONS
FROM I-70: Take I-70 to exit #61A (I-71) to Columbus, I-71 north via Exit 101A (on the left) toward Cleveland. Exit I-71 on E North Broadway St. (Exit 114). Turn east (right) on E. North Broadway St. traveling for 0.2 miles to MaizeRoad. Turn north (left) on Maize Road one block to Oakland Park Ave. Turn east (right) onto Oakland Park Ave. driving 0.3 to nursery. (Watch for signs).

GPS: N 40° 01.93', W 82° 58.97'

OHIO

WHAT YOU'LL FIND

Their classic hardy perennial collections are augmented by varieties not typically found at local garden centers, such as **tatarian statice** (*Goniolimon tataricum*);

> "One of the worst mistakes you can make as a gardener is to think you're in charge!"
> —JANET GILLESPIE, *Readers Digest*

prickly pear cactus (*Opuntia humifusa* 'Lemon Form'); **wallflower** (*Erysimum allioni*); **pussytoes** (*Antennaria dioica*); and **goldenseal** (*Hydrastis canadensis*). Emphasis is on new, unusual, and often undervalued plants.

Oakland Nursery carries the gamut of **roses**—more than 300 varieties—in an astounding selection of 20,000 plants. The potted, container-grown plants are Grade #1, hardy, well-groomed, two-year-old plants ready to be planted out in the landscape. The nursery's list includes hybrid tea roses (listed by individual colors and blends), grandifloras, floribundas, shrub, Meidiland™, rugosa, English, antique, climbing, and miniature. It carries landscape classics such as 'The Fairy', her sister 'Red Fairy', and sports 'Crystal Fairy'™, 'Fairy Queen'™, and 'Lovely Fairy'. They sell the Simplicity series of easy-care, free-flowering roses in pink, red, purple, and yellow; Buck roses 'Distant Drums' and 'Country Dancer'; and AARS winners such as the bright cherry-red 'Knockout'™ (2000), pure pink 'Bonica' (1987), carmine rose 'Carefree Delight'™ (1996), and crisp, pure white 'Starry Night'™ (2002).

My gardener's heart warmed to 'Bonanza'™ (double yellow); 'Greetings' (semi-double white overlaid with purple pink), and the white double 'Heart 'N' Soul' (apple scented, seductively edged in lipstick red). Incredibly floriferous tree roses (30 varieties) are available in 36-inch and 24-inch standards; true "miniature tree" roses, such as 'Baby Grand', 'Denver's Dream', and 'Neon Cowboy' come in diminutive 18-inch standards.

At Oakland you can find an interesting collection of perky composites: **coreopsis** (11 varieties), *Heliopsis* (**false sunflower**), *Helianthus*, *Inula*, and *Helenium* (**sneezeweed**). Late in the growing season they have **mums** (40 varieties). Customers flock for the gaggle of **yarrow**, **dianthus**, *Gaillardia*, **phlox**, **shasta daisy**, *Monarda*, and **veronica**. Ambitious gardeners eager to create stunning ornamental woodlands can find **columbine**, **jack-in-the-pulpit**,

SATELLITE LOCATION

CONTACT
25 Kilbourne Road
Delaware, OH
PHONE: (740) 548-6633

DIRECTIONS
FROM I-70: Take I-70 to I-270 north (Exit # 93B) toward Cleveland. Take I-270 to Rt-23 north toward Delaware for 14.3 miles. Turn east (right) on Rt.-36/Rt. 37/ William St. for 1.4 miles to Kilbourne Rd. Nursery on northwest corner of Rt. 36 and Kilbourne Rd.

dutchman's breeches, **false solomon's seal**, **foam flower**, **glory of the snow**, **trillium**, **anemone**, and **bloodroot**. They'll find a prodigious amount of **hosta**, **columbine** and **astilbe**. The nursery is known for its collections of **allium**, **violas**, **primulas** and **sedum**. Walking through, I found numerous cultivars of **Japanese maples**, **rhododenrons**, **dogwoods**, **viburnums**, **hydrangeas**, and **boxwoods**.

The staff advocates old fashioned flowers—beloved for their exquisite colors, alluring scents, graceful forms, and hardy constitutions. Examples are **canterbury bells** (with corolla cups and calyx saucers); queenly **delphinium**; **foxglove** (elegant flower-packed spires); bold, silky **poppies**, and staggeringly beautiful **iris**.

Popular sellers are ornamental grasses, vines, and an incredible array of tender exotics. The **salvias** and "little bananas" (*Musa sumatrana* 'Zebrina') are addictive; **alpines** in 3-inch pots are perfect for the new hypertufa troughs (available in various sizes and shapes). Gardeners short on time or ambition, but with a big need for "rockeries," can pick up troughs pre-planted with jazzy alpines enhanced by decorative rock.

"Tropicalissmo" can be found at Oakland. Bodacious temperennials of really "hot" plants for northerly climates includes *Alocasia* 'Black Velvet', *Brugmansia* 'Variegata', *Colocasia* 'Illustris', *Hedychium* 'Luna Moth', *Kaempferia rotunda* 'Raven', *Tibouchina grandiflora, Phygelius* 'Devil's Tears', and *Zingiber* 'Milky Way'.

Containerized fruit trees include **apple**, **pear**, sweet and sour **cherry**, **crab apple**, **plum**, and **peach**. Unusual woodland plants included American **fringe trees**, **bottlebrush buckeye** and **drooping leucothoe**; anything and everything from **American hop hornbeam** to **katsura trees** to weeping **hemlocks**. Some plants are grown in containers; while others, prized specimens, can have root balls four feet in diameter and price tags exceeding $1,500.

OHIO

In early spring, Oakland Nursery breaks the dreary winter blah's by offering a full range of seeds. More **Easter lilies**, interesting annuals, tropical plants, hanging baskets, and varieties of vegetables (classic and heirloom) are there than any gardener can comfortably choose. In summer, along with judicious selections of interesting lectures and seminars, the nursery sets out jumbo annuals, well-grown herbs, and a universe of potted perennials. Come autumn, bulbs, **flowering kale**, **pansies**, late season flowering plants, **pumpkins** and Halloween and Thanksgiving decorations take center stage. (The annual Pumpkin Festival, complete with tractor-pull hay rides, door prizes, face and pumpkin painting, and a giant scarecrow, also promoted a pumpkin weigh-off. The hefty winner, a gargantuan squash weighing a robust 1,360 pounds, was a mere 25 pounds short of the world record.) And for one of the merriest of all seasons, Oakland carries an excellent assortment of **poinsettias** and a world of cut greens, wreaths, rope, kissing balls, Christmas trees, and interior and exterior decorations.

The nursery's commercial attraction is further enhanced by unique and distinctive garden art, a full range of gardening supplies, an incredibly well-stocked gift shop, a highly trained and accessible horticultural staff, a large pottery assortment, vast fall bulk bulb sales, water gardening supplies, mulch, seed, fertilizer, and other products for ancillary needs. Oakland also offers lawn ornaments and statuary; printed cultivation advice, informative lists, a comprehensive rose catalog, bird houses, and outdoor works of art produced by local artists.

PLEASANT VALLEY GARDENS

❧ ❧

Pleasant Valley Gardens is a picturesque daylily garden and Clydesdale horse farm located on 38 acres of rolling land on the southwest edge of the city. The farm features an 1843 Federal style farmhouse, a number of barns, outbuildings, display gardens, and daylily propagation fields.

The nursery is owned by Joel Thomas Polston and Doug Sterling, who for the past eight years have been growing more than 1,400 named daylily cultivars (and at least 4,500 Polston seedlings) on 3 acres of their farm. Polston credits his father for igniting his passion for "getting dirt under his fingernails." Having caught the hybridization bug, in recent years Polston and Sterling have been pursuing an amazingly aggressive daylily breeding program.

Polson encourages visitors to tour the display gardens, seedling beds and production fields, and note their favorites. Peak daylily bloom is typically around the 4th of July; however, some open earlier and others later, so repeat trips are recommended.

WHAT YOU'LL FIND

Polston's specialty is breeding winter hardy, round, ruffled, "bagel" type **daylilies**. A measure of his success is the introduction in 2003 of 'When Angel's Dream', a daylily that appears diamond-dusted, with a rich peachy-pink, soft yellow throat, and lime heart. That year he also introduced 'Braided Sunset', with soft salmon-coral pink coloring, a beautiful ruffled

OWNERS: Joel Thomas Polston and Doug Sterling
TYPE: Specialty nursery
SPECIALTIES: Daylilies
HOURS: June to Mid-August. Mon.-Fri. 5:30 pm to 8:30 pm, Sat.-Sun. 9:00 am to 8:00 pm. Other times by appointment.
CATALOG AVAILABLE: Online
MAIL-ORDER AVAILABLE: Yes
DISPLAY GARDENS: Yes
CLASSES: No

CONTACT
7465 W. Third Street
Dayton, OH 45427
PHONE: (937) 835-5231
WEB ADDRESS:
www.daylilytrader.com/id148.htm
EMAIL: pleasantvalleyfa@aol.com

DIRECTIONS
FROM THE WEST OR EAST FROM I—70: Take I-70 to OH-49N/Clayton/Phillipsburg (Exit #24). Turn northeast (left) onto Brookville Sale Pike driving 0.8 miles to Diamond Mill Rd. Turn south (right) onto Diamond Mill Rd and drive 7.9 miles to Rt. 35. Turn east (left) onto Dayton Eaton Pike/US-35 (Dayton Eaton Pike/US-35 becomes 3rd Street about a mile down) for 2.5 miles to nursery on your left.
FROM THE SOUTH FROM I-75: Take I-75 to US-35W toward Eaton (Exit # 52B) driving 5.4 miles to 3rd St/US-35. Turn west (left) onto 3rd St./US-35 and drive for 1.6 miles to the nursery, on your right.

GPS: N 39° 44.76', W 84° 19.09'

OHIO

double edge (no less) of pink and gold, and a matching pink eye-halo; and 'Ah Ah Lava', a very long blooming creamy yellow daylily with a ruffled edge. But my favorite of the 2003 introductions is the eye-candy, 'Ruffles and Ribbons', an awesome coral red daylily with a golden yellow throat. The petals have large, seductive, looping ruffles that remind me of extravagant bows, parties, and stunning bridesmaid bouquets.

> "In his garden every man may be his own artist without apology or explanation. Here is one spot where each may experience the "romance of possibility."
>
> —LOUIS BEEBE WILDER

In 2004 Polston introduced 'Eye of Ra' a beautiful vibrant orange; pink 'Farscape'; 'Valley of the Kings', a soft peach-pink blend with a darker pink watermark; and 'Sea Dragon', a bright and bold purple bitone daylily with a gold and "toothy" edge (this is the one that immediately attracts all garden visitors). 'Sea Dragon' exhibits rather limited branching and a minimum of buds, but what it lacks in quantity it more than makes up for in visual quality. As is typical of greatness, Pleasant Valley Gardens was sold out of this smashingly beautiful cultivar at the time of this writing (but keep checking).

Although Polston specializes in the "bagel" types of plants, some of the seedlings held for future introductions clearly show that he doesn't limit himself

★ SIDE TRIPS ★

WOODLAND CEMETERY & ARBORETUM, ((937) 228-3221, 118 Woodland Ave., Dayton, OH 45409. Founded in 1841, this is one of America's oldest garden cemeteries. There are 230 acres of rolling terrain featuring natural beauty. Many of the 3,000 trees and shrubs are labeled for visitor education. Nine trees are Ohio Big Tree Champions. Open Year Round. **WEGERZYN GARDENS METROPARK,** (937) 277-6545, 1301 E. Siebenthaler Ave., Dayton, OH, (located 5 miles north of Dayton). This garden consists of 46 acres by the Stillwater River and 7 vignette gardens: children's, rose, English, federal, Victorian, heritage, and historical. There is a central mall featuring a 'Cimmaron' white ash allee.

OHIO

to just that venue: there are ruffles galore, blossoms resembling orchids, more "teeth" than a gardener should ever have to pick from, and rich, vibrant colors.

Pleasant Valley Gardens offers their own introductions through mail order only, sold in good sized, one-fan divisions (email them for list, ordering, and shipping information). However, the physical nursery does offer more than 1,000 varieties of named breeder cultivars at reasonable prices, giving on-site visitors a distinct advantage.

OHIO

QUAILCREST FARM

✦

Quailcrest Farm is located north of Wooster in the rolling countryside of Wayne County. What had been a dairy farm for more than a century has evolved into a family-owned retail nursery still grounded in its agricultural roots. The Quailcrest name was first established in 1957; and today is a premier Midwest resource for herbs, perennials, roses, flowering trees and shrubs. The farm sits on the crest of a hill overlooking the beautiful Killbuck Valley and, until the killing blizzard of 1978, shared the land with a large population of bobwhite quail—hence the name, "Quailcrest."

The first 200 perennials were planted at the nursery in the fall of 1974, and the nursery welcomed its first customers in April of the following year. Despite major setbacks, there's been no looking back since then.

A cutting edge nursery that continually searches for new and exciting plants, Quailcrest specializes in herbs, scented geraniums, perennials and old roses, propagated or pot-grown in the farm's greenhouses and outdoor growing beds. This beautiful destination nursery is located on the edge of Ohio's Amish country, so pick a nice sunny morning and make a day of it.

At the end of their long driveway, a welcoming committee greets visitors. This group is comprised of an assortment of cats and dogs. You'll also find innovative state-of-the-art greenhouses crammed with uncommon and classic plants,

OWNERS: Libby & Tom Bruch
TYPE: Large specialty nursery
SPECIALTIES: Herbs; perennials—sun and shade; antique roses; shrubs
HOURS: March 1 thru Nov. 15: Tues.-Sat. 9:00 am to 5:00 pm; May thru June: Sun. 1:00 pm to 5:00 pm; Christmas hours: Nov. 16 thru Dec. 27: Mon-Sat. 9:00 am to 5:00 pm, Sun. 1:00 pm to 5:00 pm.
CATALOG AVAILABLE: Online, and printed lists for perennials, roses, herbs, flowering trees, and shrubs
MAIL-ORDER AVAILABLE: No
DISPLAY GARDENS: Yes
CLASSES: Yes

CONTACT
2810 Armstrong Road
Wooster, OH 44691-8012
PHONE: (330) 345-6722
WEB ADDRESS: www.quailcrest.com
EMAIL: qcrest@bright.net

DIRECTIONS
FROM THE CLEVELAND AREA: Take I-71 southwest to Wooster/Lodi Rd/Rt. 83 (Exit 204). Drive south on Rt. 83 for 7 miles to Armstrong Road. Turn west (right) onto Armstrong Rd., drive 1.0 miles to nursery on left. From Columbus/Mansfield Area: Take I-71 northeast to Wooster/Lodi Rd./Rt. 83 (Exit 204). Drive south on Rt. 83 for 7 miles to Armstrong Road. Turn west (right) onto Armstrong Rd., drive 1.0 miles to nursery on left.

GPS: N 40° 54.05', W 81° 59.74'

OHIO

a sophisticated selection of ornamentals, a patchwork of interesting gardens, woods for wandering, and eclectic shopping.

WHAT YOU'LL FIND

Begun in 1957, the gardens are an ongoing project to this day. Changes over the years saw the addition of a good number of display gardens, including the Tea House Garden, the Formal Herb Garden, the Peony Gardens, the Phoenix Garden, the Hillside

> "A garden really lives only insofar as it is an expression of faith, the embodiment of a hope and a song of praise."
> —RUSSELL PAGE

Gardens, the Prairie Garden, the Gallery Gardens, Libby's Lake, and though technically not a garden, the beautifully planted out Pet Cemetery, with name stones, for all the numerous "dog and cat friends that have come and gone throughout the years." Various display gardens peak at different times of the year, and repeat trips would be necessary to see each in their moment of glory. However, a couple of special ones are noted here.

The Tea House was originally built for one of Quailcrest's exhibition gardens at Floralscape, Cleveland Botanical Garden's Flower and Garden show, held in years past. Dismantled and rebuilt on site, it is surrounded by lush, extensive perennial plantings—starring *Allium giganteum*, *Anemone blanda* and *Euphorbia polychroma* in the spring, *Heliopsis* and *Acanthus* in the summer, and **Russian sage**, **Japanese anemone** and **plumbago** in the fall. (Look for the Tom Torrens bell that hangs in the tea house).

Right next to the tea house, the brick building the nursery staff refer to as "The Schoolhouse," is a resurrected smoke house from the Children's Home across the road. It was reconstructed at its present location to its original size, using original bricks and trusses, with a fireplace added for comfort and warmth. Inside, there is a charming collection of antiques from that era; outside, it is surrounded by a variety of old fashioned plants: **sweetspire**, **lilac**, **southern magnolia**, **fothergilla**, **crab apples**, and **herbs** such as **artemesia**, **lavender**, **bouncing bet** and **thyme**.

The Formal Herb Garden was constructed in 1986 and is flanked by a bench at each end with an arbor of billowing climbing roses draped in sweetly scented **autumn clematis** (*Clematis paniculata*). **Mints** are grown in terra cotta tiles; there is

OHIO

a lavender border and beds of scented **geranium**, culinary herbs, more than 21 varieties of thyme, and twenty **rosemary** varieties. Located in the center is a knot garden of **germander** and crimson **pygmy barberry**.

The Phoenix Garden has its own interesting tale. The place has a spirit that just won't be put down. A century old bank barn, used as a gift shop, burned down in 1986. After the replacement barn named for the rising Phoenix burned down Christmas Day,

★ **SIDE TRIPS** ★

SECREST ARBORETUM (330) 263-37761, 1680 Madison Ave., Wooster, OH 44691. This 85 acre arboretum is highlighted with more than 2,000 species, varieties, and cultivars for evaluation. Over 500 varieties of roses of antiquity, legend, and romance are featured in a 2.7-acre garden.

1999, Libby Bruch says it was decided "the karma's wrong over there." A special garden was established on the spot as a "lasting memorial to the buildings of the past."

The Tracy Barn is an historic 170 year-old building rescued from a local farm that was sold for commercial development. It was dismantled in the early part of the year 2000, "raised" in June and finished off as a gift shop by November of the same year. The barn's timbers, size and shape are all original (though a cedar timbered "half barn" was added to the side). Garden plantings surround the barn, and the massive stone horse trough gracing the front of the barn (as it would have 140 years ago), as well as the sitting area are constructed from stones from the original Tracy Barn.

Quailcrest offers more than 350 varieties of herbs: **sage** (15), **thyme** (30), **oregano** (20), mint (30), **lavender** (23), **basil** (20), scented geraniums (40-plus types—fruit or specialty scents, citrus, rose, and mint), and hundreds of superior perennials.

Antique **roses**, dating back to the 1800's include 'Camaieux' (1830), 'Baronne Prevost' (1842), 'Louise Odier' (1851), 'La Ville de Bruxelles' (1849), and 'Soupert et Notting' (1874). The nursery's rose list also includes climbers, David Austin™, shrub, Buck, musk and rugosa varieties.

Quailcrest's motto: "A clump of good Wayne County soil goes with each plant," seems to launch a kind of potting frenzy every spring. Outside the greenhouse, the nursery offers a collection of hardy perennials, ornamental grasses, ferns, ground covers, vines and flowering trees and shrubs, all well labeled and easy to find. The perennials include a bevy of **daylilies, artemisia, yarrow, aster, delphinium** and **dianthus**; a bunch of **foxglove, coreopsis, veronica,** hardy geranium, **iris, phlox**; and a den of **columbine, astilbe, hellebores,** and **pulmonaria**.

The Farm is known for its decorative topiaries and hanging baskets. In recent years Quailcrest has really excelled in its selection of greenhouse grown annuals, tender perennials and "exotics." The nursery grows scads of **abutilon, calibrachoa, diascia, impatiens, begonia** and **anagallis**. It has a universe of **coleus,** in all forms, shapes and colors; a world of annual **salvias, fuchsias, nemesias,** and **osteospermum**; and an amazing array of **bacopa, scaevola, supertunia,** and **verbena**. There are trailers, such as **licorice plants, ivy, vinca, plectranthus,** and **sweet potato vine**.

Tracy Barn carries a unique collection of gifts, including books, home accessories, picnic and patio ideas, bath treats, gourmet food, music, jewelry, off beat clothing, and a bridal registry. The Statuary Pavilion carries a wide selection of garden ornaments (Campania International brand), including birdbaths, troughs, statuaries, and containers in all sizes, shapes, and glazes. There are wooden window boxes, iron trellises, plaques, dish gardens, and stepping stones. The holidays bring their own kind of magic. Tracy Barn and Plant Barn are converted into winter wonderlands with the addition of holiday decorations, artificial trees, swags, wreaths, garlands, santas and snowmen.

Festivals are held in June (Spring Garden Fair, Second Chance Dog Walk), July (Summer Celebration Fair…a Time for Women), and September (Herb Fair), in addition to special events planned throughout the year.

OHIO

ROSE FIRE, LTD.

❧ ❧

Rose Fire, Ltd., a delightful little nursery, focuses exclusively on well-grown, well-established, own-root hardy roses able to withstand northern Ohio's cold, bitter winters as well as the hot, humid summers of the Midwest. This country nursery, the brainchild of Conrad Alexander, currently offers more than 55 varieties of old-fashioned roses including climbing, damask, Gallica, hybrid perpetuals, Portland, polyantha, rugosa and shrub.

Conrad Alexander, an International Harvester design engineer, avid gardener, and passionate rosarian, started Rose Fire Ltd., after his enthusiasm for gardening and propagating got the upper hand. The nursery is located southeast of rural Edon, and is picturesquely situated on grounds surrounding a farmstead of 100 acres. While not huge, this charming nursery offers an excellent range of well-chosen roses, propagated on site and grown out on their own roots. The year 2004 marks Alexander's sixth season in the nursery business, and in that time he has provided his long list of customers with a laudable palette of antique roses. These are hardy roses that grow well in landscape conditions with no need of coddling. Alexander explains, "Just plant them and keep them well watered for the first six weeks. You will be rewarded with roses that can bloom for a lifetime."

All roses, robust one- or two-year old plants, are sold at the nursery in 1-gallon containers. Own-root roses are slower to propagate and initially appear to be somewhat sluggish growing plants. However, they are tougher, more resilient, and better prepared to handle the rigors of our notorious Midwest winters with minimal harm to the plant's root systems. Even total cane die-back after an

OWNERS: Conrad Alexander
TYPE: Small specialty nursery
SPECIALTIES: Roses
HOURS: First weekend in May through June (call ahead for dates): Mon. - Fri. after 6:00 pm, Sat.-Sun. 9:00 am to 4:00 pm. Also, by special appointment throughout summer.
CATALOG AVAILABLE: Online, and printed availability list
MAIL-ORDER AVAILABLE: Yes
DISPLAY GARDENS: Yes
CLASSES: No

CONTACT

09 394 State Route 34
Edon, Ohio 43518
PHONE: (419) 272-2787
MESSAGE CENTER: (419) 388-8511
WEB ADDRESS: www.rosefire.com
EMAIL: info@rosefire.com

DIRECTIONS

FROM EDON: Drive 2 miles east and 0.5 miles south on SR-34. (SR 34 makes a sharp, 90 degree turn). Nursery is located on the east (left) side.

GPS: N 41° 32.96', W 84° 43.82'

OHIO

exceptionally harsh winter will bring forth armloads of blossoms come summer.

Rose Fire's availability list provides information on the origin, history, date of introduction, size,

and shape of blossoms as well as the overall dimensions of each shrub offered. The web site, with an option to access the rose collections alphabetically by class, color, or size, also includes a color photo of the blossom and the availability status for each plant. Shipping of roses ordered by mail ceases mid-June (due to excessive heat), and picks up mid-September, once the weather cools down again.

Rose Fire's display beds are a lusty lot, making up approximately 1 acre of landscaped gardens surrounding the Alexander residence and long driveway. Although their refined beauty makes them a striking addition to any garden, roses are often regarded as fussy plants that require too much coddling. One look at the nursery's exquisite rose collection immediate puts an end to that notion. Says Alexander, "The idea that roses need pampering is the mindset of a purist in search of that flawless bloom. Roses for the garden don't have to be perfect, but they do need to survive the region's mercurial climate of sweltering summers and bone-chilling winters with minimal care." And one look at the vibrant palette of 200 (or more) varieties of roses in these display gardens (some still in the trial stage) certainly lends credence to Alexander's theory.

WHAT YOU'LL FIND

Viewing these plants as mature roses in a landscape is an invaluable benefit to help shoppers sort through the enticing choices before them. It gives the opportunity to glean a sense of the plant's essence—such as mature shape, height, blossom, leaf color, leaf shape, and fall hips, if any. Pictures can't do them justice. To see these roses in full bloom, to inhale the sweet fragrance, to behold the plentiful blossoms, is to understand why the antiques are back in vogue. A dear friend and **rose** fanatic, rated her favorites: 'Carefree Beauty'™, (very large, medium pink, double blossoms in profuse waves), 'Hawkeye Belle', (one of the loveliest of the Buck roses), another Buck rose 'Winter's Sunset', (the gardener's answer for hardy, disease resistant yellow), 'Marchessa Boccella' (very fragrant, light pink, fully double and quartered blooms produced in succession from summer to fall), and the beautiful Gallica, 'Duchesse de Montebello' (because the shell pink blooms often look like pink saucers with white centers). I found 'Mary Rose' with her shy habit for shedding spent blooms rather inviting; the dense, vigorous, thorny, dark red, highly fragrant 'Duc de Fitzjames' a beautiful means of keeping my neighbors pets at bay; 'Barrone Prevost' providing the most attractive cut flowers; and the only rose I know exhibiting a "voice," 'Autumn Damask' (if it's happy, its crumpled bed of blowsy petals will be strongly perfumed, otherwise, they won't).

These and other lovely antique and shrub roses can be viewed at peak bloom at Rose Fire from late May thru mid-June (always weather dependent). The display beds with re-blooming roses remain quite attractive throughout the entire growing season.

OHIO

Valley of the Daylilies

Valley of the Daylilies is an official American Hemerocallis Society (AHS) display garden. It is comprised of a series of colorful, sweeping beds and borders around the Bachman residence, and contains more than 500 well-labeled, exceptional daylily cultivars.

Valley of the Daylilies is located in rural southwestern Ohio near the historic village of Lebanon, approximately 30 miles northeast of Cincinnati and 70 miles southwest of Columbus. Specializing primarily in hardy, field-grown daylily spiders and unusual forms, the picturesque nursery situated on nearly 12 acres of pastureland moved to its present site in 2001.

Owner Dan Bachman only met his first daylily in 1984, yet today he grows 3,200 registered cultivars, along with several thousand seedlings from his hybridization program. Although Dan Bachman's principal interest is in hybridizing spiders, he initially cultivated more of a hit or miss attitude as he made random crosses in a haphazard manner with no concerted aim or focus. As with other hybridizers before him, he learned the importance of having a main focus or goal on which to concentrate his efforts. Bachman says "I decided on spider variant forms for the same reason that I started collecting them avidly— there were few people in the field." Spiders, once considered the outcasts of the daylily world, are the *Hemerocallis* darlings of today.

Peak bloom is typically the first two weeks of July, with July 5th generally marking the start of a week-long open house. Visitors by the hundreds come to the nursery to take a self-guided tour of the display beds, walk the production fields, or catch a master hybridizer at his art.

OWNERS: Jackie and Dan Bachman
TYPE: Specialty nursery
SPECIALTIES: Daylilies; hosta
HOURS: May thru end of Sept.: Tues.-Fri. 9:00 am to 5:00 pm, Sat. 10:00 am to 4:00 pm. Other times by appointment.
CATALOG AVAILABLE: Yes
MAIL-ORDER AVAILABLE: Yes
DISPLAY GARDENS: Yes (AHS Display Garden)
CLASSES: No

CONTACT
1850 S. State Route 123
Lebanon, OH 45036
PHONE: (513) 934-1273
WEB ADDRESS: www.valleyofthedaylilies.com
EMAIL: valleydan@earthlink.net

DIRECTIONS
FROM I-71: Exit I-71 at Rt. 123 (Exit 32). Take Rt. 123 southeast for 1 mile; the nursery's on the right hand side—look for signs.

GPS: N 39° 24.06', W 84° 08.32'

OHIO

Through many purchases, trades, and various other "means of acquisition," Bachman was able to grow enough **daylily** varieties by 1994 to put out his first catalog. Then his work really shot into high gear, and in 2001 he registered his first three introductions: 'Big Ross' (a $10^1/_2$-inch, light rose with deeper halo), 'Jackie Bachman' (a 7-inch, orchid pink beauty), and 'Suzy Cream-cheese' (a 7-inch, light peach self).

> *"How often I regret that plants cannot talk."*
> —VITA SACKVILLE-WEST

His earliest efforts were with old standards. Some seedlings would show promise of a pretty face, but lack dreadfully in substance. It wasn't until he added 'Spider Miracle' and 'Coburg Fright Wig' to his hybridization efforts that the seedling bed began to show great promise. Bachman's hybridization program is geared to achieving a "big" and "pretty" spider face; but to pass muster, his hybrids must also possess good branching and a high number of buds per scape (stem). "What a difference," he notes, "when you can finally show off your seedlings, instead of continu-ally trying to steer people to different parts of the garden."

In 1998, when hybridizer and AHS treasurer Curtis High passed away, the Valley of the Daylilies nursery acquired much of his Hillside Gardens stock, including several promising seedlings hybridized by High. By 2002, Bachman had worked out a "formula" for his spider hybridization program introducing four more win-ners: 'Ben Bachman' (a 7-inch, bright yellow daylily named after Bachman's son); 'Chicken on the Run' (a tall, $6^3/_4$-inch, coral pink with an orange watermark, named after a neighbor-

EXTRAS

The nursery offers to its on-site visitors daylilies that are not listed in the catalog—defi-nitely a distinct advantage. Buyers have the choice of pur-chasing pre-potted daylilies or fresh-dug, "right out of the fields" plants. Worthy seed-lings from the Bachman hybridization efforts, rejects from the registration program (but far superior to a great many named cultivars) are sold at the nursery for $15 per hefty clump. All seedling clumps, 6 to 20 fan plants, are in their 3rd blooming season.

OHIO

hood bar and grill once owned by Bachman); 'It's Soul Time' (a 5^3/$_4$-inch, yellow bloomer which won Best Seedling with a purple ribbon in the Cincinnati AHS show); and 'Rachel Frye' (a 7-inch coral-rose color). Also in 2002, in honor of High, Bachman introduced 'Curtis High Memorial' (a light yellow hybridized by High). His formulas didn't stop there, as Bachman registered seven more daylilies in 2003 and six in 2004.

Bachman follows the charming convention of naming hybrids in honor of friends and relatives—and man's best friend, as well. 'Nate' is a bitone of dark rose petals, lighter sepals, and a coral rose halo with a ruffled fine gold edge. This one is named after Bachman's constant canine companion and official garden greeter, his yellow Labrador Retriever.

Additionally, Bachman has been fascinated with the work of the "pioneer" breeders of the early twentieth century. Called "nostalgic daylilies" by Bachman, the nursery offers an impressive collection of named cultivars that were registered prior to 1960. Many are hard-to-find, noteworthy, older varieties possessing unique refinements that have been pushed aside by the newer, flashier, more flamboyant upstarts of today.

Though there are more than 350 spiders included in Valley of the Daylilies' 3,200 registered daylily cultivars, the Bachmans sell through their catalog only those daylily varieties whose numbers are great enough to support mail order customers. These are freshly dug, field-grown, hardy daylilies; bonus plants are included with each order. Although the nursery's new introductions can run upwards of $100, Bachman also offers stout, wonderful, named cultivars for as little as $5, $6 and $8.

OHIO

WADE & GATTON GARDENS

❧ ❧

Where do I even begin to describe a place like Wade & Gatton? No matter how many superlatives I pile on, you cannot appreciate the size and magnitude of its holdings, except by visiting the nursery and the incredible gardens for yourself. The main portion of Wade & Gatton includes the display gardens, the retail area, daylily and hosta growing beds (growing "American Hostas, Daylilies and other Perennials™"), as well as various plant collection beds. It is located on 390 acres primarily devoted for the growth of deciduous trees and shrubs. Another 400 acres grow out ever-green trees chiefly for the Christmas trade. These immense holdings, started in 1928, presently are owned and operated by three generations of Wades—Shirley and Van Wade along with their three sons and grandsons. For the hosta collectors or aficionados, a pilgrimage to this Hosta Mecca is a must!

In this day of unrelenting adver-tising, Wade & Gatton does not advertise. Instead Van chooses to give back to his community as his way of advertising. He donates plants exten-sively to gardens, plant conventions, and his customers. (A free hosta plant is given to each customer who comes from a substantial distance. Just call and let them know you are coming.) Regarding the latter, his philosophy is that he would like to see each private garden in the nation with its own "pas-salong plant," what he hopes will be a

OWNERS: Van & Shirley Wade
TYPE: Exceptionally large retail and wholesale nursery (and landscaping)
SPECIALTIES: Hostas; daylilies; trees; shrubs; perennials, roses, grasses
HOURS: Jan. thru Mar. Mon.-Fri. 8:00 am to 5:00 pm, Apr.-Dec. Mon.-Sat. 8:00 am to 5:00 pm.
CATALOG AVAILABLE: Hosta catalog
MAIL-ORDER AVAILABLE: Yes
DISPLAY GARDENS: Yes
CLASSES: No

CONTACT

1288 Gatton Rocks Road
Bellville, Ohio 44813-9016
PHONE: (419) 883-3191
FAX: (419) 883-3677

DIRECTIONS

Located midpoint between Cleveland and Columbus near the center of Ohio, they are 15 miles south of Mansfield, 3 miles east of Bellville, and 2 miles west of Butler. **FROM THE SOUTH:** I-71 to SR-97 East (Exit 165) approx. 2 miles to Bellville. Take a left at the first traffic light in Bellville, go through the center of town following the SR-97 East signs carefully for approx. 3 miles to Dill Road. Turn right on Dill and drive 1.5 miles following signs for the nursery. **FROM THE NORTH:** I-71 to St. Route 13 – South (Exit 169) near Mansfield. Take SR-13 south, 8 miles, to Bellville. Take a left onto SR-97 East and drive approx. 3 miles to Dill Road, turn right and 1.5 miles to nursery following signs.

GPS: N 40° 35.92', W 82° 27.99'

Wade & Gatton hosta. His only request is that if he passes a plant on to you, please be sure to share another of yours with a friend. All garden club members receive special purchase discounts.

Customers are received warmly, and wandering the Botanical Gardens is greatly encouraged. To that end, there are eight picnic areas scattered about the premises (plus for those unforeseen wet days, a picnic garage area complete with tables). Comfortable shoes and picnic lunches are recommended.

WHAT YOU'LL FIND

It is incredible to think that the immense display gardens here (known as the Wade Botanical Gardens) were started as recently as 1984. They comprise 15 to 20 acres and can take up to a full day to view. Currently the gardens contain more than 2,300 different varieties of **hosta**, 2,000 varieties of **daylilies**, hundreds of **daffodils**, more than 40 varieties of rare and unusual **ferns**, a few thousand perennials, shade and ornamental trees, shrubs, ground covers, and more bulbs. Dozens of hosta and daylily hybridizers maintain test gardens, where they evaluate and grow their plants. Everything is clearly labeled. The evaluation fields will someday yield new winners.

Daylily beds are alphabetized, i.e., all daylily cultivars whose name starts with the letter A are planted in the A bed, those starting with the letter B in the B bed, and so on. These beds are scattered, in a somewhat random order, throughout the gardens. The hostas, on the other hand, are planted out with landscape design and collections in mind. Though each bed is clearly labeled, they are also scattered about the gardens; and the only way you'll find them is to walk the gardens reading labels, ask the staff, or buy the hosta catalog. Also, there are a few hosta cultivars that are not in the gardens, and the only way a customer can glean which ones are (or are not) in the gardens is from the hosta catalog.

The catalog titled "The American Hosta Guide," (or as I like to refer to it, the "hosta bible"), is a gigantic 8½-inch × 11-inch, soft cover, 511-page catalog, listing approximately 1,500 hostas currently for sale at Wade & Gatton. Including those not for sale, the polyhouses in the retail area contain a whopping 2,300. The catalog is updated every two years, with an addendum published in alternate years.

All hostas are in alphabetical order, including species, sports, cultivars, duplications, as well as some obsolete, older names for use as reference. Crammed full of information, it contains pictures of the gardens, a few individual plants, cultural and other miscellaneous information. You will also find all vital statistics on hosta cultivars, the "blood" lines, what collection they reside in (and where), and the prices. An added benefit is an inclusive listing of local accommodations, restaurants, and attractions.

Now, about the pricing. This method of pricing is not something that I, living in the western suburbs of Chicago, have experienced or am used to. I'm not saying it's right or wrong. What is important is that it works for Wade & Gatton, and the buyer will need to understand it. Van Wade explains it best in their catalog. Each price indicates the price for one, 1-2 eye/crown plants, available bare root or in #1-1.5 containers. If you're purchasing plants from the sales area, and a pot contains more than 1-2 crowns, you will be charged per extra crown. For example, if a hosta is priced at $12.00 each (for up to 2 crowns), then customers will be charged $6.00 per crown, per pot for hostas containing more than 2 crowns.

Wade & Gatton will dig daylilies out of the gardens on the day of your visit (when in bloom). They won't do the same for hostas though. In other words, if the hosta to make your heart aflutter has to be dug up from the garden (this is noted in the catalog), you'd better notify them ahead of time. Daylilies get special treatment probably because there is no daylily catalog (how would one know what is available before arrival?). But don't quote me on that.

As you might have gathered, hosta is the greatest seller here, followed by the daylilies. But there are other tempting areas as well. Wade & Gatton carries roses, some ornamental grasses, trees, and shrubs. There is no gift shop or inside sales area.

Wade & Gatton's wholesale division comprises the greatest volume of sales, most of them involving deciduous shrubs and trees. For the last mile of the drive prior to arriving at the nursery gates, you are surrounded by thousands of rows of extremely well grown trees in every shape, size, and color. Trees with a 5- to 6-inch (and up) caliper are routinely shipped to the five surrounding states.

EXTRAS

Presently, plants in the evaluation fields are not for sale; however, if something catches your eye that falls into the "must have" category, you can register for the "wish list." When that plant is ready and they have enough to sell, those on the wish list get first priority.

OHIO

Searching Wisconsin

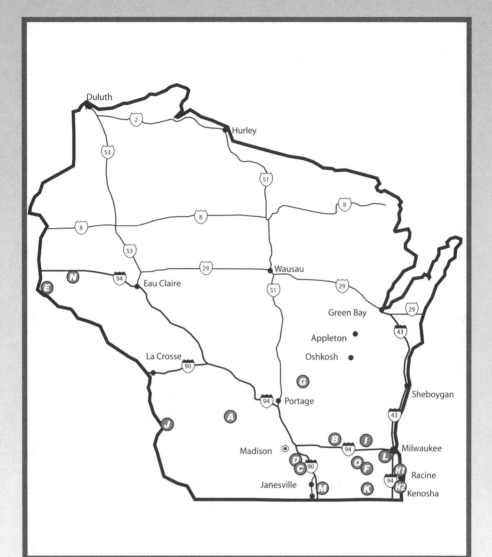

BEAR VALLEY PERENNIALS

ꙮ ꙮ

Bear Valley Perennials is a small family-run nursery nestled amid the scenic hills of Bear Valley, Wisconsin. Specializing primarily in hardy, field-grown **daylilies,** it was started by Billie Lee Jones with the aim of selling quality, well-grown daylilies at the Madison Farmers Market. As word spread of the high-quality yet reasonably priced plants, she found herself lugging more and more daylilies to the market every week, only to sell out before the day was through. So, in 1997 Jones expanded her line of daylilies to encompass more than 400 named daylily hybrids, developed a line of hardy perennials for both sun and shade, and added a few hosta, prairie plants, wildflowers, and more recently, some aquatic plants. Hybrid daylilies are the only daylilies the nursery offers by mail-order, but these are tough, lovely plants.

Customers are encouraged to bring a camera, stroll the garden paths, and view mature plants in a natural setting.

WHAT YOU'LL FIND

Bear Valley may not carry the latest decorator dazzlers, but for reliable performance in a cold climate, the nursery offers named cultivars (many are designated award winners) that are beautiful, vigorous, trouble free plants with decent foliage for most of the growing season. Dormant **daylilies** are considered the most suitable choices for cold climates, although some semi-evergreen cultivars are hardy, too. To that end, Bear Valley Perennials has field tested and eliminated those semievergreen cultivars too dainty for this rugged environment.

If you normally wouldn't hit the road for daylilies, keep in mind that for the beginner as well as the seasoned gardener, daylilies are a no-brainer.

OWNER: Billie Lee Jones
TYPE: Small specialty nursery
SPECIALTIES: Daylilies; hosta; perennials
HOURS: Last week in April thru mid-Oct. (weather dependent—call ahead): Tues.-Sun., 10:00 am to 5:00 pm or by appointment.
CATALOG AVAILABLE: Daylily list
MAIL-ORDER AVAILABLE: Daylilies only
DISPLAY GARDENS: Yes
CLASSES: No

CONTACT

S7225 Hwy 130
Hillpoint, WI 53937
PHONE: (608) 986-3096
EMAIL: bljones@jvlnet.com

DIRECTIONS

FROM THE MADISON AREA: Take Hwy-14 west to Hwy-130. Turn north (right) onto Hwy-130 and drive 13 miles to nursery (watch for sign).
FROM THE LACROSSE AREA: Take Hwy-14 southwest to Hwy-130. Turn north (left) onto Hwy 130 and drive 13 miles to nursery.

GPS: N 43° 21.66', W 90° 10.68'

They shake off pests, tolerate bright sun and light shade, thrive in wet or dry soil, and are even drought resistant once established. They provide bold color and come in a wide range of flower sizes, colors, and plant heights. Daylilies are fast growers but not invasive; the flowers encompass the entire rainbow of colors (except true blue) in palettes of red, yellow, bronze, gold, cream, pink, lavender, and purple. They also come in a tremendous variety of patterns in shades that are dark, light, or bitone.

Bear Valley carries about 80 varieties of **hosta**, and a full line of perennials such as: **lilies**, **delphiniums**, **ferns**, **astilbe**, **coneflowers**, **iris**, **beebalm**, **coral bells**, **rudbeckia**, **pulmonaria**, and **tiarella**. All plants are grown in a 1-acre production field and are guaranteed to have survived at least one winter in the harsh, wind-swept environment.

Bear Valley offers classic plants at reasonable prices. Some striking examples are the 1991 Stout Medal Winner 'Betty Woods' (yellow blossoms like tissue paper pom-poms); 'Condilla' (a smashing gold with extra petals gathered together in a frilly bunch, hose-in-hose); 'Pearl Lewis' (exquisite shape); and the ever-so-popular 'Lullaby Baby' (in a ruffled baby-ribbon pink). Bear Valley carries 16 varieties of the Marsh Chicago series and 17 of "Siloam."

Daylilies are field grown, dug up and divided in late summer and fall, and potted up to overwinter in a daylily sanctuary (the remains of a rustic old barn and silo). Mail-order plants, at least two fans, are freshly dug and shipped bare root. (Look for overstocks, end-runs, and discontinued cultivars, when available, out on long tables for just a few dollars per plant.)

★ SIDE TRIPS ★

Less than thirty minutes to the southeast is the town of **SPRING GREEN.** There you will find **TALIESEN,** Frank Lloyd Wright's estate, (608) 588-7900; **AMERICAN PLAYERS THEATRE** where classic plays are presented in an outdoor setting, www.AmericanPlayers.org; and the world famous **HOUSE ON THE ROCK,** with mind-boggling attractions (including an indoor carousel), www.Houseontherock.com (near the Wisconsin River). About thirty minutes to the northeast is **BARABOO,** the home of the Circus World Museum and Devil's Lake State Park, www.baraboo.com. Less than thirty minutes to the north is Reedsburg, which hosts the **NORMAN ROCKWELL MUSEUM,** (608) 524-2123. **WISCONSIN DELLS,** home to magnificent scenery, the famous Ducks, theme parks, and water parks, is less than forty-five minutes away, www.wisdell.net.

WISCONSIN

EBERT'S GREENHOUSE

❦

Started in 1976 as a small-truck farm growing fresh vegetables for sale at the local farmers market, Ebert's Greenhouse has grown into a "village" of twenty-eight greenhouses packed with a wonderful variety of plants, and famous hanging baskets. Today's hottest horticultural trend is toward tropicals and annuals, and Ebert's, on the cutting edge of container gardening and the rehabilitation of annuals, revels in this. Add to all that a huge display of trees and shrubs (brought in from northern growers); a good selection of sought-after annuals and perennials; organically grown herbs and vegetables (mainstream and heirloom varieties); and a vast assortment of roses (both own-root and grafted). There's a country store full of garden accessories and décor including gloves, gazing balls, arbors, and statuary.

Caramel apples, pumpkin bars, and just plain ol' "yummy" sweets can be had in the log cabin—the Sweet Shop—located near the silo. Flower beds, a testing area, as well as a showcase for the newest varieties, are interspersed throughout the nursery and surrounding the old farmstead. They are vibrant and fragrant, flaunting shades of glorious color.

In the fall, Eberts pulls out all stops with beautifully flowering mums, horse drawn hayrides, pumpkin patches,

OWNERS: Ron and Mark Ebert
TYPE: Large retail nursery
SPECIALTIES: Annuals; hanging baskets; perennials—sun and shade; roses; herbs; trees; and shrubs
HOURS: April 15 thru July 18: Mon. – Fri. 8:00 am to 9:00 pm, Sat. 8:00 am to 6:00 pm, Sun. 11:00 am to 6:00 pm; July 19 thru Sept. 24: Mon.-Fri. 9:00 am to 6:00 pm, Sat. 9:00 am to 5:00 pm; Sun. 11:00 am to 5:00 pm; Sept. 25 thru Oct. 31: Mon.-Fri. 9:00 am to 6:00 pm, Sat. 11:00 am to 6:00 pm, Sun. 11:00 am to 6:00 pm; Nov. 1 thru Dec. 24: Mon.-Fri. 9:00 am to 5:00 pm, Sat. 9:00 am to 5:00 pm, Sun. 11:00 am to 5:00 pm.
CATALOG AVAILABLE: Printed information sheet
MAIL-ORDER AVAILABLE: No
DISPLAY GARDENS: Yes
CLASSES: Yes

CONTACT
W1795 Fox Road
Ixonia, WI 53036
PHONE: (920) 261-5645
FAX: (920) 261-0467
WEB ADDRESS: www.ebertsgreenhouse.com
EMAIL: eberts@execpc.com

DIRECTIONS
FROM WATERTOWN: Take Hwy WI-16 East for 5 miles to Hwy WI-SC. Turn left onto Hwy WI-SC and drive 2 miles to Fox Road. Follow the signs. **FROM OCONOMOWOC:** Take Hwy WI-16 west 6 miles to Hwy WI-SC. Turn right onto Hwy WI-SC, and drive 2 miles to Fox Road. Follow signs.

GPS: N 43° 11.26', W 88° 37.52'

scarecrows, and yummy treats. For the kids there is storytelling and an adventurous trip through a maze of straw. For the Christmas season, the nursery offers colorful poinsettias, Christmas trees, live wreaths, and unusual "green" decorations for the home.

WHAT YOU'LL FIND

A hanging basket makes an instant garden, and Ebert's creates them by the bushel every spring—15,000 gorgeous flowering baskets. That is their claim to fame. (And if you can't find one that suits you from those already out, they'll gladly custom make one for you.) These scrumptious works of art, planted out in single, double, and multiple varieties, are typically potted in 12-inch containers but are also available in 16- to 20-inch moss baskets (800 of these every spring).

"See! The winter is past; the rains are over and gone. Flowers appear...The season of singing has come..."
—Song of Solomon 2:11, 12 NIV

From classic favorites to all-new creations, Ebert's line of spring annuals in flats, 4½-inch pots, and hanging baskets includes the best examples of the most desirable varieties. Ebert's grows scads of **abutilon**, spreading **petunias** (Wave™ petunias, Supertunias™, Surfinias™, and Suncatcher™ series), small petunia-like flowers (tiny tunias, Million Bells®, mini famous, and Super Bells®), **bacopa**, various **daisies** (*Osteospernum, Marguerite, Leucanthemum*), and **comets** (*Argranthemum, Nemesia*), *Diascia*, **trailing snapdragons**, **trailing verbenas**, *Dichondra*, **ivy geranium,** *Helichrysum,* and **purslane**. It has yards of **dahlia**, **coleus**, **fuchsia**, **hibiscus**, **impatiens** (double, mini, new Guinea, and single), **lisianthus**, **lobelia**, **pentas**, and **salvia** in all colors and forms. There's *Brugmansia* and *Strobilanthes* for bold architectural interest; **sweet potato vines**, both the chartreuse and the dark-leaved, to drape skirt-like down the sides of containers; **nasturtiums** to tumble out of jars; and other trailing plants to sprawl, creep, or wander across decks, patios, terraces, and gardens.

Ebert's carries paddle-leaved **cannas**, admired in Victorian days; luxuriant and sleek **taro**, delicious in borders and containers; *Alternanthera,* playful plants of our grannies era; the dazzling **prayer plant**, striped in green and purple; the **caricature plant**, *Graptophyllum;* from Down Under; brilliantly flame colored **Mexican fire bush** (*Hamelia*)*;* and **bloodleaf** (*Iresine*) a fancy foliage plant in all incarnations of puckered, painted, streaked, and striped leaves.

Ebert's specializes in superior, cutting-edge perennials of the kind rarely encountered elsewhere. On my trip, I saw Orange Meadowbrite™ (*Echinacea* 'Art's Pride'), 'Razzmatazz'®, 'Rocky Top', and 'Doppelganger'; tall garden *Phlox paniculata* 'Fancy Feelings' and 'Natural Feelings'; the Junior series of short *Phlox paniculata* 'Jr. Bouquet', 'Jr. Dance', 'Jr. Dream', and 'Jr. Fountains'; *Gaillardia* 'Fan Fare'®, *Physostegia* 'Olympus Gold' and *Geranium* 'Okey Dokey'. With the addition of the Planet series, *Heuchera* 'Saturn', 'Venus', and 'Mars', Ebert's line of **coral bells** grows in stature every year.

ENCHANTED VALLEY GARDENS

❧ ❧

Enchanted Valley Gardens is a popular, family owned nursery located on 13 pastoral acres just outside the pleasant town of Evansville. The nursery is an extraordinary find for the discerning plant lover and a highly recommended destination outing. Enchanted Valley is renowned for its collection of well-grown, healthy stock. The nursery built its reputation on fine plants pot-and field-grown in the greenhouses, fields, or outdoor growing beds.

Enchanted Valley specializes in superior perennials that flourish in northern landscapes, boasting "We are not only producers of plants, but we are also passionate gardeners as well." They grow and cultivate as many of the plants as possible—both in the display and private gardens in Evansville (Zone 5), but also in a private garden in Northwest Wisconsin (Zone 3).

Plants in the display gardens near the parking area can be viewed any time throughout the season. However, the beds and borders around the old farmstead are all part of a personal residence and are open to the public only during the month of July, coinciding with the daylily festival.

WHAT YOU'LL FIND

The mainstay of Enchanted Valley Gardens is its amazing collection of hardy perennials and shrubs. The cultivar listing is interesting for its depth, featuring many spectacular

OWNER: Steve Evers
TYPE: Large retail and wholesale nursery
SPECIALTIES: Perennials—sun and shade; trees and shrubs; daylilies; roses; vines; annuals; aquatics; herbs; vines; ornamental grasses
HOURS: April 1 thru November 30 (opening and closing dates vary, call ahead): Mon.-Fri., 8:00 am to 7:00 pm, Sat.-Sun. 9:00 am to 4:00 pm. Other hours by appointment.
CATALOG AVAILABLE: Internet listing
MAIL-ORDER AVAILABLE: Daylily only
DISPLAY GARDENS: Yes
CLASSES: No

CONTACT
9123 North Territorial Road
Evansville, WI 53536
PHONE: (608) 882-4200
FAX: (608) 882-4280
WEB ADDRESS: www.enchantedvalleygardens.com
EMAIL: evgdaylily@aol.com

DIRECTIONS
FROM MADISON AREA: Take WI-14 south to Bullard Rd (just past the town of Union). Turn east (left) onto Bullard Rd., and drive for 0.5 miles to Territorial Rd. Turn south (right) onto Territorial. Nursery is 0.1 miles down on the right. Watch for signs. **FROM JANESVILLE AREA:** Take WI-14 west to CR-M (east of Evansville) Turn north (right) onto CR-M driving 1.1 miles to Territorial Rd. Turn northwest (left) onto Territorial and drive for 1.4 miles to the nursery on your left.

GPS: N 42° 48.49', W 89° 17.37'

WISCONSIN

daylilies, **hosta**, **phlox**, **coneflower**, **iris**, **campanula**, and **lobelia** as well as **bee-balm**, **cranesbill** (hardy geranium), **monkshood**, **salvia**, **coreopsis**, **rudbeckia**, **sedum**, and **peony**. Two years ago, I purchased three pots of Himalayan **maiden-hair fern** (*Adiantum venustum*) for my woodland garden. Planted out, they sat there the whole season with no sign of life other than the few fronds present when I first plunged them into the ground. I don't know who sulked more, the ferns or me. But much to my delight, fresh growth emerged this spring.

> "A morning-glory at my window
> satisfies me more than the
> metaphysics of words."
> —WALT WHITMAN

Playmates for the fern that I picked up on this trip included *Helleborus* × *hybridus* (lusty **lenten rose**), *Dryopteris filix-mas* (handsome male fern), and a harmonious collection of bells: *Uvularia grandiflora* (majestic great **merrybells**), *Kirengeshoma palmata* (personable **Japanese yellowbells**), and *Heuchera* (**coralbells**). I have a passion for *Heuchera* that borders on obsession, and every visit to the nursery leaves me smitten with a cultivar or two. This trip I picked up 'Royal Velvet', 'Frosted Violet', 'Frosted Spice', 'Venus', 'Saturn', "Vesuvius', and 'Obsidian'.

No other perennial blooms so generously in the baking sun or can even begin to match the beauty of the daylilies' large, exotic flowers. Without a doubt, they are the shining stars of any midsummer garden. Enchanted Valley grows more than 300 varieties of daylilies in bold or subtle colors and various surface textures. Pot-grown daylilies are always available in containers at the nursery; however, they can also be had bare root (2 fans or greater) both on site and by mail-order. Though there is a slight overlap between field-grown and pot-grown plants, the field-grown lilies have quantity price breakpoints that are, understandably, unavailable on container plants.

With acres of varieties in full bloom from mid-July to mid-August, roaming the fields, viewing mature specimens, and choosing favorites is a wonderful experience. One caveat, though: Although bare-root and field-grown daylilies are available for the asking, the nursery is not able to dig field stock "on the spot" due to weather, field conditions, and time constraints. They need atleast four to seven days advance notice before they can have your plants "clean and ready." As a result, though field-grown daylily prices are surely attractive, you must factor in shipping charges or a return trip.

The perennials at Enchanted Valley Gardens are nursery-grown gallon-sized (or larger) container plants that are at their best in spring but look remarkably healthy even at summer's end. Additions are constant, for plant selections change as newer varieties mature and are put out. What makes this nursery special is its innovative selection—splendid old favorites, choice new cultivars, and plants you may not recognize. Assembled by category on large expanses of landscape-cloth covered fields, the diverse stock is laid out in an orderly manner and clearly marked with large, easy-to-read informative placards with a full description of the name, characteristics, and cost.

Enchanted Valley Gardens carries an expanded selection of own-root **roses** including tea, floribunda, grandiflora, shrub, climbing, Buck, Canadian Series (Parkland™ and Explorer™), Towne & Country™, Gallica, David Austin™, and landscape—well over 150 varieties in all. Last summer, 'Knock Out'™ and 'Carefree Sunshine' disappeared as if by magic even before the season started.

The marriage of clematis and climbing roses was made in heaven. Clematis clambers up a rose's thorny canes, opening its splendid blossoms and providing cascades of color while hiding the rose's bare legs. Enchanted Gardens carries more than 40 varieties of **clematis** vines, so choosing, say, a bodacious purple clematis like long-blooming 'Jackmanii' or 'Etoile Violette' to consort with a gracious pink rose can be easily done.

Besides perennials and roses, the nursery offers an excellent choice of woody plants, including **lilac** (the hard to find Father Fiala series), **viburnum**, **hydrangea** (the new 'Endless Summer'), **fothergilla**, **forsythia**, **mockorange**, **daphne**, and **dogwood**. A good selection of evergreen shrubs including **azaleas**, **rhododendrons**, and conifers, stand needle to leaf with **weigela**, **elderberry**, and **pussy willow**. Small ornamental trees include **silverbells**, **crabapple**, **serviceberry**, **European beech**, **Japanese maple**, and a good assortment of **fruit trees**.

Enchanted Gardens has expanded its line of aquatics, including hardy **water lilies** and **lotus**, **marginals** such as **cattails**, **water pickerel**, **parrot's feather**, **water lettuce**, **hyacinth**, **water clover**, and oxygenators. And for those last minute needs, the nursery supplies a basic line of chemicals, fertilizers, insecticides, and potting needs.

THE FLOWER FACTORY

The Flower Factory was founded seventeen years ago by self-confessed "plantaholics," Nancy and David Nedveck. This nursery offers hardy, winsome plants for cold-climate gardens. Initially, the Nedvecks did a little bit of everything. "We grew annuals, perennials, cut flowers—even went the dried flower route," says Nancy, a degreed horticulturist. "Yet very early on we saw the need to specialize. So, we no longer grow annuals or vegetables."

For first-timers, the sheer magnitude of this place can be daunting and overwhelming. The Flower Factory is a charming country destination, and features one of the largest selections of perennial plants in southern Wisconsin, if not the Midwest. The cultivar list, more than 3,000 varieties of perennials, is uncommonly captivating and deep. Nearly all of the plants are propagated and grown on site, an almost improbable feat when the scope and magnitude of the undertaking is considered.

The nursery has a total of 5 acres in production, in greenhouses scattered throughout the grounds. Eight of these greenhouses are open to the public. While every gardener will surely find old favorites, it is the joy of discovering new choices that makes this trip worthwhile. The selection is unbelievable—and unbeatable.

WHAT YOU'LL FIND

Telling you about the stock can easily become a numbers game: 102 varieties of **aster**, 84 **astilbe**, 67 **campanula**, 68

OWNERS: Nancy and David Nedveck
TYPE: Large retail nursery
SPECIALTIES: Perennials—sun and shade; hosta; daylilies; ornamental grasses; ground covers; vines
HOURS: Last week in April thru the end of the season (weather dependent, call ahead): Mon.-Fri. 10:00 am to 7:00 pm, Sat.-Sun. 10:00 am to 6:00 pm.
CATALOG AVAILABLE: Printed catalog
MAIL-ORDER AVAILABLE: No
DISPLAY GARDENS: Yes
CLASSES: No

CONTACT
4062 Hwy A
Stoughton, WI 53589
PHONE: (734) 461-1230
FAX: (608) 873-0339

DIRECTIONS
(Note: This nursery is located near Oregon, Wisconsin, although the mailing address is Stoughton.) **FROM MADISON:** Hwy. 14 south to Hwy-A. Turn left (east) on Hwy-A for l.5 miles to nursery on your left at the bend in the road. **FROM I-90:** North of Janesville. Exit I-90 at the Stoughton exit (Exit # 156) Rt.-138 Travel westbound on Rt-138 to Rt-14. Turn south (left) onto Rt-14 for approx. 1.5 miles to Hwy-A. Turn left on Hwy-A and drive for 1.5 miles to nursery on your left, at the bend in the road.

GPS: N 42° 53.57', W 89° 19.16'

pinks, 71 **ferns**, 82 hardy **geraniums**, 185 ornamental grasses, 400 **day-lilies**, 500 **hostas**, 70 true **lilies**, 33 **monarda**, 45 **peonies** (plus 11 tree peonies), 88 **sedum**, and 65 **veroni-**

> *"When it comes to love—flowers sing where words merely talk."*
> —Anonymous

cas, to note but a few of the major categories. If you think this is mind-boggling, you're right.

The backbone of The Flower Factory is its commitment to native Wisconsin wildflowers and shade plants, of which the hosta is a major player. I am lukewarm in my feelings about the flowers of *Hosta* species and cultivars; however, my admiration for the foliage knows no bounds. In particular, I am enamored of the extra-large varieties like 'Sum & Substance' or those with bright leaves like 'Piedmont Gold', which stand out in the deep shade like glowing shafts of sunlight. The Flower Factory carries some rather admirable cultivars in both these categories: 'Blue Mammoth' (large, thick, blue-green leaves); 'Mr. Big' (a blue-green equivalent to 'Sum & Substance'); 'Samurai' (blue-green leaves with a yellow edge); 'Satisfaction' (the green equivalent of 'Piedmont Gold'); 'Vim & Vigor' (green and shiny); 'Aspen Gold' (solid gold); 'Fort Knox' (precious gold, of course); and 'Glory' (bright yellow, and ruffled). On the other end of the spectrum, all under 6 inches, there is 'Baby Bunting', 'Bitsy Gold', 'Bitsy Green', 'Cat's Eyes', 'Crepe Suzette', 'Gaijin', 'Green Eyes', 'Haku Chu Han', 'Heart and Soul', 'Kifukurin Ko Mame', 'Little Aurora', 'Little Razor', 'Sultana', 'Vanilla Cream', 'Warwick Delight', and 'Little Sunspot'.

The Flower Factory carries an exciting line of ephemerals—native spring bloomers that burst into flower to welcome the season, then disappear only to resurface again next spring. Although they bloom for only a couple of weeks before dying back, **Dutchman's breeches**, **shooting stars**, **trilliums**, **Virginia bluebells**, **umbrella leaf**, **liverleaf**, **fairy bells**, and **merrybells** can add indescribable charm to your shady borders.

This nursery has unusual North American native plants, such as species of *Scutellaria* (whorled spikes of tubular flowers), *Pedicularis* (snapdragon spikes from ferny, green leaves with splashes of red), *Panax* (**ginseng**, a root worth its weight in gold), and *Cortusa* (hanging bells above geranium like leaves). They also carry the rarely available **St. Bernard's lily** (*Anthericum*); true-blue flowering **alkanet** (*Anchusa*); clover-headed **lady fingers** (*Anthericum*); snapdragon-like **dragonhead** (*Dracocephalum*); **silver horned poppy** (*Glaucium*); the **Japanese bluebell** *Mertensia*

WISCONSIN

pterocarpa v. *yezoensis* (which, unlike our native, does not go dormant); and horned **rampion** *(Phyteuma)*, a campanula relative.

Gardeners will hanker for the white candelabra **Martagon lily** *(Lilium martagon)*; the blue **gentian** *(Gentiana crinita)*; the huge ornamental **rhubarb** *(Rheum)*; the 6-foot **snakeroot** *(Cimicifuga)*; the tiny, furry, kitten-footed **pussytoes** *(Antennaria)*; the 2-foot **green dragon** *(Arisaema)*; the giant scabiosa-like *Cephalaria*; and the dwarf perennial **snapdragon**, *(Chaenorrhinum)*. The unusual color and arching habit of burnished bronze **sedge** *(Carex* sp.'Bronze Glow') is sure to provoke comment; tall ornamental grasses such as **switchgrass** *(Panicum virgatum'* Cloud Nine') present a striking focus alone or in combination with other plants. Arching stems of **Solomon's seal** *(Polygonatum commutatum* 'Giganteum') dangling a bevy of white lockets make for a fine architectural display.

Some plants offered here are sufficiently unusual to lack common names, such as some species of *Acantholimon, Acerphyllum, Scrophularia, Bolax, Pterocephalus, Micromeria,* and *Hutchinsia.* The nursery also carries trusty alpines, good pond plants, ornamental vines, and native Wisconsin prairie plants. For alpine growers, there is a good selection of troughs in various sizes and shapes.

The Flower Factory offers exceptionally well-grown, acclimated plants at very reasonable prices. Each container is clearly identified and coded for price. There are eighteen price points, and the easiest way to keep them straight is to pick up a catalog as soon as you arrive. The price points are on the last page. If you wear reading glasses, you might consider bringing them along—the type is small and the pages full.

The greenhouses are clearly marked as to the type of plants within, and the friendly and accessible sales staff carries a master identifier list pinpointing the exact location of each plant (also available hanging by the side of the door at the checkout counter in the hosta greenhouse).

Mature display gardens weave gracefully around the Nedveck's farmhouse and barn; a railroad garden jostles for attention with a shed sporting an innovative, quilted "green roof;" and the long, expansive shade border (just beyond the peony area) gives gardeners cause for celebration. Two new display gardens, planted just recently, are the woodland garden under the large maple trees, and the combination rain and butterfly garden, behind greenhouse No. 3.

A water garden, a soothing oasis on hot, humid days, takes center stage between the parking lot and checkout area. For many gardeners, a water garden is a source of spectacular color, lush foliage, and cooling sounds. At the Flower

Factory, the water garden is also the place to sit a spell, to rest, to snack, and to trade lists with a new-found friend in the shade of old, majestic trees. This was the same spot Dolores—my fearless, and equally "nutty" good friend—and I sat delirious with indecision, trying to figure out how the heck we were going to cram four carts full of snazzy perennials, into one single, solitary car. Laugh, if you must. However, possibly on my next trip out, the person standing by the car next to mine with the same problem could be you! And, yes, I understand, you only meant to buy a few.

FUNKIE GARDENS

❧ ❧

Located in town on 3¹/₂ acres (a full city block) in the sleepy river town of Prescott, a gorgeous 1859 white-frame house and pre-1900 carriage house are settled snugly under ancient trees. "Where the St. Croix River meets the Mississippi River on the border of Wisconsin and Minnesota," this location provides a spectacular setting for Funkie Gardens. Started in 1995 by Baard and Diane Webster, Funkie Gardens gets its name from the melding of two words. "We thought of Webster Gardens, Pearl Street Gardens, and others," says Baard, "but they sounded too formal. Gardening is supposed to be fun, so while I was reading George Schmid's book on hostas, I came upon the word 'funkia,' which is what hostas used to be called. I then looked up the term 'funky' in the dictionary and found the definition as, 'something earthy and unsophisticated.' That sounded just right, and we had our name." The style might not be sophisticated, and the feeling may be casual—but the quality of the plants at Funkie Gardens is nothing if not first class!

WHAT YOU'LL FIND

The Websters and their helpful and knowledgeable staff welcome customers warmly with a full pot of delicious coffee and a staggering range of truly remarkable plants. Of course

OWNERS: Baard and Diane Webster
TYPE: Specialty nursery
SPECIALTIES: Hosta; perennials— shade and sun; trees; shrubs; vines
HOURS: Last weekend in April thru mid-Sept. (call for exact dates): Wed.-Thurs. 9:00 am to 8:00 pm, Fri.-Sat. 9:00 am to 5:00 pm, Sun. Noon to 5:00 pm. Other hours by appointment.
CATALOG AVAILABLE: Online
MAIL-ORDER AVAILABLE: No
DISPLAY GARDENS: Yes
CLASSES: Yes

CONTACT
618 Pearl Street
Prescott, WI 54021
PHONE: (715) 262-5593
WEB ADDRESS: www.funkiegardens.com
EMAIL: info@funkiegardens.com

DIRECTIONS
Funkie Gardens is located southeast of the Twin Cities in Prescott, WI, just across the Mississippi River from Hastings, MN. **FROM MINNEAPOLIS AREA:** take Hwy-61 south to Hwy-10, turn east (left) for approx. 3 miles (you will cross the Bridge into Prescott), and continue straight ahead (across Rt.-35) on Cherry Street straight up the hill for 5 blocks. Turn northwest (left) on Young Street, drive for 3 blocks to the nursery on your right. (Young St. becomes Pearl St. at the slight jog in the road). **FROM I-94 (AND RIVER FALLS AREA):** Take I-94 to Hwy-35 south (Exit 3) to Hwy-10 in Prescott. Go west (right) on Hwy-10 to Pearl St. Turn south (left) on Pearl and continue a few blocks. Nursery is on left.

GPS: N 44° 45.22', W 92° 48.01'

WISCONSIN

it is obvious that the specialty of the house, with a rich collection of about 200 varieties, is the **hosta**—treasured not so much for its flowers as for its foliage. Rippled, smooth, ruffled, or ribbed, these aristocrats of the shade garden have leaves that may be large or small, wide or narrow, smooth or quilted, solid or variegated. Foliage colors include bright yellows, cool blues, and just about every shade of green imaginable. Leaves are piped in white, streaked with gold, or striped in contrasting tones of emerald and cream on a background of yellow, green, or blue. They range in size from 4-foot giants to tiny, 3-inch midgets, providing incredible opportunities for designing one-of-a-kind beds and borders.

> *"What a pity flowers can utter no sound—a singing rose, a whispering violet, a murmuring honeysuckle—Oh, what a rare and exquisite miracle would these be!"*
> —HENRY WARD BEECHER

Regarding the countless numbers of new hosta cultivars flooding the market each and every year, Baard Webster's philosophy is simple. He chooses new hostas not because they are the newest but rather because they enhance gardens. To that end, he offers exciting selections for the intrepid gardener. I was won over by 'Fatal Attraction', 'Ebb Tide' (a smaller version of 'Aureo-Marginata'), 'Center of Attention', 'Afternoon Delight', 'Grey Ghost', 'Ice Cream' (how can you not love a plant named after everyone's favorite comfort food?), 'Ultramarine', 'Jimmy Crack Corn', and 'Merry Sunshine'.

Baard, who switched careers from marketing to nursery owner, credits Lillian Maroushek, a locally well-known plant expert, with encouraging them to open the nursery. Today, impressive display gardens surround the nursery, the Webster's beautiful home, carriage house, and propagation beds. These glamorous display beds are Diane's domain, and she spends much time tending them. "This is so much hard work. I don't think you could do it

EXTRAS

Funkie Gardens' Hosta Jamboree is a daylong event of food fellowship and fun. The nursery is host to booths of hosta growers, and visitors can enjoy plant raffles, auctions, table-top demos, speakers, and even a BBQ lunch and ice cream social. You might even pick up a t-shirt.

WISCONSIN

without loving it." She noted. "But, at the end of the day, you really feel like you've accomplished something."

In the shade under a massive pine, robust hosta clumps bursting with a chorus line of perfectly shaped leaves are surrounded by a stage full of supporting actors—**primula, fern, trillium, bleeding heart, shooting star, toad lily, barrenwort, mayflower, Jack-in-the-pulpit,** and **foam flower.** On the sunny podium, **daylilies, monarda, salvia, sedum, aster,** and **peony,** jostling and rubbing elbows with one another, nervously await their turn in the spotlight. Beginning gardeners would be wise to bring their notebooks to record these elegant effects.

Currently, Funkie Gardens stocks about 240 hosta varieties and more than 700 varieties of shade and sun perennials. Additionally, they have added a small but very special collection of vines, flowering shrubs, and trees. It's easy to spend time poking around, discovering plenty of tasty surprises—unusual varieties guaranteed to make any plant lover's pulse quicken. I found evergreen **Solomon's seal** *Disporopsis pernyi* (with its arching stems of dark green leaves); **Joe-Pye weed** *Eupatorium* 'Carin' (a breakthrough color of unique silvery-pink flowers and deep purple stems); and an interesting **cushion spurge,** *Euphorbia* 'Mini Martini' (a rare, dwarf selection of greenish-yellow bracts and purplish stems). There was the **giant coneflower** *Rudbeckia maxima* (an impressive giant of blue-green foliage and yellow flowers); the native hardy **geranium** *Geranium* 'Espresso' (attractive red-brown foliage); and, of course, *Opuntia humifusa* (who couldn't use a little prickly pear in a Zone 4 garden?).

They offer a dazzling assortment of alpine plants, an excellent selection of ornamental grasses, and an incredible number of true **lilies** including: Asiatic,

WISCONSIN

trumpet, LA (longiflorum-asiatic) hybrid, Oriental-trumpet, Oriental, leopard, and (at last count) 8 spectacular cultivars of the **Martagon lily**, a must for any woodland garden.

Hostas are set out on the ground in rows by size and color rather than by name. (The sales staff has a master list for those in search of that elusive cultivar.) The rest of the plants are located aesthetically in clearly marked groupings, and one section is devoted to ornamental vines, trees, and shrubs.

Container gardeners will be happy to know that the nursery is introducing some "temperennials" (tender perennials) including **begonia**, **angel's trumpet**, **pelargoniums**, **dahlias**, and non-hardy **hibiscus**. My warm feelings for Funkie Gardens extends to its catalog, *The Dirt*, which provides clear and intelligent information about each plant offered at the nursery. If you are lucky enough to live nearby you'll certainly know about their sales (in June) and the occasional "Hosta Jamboree." Do not miss this exceptional nursery and its quality plants.

WISCONSIN

Heritage Flower Farm

❦ ❦

Heritage Flower Farm is a small specialty nursery devoted exclusively to growing heirloom (antique) plants and educating gardeners about them. Heirloom plants, those that predate the plundering and innovations of the twentieth century, often carry fascinating histories—sometimes legend, sometimes lore, and, other times true stories of their discovery and use by man. In growing heirloom plants, Heritage Flower Farm helps to illuminate the progress of human industry.

By ascribing profiles to each plant, owner Betty Adelman showed us how they were grown and used and, at the same time, amused us by noting which gardeners grew them (famous or infamous). Betty, a practicing municipal law attorney, became interested in the histories of plants shortly after she and her husband purchased the 10-acre farmstead from a descendant of the original homesteaders. The previous owner, Ann Patterson (who lived to be 104), regaled Betty with her personal history of the plants surrounding the house and, at the same time, ignited in her a new passion for heirloom plants.

Heritage Flower Farm offers special events throughout the summer, holds genuinely interesting classes, and leads a garden design school. They also conduct theme-oriented garden walks, such as, plants exhibiting historical associations with "love," plants grown by Jefferson or Washington or discovered by Meriwether Lewis, etc.

OWNERS: Betty Adelman
TYPE: Small specialty nursery
SPECIALTIES: Perennials; heirloom
HOURS: April 15 (approx.) thru Sept: Wed.-Sun. 9:00 am to 5:00 pm. Other times by appointment.
CATALOG AVAILABLE: Online
MAIL-ORDER AVAILABLE: Yes
DISPLAY GARDENS: Yes
CLASSES: Yes

CONTACT

33725 Highway L (Janesville Rd.)
Mukwonago, WI 53149
PHONE: (262) 662-0804
FAX: (262) 662-3864
WEB ADDRESS: www.heritageflowerfarm.com
EMAIL: betty@heritageflowerfarm.com

DIRECTIONS

FROM MILWAUKEE AREA: Southwest on I-43, to Hwy 164 (Exit 50), south on Hwy 164 to the town of Big Ben, Hwy L. Turn west (left) on Hwy L and proceed for 4.6 miles to the nursery. **FROM CHICAGO:** I-94 (Tri-State) north to Rt. 20 (WI). West on Rt. 20 to Rt. 83. Turn north (right) on Rt. 83 (Northwest Hwy) for 3.5 miles to CR-O. Turn north (right) onto CR-O and drive for 1.7 miles to CR-L. Turn west (left) on Hwy L and watch for nursery signs. **FROM MADISON AREA:** Take I-94 to Rt. 83 (Exit 287), drive south on Hwy 83 for 17 miles to CR-L. Turn east (left) onto CR-L and proceed for 1.3 miles to Nursery (Watch for signs).

GPS: N 42° 50.11', W 88° 16.63'

At present, Heritage Flower Farm grows 450 varieties of heirloom perennials as well as some roses, vines, and shrubs. Heritage Flower Farm is an excellent source for historically accurate plants for garden restorations or for those gardeners simply interested in the fascinating—real or mythical—histories of heirloom plants.

Display gardens surround the residence and the 1850s barn that serves as a gift shop. These gardens include themed borders (the Emily Dickinson bed contains all the plants mentioned in her poetry), rose borders, and ornamental grass beds, as well as 3½ acres of production fields. Heritage Flower Farm grows quality "old fashioned plants in the old fashioned way—in the ground in rows—digging and potting them up in the spring and summer as needed." Each plant, sold in trade gallons, comes with a profile of its ancestry, the origins of its name (if available), and known medicinal uses.

> "A garden is a delight to the eye, and a solace to the soul."
> —SA'DI

Anyone who thinks old-fashioned plants yield no surprises must have spent their gardening years under a rock. Did you know that the current ornamental darlings, *Miscanthus sinensis* 'Variegatus' and *M. sinensis* 'Zebrinus' have been cultivated in American gardens since the late 1800s? Or that *Miscanthus sinensis* 'Gracillimus', so prominent in current landscape design, was one of the first imported grasses to the west and is the oldest variety grown today?

Because Betty is a horticultural detective and plant sleuth, this nursery is a treasure trove of curious and rare vintage plants. This is home to many long-forgotten plants. You'll find the original **marshmallow** (*Althaea officinalis*), whose roots, plenty of sugar, and tons of pounding produced the original marshmallows which were a sweet tasting medicine. Saxifrage (*Saxifraga virgineaensis*) is an uncommon Wisconsin native. Liberty Hyde Bailey called it "much prized by fanciers, particularly abroad [but] very rare in American gardens." There is **mouse ear** *Cerastium biebersteinii* (frosted, felt-like foliage favored by Victorians under tropical plants); **kankakee mallow** *Iliamna remota* (pale rose mallows, endemic to Illinois and Virginia); and **globe mallow,** *Sphaeralcea ambigua* (orange mallow shaped saucers).

Among the nursery's holdings, gardeners can find plants with lengthy histories of cultivation. **Feverfew** (*Chrysanthemum parthenium*) is a plant that reputedly cush-

WISCONSIN

ioned the fall and saved the life of a construction worker who fell from the Parthenon. There is **lily-of-the-valley**, *Convallaria majalis* (cultivated since at least 1000 BC), and the poppy (*Papaver*), dating from "at least the time when Homer wrote the Illiad, in which he used the poppy's hanging bud as a symbol for a dying soldier." **Meadowrue** *(Thalictrum aquilegifolium)* was used by ancient Romans to cure ulcers and the plague. *Hosta plantaginea* 'Grandiflora' was a popular Chinese plant as long ago as the Han Dynasty (202 BC – 220 AD). Flag iris (*Iris ono-cyclus*) dates back to 1959 BC "when Egyptian Pharaoh Thutmosis I brought it back from Syria. Its representation still lives today as a carving on temple walls at Karnak, along the Nile."

Heritage Flower Farm issues an engrossing, history-laden catalog that chronicles the details surrounding a plant's name, describes its virtues, documents its medicinal trials and legacies, regales us with the names of the luminaries that grew it, and recounts historical gems to entertain and educate. The catalog notes that **lady's mantle** (*Alchemilla mollis* syn *A. vulgaris),* was named for alchemists (medieval chemists who believed they could change ordinary substances into gold) who used the dewdrops from lady's mantle as one of the secret ingredients. It also notes plants whose curative properties were far-reaching, such as *Corydalis lutea*, which in the sixteenth century was credited with curing leprosy, scabs, itches, cholera, salty blood (whatever that is), jaundice, melancholy, plague, pestilence, red eye, and diseases of the liver and spleen.

The catalog recounts bewitching historical vignettes, which tug at the heart, make us laugh, and somehow invest these humble plants with a renewed glamour. For example, Betty's research shows that **rattlesnake master** (*Eryngium yuccifolium),* a Wisconsin native, got its name because Chickasaw shamans "chewed the root, blew on their hands, and then picked up rattlesnakes without injury." English brides carried **sneezewort** (*Achillea ptarmica* 'The Pearl') at their weddings and called the plant "seven years' love." **Lobelia** (*Lobelia cardinalis*) was used to cure the

WISCONSIN

seven year itch. According to German legend, **forget-me-not** (*Myosotis palustris*) got its common name when a lover who died gathering the flowers cried out "forget-me-not" as he fell into a river.

All references to plants at Heritage Flower Farm (via catalog, on premises, and online) are listed alphabetically by botanical name and then by common name, if there is one. Despite the sometimes difficult pronunciations, as Betty puts it, "We use botanical names because they accurately identify the plant. Come on, how hard can it be? The Romans could do this 2000 years ago."

Due to low quantities, or plants received after the catalog is printed, not all plants available at the nursery are listed in the catalog. It is highly recommended that you visit the nursery several times during the season. Otherwise you could miss out on some unadvertised treasures such as *Hesperaloe parviflora*, a yucca look-alike with red flowers.

All-in-all, visiting Heritage Flower farm is a great way to spend the day while picking out sometimes rare, often historical, always interesting plants.

WISCONSIN

McClure & Zimmerman

❧ ❧

McClure & Zimmerman is a tried-and-true bulb supplier that offers both spring- and summer-flowering choices. Known for its superior quality of unusual flower bulbs for "the dedicated bulb enthusiast," McClure & Zimmerman, are "quality flower bulb brokers." McClure & Zimmerman features more than 600 quality bulb varieties, tubers, corms, and other rootstocks. They have a large selection of top of the line standards, but really shine in their offerings of species, exotic, and rare bulbs.

OWNERS: Richard Zondag
TYPE: Specialty bulb house
SPECIALTIES: Tulips; daffodils; minor bulbs; spring planted bulbs; amaryllis
HOURS: Orders 8:00 am to 4:30 pm (not open to the public).
CATALOG AVAILABLE: Printed and online
MAIL-ORDER AVAILABLE: Yes
DISPLAY GARDENS: No
CLASSES: No

CONTACT
108 W. Winnebago
P.O. Box 368
Friesland, WI 53935-0368
PHONE: (800) 883-6998
FAX: (800) 374-6120
WEB ADDRESS: www.mzbulb.com

WHAT YOU'LL FIND

There are several hundred premium **tulip** cultivars. Some of the categories are: Kaufmannia varieties (blossoms resemble waterlilies, some have mottled leaves); Fosteriana (single and double, producing some of the largest flowers); Triumph Greigii (eye-catching foliage, large colorful blooms); informal Parrot (brought to fame in Dutch still life oils); tall Darwin, Fringed Tulips, Viridiflora, elegant Lily Flowered Tulip; and Multiflowered Tulip.

They also have representative examples of tulips one would find growing in woodlands and mountains throughout the world (which have been nursery propagated). Wild tulips are fascinating miniatures. I especially enjoy *Tulipa tarda* (formerly *T. dasystemon*) whose star-like yellow blossoms open wide when kissed by the sun; and the showy gem, **lady tulip** or **lipstick tulip** (*T. clusiana*) with its broad red bands from top to bottom and cream inside, flaunting a deep purple center. The first one delightfully reseeds itself; the second is a bit harder to keep.

Then there are the **daffodils**, one of the showiest and probably the most popular of all spring bulbs. Many divisions can be found, such as: Trumpet, Single, Double, Long Cupped, Short Cupped, Triandrus (petite, graceful, and attractive multiple florets on a single stem); Cyclamineus (petals stream backward and away

WISCONSIN

from the long, slender trumpet); Jonquilla (sweetly-scented); Tazetta (bunch or cluster flowering); Poeticus (**pheasant's eye** once considered to be the only "true" daffodils); and species and wild forms that can be as little as the tip of your little finger. Others include Split-Corona, commonly known as **butterfly daffodil**, with divided, ruffled cups; and miscella-neous bulbs such as 'Tete-a-Tete' (an 8-inch hybrid that is often sold in pots in supermarkets or greenhouses).

> *"I love spring anywhere, but if I could choose, I would always greet it in a garden."*
> —RUTH STOUT

My favorite daffodil has always been the small yet delightful 'Hawera' that is like a fragrant "cloud of lemon-yellow butterflies" winging in on 8-inch stems. McClure & Zimmerman offers many tantalizing and economical mixtures of bulbs, including their fragrant Cluster-Flowered mix, Elfin Charm mix, Southern mix, Pretty in Pink mix, and mixes of all yellow.

There are **amaryllis** bulbs galore, including single, double, miniature, and but-terfly. For those too stressed out to pick one, four mixtures of bulbs are also available. And finally, there are McClure & Zimmerman's miscellaneous bulbs such as **allium** (34 varieties), **camassia**, **hardy cyclamen**, **foxtail lily** (12 varieties), **fritillaria** (19 kinds, including the North American native *F. pudica*), **hyacinths** (26 varieties), **iris** (Dutch, English, Juno, Dwarf, Spanish, and Siberian), and **calla lily**. There are indoor bulbs for forcing and early bloomers heralding the ancient pull of spring: **grape hyacinth**, **scilla**, **snowdrops** (7 varieties), **squill**, **winter aconite**, and **anemone**. There are exceptional lily hybrids and species (mainly Asiatic, the hard-to-find **martagon lily**, and **turk's cap**), a generous sampling of *Colchicum* (unique fall-flowering bulbs that actually bloom while still dormant), some autumn flowering **crocuses**, and the brilliant-yellow, crocus-like *Sternbergia lutea*.

McClure & Zimmerman's spring catalog showers us with bulbs for summer bloomers: everything from *Achimenes* to *Zephyranthes*. There are impressive selec-tions for container gardening: **lily-of-the-Nile** (*Agapanthus*), **angel's trumpet** (both *Brugmansia* and *Datura*), **caladium** (16 varieties), **canna** (31 varieties), **pineapple lily** (*Eucomis*), and **elephant ears** (*Colocasia*). For woodland gardening: **Jack-in-the-pulpit** (*Arisaema*), **wild ginger** (*Asarum*), **Chinese ground orchid** (*Bletilla*), hardy versions of florists' **cyclamen** (*Cyclamen*) and **Virginia bluebells** (*Mertensia virginica*). For the sun garden there are lily hybrids and species, and even daylilies. With **clivias,** or **Kaffir lilies** all the rage here, for me the crown jewel of the spring

WISCONSIN

selection was a mature, potted (once bloomed), incredibly priced, Kaffir lily (*Clivia miniata* var. 'Citrina')—that elusive, much heralded, rare yellow clivia.

The catalog is liberally sprinkled with exquisite botanical illustrations. They guarantee to sell only the largest hybrid tulip bulbs that Holland exports to the United States, as well as the largest daffodil bulbs. They provide their own "Floradapt" hardiness map to help their customers choose bulbs that will survive in their climate. In addition to all this, McClure and Zimmerman also provides books, bulb boosters, and friendly service.

WISCONSIN

MILAEGER'S

❧ ❧

Shortly after their engagement in 1946, in what can only be described as a prophetic moment, a lighthouse keeper's daughter sent her favorite postal worker this poem:

Our love is like a garden, Dear
With beauty everywhere.
And every time we kiss, we plant
Another flower there.

Two years after their marriage, Dan and Joan Mileager built their first greenhouse where they grew vegetable plants and annual flowers to supplement their income. In 1960, the Milaegers purchased the original 2 acres of the site that today is known as the Racine central store, propagation, and growing area. They reworked an old greenhouse and successfully grew their first crop—hot-house tomatoes. Later geraniums and annuals were added.

Forty-three years and 20 acres later, surrounded by a bevy of picturesque farmsteads, that old greenhouse has grown into a complex of eighty-seven greenhouses covering more than 3 acres and producing what is arguably one of the largest retail operations in the Midwest.

The nursery's lure is enhanced by exceptionally well grown plants, an extensive selection, a trained horticul-

OWNERS: Dan and Joan Milaeger
TYPE: Large retail nursery
SPECIALTIES: Perennials—sun and shade; annuals; hanging baskets; roses; vines; trees; shrubs; herbs; aquatics; grasses; garden art; seeds; containers; clothing; accessories; patio furniture; year-round christmas shops
HOURS: Open year round except for Christmas Day. Jan. thru Apr. 23 (approx.): Mon.-Fri. 9:00 am to 8:00 pm, Sat. 9:00 am-5:00 pm, Sun. 9:30 am-5:00 pm. April 24 thru mid June: Mon.-Fri. 8:00 am to 9:00 pm, Sat. 8:00 am to 8:00 pm, Sun. 9:00 am to 6:00 pm, Mid June thru end of year, Mon.-Fri. 8:00 am-8:00 pm, Sat. 8:00 am to 6:00 pm, Sun. 9:30 am to 5:00 pm.
CATALOG AVAILABLE: Separate versions for annuals; perennials; roses, and nursery stock. Specials listed online.
MAIL-ORDER AVAILABLE: No
DISPLAY GARDENS: Yes
CLASSES: Yes

CONTACT
4838 Douglas Avenue
Racine, WI 53402-2447
PHONE: (262) 639-2040; (800) 669-1229
FAX: (262) 639-1855
WEB ADDRESS: www.milaegers.com
EMAIL: kara@milaegers.com

DIRECTIONS:
FROM I-94: Exit I-94 County Hwy K, Exit will put you on frontage road. Continue north on the frontage road across County Hwy K to 4 Mile Road. Turn east (right) onto 4 Mile Road and drive 4.5 miles to Rt. 32. Turn south (right) onto Rt. 32, nursery is 0.3 miles on right.

GPS: N 42° 46.80', W 87° 48.45'

WISCONSIN

> *"When it comes to love—flowers sing where words merely talk."*
> —ANONYMOUS

tural staff, free lectures, demonstrations, and seminars. They also offer landscape design and installation, horticultural consultations, user-friendly catalogs, online specials, enormous quantities of containers, and good seed and bulb selections. A vast assortment of garden accessories, garden art, statuary, arbors, and trellises can be purchased. Two separate shopping areas overflow with gifts, home accents, patio furniture, clothing, footwear, and an amazing year-round array of Christmas ornaments, decorations, and collectibles.

The most important bit of advice I can give anyone visiting Milaeger's for the first time is to ignore those supermarket carts and head straight for the three-tiered, oversized rolling carts. Under no circumstances are you to share one cart with your companion! Otherwise, you'll waste time and energy later, transferring plants to an additional cart—probably by the time you reach the second greenhouse. Learn from my mistakes—make sure your friend has one of his or her own! Also, allow sufficient time, wear comfortable walking shoes, have some idea of your plant needs and requirements, and have ample room available in your car for your many purchases.

Milaeger's is in a controlled "total chaos mode" for the period from Mother's Day through Memorial Day. They are completely jammed on weekends but, despite the crowds, the staff is always courteous, helpful, and fast. The plant selection is fresh and top-notch, and though you may have to walk a bit on weekends, there is ample room to park. Milaeger's is both popular with hands-on gardeners and shopping tourists, successfully accommodating all groups, even those coming in by the busload.

WHAT YOU'LL FIND

Mileager's grows more than 42,000 flats of annuals and 12,000 hanging baskets in more than 1,000 varieties of traditional and new annuals. Some of the larger categories are: **geraniums** (nearly 90 varieties, including trailing and scented), **impatiens** (95, including New Guinea), **petunias** (80, including the trailing forms), **pansies/violas** (35), **snapdragon** (28), **lisianthus** (15), **nicotiana** (11), **marigold** (25), **verbena** (23), **vinca** (15), and **zinnia** (15).

In some of the newer categories, you'll find: *Bacopa* (7 different varieties of this genus, in white, pink, or lavender), **sun coleus** (25, brightly colored), ornamental **sweet potato vine** *Ipomea batatas* (5), **licorice plant** *Helichrysum* (4), and **Million Bells®** *Calibrachoa* (10). At Mileager's you can also find some of the more unusual plants perfect for landscapes, such as green **nicotiana**, *Nicotiana alata* 'Lime Green'; **spider flower**, *Cleome* 'Linde Armstrong' (a new, shorter variety); and yellow **trumpet flower**, *Datura meteloides* 'Triple Lavender' (lavender-edged).

Hanging baskets are sold in different sizes and in all manner of combinations from single plant (such as impatiens, **fuchsia**, or **diascia**) to snazzy and colorful amalgamations blending the newest, hottest, and trendiest varieties available today. Unusual plants for containers include **lilac hibiscus**, *Alyogyne huegelii* 'Santa Cruz' (purple-flowered); the colorful **Joseph's coat**, *Alternanthera ficoidea* 'Trailing Ruby Red'; **angelflower**, *Angelonia* (resembling miniature snapdragons); **elephant's ear**, *Colocasia* 'Illustris' and 'Black Magic'. You'll also find *Dichondra argentea* 'Silver Falls' (incredibly different, silver foliaged and cascading), impatiens, *Impatiens hybrida* 'Fanfare' (trailing); and the darling of the 2003 new introductions, *Perilla frutescens* 'Magilla' (with coleus-like foliage).

For vertical accents, Milaeger's carries twining **snapdragon**, **golden trumpet**, **cardinal climber**, **love in a puff**, purple **cup and saucer**, and **cypress vine** (representing both *Mandevilla* and *Dipladenia*). You'll also find climbing yellow **bleeding heart**, **Chilean glory flower**, **firecracker vine**, **hyacinth bean**, **star Jasmine**, **candy corn vine**, **orange glow**, **morning glory** (8 varieties), **moon vine**, climbing **nasturtium**, **bower vine**, **snail vine** (Thomas Jefferson's favorite), **black-eyed Susan vine**, and **purple bells**.

In the vegetable category, sold in packs of two and four or in 3½-inch containers, Milaeger's carries the entire gamut from **artichoke** and **asparagus** to **squash** and **strawberries**. The nursery offers sweet **peppers** (12 varieties), hot peppers (10), and **tomatoes** (21 hybrid varieties, 47 heirlooms). I was especially pleased to see my favorites: 'Cherokee Purple' (dusky pink), 'Black Krim' (dark red), 'Green Zebra' (yellow-green), and 'Marmande' (scarlet red).

Milaeger's carries more than 1,000 varieties of perennials, arranged alphabetically by botanical name according to category, and artfully displayed on and under long, slat tables. If you are less familiar with botanical names, you can pick up a "Common Name Cross Reference Guide" posted in several places throughout the nursery. Classic hardy perennials are augmented by unusual varieties in limited quantities in a separate, "Collector's Corner." These are considered trial plants and, therefore, not guaranteed.

For neophyte gardeners, as well as seasoned pros confused by the great numbers of available plants, Milaeger's has extrapolated foolproof, tough garden performers that are plants of extra high merit. They have created lists of these plants arranged both by color and use. Lists in hand, it is now incredibly easy to answer such questions as "What will grow in the shade and has a white blossom?" You can cross-reference the lists to come up with several fine choices. Milaeger's also has handouts for successful plant combinations, offering suggestions for various sites and situations. Ask for the "Best for the Midwest" handouts.

Mileager's is much appreciated for its vast holdings of commonly sought-after perennials. Their superior collection tends to be more mainstream but does contain enough distinctly different and interesting cultivars to lure me back time and

★ SIDE TRIPS ★

CHARLES WUSTUM MUSEUM OF FINE ARTS (414) 636-9177, 2519 Northwestern Avenue, Racine. This is an historic Italianate farmhouse surrounded by 13 acres of magnificent gardens and filled with a permanent collection of more than 2500 works of art. LOG CABIN MUSEUM (414) 767-2884, Echo Lake Veterans Park (Hwy 36), Burlington. This is a completely furnished (period pieces) log cabin. OLD ENGINE HOUSE No. 3 MUSEUM (414) 637-7395, 700 Sixth Street, Racine. Once a working firehouse, today it features an exhibit of antique fire fighting equipment. WINDPOINT LIGHTHOUSE, Lighthouse Drive, between Three and Four Mile Roads, Racine. Built in 1880, the lighthouse has become an outstanding landmark. Though the interior is not open to the public, visitors can stroll the grounds and enjoy the view.

again. In addition, Dan and Joan offer hundreds of varieties of **roses** that perform well in Wisconsin's harsh climate. These roses are available as grade #1, two-year old plants. There are own-root and grafted, hand-potted in $1^{1}/_{2}$- and 2-gallon pots. Included in their collections are climbing, hybrid tea, grandiflora, floribunda, rugosa, polyantha, David Austin™, Meidiland™, Canadian, miniature, and tree (standards).

SATELLITE LOCATION

CONTACT
8717 Hwy 11
Sturtevant, WI 53177-2011
PHONE: (262) 886-2117, (262) 552-7118
FAX: (262) 886-5166
EMAIL: johnw@milaegers.com

DIRECTIONS
FROM I-94: Exit I-94 at County Hwy. K, exit will put you on Frontage Road. Proceed south on Frontage road to Hwy 11. Turn east (left) onto Hwy 11 and proceed for 2 miles to the nursery on your right.

This nursery is a promising resource for an interesting selection of well-grown, specimen-sized, cold-hardy trees and shrubs. Its stock is wide-ranging, and therefore hard to summarize. The nursery's focus appears to be on deciduous ornamental trees including superb varieties of **maple**, **serviceberry**, **birch** (unusual 'Purple Rain' weeping birch), **redbud** (purple leafed 'Forest Pansy'), **dogwood**, **beech** (including the hard to find **European Beech** 'Tricolor'), **flowering cherry**, and **mountain ash**. Flowering shrubs include **Japanese maple**, **butterfly bush**, **azalea**, **summersweet**, **smoke bush**, **witch hazel**, **rose of Sharon**, **hydrangea** (including Endless Summer™) **bidleaf**, **mockorange**, **potentilla**, **spirea**, **lilac**, **weigela**, **yucca**, and **viburnum**. Its **clematis** selection includes big-flowered, small-flowered, and non-vining clematis.

What would I change about Mileager's? Well, if I had my way they could really use a food court, tea room, or better yet, an herbal spa for happy shoppers' stressed and vanquished muscles.

WISCONSIN

Monches Farm

❧ ❧

Monches Farm, treasured by serious gardeners, is a horticultural wonderland that grows an engaging abundance of perennials, herbs, grasses, ground covers and a few unusual shrubs on a delightful old farmstead. This 7-acre floral extravaganza is in the heart of Wisconsin's Kettle Moraine, about 30 miles northwest of Milwaukee in a scenic woodland area on a designated "Rustic Road."

The two-story gift shop (not wheelchair accessible) overflows with dried arrangements (a nursery specialty), spectacular candles, an incredible selection of soaps, wall hangings, table decorations, antiques, linens, blankets made from Scott's own sheep, pottery, and art glass—everything from the elegant to the whimsical, and some items that are simply different. Founded in 1981 by Scott Sieckman, a former anthropology and art major turned horticulturist, Monches carries an exceptional range of captivating plant material that is hardy to the area, aesthetically pleasing, and passes Scott's rigorous standards.

Monches Farm looks deceptively like a working farm, with its barn, rare breed poultry, heirloom sheep bred for superior wool, and geese in summer. However, the fenced in animals and the aviaries in the greenhouse are simply to add ambiance, country atmosphere—and fun. (Monches sells farm-fresh eggs in season in beautiful hues ranging from light beige to sky blue.)

OWNERS: Scott Sieckman
TYPE: Specialty nursery
SPECIALTIES: Field-grown perennials—sun and shade; grasses; herbs; unusual shrubs; ground covers; annuals
HOURS: April 1 thru Dec 31: Tue.-Fri. 10:00 am to 6:00 pm, Sat. 10:00 am to 4:00 pm, Sun. Noon to 4:00 pm (for classes only); Feb. 1 thru Mar. 31: Thurs.-Sun. 10:00 am to 4:00 pm.
CATALOG AVAILABLE: Online
MAIL-ORDER AVAILABLE: No
DISPLAY GARDENS: Yes
CLASSES: Yes

CONTACT
5890 Monches Road
Colgate, WI 53017
PHONE: (262) 966-2787
WEB ADDRESS: www.monchesfarm.com

DIRECTIONS
FROM MILWAUKEE: Take US-41/US-45 northwest to CR-Q (County Line Road). Turn west (left) onto CR-Q driving for approx. 11 miles to Monches Road. At Monches Road turn northeast (right) and drive 0.5 miles to the nursery which is on your left. **FROM MADISON AREA:** Take I-94 to WI-83 (exist 287). Take WI-83 north for 8.4 miles to CR-VV in North Lake. Turn east (right) onto CR-VV and drive for 1 mile to CR-E. Turn north (left) onto CR-E and proceed for 2.4 miles to Monches Road (Hartley Road). Turn northeast (right) onto Monches/ Hartley and drive one mile to the nursery which is on your left.

GPS: N 43° 11.93', W 88° 19.75'

WISCONSIN

The scenery around the nursery is breathtaking. Benches scattered throughout the property invite moments of rest and quiet contemplation. Customers should not miss the gorgeous container displays scattered casually throughout the gardens and randomly framing the gift shop entrance, for they exhibit exciting artistry and interesting originality in their plant combinations. There are stunning pastoral views of Holy Hill in the distance, and for those with a yen for exploring, entrances to Wisconsin's Ice Age Hiking Trails are close by.

In the greenhouse with cooing doves for company, the sedums with their descriptive placards are attractively arranged on several tables. The nursery's stunning display gardens are scattered about the property, enveloping the gift shop and the original 1840s post and beam house (Scott's residence). These gardens are masterpieces of design deserving of close inspection.

WHAT YOU'LL FIND

In addition to the rare and unusual, Monches Farm offers plants in the normal nursery categories—**hosta**, **daylilies**, **yarrow**, **astilbe**, **phlox**, and other stalwarts of the garden, yet little, if any, of its stock selection is ordinary. Scott's seductive choices betray a palate of cutting-edge plants gleaned through top-notch horticultural contacts across the country. Choosing from this group can lead to a fair amount of indecision and head scratching. They have **monkshood**, *Aconitum carmichaelii* 'Pink Sensation' (powder pink and cream); **bugleweed**, *Ajuga* 'Rainbow' (burgundy-bronze mottled with pink, gold, and yellow); **Dutchman's pipe**, *Aristolochia clematitis* (seldom grown, non-vining); and *Geranium* 'Spinners' (deep-purple flowered, tall) to name a few. Each of these is appealing in its own way, but personally, I was blown away by the choices of exceptionally stocky *Campanula*. For most of us, the easiest and most rewarding *Campanula* are the tall border species, so the prize for the best border **campanula** at Monches Farm goes to *C. lactiflora* (fat and opulent, with large branched panicles of flared, skim-milk blue blossoms).

Monches' collections of ornamental grasses, **iris**, hardy **lilies**, **beebalm**, **salvia** (mealy-cup sage), **sedum**, and **toad lily** are also impressive. And practically every one of the 250 or so prismatic cultivars of field-grown daylilies (*Hemerocallis*) will charm the pants off you if you let them—and that can get you into a whole mess of trouble. On my visit, unusual perennials included **St. Bruno's lily** (*Anthericum*); upscale **Japanese tree peony** (*Paeonia suffruticosa*); native swamp **sedge** (*Carex muskingumensis* 'Bad Hair Day'); unusual clumping *Descampsia cespitosa* 'Fairy's

> *"...alliums have high value in the garden...and as for smelling nasty when crushed—well, who in his senses would wish too crush his own flowers?"*
> —VITA SACKVILLE-WEST
>
> ❧

Joke'; short, powerful violet beard-tongue (*Penstemon hirsutus* 'Pygmaeus'); and dark purple beebalm (*Monarda* 'Mahogany').

There are interesting finds for the woodland garden: the checkered lily (*Fritillaria meleagris*) usually available in the fall; **bowman's root** (*Gillenia*); and yellow **waxbells** (both the *Kirengeshoma palmata* and the harder-to-find *K. koreana*). Singular choices for shade include: orange-flowered **barrenwort** (*Epimedium pubigerum* 'Orangekonigen'); a cute pink mini **meadowsweet** (*Filipendula vulgaris* 'Kahome'); and, sporting huge blue flowers, **Jacob's ladder** (*Polemonium* 'Heavenly Habit').

There are noteworthy assets for any sunny border: giant **scabiosa** (*Cephalaria gigantea*); the pink with a red eye phlox (*Phlox paniculata* 'Dodo Hanbury Forbes'); double **rudbeckia** (*Rudbeckia laciniata* 'Golden Glow'); and hardy **petunia** (*Ruellia*). Some classic prairie plants included **goldenrod**, 8 varieties of **liatris**, **hawkweed**, impressive **Indian plaintain**, **mountain mint**, and wild **quinine**. Annual and perennial herbs include a good selection of **basil**, several **lavender**, unusual **ornamental thyme**, several extraordinary **chives**, **French sorrel**, fragrant **rosemary**, and **mint** for every taste—lemon, peppermint, pineapple, apple, and chocolate.

For his dried arrangements, Sieckman initially grew everything, including the flowers used in his unique dried arrangements, "on 3 acres out back." But as tastes and the subtle nuances of fashion changed, the demand for arrangements, garden accessories, and unusual plants increased. So he started importing items from all over. "It's difficult to grow some of the flowers we currently need for our dried arrangements," says Sieckman. "But that doesn't mean we don't grow quite a few." Indeed, most plants are propagated on site and are field grown for at least a year. They are "survivors of at least one winter" he says. Plants

WISCONSIN

★ SIDE TRIPS ★

FOX & HOUNDS, (262) 628-1111, 1298 Friess Lake Road, Hubertus, WI. This rambling log cabin-style restaurant has been winning the hearts and palates of local diners for many years. **DELAFIELD ANTIQUES CTR.** is a popular local attraction for lovers of antiques. (608) 764-1454, Delafield, WI.

in the sales area are grouped by category and arranged alphabetically by botanical name. They are potted out, pots and all, in the ground, giving customers a true perspective of the plant's nature, size, blossoms, and staying power.

Scott is an avid collector of unusual woody plant material—planted out throughout the property, though a number of them at Monches Farm are unavailable. Should some beautiful shrub catch your fancy, ask the ever-so-helpful staff to direct you to some great sources. Visitors are welcome to tour the show gardens which include a large mature shade garden with an impressive hosta collection, a **boxwood**-edged formal herb garden, and a sun border with some fashionably witty plant combinations. In fact, there are so many areas and varieties planted out on the premises that sometimes the lushness of the plantings makes it hard to know where the display gardens end and the production fields begin.

Monches is a wondrous find for the discerning plant lover. Special events include May Day, a lavish summer Fairy Festival (kids come dressed as their favorite fairy), Fall Festival, and Christmas.

NORTHERN GROWN
PERENNIALS

ꞏꞏꞏ

Northern Grown Perennials is a charming specialty nursery located south of LaCrosse, and is a treasure trove of hardy field-grown daylilies, hostas, and **peonies** suitable for northern gardens. Owner Rod Lysne operates this popular enterprise on the various scattered fields of a former dairy. As a sophisticated hybridizer, he creates cold-hardy plants endowed with elegant, prizewinning characteristics. Gardeners are invited to view gardens and growing fields, just let them know in advance that you are coming.

Northern Grown Perennials offers more than 650 daylily (*Hemerocallis*) cultivars and 550 hosta varieties, products of both the owner's and other breeders' hybridizing efforts. These plants are some of the newest and finest hybrid hosta and daylily varieties available today, suitable for the hosta and daylily collector, amateur hybridizer, or the gardening enthusiast in search of a spectacular plant. In addition, Rod grows 150 named peonies (*Paeonia*) plus several thousand of his own daylily and hosta seedlings garnered from his ongoing hybridizing efforts.

The natural surroundings serve as a foundation from which to draw inspiration. Rod's breeding goals are to produce memorable plants that, while stunning, decorative, and picturesque, also survive and thrive in this part of the country. His skill in crossing choice plants, both his own seedlings as well as parent stock from other

OWNERS: Rod Lysne
TYPE: Specialty nursery—mail-order only (or pick-up)
SPECIALTIES: Hosta; daylilies; peonies
HOURS: By appointment only.
CATALOG AVAILABLE: Printed and Online
MAIL-ORDER AVAILABLE: Yes
DISPLAY GARDENS: Yes, by appointment
CLASSES: No

CONTACT
54779 Helland Road
Ferryville, WI 54628
PHONE: (608) 734-3178 (after dark or 6:30 to 7:00 am CST)
WEB ADDRESS: www.hostalink.com
Email: ngp@mwt.net

DIRECTIONS
FROM THE NORTH (LaCROSSE AREA):
Directions from US-14: Take US-14 south to SR-27 (approx. 33 miles from LaCrosse). Turn west (right) onto SR-27 and proceed for 16.7 miles to Helland Rd. Turn west (right) onto Helland Rd. and drive 1.4 miles to address.
FROM MADISON AREA: Direction from US-14: Take US-14 West to SR-27. Turn southwest (left) onto SR-27 and drive for 15.7 miles to Helland Road. Turn west (right) onto Helland Rd and proceed for 1.4 miles to address.

GPS: N 43° 19.49', W 90° 57.23'

breeders, has resulted in exceptional cultivars with good bud count and branching habits. These plants have great looks, and of course, cold-hardiness.

WHAT YOU'LL FIND

Some of the outstanding Northern Grown **daylily** introductions are: 'Turtledove' ("pony-sized bloomer" in the colors of warm sand with a large, pure pink eye and chartreuse throat); 'Early Edition' (small irresistible creamy pink flirt); 'Hey Lookie' (champagne-pink cutie with dark purple eye); and 'Sable Song' (scintillatingly morose, sultry black-red beauty). They also carry huge, ruffled, picotee-edged (very popular), bicolored, frilled, edged, gilded, and ornamentally-eyed daylilies from numerous other well-known breeders.

> *"Some people like to make a little garden out of life."*
> —JEAN ANOUILH

Northern Grown Perennials offers four daylily categories that appeal to different collectors or garden situations: cream-of-the-crop, spider, double, and small/miniature daylilies. A serious daylily collector from my neck of the woods continually adds daylilies of all categories from Northern Grown Perennials. She claims they provide "husky plants of exceptional value." There are stunners in each group; however, what attracted me were the gregarious spiders: 'Chevron Spider' (creamy peach with red); 'Angelus Spider' (polychrome); 'Green Spider' (green-toned yellow); 'Pink Super Spider' (clear rose stud); 'Spider Lady' (light pink, ladylike); 'Ruby Spider' (scarlet gem); 'Spider Spirits' (soulful yellow); 'Spider Miracle' (marvelous yellow); 'Spiderman' (commanding stealth); 'Tarantula' (bronze); and 'Wilson Spider' (my favorite, lavender-pink). When you think about it, doesn't that selection constitute the perfect excuse for a theme bed?

Rod's hybridizing efforts with the genus *Hosta* has also garnered incredible results. The description on his 2000 introduction, *Hosta* 'Jurassic Park', is just too good to pass up without sharing: "To this beast we attribute the loss of 3 shovels, a John Deere riding mower, 2 garden tillers, 3 cats, 6 raccoons, a Guernsey cow, and 2 little old ladies on a garden visit. Hence we give it wide berth when working close to it. It has been recommended that we spray it with Roundup™ once or twice a year just to keep it from hurting anyone." Regarding pests, "Due to its heavy substance, slugs have never been a problem—basically because it eats them!" Now, if you were me and you already had 'T. Rex' and 'Behemoth' stomp-

WISCONSIN

ing about in the shade garden, could you pass up 'Jurassic Park'? I didn't think so!

Other imposing **hosta** introductions include Rod's personal favorite, the sparkling, bright gold confection 'Lemon Drop' (a wonderful companion for early woodland ephemerals); the aptly named 'Shade Babe'; the ever-so-toney 'Glad Rags'; stippled 'Lucky Stripes'; and the perfect gift for any college graduate, 'Streets of Gold'.

Northern Grown Perennials is the repository of a great many cultivars of the late Chet Tompkins (of iris, daylily, and hosta fame), as well as his mother Mrs. Tompkins' daylily and hosta plants. (This astute, dear lady was hybridizing hostas as far back as the 1920s, when hostas were not even considered fashionable.) Rod has compiled a descriptive listing of all the standard Tompkins hostas and daylilies, along with many never-before-available hybrids, which he'll gladly send to anyone interested in acquiring these choice cultivars.

> ### EXTRAS
>
> Northern Grown Perennials offers some interesting daylily deals for those gardeners capable of picking up their plants directly from the nursery. He offers overstocks and end-runs (all named varieties) as well as unnamed, tetraploid, multi-fan, hybrid daylily seedling clumps (products from his hybridizing projects) for $5 per clump (with a 10-clump minimum, Rod's choice). The latter can produce some delightful bargains, for the passed-over seedlings of a talented hybridizer are often "drop dead gorgeous" plants of unrivaled beauty, costing far less than the named ones. Northern Grown also includes bonus plants with each order.

Northern Grown Perennials sends out freshly dug, mature, big root daylily cultivars (many with double or triple fans on them), with 3 to 5 fans on the mini's and diploids. They supply blooming sized singles of the few slow growers, or those that are new and scarce. The same applies to the hostas. These are freshly dug, mature, big root, and have two or three eyes for the majority of the hosta plants, three to four eyes for the *H. fortunei* types, and a single established eye for the slow growers or the new introductions. Being a smaller nursery, they have a limited supply of each variety, and it is the wise gardener who orders early.

Northern Grown Perennials' guarantee on their daylily and hosta introductions is indeed a generous one. In their own words, if you purchase an introduction that is over $20, "grow the undivided plant for two seasons and at the end of that time if you are not happy with it, just return it to us 'undivided' with the original label and we will be glad to refund the original purchase price, plus postage." Depending on weather conditions, Northern Grown begins shipping hostas about the middle of May, followed by daylilies a couple of weeks later.

Rod's **peony** selection is tantalizing yet compact, but as peonies are still "new" to this nursery, I expect the numbers in the coming years to grow substantially. Currently he is growing approximately 100 varieties and is propagating those he considers "the best of the best." Presently, 'Coral Charm' and the attractively priced 'Fernleaf' are the most popular, but what pulled me in were: 'The Fawn' (double pink with flecking); 'Picotee' (white edged with lavender-pink and hard to come by); and 'Illini Belle' (rich mahogany-red). All peonies are freshly dug, field-grown plants shipped only in the fall. For peak bloom time, I suggest you email the nursery, as Mother Nature follows her own agenda and bloom times vary from year to year.

NORTHWIND PERENNIAL FARM

❧ ❧

On a picturesque century-old farm, nestled between sleepy rolling pastures north of Lake Geneva, lies Walworth County's very own blockbuster field of dreams. The stately farmhouse, colorful dairy buildings, and 10 acres of productive fields are home to Northwind Perennial Farm. Co-owners Roy Diblik, Colleen Garrigan, and Steve Coster started their horticultural venture as a wholesale endeavor. Never conceived as a retail operation, the staff simply threw up a bench one fine autumn day, put out some mums and other overstocks, and watched in amazement as customers quickly snatched them up. The following year they added more benches and more plants, and before long a new branch of the existing enterprise was born. As the website notes, "It is the quintessential example of the field of dreams motto: If you build it, they will come."

Northwind Perennial Farm is an excellent resource for classic, hardy ornamental perennials ideally suited to the vagaries of Midwestern climates. The field-grown plants, deemed hardy after spending at least one winter in the ground, are dug up and potted out in 1- and 2-gallon containers, and set out on various benches in the sales area. The varieties of plants available at Northwind Perennial Farm are an interesting blend of proven classics, reliable stalwarts, and new forms with superior ornamental interest that add spice, pizzazz, and excitement to any gardener's landscape.

Visitors are invited to stroll the Farm's extensive production fields for

OWNERS: Roy Diblik, Colleen Garrigan, and Steve Coster

TYPE: Large retail and wholesale nursery

SPECIALTIES: Perennials—sun and shade; annuals—tender perennials; tropicals; summer bulbs; hanging baskets

HOURS: April 10 thru Oct. 13 (dates vary; check before coming out): Thurs.-Mon. 10:00 am to 6:00 pm; July and Aug: Fri. and Sat. 10:00 am to 6:00 pm. Also by appointment.

CATALOG AVAILABLE: Plant list printed and online

MAIL-ORDER AVAILABLE: No

DISPLAY GARDENS: Yes

CLASSES: Yes

CONTACT
7047 Hospital Road
Burlington, WI 53105
PHONE: (262) 248-8229
WEB ADDRESS: www.northwindperennial-farm.com
EMAIL: info@northwindperennialfarm.com

DIRECTIONS
FROM LAKE GENEVA: Take I-120 north for 3.3 miles to Hospital Road. Turn east (right) and drive 0.25 miles to nursery. (Look for signs)

GPS: N 42° 39.27', W 88° 24.53'

a better feel of the nature of mature plants. As compliments to the lusty perennials, the Farm offers an immense selection of garden ornaments and planters; "cutsey" plaques; birdfeeders

> *"Nature works no faster than need be."*
> —Henry David Thoreau

of every color, shape, and size; dried flowers; and good, sturdy gardening tools.

The big red barn houses Colleen's personal antique collection consisting of quilts, folk art, and weathered antiques. It is part museum, part history lesson, and part treasure hunt (open for exploration, but nothing is for sale).

What You'll Find

The Farm grows mainstays of the summer garden with cottage garden appeal, such as **bellflower**, *Campanula punctata* 'Sarastro' (continuously blooming, glistening royal purple); double lavender *Delphinium* 'Wishful Thinking'; and miniature **hollyhock**, *Sidalcea* 'Little Princess' (hardy and vigorous). It offers such **hosta** curiosities as 'Sweet Home Chicago' and 'White Triumphator'. Interesting denizens of the shade include: **painted fern**, *Athyrium* 'Ghost' (delicate gray green tints on celadon porcelain; *Astilbe* 'Flamingo' screams to be noticed with hot pink plumes thrust pointedly in the air.

The nursery carries big, bold architectural plants such as **Joe-Pye weed**, *Eupatorium maculatum* 'Bartered Bride' (foaming heads full of pure white blossoms) and *Boltonia* 'Snowbank' (statuesque white beauty, sizeable but showy, floating clusters of flowers high above its neighbors). You can also find old-fashioned prairie **coneflowers**, *Echinacea purpurea* 'Magnus' and 'Rubinstern', among others.

For late-season bloom, a time when summer's heat and humidity shows up like unwanted dinner guests, the Farm has some cooling choices including the rugged native **culver's root** *Veronicastrum virginicum* 'Rosea' (well adapted to brutal August heat); **rose mallow**, *Hibiscus moscheutos* 'Lord Baltimore' (heartstopping, red-flowered); **Russian sage**, *Perovskia atriplicifolia*; (profuse spikes of lavender-blue); and **turtlehead**, *Chelone lyonii* 'Hot Lips' (hooded, two-lipped pink). The Farm grows **clematis**, decorative **elderberry**, the various tribes of the **phlox** family, trouble-free **speedwell**, and the ever-so-popular, all season classic *Sedum* 'Autumn Joy'.

For year-round landscape interest, Northwind Perennial Farm offers grasses to fit every garden need. Of particular interest is the naturally occurring selection of *Panicum virgatum* 'Northwind', a cultivar of the native **switchgrass** found by Diblik.

WISCONSIN

The nursery's sales area is wrapped in well-designed, well-executed, extensive display gardens that showcase the Farm's incredible design talents. These enchanting gardens, a destination in their own right, cleverly demonstrate that with forethought and flair artistry can be achieved. Paths of all substances lead through dappled shade gardens and bright sunny borders. A unique, awesome water garden is meshed with intricate passageways of boulders and stone, yet the simple but colorful hedgerows planted along two interesting fences should not be missed, either. There are wood and metal benches and stone niches for resting; trellises, arbors, and pergolas both elaborate and simple; and a choice of funky garden art providing whimsical touches (sold directly from on-site inventory). As you wander about, keep an eye out for a trio of well-weathered, interesting, vintage "privies" scattered about the shady gardens.

WISCONSIN

SHADY ACRES PERENNIAL NURSERY

❧ ❧

Shady Acres Perennial Nursery is a large, popular nursery on the outskirts of Milwaukee. They specialize in mature ornamental perennials (there are no trees or shrubs), combining familiar favorites with worthy new introductions. Less than 15 miles southwest of the city, the nursery is a treasure trove of lusty, container-grown hardy perennial plants suitable for gardens in the Midwest. The nursery's layout is well thought out, and boasts ambitious display beds full of bodacious plants attractively interspersed throughout the sales areas. These are an attractive lure to the joyous array of interesting and desirable plants found within. Owner Jim Garbe, an accomplished nurseryman, deserves much of the credit for the nursery's impressive plant list, which currently features more than 1,400 varieties of perennials with a broad selection of companion annuals, herbs, ground covers, and vines.

The Shady Acres shop offers such upscale items as the Trapp Candle collection, garden art from around the country and abroad, Malaysian pottery, birdbaths, fountains, garden furniture, and trellises. As always, customers have access to decent selections of potting soil, peat moss, cocoa beans for mulch, and mushroom and cow compost.

OWNERS: Jim Garbe
TYPE: Large retail nursery.
SPECIALTIES: Perennials—sun and shade; ornamental grasses; herbs; vines.
HOURS: April: Mon.-Fri. 9:00 am to 6:00 pm, Sat. 8:00 to 4:00 pm, Sun. 10:00 am to 4:00 pm; May and June: Mon.-Fri. 9:00 am to 7:00 pm, Sat. 8:00 am to 4:00 pm, Sun. 10:00 am to 5:00 pm; July thru Sept.: Mon.-Fri. 9:00 am to 6:00 pm, Sat. 8:00 am to 4:00 pm, (closed Sun, July 4th and Labor Day); Oct.: Mon.-Fri. 9:00 am to 5:00 pm, Sat. 8:00 am to Noon, closed Sun.
CATALOG AVAILABLE: Printed and Online.
MAIL-ORDER AVAILABLE: No
DISPLAY GARDENS: Yes
CLASSES: Yes

CONTACT
5725 South Martin Road
New Berlin, WI 53146
PHONE: (262) 679-1610
WEB ADDRESS: www.shadyacresnursery.com
EMAIL: ShadyAcresNursery@juno.com

DIRECTIONS
FROM MILWAUKEE AREA: Take Rt. 43 southwest. Exit at CR-Y (Exit 54) northbound. Drive 0.7 miles to National Avenue. Turn east (right) on National and drive 0. 5 miles to Martin Road. Turn south (right) onto Martin and drive to the nursery a short distance on your right.

GPS: N 42° 56.91' W 88° 08.80'

WISCONSIN

The seductive display gardens include a shade garden, a hosta bed, a bog garden, and a number of rather distinct, sun tolerant perennial borders. Sun perennials are grouped alphabetically by botanical name in two groups, A-P (large section beyond the gift shop) and P-Z (across the walkway). Shade perennials, tucked under protective lattice, share space with a good selection of hanging baskets, which are referred to here as "hanging gardens."

> *"I come from fields once tall with wheat, from pastures deep in fern."*
> —E.B. WHITE

Shady Acres offers a dazzling assortment of rock garden plants as well some good residents for the woodland, including an interesting selection of hardy **ferns**. You can find **Jack-in-the-pulpit** (*Arisaema*), species of *Corydalis,* **Dutchman's breeches** (*Dicentra*), **shooting star** (*Dodecatheon*), **hellebore** (*Helleborus*), **liverwort** (*Hepatica*), **Virginia bluebells** (*Mertensia*), **bloodroot** (*Sanguinaria*), some *Trillium*, and **merrybells** (*Uvularia*). Gardeners spicing up an existing landscape can find superior selections of **campanula**, hardy **geranium**, **coral bells**, **sedum**, **iris**, and **phlox**. The phlox types alone include garden, Carolina, woodland, meadow, spring pearl, and creeping.

The specialties of the house, however, are **daylilies** (*Hemerocallis*) and hosta. For gardeners from the Windy City, Shady Acres offers a number of the Marsh Chicago series of daylilies along with collections from the Siloam, Little, and Eenie miniature series.

Often I have confessed a weird attraction towards plants with humorous, inexplicable, idiotic, or simply amusing names. *Hosta* 'Fire & Ice' is one such attraction. Acquired several years ago, mine has been waiting for a playmate. Today, Shady Acres has provided it with companions such as *Hosta montana* 'Mountain Snow'. Anyone desiring to incorporate more selections into their shady hosta glade might easily gravitate toward the impressive, gallon-sized specimens of 'Super Nova', 'Thunderbolt', 'Bright Lights', 'Sun Power', 'August Moon', and 'Daybreak'. Hostas 'Snowmound' and 'Snowcap' can also be found.

Graber obviously gave some serious thought to his customers when he set out his hosta and daylily collections. Instead of lining them up in a row alphabetically, he grouped the daylilies by blossom color and divided the hosta into blue, green, yellow-gold, cream-gold margins, white margins, and variegated types

WISCONSIN

(also in the catalog, further broken out by size).

For container gardeners, a good choice of colorful annuals and tender perennials (temperennials) is stocked in spring and early summer, while cottage gardeners will turn to **pinks**, **delphinium**, and **foxglove**. For shoppers seeking that rare gem to get a gardener's heart a-flutter, Shady Acres certainly doesn't disappoint. I noticed **rose mallow** *Hibiscus* 'Old Yella'; coral bells *Heuchera* 'Ring of Fire' (silver or purple leaves edged in bright coral); 'Mars' (pale purple-red foliage with darker veins); and 'Mint Frost' (minty green leaves iced in silver). There was compact **cranesbill** *Geranium sanguineum* 'New Hampshire Purple' (deep purple blossoms effervescing above green foliage); and **peony** *Paeonia* 'Doreen', (single, fuschia with fringed yellow center).

Every gardening season, based on how well plants performed during the previous growing season, Shady Acres creates their own inimitable list of the top 10 must-have plants. The list is yours for the asking. Special events include nursery garden walks, some short seminars, the traditional "Riot of Color" on Mother's Day weekend, and a not-to-be-missed nursery tour day (your chance to see what goes on behind the scenes).

WISCONSIN

SONG SPARROW
PERENNIAL FARM

Roy Klehm, internationally known plant grower and world famous for peony and daylily breeding, is continually expanding the selections offered at Song Sparrow Perennial Farm. His plants include the newest and the best in perennials, trees, and shrubs. The fourth-generation hybridizer and owner of Song Sparrow Perennial Farm specializes in peonies, daylilies, hostas, and woody plants. The Klehm reputation for estate peonies goes back generations; they originally bred them for the cutflower trade. In those days, they focused on cultivars producing blooms in clear colors that opened well and readily took up water.

Named for the Greek physician Paeon, who used them to treat the battle wounds of the gods, peonies signify healing. Planted along the path to your door, they are said to keep evil from your home. "Peonies are an old-fashioned flower: healthy and vigorous, and seldom fail even with neglect," says Klehm.

OWNERS: Roy Klehm
TYPE: Specialty mail order nursery
SPECIALTIES: Peonies—deciduous and tree; daylilies; hosta; clematis; perennials—sun and shade; woody plants
HOURS: Not open to the public. Business hours for mail-order: Dec. thru Feb.: 8:00 am to 4:00 pm; Mar. thru Nov.: 7:30 am to 4:30 pm.
CATALOG AVAILABLE: Printed and Online
MAIL-ORDER AVAILABLE: Yes
DISPLAY GARDENS: No
CLASSES: No

CONTACT
13101 East Rye Road
Avalon, WI 53505
PHONE: (800) 553-3715
FAX: (608) 883-2257
WEB ADDRESS: www.songsparrow.com
E-MAIL: info@songsparrow.com

WHAT YOU'LL FIND

The scenery at Song Sparrow is breathtaking. Plus, walking the fields of **peonies** in full bloom with Roy is like walking with a living encyclopedia on the subject. He notes, for instance, that the flower color of choice for the early 1950s and 1960s was white. He should know. There's 'Bowl of Cream' (American Peony Society Gold Medal Selection); 'Bridal Gown' created by his dad; and Roy's own introductions, 'Princess Bride', 'Snow Princes', and 'Bridal Shower', in their pristine, glistening white splendor. Ranging in colors including white to cream, and

WISCONSIN

pink to deep red, the options are endless (except for pure yellow). In the fields, I found Roy's creations simply enthralling, such as 'Petticoat Flounce' (a tulle confection in soft pink and creamy white), 'Best Man' (a handsome, deep red stud), and 'Blitz Tort' (a fluted, flared and twisted cactus-dahlia type peony). An unusual type, the lovely fernleaf *Peony tenuifolia* (a dainty cut-leaf peony), is among the first to bloom. Klehm's hybrid cultivar 'Early Scout' took the American Peony Society's Gold Medal in 1991 (an impressive honor for a peony, though Roy is rather nonchalant about it).

Along with the herbaceous, Song Sparrow Perennial Farm also offers a selection of **tree peonies** bred by various American hybridizers including Roy, Don Hollingsworth, and Arthur Saunders. In contrast to the dearth of yellow herbaceous peonies, there are several good yellows in the tree peony family, and Song Sparrow Perennial Farm offers some of the best: 'Antigone', 'Narcissus', and 'Golden Bowl'.

Additionally, Klehm offers five Itoh's—rare treasures indeed! Itohs (or intersections), possess the attractive foliage of tree peonies while still retaining their herbaceous nature. These crosses are difficult to make and demand extreme patience, the seedlings take years to mature, and propagation is dauntingly slow. 'Bartzella', considered by peony fanciers as the world's most desirable peony, is definitely priced quite attractively here, though it's not inexpensive.

Each year Song Sparrow Perennial Farm offers new hybrids of herbaceous, tree, and intersectional peonies plus a rotating group of peony hybrids (the current catalog lists 135 herbaceous, 50 tree, and 5 Itoh) selected from its collection of more than 300 stock peony varieties. Propagated on site, the deciduous peony roots (shipped in fall) are much larger than normal—three to five eye roots— while the tree peony and Itoh are two- to four-year-old container-grown plants (shipped spring to fall). These are superior in size and age to most mail-order offerings. Herbaceous peonies, the very epitome of a border perennial, are very cold hardy, deer-proof, and extremely long lived – some are known to survive for more than a century. Can you think of a more lasting gift for a wedding, birthday, or graduation?

Song Sparrow Perennial Farm is also known for its immense collection of field-grown **daylilies** amassed (and hybridized) by Roy Klehm, ranging from old-fashioned classics to colorful, bright new hybrids. I am a big fan of daylilies introduced by the late Brother Charles Reckamp, one of the first hybridizers of tetraploid daylilies. Brother Charles Reckamp is probably best remembered for his daylily, *Hemerocallis* 'Angels Smile', favored by key hybridizers, which led to the development of many new and distinctive cultivars. At Song Sparrow Perennial Farm, I found 'Angels Realm' (one of his cornerstones), 'Live Jazz' (ruffled, old-gold), and 'Peaceful Prairie' (fragrant, pastel-pink), just a few of the many varieties of daylilies that he developed and partnered with Roy Klehm.

> "No occupation is so delightful to me as the culture of the earth, and no culture comparable to that of the garden."
>
> —THOMAS JEFFERSON

The long list of Roy Klehm's introductions spans the rainbow of colors from elegant whites and creams to some really gorgeous pinks, melons, apricots, lilacs, purples, crimsons, and black-reds. Song Sparrow's collection includes several types of his daylilies, such as delicate small-flowered, daring spider, breathtaking large-flowered, double, and bitone. Some are long blooming; some re-blooming, and still others open in the evening for a good show the next day. I had to keep myself from nibbling on spicy 'Pumpkin Ruffles', ripe 'Banana Cream Pie', or delightful 'Papaya Delight'.

All daylilies are hardy, freshly dug, have field-grown roots, and are shipped bare-root, in double fan divisions. (New varieties with low inventory may be sold as single fan divisions.)

Song Sparrow Perennial Farm grows most of its stock, offering well-grown, robust, and vigorous perennials, trees, and shrubs. I certainly was enamored of its excellent selections of **magnolia, lilac, hydrangea,** and **crabapple.** Plants that add interest—whether through size, texture, or unusual color—have soared in popularity in recent years, and what could be more inviting than variegation? The variegated plants have their own mischievous personalities: **dawn redwood,** *Metasequoia glyptostroboides* 'Jack Frost' (white-tipped); the attractive **Chinese dogwood,** *Cornus kousa* 'Wolf Eyes'; **Korean forsythia,** *Forsythia koreana* 'Kumson' (new and still hard to find); **sweet pepperbush,** *Clethra alnifolia* 'Creel's Calico' (delightfully fragrant, irregularly variegated); or variegated **lilac,** *Syringa vulgaris* 'Aucubaefolia' (unique, irregularly splashed with yellow).

The overriding focus of the 104-page catalog, crammed full of glossy photographs, is on peonies, daylilies, and **hostas.** Song Sparrow Perennial Farm offers a selection of perennials including: **ferns, coral bells, bleeding heart, astilbe, martagon lily, lungwort, tiarella,** and **toad lilies** for shade. They have coneflower

(Orange Meadowbrite™, also known as 'Art's Pride'), **campanula** (the lacy white 'Beautiful Trust'), **phlox**, **iris**, **lobelia**, hardy **geranium**, **clematis** (from tree-climbing montanas to large-flowered vines all the way down to a small non-vining prairie species), and **verbascum** for sunny spots. Green pages in the back of the catalog offer information and answers to frequently asked questions about cultivation, planting, soil preparation, and general plant habits. On the website, seek out the "Sparrow's Nest" section, which lists plants that didn't make the catalog or were simply in short supply.

Most perennials are shipped in half-gallon pots with good-root systems. Shipping charges are a bit pricey; however, the care and detail exhibited in packaging makes the increase in price worth it.

SPRING VALLEY ROSES

❦❦

Spring Valley Roses, a specialty nursery nestled on rolling land near the small town of Spring Hill on the western fringes of Wisconsin, carries over 200 varieties of roses and sells close to 10,000 of them each year. Founded in 1990 as a mail-order nursery, Spring Valley expanded its operations in 1995 to include an on-farm walk-in nursery division. I love old roses yet was totally unprepared for the utter beauty of this place. To say it's awesome just wouldn't begin to do it justice! Repeat-blooming shrub roses are intermingled with scads of lilies, peonies, perennials, and Gallicas on a terraced hill.

A sea of roses surrounds the 1901 farmhouse occupied by the owners. All roses are own-root, grade #1, two-years old, field-grown or container-grown plants. (Own-root roses are initially slow growing and time consuming to produce but are tougher and longer-lived.) Initially, the Wielands self-propagated all roses; however, as the rose industry became more complex and restrictive, they more often turned to propagated cuttings for growing out.

All roses are one price, unless you buy three of a kind, whereupon a discount kicks in. Super-sized plants (three- or four-year-olds) are available on site in 5-gallon containers for extremely appealing prices. Catalog orders are shipped bare root from early April through mid-May, while on-site sales offer healthy containerized plants in 3-gallon pots.

OWNERS: Andrea and Mike Wieland
TYPE: Large Specialty nursery
SPECIALTIES: Roses
HOURS: Early May thru mid July (dates vary, check before coming): Saturdays only, 9:00 am to 5:00 pm. Other times by appointment.
CATALOG AVAILABLE: Online information and printed handouts
MAIL-ORDER AVAILABLE: Yes
DISPLAY GARDENS: Yes
CLASSES: No

CONTACT

N7637 330th St. (P.O. Box 7)
Spring Valley, Wisconsin 54767
PHONE: (715) 778-4481
FAX: (715) 778 4580
WEB ADDRESS: www.springvalleyroses.com
EMAIL: svroses@svtel.net

DIRECTIONS

FROM I-94 EASTBOUND: Take I-94 to Hwy 63 Baldwin (Exit # 19) exit. Go south on Hwy 63 7 miles to Hwy 29. Turn east (left) on Hwy 29 about 5 miles to 330th Street. (You'll see a red brick church on your left at the intersection) Turn south (right) on 330th St. driving for 0.5 miles. Spring Valley Roses is the first place on your right (west side). **FROM I-94 WESTBOUND:** Take I-94 West to Rt. 128 (Exit # 28) exit. Go south on Hwy 128 to Rt. 29. Turn east on Rt. 29 to 330th St. (You'll see a red brick church on your right at the intersection. Turn south (left) on 330th driving for 0.5 miles.

GPS: N 44° 49.31', W 92° 17.88'

Admirers of the beauty of birds, the Wielands have a sideline of bird-friendly shrubs and vines.

When you visit, wear comfortable shoes; the production and sales areas cover 2 acres. Check out the handsome website for a map, directions (or use mine), photos of the gardens and nursery, and an online catalog listing of plants. Be sure your car trunk is empty, as temptation runs high here. A small gift shop carries rose accessories from fertilizer to trellises.

This is a destination nursery. Bring a lunch, nestle up in a couple of chairs, and enjoy the experience.

WHAT YOU'LL FIND

Traditionally, gardeners have more or less isolated roses from other plants in the garden. I'm sure we've all seen whole beds or parts of a garden devoted exclusively to teas, floribundas, and grandifloras. One reason they're separated is that their beauty has earned them a sort of exalted stature; another is for more practical, cultural reasons. Unfortunately, when not in bloom, most "modern" roses are rather unappealing. Spring Valley aims to change this perception.

> *"The amen of Nature is always a flower."*
> —OLIVER WENDELL HOLMES

The climbing, landscape, shrub, and rugosa **roses** carried by Spring Valley are beautiful, fragrant, and sport a noble year-round presence in the garden. But they also exhibit additional compelling qualities. They tolerate soils too poor for most roses, shrug off diseases that traditionally fell their more tender relatives, and endure temperatures too cold for all but a few hardy canes. (Some rugosas in their collection are stout enough to endure bone-chilling winter temperatures of −40 degrees Fahrenheit.) All roses are first field tested for three winters on the farm before they are offered to customers. Andrea is a firm believer that roses grown on their own roots are better, especially where winters are harsh.

Andrea's large display gardens (her "catalog in the ground") show off lusty plant combinations and admirably showcase plants—roses, perennials, shrubs, and vines—that grow well in landscape conditions. A stroll through the immense, mature gardens comprised of over 200 rose bushes is a comparison shopper's dream. The showcased roses offer bountiful blooms and a luscious diversity of

WISCONSIN

★ SIDE TRIPS ★

In nearby Spring Valley, The **RED BARN CAFÉ,** W4890 State Hwy. 29, (715) 778-5522, is justly famous for its homemade pies. Be sure to enjoy a slice.

scents—some light and charming, others deep and intoxicating. How better to choose a rose than by having the ability to scrutinize each mature plant's characteristics—its color, texture, size; leaf shape, shrub size; and hips—information that cannot be had from any catalog or photo.

An old building foundation is filled to its stone and block gills with hybrid Perpetuals, shrubs, rugosas, and Canadian Explorer™ climbers. Lusty, pink, semi-double 'John Cabot' cavorts up an old post while my grandmother's favorite, blended pink 'Seven Sisters' hugs another. And what can be more alluring or romantic than Wisconsin's own, fully double, rich and velvety blossoms of crimson on a 'Ramblin' Red' rose? These and other exemplary roses can be seen through mid-July, though the garden remains colorful throughout the growing season. Just remember to bring your camera!

The top sellers, 'Natchez'™, 'Nashville'™, 'Pebble Beach'™, and 'Santa Barbara'™, are special landscape roses from Denmark—prolific bloomers propagated by Poulson. The newer dark red 'Hope for Humanity', named to commemorate the one-hundredth anniversary of the Canadian Red Cross, is also a favorite.

WISCONSIN

WINDY OAKS AQUATICS

⚬⚬⚬⚬

Windy Oaks Aquatics, a retail and wholesale enterprise, has been propagating, growing, and selling aquatics for more than two decades. Located in the scenic Kettle Moraine State Forest, just south of the picturesque town of Eagle, the nursery is a family-owned business that caters to the needs of pond enthusiasts and aquatic devotees. There are seven greenhouses, well over 10,000 square feet, devoted exclusively to water plants, and an outdoor growing area that may even be greater. According to Marilyn Buscher, enthusiastic hobbyist turned businesswoman, there are always upwards of 10,000 water lily and 300 lotus plants from which to choose.

Plants that grow in and around water offer an incredible kaleidoscope of colors, textures, and patterns to please every visitor to the pond. Ranging in size from about that of a bathtub to almost 50 feet across, the nursery display gardens, on 1 1/2 acres, showcase seven water ponds, each one unique. "It is gardening for all senses," notes Buscher, "the soothing sound of water, the exquisite blossoms, the incredible perfume of the flowers, plus the anticipation of new ones to come." The area was designed with the customer in mind by showcasing many of the different elements and techniques typically implemented in pond construction. You'll find a beautiful array of waterfalls, streams, and bog gardens as well as a wide spectrum of hardscaping materials such as flagstone, holy boulders, chestnut boulders, granite, and native fieldstones.

WHAT YOU'LL FIND

Although it's the Victoria **water lily** that knocks the socks of anyone seeing

OWNER: Marilyn Buscher
TYPE: Specialty nursery and wholesale
SPECIALTIES: Aquatic plants: waterlilies; lotus; Victoria; hardy marginals; tropical marginals
HOURS: May thru Labor Day: Wed.-Sun. 10:00 am to 4:00 pm. Other times by appointment.
CATALOG AVAILABLE: Printed and online
MAIL-ORDER AVAILABLE: Yes
DISPLAY GARDENS: Yes
CLASSES: No

CONTACT
W377 S0677 Betts Road
Eagle, WI 53119
PHONE: (262) 594-3033
FAX: (262) 594-3414
WEB ADDRESS: www.windyoaksaquatics.com

DIRECTIONS
FROM EAGLE, WI.: Take WI-67 south for 2 miles from the town of Eagle to Betts Road, turn east (left) onto Betts, nursery is the 5th on your right.

GPS: N 42° 51.00', W 88° 29.80'

WISCONSIN

it for the first time, Windy Oaks is justifiably well known and respected for a wide selection of other plants that grow in or near the water. The nursery carries exotic water lilies—both hardy and tropical varieties. As the names imply, the main difference is simply this: tropical waterlilies don't like the cold, while hardy waterlilies will tolerate it. Still, both will go dormant in cold conditions.

Hardy lilies are dependable and easy to plant—a good choice for a beginner. Daytime bloomers, they blossom in the morning and close after sunset, lasting three or four days before sinking beneath the surface. They are available in white, all shades of pink, yellow, and sunset and have thick and leathery pads. A hardy water lily always in great demand at Windy Oaks Aquatics is the bright rose-red 'Attraction'; however, what caught my attention was a shimmering pale pink changing to white as it matures, fully double 'Glorie du Temple'. My dear friend, on the other hand, was positively captivated by the gargantuan bright yellow blossoms of 'Texas Dawn'. All water lilies sold at the nursery are mature plants, grown in 10-inch containers.

Tropicals, flowering in rather exotic shades of color, can be either day or night bloomers. Their flowers are larger and more prolific. Day bloomers are blessed with a sizzling rainbow of color including white, all shades of pink, yellow, shades of autumn, purple, and undertones of green. On my visit, I was particularly charmed by the blossoms of 'Green Smoke', a truly unique blend of blues, violets, and silver gray—though the deep purple blossoms of 'Purple Zanzibar' certainly came in a close second. My intrepid companion—a first year pond owner—and I were drawn like flies to a web by the glistening, vivid blue blossoms of the bewitching arachnid, 'Blue Spider'. Night blooming varieties have vibrant, almost electric colors but are limited to white, all shades of pink, and near red. 'Woods White Knight', a very fragrant, free-flowering, double white lily, definitely caught our eye. (My friend immediately put in her order for what will surely turn out to be one awesome moonlight garden.)

In the world of pond plants, one word says it all. Victoria! The giant water platter Victoria has captured the imagination of the world from the instant it was first seen in South America in 1801. Named for Queen Victoria, it took nearly fifty years "in captivity" to bring about its first blossom. But when it did, it inspired a new wave of enthusiasm for the plant. As beautiful as the blossoms are,

WISCONSIN

and they are exquisite, it's the size and structure of the pads that attract. The undersides of the leaves, armed with thorns, are a marvel of structural engineering.

Victoria is generally regarded as an annual in most climates. It grows only from seed. But because the seeds don't keep well, they need to be remade every year, and plants must be regrown from those seeds annually resulting in an expensive price tag. In short, it grows from a pea-sized seed to a huge blooming plant (leaves 5 to 6 feet across) in a matter of months. It fruits, declines, and dies as cold weather approaches. Windy Acres is one of the few aquatic nurseries that sells and showcases Victoria—not exactly inexpensive for an annual ($75.00). However, if you have a pond large enough to accommodate it, you certainly will make a splash in your local horticultural community. Guaranteed!

With its leaves and flowers held boldly above the water, enthralling in its brilliance, the most mysterious of all pond plants is the **lotus**. Architecturally elegant in stature, the ethereal beauty of the plant never ceases to captivate. The mature plants, typically grown in 16-inch containers, can be planted in multiples in a single container as large as 30 inches, thereby putting off the need to repot the plants for several years. Some showstoppers available at the nursery include: 'Maggie Bell Slocum' (majestic mauve-pink blossoms); 'Giant Sunburst' (huge creamy yellow blossoms a good 12 inches across); two ideal container plants, 'Baby Doll' (small, white, free blooming) and 'Chawan Basu' (blossoms of sparkling white with red edges); and 'Mrs. Perry D. Slocum' (large double pink and yellow).

The nursery also offers many iris varieties, including selections of Japanese, Louisiana, and Siberian). Shallow water marginals from the "animal world" include **horsetail**, **elephant ear**, **cattail**, and zebra striped. Windy Oaks Aquatics carries every size, shape, habit, and color grow in an around the pond including **rush**, **water spurge**, **cotton grass**, **bulrush**, **mini-cattail**, and various floating and oxygenating aquatic plants. Tropical marginals include **taro** (*Colocasia* 'Imperial' and 'Black Magic') **alligator weed** and **aquatic**

★ SIDE TRIPS ★

Sometimes called the water chinquapin, the rich lemony-yellow AMERICAN LOTUS can be viewed in Antioch, IL. (50 miles northwest of Chicago). There is a famous lotus bed in Grass Lake, where 600 acres of these lovely flowers can be seen in full bloom each August.

WISCONSIN

pea, **umbrella palms** and **canna**, **paper plants** and **water hyacinths**, **powderpuffs** and **water poppies**, and **water lettuce** and **spider lilies**. All plants are potted in $7^1/_2$- to 10-inch containers and kept in warm greenhouses, giving customers a jump on the season. The nursery carries a good selection of pond fish, including koi, goldfish, orfes, shubunkins and comets. The showroom is stocked with filters, pumps, lights, fish food, pond treatments, and "just about everything else vaguely associated with water gardening."

Buscher, an accomplished artist, displays her realistic metal sculptures (the pig was our favorite) throughout the grounds. It is best to get there early in the summer as she welds during the winter months and the best selections are quickly snapped up by eager and savvy shoppers.

ALPHABETIC NURSERY LISTING

⟋⟍

NURSERY LISTING

Index By Plant Groups

INDEX

Munchkin Nursery & Gardens,
  L.L.C., IN, 110
The National Garden, Inc., IL, 63
Northwind Perennial Farm, WI, 288
Pleasant Valley Gardens, OH, 235
Quailcrest Farm, OH, 238
Renaissance Acres Organic Herbs, MI, 165
Rich's Foxwillow Pines Nursery, Inc., IL, 72
Rose Fire, Ltd., OH, 242
Saguaro Nursery & Gardens, MI, 168
Shady Acres Perennial Nursery, WI, 291
Shields Gardens, Ltd., IN, 113
Soules Garden, IN, 115
Spring Valley Roses, WI, 298
Sunshine Perennial Nursery, MI, 171
Taylor's Ornamental Grasses, IN, 118
Telly's Greenhouse, MI, 174
Valley of the Daylilies, OH, 245
Wade & Gatton Gardens, OH, 248
Wavecrest Nursery, MI, 177
Windy Oaks Aquatics, WI, 301
Winton's Iris Hill, IN, 120

EVERLASTINGS
Lewis Mountain Herbs & Everlastings, OH, 222
Monches Farm, WI, 280

FERNS
Arrowhead Alpines, MI, 124
Craig Bergmann's Country Garden, IL, 28
The National Garden, Inc., IL, 63
Planter's Palette, IL, 69

GERANIUMS (SCENTED, PELARGONIUMS)
Bordine's Nursery, Ltd., MI, 128
The Growing Place, IL, 40
Kleiss Farm & Nursery, IL, 54
Lewis Mountain Herbs & Everlastings, OH, 222
Milaeger's, WI, 275
Quailcrest Farm, OH, 238
Shady Hill Gardens, IL, 79
Ted's Greenhouse, IL, 83

GROUND COVERS
Baker's Acres Greenhouse, OH, 184
Bakers Village Garden Center, OH, 188
Blue River Nursery, IN, 89
deMonye's Greenhouse, OH, 301
The Flower Factory, WI, 260
Hallson Gardens, MI, 153
Homewood Farm, OH, 218
Milaeger's, WI, 275
Miller's Manor Gardens, IN, 104
Monches Farm, WI, 280
Oakland Nursery, OH, 231
Planter's Palette, IL, 69
Quailcrest Farm, OH, 238
Ted's Greenhouse, Inc., IL, 83

HANGING BASKETS
Alwerdt's Gardens, IL, 14
Avon Perennial Gardens, IN, 86
Baker's Acres Greenhouse, OH, 184

Bakers Village Garden Center, OH, 188
Bordine's Nursery, Ltd., MI, 128
Country Arbors Nursery, IL, 25
deMonye's Greenhouse, OH, 211
Ebert's Greenhouse, WI, 254
The Fields on Caton Farm Road, IL, 35
Gee Farms, MI, 144
The Growing Place, IL, 40
Jones Country Garden, IL, 51
Kleiss Farm & Nursery, IL, 54
Milaeger's, WI, 275
Northwind Perennial Farm, WI, 288
Oakland Nursery, OH, 231
Planter's Palette, IL, 69
Quailcrest Farm, OH, 238
Shady Hill Gardens, IL, 79
Ted's Greenhouse, Inc., IL, 83
Telly's Greenhouse, MI, 174

HERBS
Alwerdt's Gardens, IL, 14
Baker's Acres Greenhouse, OH, 184
Bakers Village Garden Center, OH, 188
Blue River Nursery, IN, 89
Bluestone Perennials, OH, 192
Bordine's Nursery, Ltd. MI, 128
Companion Plants, OH, 202
Country Arbors Nursery, IL, 25
Craig Bergmann's Country Garden, IL, 28
deMonye's Greenhouse, OH, 211
Ebert's Greenhouse, WI, 254
Enchanted Valley Gardens, WI, 257
The Fields on Caton Farm Road, IL, 35
The Flower Factory, WI, 260
The Growing Place, IL, 40
Homewood Farm, OH, 218
Kleiss Farm & Nursery, IL, 54
Lewis Mountain Herbs &
  Everlastings, OH, 222
Mary's Plant Farm, OH, 225
Milaeger's, WI, 275
Monches Farm, WI, 280
Mulberry Creek Herb Farm, OH, 228
The National Garden, Inc., IL, 63
Northwind Perennial Farm, WI, 288
Oakland Nursery, OH, 231
Planter's Palette, IL, 69
Quailcrest Farm, OH, 238
Renaissance Acres Organic Herbs, MI, 165
Shady Acres Perennial Nursery, WI, 291
Ted's Greenhouse, Inc., IL, 83
Telly's Greenhouse, MI, 174
Westview Farms, MI, 180

HOSTA
AAA Ornamentals, IL, 12
Bear Valley Perennials, WI, 250
Carol Kerr Perennials, MI, 131
Coburg Planting Fields, IN, 96
Cottage Garden, IL, 21
Country Arbors Nursery, IL, 25
Daylily Lane, OH, 208
Dogwood Farm, IN, 99

Bordine's Nursery, Ltd., MI, 128
Carol Kerr Perennials, MI, 131
Companion Plants, OH, 202
Cottage Garden, IL, 21
Counry Arbors Nursery, IL, 25
Craig Bergmann's Country Garden, IL, 28
deMonye's Greenhouse, OH, 211
Dogwood Farm, IN, 99
Ebert's Greenhouse, WI, 254
Enchanted Valley Gardens, WI, 257
Englerth Gardens, MI, 136
The Fields on Caton Farm Road, IL, 35
The Flower Factory, WI, 260
Funkie Gardens, WI, 264
Garden Crossings L.L.C., MI, 141
Gee Farms, MI, 144
The Growing Place, IL, 40
Hallson Gardens, MI, 153
Hidden Gardens Nursery, IL, 44
Hidden Hill Nursery, IN, 101
Homewood Farm, OH, 218
Hornbaker Gardens, IL, 47
Jones Country Garden, IL, 51
Kleiss Farm & Nursery, IL, 54
Lee's Gardens, IL, 57
Long's Garden, IL, 60
Mary's Plant Farm, OH, 225
Milaeger's, WI, 275
Miller's Manor Gardens, IN, 104
Monches Farm, WI, 280
Morningside Gardens, IN, 107
Mulberry Creek Herb Farm, OH, 228
Munchkin Nursery & Gardens, L.L.C., IN, 110
The National Garden, Inc., IL, 63
Northwind Perennial Farm, WI, 288
Oakland Nursery, OH, 231
Planter's Palette, IL, 69
Quailcrest Farm, OH, 238
Saguaro Nursery & Gardens, MI, 168
Shady Acres Perennial Nursery, WI, 291
Shady Hill Gardens, IL, 79
Song Sparrow Perennial Farm, WI, 294
Soules Garden, IN, 115
Sunshine Perennial Nursery, MI, 171
Ted's Greenhouse, Inc., IL, 83
Telly's Greenhouse, MI, 174
Wade & Gatton Gardens, OH, 248
Wavecrest Nursery, MI, 177
Westview Farms, MI, 180
Winton's Iris Hill, IN, 120

POINTSETTIAS
Shady Hill Gardens, IL, 81

ROSES
Alwerdt's Gardens, IL, 14
Baker's Acres Greenhouse, OH, 184
Bakers Village Garden Center, OH, 188
deMonye's Greenhouse, OH, 211
Ebert's Greenhouse, WI, 254
Enchanted Valley Gardens, WI, 257
Gee Farms, MI, 144
Great Lakes Roses, MI, 150

The Growing Place, IL, 40
Mary's Plant Farm, OH, 225
Michigan Mini Roses, MI, 156
Milaeger's, WI, 275
Oakland Nursery, OH, 231
Planter's Palette, IL, 69
Quailcrest Farm, OH, 238
Rose Fire, Ltd., OH, 242
Roses & Roses & Roses, IL, 76
Spring Valley Roses, WI, 298
Telly's Greenhouse, MI, 174
Wade & Gatton Gardens, OH, 248

SEEDS
Bordine's Nursery, Ltd., MI, 128
Milaeger's, WI, 275
Telly's Greenhouse, MI, 174

SHRUBS
Alwerdt's Gardens, IL, 14
Arrowhead Alpines, MI, 124
Avon Perennial Gardens, IN, 86
Baker's Acres Greenhouse, OH, 184
Bakers Village Garden Center, OH, 188
Blue River Nursery, IN, 89
Bluestone Perennials, OH, 192
Bordine's Nursery, Ltd., MI, 128
Cottage Garden, IL, 21
Country Arbors Nursery, IL, 25
Craig Bergmann's Country Garden, IL, 28
deMonye's Greenhouse, OH, 211
Ebert's Greenhouse, WI, 254
Enchanted Valley Gardens, WI, 257
Essentially English Gardens, OH, 214
Funkie Gardens, WI, 264
Gee Farms, MI, 144
The Growing Place, IL, 40
Hidden Gardens Nursery, IL, 44
Hidden Hill Nursery, IN, 101
Homewood Farm, OH, 218
Hornbaker Gardens, IL, 47
Kleiss Farm & Nursery, IL, 54
Long's Garden, IL, 60
Mary's Plant Farm, OH, 225
Milaeger's, WI, 275
Miller's Manor Gardens, IN, 104
Monches Farm, WI, 280
The National Garden, Inc., IL, 63
Oakland Nursery, OH, 231
Planter's Palette, IL, 69
Quailcrest Farm, OH, 238
Rich's Foxwillow Pines Nursery, Inc., IL, 72
Saguaro Nursery & Gardens, MI, 168
Song Sparrow Perennial Farm, WI, 294
Sunshine Perennial Nursery, MI, 171
Ted's Greenhouse, Inc., IL, 83
Wade & Gatton Gardens, OH, 248
Wavecrest Nursery, MI, 177
Westview Farms, MI, 180

TOPIARY
Avon Perennial Gardens, IN, 86
Kleiss Farm & Nursery, IL, 54

MEET THE AUTHOR

❧ ❧

Betty Earl is a garden writer, photographer, lecturer, and garden tour guide living in Naperville, IL, a western suburb of Chicago. Betty is a Garden Scout and Field Editor for *Better Homes & Gardens* magazine. Her articles and photographs have appeared in various other magazines including *Chicagoland Gardening*, *Small Gardens*, *Old Farmer's Almanac's Gardener's Companion*, *Le Bep's*, and *Birds and Blooms*. Betty is also a regional representative for the Garden Conservancy's Open Days Program. She actively seeks out generous American gardeners willing to include their spectacular gardens in this worthwhile program.

Betty formed a lasting love affair with gardening at a very early age. While working as an International Information Scientist and International Compensation Analyst, she found enjoyment and fulfillment in the seductive delights of the garden. A self-professed "plant nut," she has never met a plant that she didn't like.

When not writing, photographing, or speaking, Betty can be found "playing in the dirt" in the beds and borders surrounding her home.